DATE DUE			

The Evolution of Human Social Behavior

Edited by
Joan S. Lockard

Elsevier · New York
New York · Oxford

Exclusive Distribution
throughout the World by
Greenwood Press, Westport,
Ct. U.S.A.

Elsevier North Holland, Inc.
52 Vanderbilt Avenue, New York, New York 10017

Distributors outside the United States and Canada

Thomond Books
(A Division of Elsevier/North-Holland Scientific Publishers, Ltd.)
P.O. Box 85
Limerick, Ireland

Library of Congress Cataloging in Publication Data

Main entry under title:

The Evolution of human social behavior.

  Bibliography: p.
  Includes index.
  1. Social evolution—Addresses, essays, lectures. 2. Human
  ecology—Addresses, essays, lectures. 3. Social behavior in
  animals—Addresses, essays, lectures. 4. Sociobiology—Addresses, essays,
  lectures. I. Lockard, Joan S.
HM106.E96   301.1   79-25232
ISBN 0-444-99072-0

Assistant to the Volume Editor   Joyce O'Brien
Desk Editor   Louise Schreiber
Design   Edmée Froment
Art Editor   Virginia Kudlak
Production Manager   Joanne Jay
Compositor   General Graphic Services, Inc.
Printer   Haddon Craftsmen

Manufactured in the United States of America

The motivation for this book arose in part from a Spectrum course of lectures I was asked to organize at the University of Washington, and for that impetus and opportunity I am grateful. Any wisdom that my own chapters may contribute stems from my casual and systematic observations of others and in particular my children, Eric Neil and Kim Ann. The mechanics of assembling an edited volume are prohibitive without the help of individuals who spell, type and tolerate reworking and retyping much better than I, and in this endeavor I especially wish to thank Joyce O'Brien and Sandy Brice-Nicolls.

Contents

Acknowledgments

Chapters 1 and 15. Some of the research presented in these two chapters was partially supported by a grant from the Harry Frank Guggenheim Foundation.

Chapter 3. The author's work on the theory of habitat selection and testing of the ideas with blackbirds has been supported by the National Science Foundation. Several of the concepts in this chapter have been facilitated by Lionel Tiger and Eric Charnov.

Chapter 8. The research described here has been supported by several grants from the National Science Foundation, and from a Research Fellowship from the U.S.–France Cooperative Science Program. This manuscript was prepared while the author was a Fellow at the Center for Advanced Study in the Behavioral Sciences, Stanford, California (1977–1978), under the directorship of Gardner Lindzey.

Chapter 9. This manuscript was completed with the assistance of Jan Lauridsen and Jean Gladstone, and supported by a grant from the Public Health Service (MH 15181).

Chapter 11. Some of the ideas and parts of the discussion in this chapter have been drawn from other papers by the authors: Hirsch (1978), Hirsch and Vetta (1978), McGuire and Hirsch (1977).

Chapter 13. Several sections are reprinted from a forum on self-deception by the author, which appeared in the *Human Ethology Newsletter*, March (No. 21) 1978.

Chapter 14. This manuscript is based on a talk entitled, "Challenging the Psychic Unity of Mankind," given at the June 1976 meetings of the Animal Behavior Society, Boulder, Colorado.

Contributors

Robert M. Adams
Department of Psychology, Eastern Kentucky University, Richmond, Kentucky

David P. Barash
Departments of Psychology and Zoology, University of Washington, Seattle, Washington

Jerome H. Barkow
Department of Anthropology, Dalhousie University, Halifax, Nova Scotia

Gerald Borgia
Department of Biology, University of Chicago, Chicago, Illinois

Penelope J. Greene
Department of Statistics, Harvard University, Cambridge, Massachusetts

Jerry Hirsch
Departments of Psychology and Ecology–Ethology–Evolution, University of Illinois, Urbana-Champaign, Illinois

Jonathan K. Lewis
Child Development and Mental Retardation Center and Department of Psychology, University of Washington, Seattle, Washington

Joan S. Lockard
Departments of Psychology and Neurological Surgery, University of Washington, Seattle, Washington

Terry R. McGuire
Department of Biology, Livingston College, Rutgers University, New Brunswick, New Jersey

Charles J. Morgan[1]
Institute for Environmental Studies, University of Washington, Seattle, Washington

[1]Present address: Environmental Protection Agency, 1200 Sixth Avenue, Seattle, Washington, 98101.

Gordon H. Orians
Department of Zoology and the Institute for Environmental Studies, University of Washington, Seattle, Washington

Halbert B. Robinson
Department of Psychology, University of Washington, Seattle, Washington

Gene P. Sackett
Department of Psychology and the Regional Primate Research Center, University of Washington, Seattle, Washington

Daris R. Swindler
Department of Anthropology, University of Washington, Seattle, Washington

Bruce Ullock
Department of Psychology, University of Washington, Seattle, Washington

Pierre L. van den Berghe
Department of Sociology, University of Washington, Seattle, Washington

Atam Vetta
Department of Mathematics, Oxford Polytechnic, Oxford, United Kingdom

Nathaniel N. Wagner (Deceased)
Departments of Psychology and Obstetrics-Gynecology, University of Washington, Seattle, Washington

Allan E. Williams
Department of Psychology, University of Washington, Seattle, Washington

Stephen C. Woods
Department of Psychology, University of Washington, Seattle, Washington

Introduction
Origins of Human Social Behaviors

Joan S. Lockard

Most behavioral scientists, at some time or other, have longed for the opportunity to expound on their research philosophies without fear of peer criticism, without the restraint of scientific rigor, and with prior knowledge that the audience would benefit from the discourse. It is such a wish on which this book is predicated. My colleagues and I have taken several scientific liberties and in spite of, or perhaps because of, this freedom, we hope to stimulate the reader to more productive thinking. Instead of rationalizing the meager progress in this area to date with statements that human social behaviors are very complex, we will attempt to strip the complexity to ridiculous essentials. However, what is proposed here should *not* be regarded as truths, but as models to be eventually rejected, in part or total, modified and/or extended by new data. The value of these discourses is the discussion they evoke and the ideas that they generate.

In the world of "what if" let us assume that all evidence of cultures as we know them today vanished and that the human population of the earth was reduced one millionfold. Given ecological selective pressures such as the availability of natural resources and changing climatic conditions, what then in the way of genetic predispositions would an adult need to have in order to survive and reproduce? In other words, what are the adaptive behaviors of individuals that perpetuated our species in the distant past? How did our social structure evolve to what it is from what it was? What were the origins of human social behaviors?

We were by descent, at the very least, reproductive Old World primates with an extended infancy. Even our early ancestors could no longer contribute differentially to the next generation by birth rate alone since survival of offspring to reproductive age was essential. Adult existence was dependent on learning in childhood from others about the environment, the local geography and available resources. We were, also, well on the evolutionary pathway to a division of labor between the sexes (i.e., different roles), with infant care and food foraging the primary responsibilities of the female and protection and occasional hunting that of the male. The acquisition of these skills and social behaviors necessary to assume these adult roles required communication among individuals.

Until recently, the study of human communication had concentrated on situational or immediate variables (i.e., *proximate* causation) with little emphasis on more historical or evolutionary considerations (i.e., *ultimate* causation). The first chapter of this book considers studies of human social signals and their possible origins. Hominids have had a history of at least several million years in which natural selection was a reality. During that time their survival was contingent on communicative behaviors. Social signals require predictability and, therefore, were particularly amenable to selective pressures. Chapter 1 considers some of the possible origins of human social signals in terms of phyletic precursors and ontogenetic development. It sets forth the methods by which the past and present functions of certain facial, gestural and postural signals can be studied and compared.

To understand human social behavior today it is essential to trace some of the likely pathways from which it may have emanated in the past. Chapter 2 considers primate and human evolution, regarding behavior as a function of the physiological and anatomical apparatus with which an organism is endowed. The origin and evolution of the members of the order Primates are discussed in a paleontological framework. The radiations of the early groups of primates are set forth briefly as an underpinning for a more detailed discourse on the higher primates and the Hominidae.

Chapter 3 considers the influence of ecology on human social behavior in terms of habitat selection and human niche preference. Since selection of habitat determines the context for subsequent behavioral activities of an animal, the choice is under strong natural selection. The quality of a habitat for a particular organism depends on the resources it provides, the protection it offers from the physical environment, and the risk of predation per unit time while engaged in different activities within the habitat. If the area serves as a breeding site, its value is also a function of the features that influence breeding success. Habitat selection is explored in terms of (a) time span of occupancy, (b) time available for searching and the cost of searching, (c) extent of knowledge the organism possesses or can be expected to possess, and (d) the activities that will be carried out in the area. These considerations are discussed in terms of human preferences for savannalike environments and the aesthetic aspects of "wide-open spaces."

From phyletic origins and ecological selective pressures on human social behaviors, we consider in Chapter 4 the basic social unit—the family. The evolution of human mating systems is discussed in terms of a biosocial view, with particular focus on polygyny. Mating strategies have long preoccupied sociologists and anthropologists, but they have been dealt with in overwhelmingly culture-deterministic terms. The reasons for the resistance of social scientists to biological concepts are examined and the need to incorporate a biological perspective in the social sciences is discussed, with special reference to the family.

It is a natural sequence from the considerations of the evolution of the family unit to determinants of human population patterns as presented in Chapter 5. A review and integration of theories concerning population trends in human and nonhuman groups from the point of view of two widely separate disciplines, demography and ethology, are presented. Theorists in both disciplines have analyzed population patterns in terms of the relation between death and birth rates. In reiterating the determinants of both factors, particularly those controlling birth rates, demographers and ethologists present very different explanatory paradigms. The former emphasize social and economic variables and the latter genetically programmed behavioral patterns. It is argued that among the most important determinants of human population trends are (a) the desire for children for their own sake, this desire being in large part a function of biological systems organized during the formative years, and (b) the number of family members who will contribute energy to the care of children, this energy distribution being mostly a function of the evolutionary process.

With the stage set for the importance of development on human social behavior, we return once more to nonhuman primates to consider rearing conditions and sex differences. Similar to other primates, human survival is contingent on the young who interact with and learn about the environment in which they must function as adults. During this development, if what is learned turns out to be inappropriate interactions for the world in which the organism is destined, then the individual's behavior is maladaptive. Chapter 6 provides an overview of the effects of varied rearing experiences on social development and other behaviors in a monkey model. It considers the influence of gender on "bad" rearing conditions and suggests an ontogenetic program to study the interaction of infancy, sex and rearing conditions in the production of species-atypical (abnormal) behavior.

The importance of early environment and adequate experiences in the development of adult sexual behavior sets the background for the changed role of human sexual behavior as addressed in Chapter 7. The evolution of sexual behavior from a largely reproductive activity to one with considerable social and psychological implications is presented. Particular emphasis is placed on a comparison of two interrelated functions, namely, species perpetuation and pair bonding. Whereas sexual behavior may have originally subserved mainly reproduction, the increasing dependence of individual survival on social interactions probably expanded its affiliative role. The evolutionary and psychological components of human sexual behavior are discussed and contrasted.

From the previous chapters it is increasingly evident that evolution can be used as a valuable tool in the analysis and prediction of human social behavior. To illustrate how this tool is productively employed, Chapter 8 considers some evolutionary strategies of parental behavior. This book is based on the assumption that living things will be selected for behaving in such a way as to maximize their fitness, i.e., contributing the greatest number of reproducing offspring to the next generation. Studies of animal sexual behavior (including adultery and rape), care of young, choice of mates and defense against predators provide instructive models for the role of evolution in mediating these complex patterns in humans as well.

Only after some introduction to sociobiology and the promise of its concepts and theories for the understanding of human social behavior, as depicted in Chapter 8, is the reader ready for a topic such as human aggression in Chapter 9. This subject matter has been frought with mistaken applications and overgeneralizations of evolutionary theory for some time, which make the task of illustrating biological influences on human agonistic behavior most difficult. A conservative discourse is attempted in the present treatice on the role of aggression in the history of warfare. An argument is set forth of the importance of aggression on fitness and, therefore, on hominid evolution. An idea is proposed that warfare is not merely the product of aggression run rampant but has adaptive significance. The discussion is closed with meaningful speculations as to the contribution of cultural laws in the regulation of human aggression.

At this stage in the treatment of human social behavior from the point of view of natural selection, it seems appropriate to outline the fundamental principles of evolution. In Chapter 10, specific focus is given to concepts such as heritability, genetic drift, evolutionary stable strategies and the biology of altruism. An understanding of these mechanisms and their social utility is essential to an appreciation of the approach taken herein.

It is fitting after a thesis on evolution to consider the misapplication of behavioral genetics to human behavior. Scientists are charged not only with pointing out proper employment of techniques but, equally important, their misuse. In Chapter 11, the basic concepts of behavioral genetics are presented in a readable fashion and their relevance and irrelevance to human behavior illustrated. One is left with the impression that a genetic understanding of our behavior will be a matter of biological faith from the study of simpler organisms for sometime to come. However, this faith may be bolstered occasionally, and most likely fortuitously, by a rare occasion to conduct an appropriate human study.

No endeavor to hypothesize about the evolution of human social behavior would be successful without some coverage of the applied significance of such theorizing. Chapter 12 considers the area of human nonverbal communication in this light and discusses the limitations and findings of such studies. Although basic science is ideally *not* frought with application, it is largely through this latter avenue that "control" in the scientific sense is realized and, thus, understanding achieved. If in fact "basic principles" are operating in the clinical setting and are amenable to detection and, subsequently, to systematic application, no better test-bed could be had. It was this belief that the everyday behavior of humans had some underlying evolutionary foundation that the title of this book was coined.

In the last 10 years, the idea that deception can be adaptive and that it is an evolutionary strategy (with many different manifestations) is gradually being accepted in animal behavior. More recently, in human behavior, the concept of self-deception has been addressed in terms of its possible biological aspects. The "unconscious" can no longer be regarded as an elusive phenomenon unamenable to objective study. It is being seen as a mechanism of survival where self-ignorance of one's actions may not only be in the individual's best interest at times, but for which there may be some genetic predisposition. It may be advantageous in the deception of others to be self-deceived as to one's own motives. Moreover, how much more palatable it is to expend enormous amounts of energy, say, in the care of offspring, if you can "chalk it up" to parental love rather than reproductive success. It seems fitting that Chapter 13 has the distasteful task of opening our eyes and depressing our souls by showing how selfish genetic evolution really is.

The reader would have considerable difficulty with Chapter 14 if its contents appeared earlier in this volume. It is only when the audience is convinced that all is not what it appears to be, that the idea that culture is itself an evolutionary strategy could be contemplated as something other than a contradiction in definition. It is bad enough to be merely a "gene machine," but when our possible "salvation," namely, *culture* is described as just another tool of genetic evolution, we perhaps appreciate (for really the first time) the role of human behavior in natural selection. We are a species whose genetic immortality depends upon having considerable "freedom" to adjust to environmental contingencies. In essence, our future existence will depend on decisions that continue to be good for our genes.

An attempt at some degree of closure on biological and cultural factors that systematically influence human social behavior is presented in Chapter 15. An integration and summary of the preceding chapters, with an emphasis on the history and state of the science today, is provided. The book ends on the note that however primitive these initial efforts will appear some years from now, the biological synthesis has at last caught up with human behavior.

Studies of Human Social Signals:
Theory, Method and Data

Joan S. Lockard

1

Few behavioral scientists, or for that matter biologists, take evolutionary theory seriously as a means to understanding human social signals. The intention of this chapter is to do just that, discussing its application, sketching the methods by which it is done and illustrating the scientific productivity in so doing. Implicit in the application of any scientific theory is the use of models. An appreciation of physical and mathematical models is long standing in the behavioral and life sciences. In the employment of evolutionary theory, biological models that share some degree of common descent with the species under study are often used. Such models are the very basis of the comparative method. They are usually most fruitfully applied in the study of closely related animals, such as species or subspecies, with the species about which the most is known serving as the model. However, there is nothing inherent in the scientific application of models that necessitates genetic compatibility. A biological model could be utilized to understand behavior with no implication of relatedness. Problems arise only when such models are retained in spite of empirical evidence to the contrary, simply because of superficial similarities in morphology and/or ecology.

Research Concepts and Assumptions

With the above caution in mind, social signals in nonhuman primates become a fertile source of biological models for the study of human communication. Signals selected for scrutiny could be acquired, genetically programmed or, as is most often the case, an interaction of the two. *Analogous* similarities in signal function could be investigated or, if common descent is implicated in the origin of the signals, *homologous* comparisons could be instigated. Signals that serve the same function but have not evolved as a consequence of recent genetic sameness in morphology and physiology are often a product of *convergent evolution* where similarities in environment have imposed similar selective pressures. For example, New World primates (infraorder, *Platyrrhines*) have been geographically separated in their evolution for about 30 million years from Old World primates (*Catarrhines*). Although many social signals of these two groups may still be homologous, similarities in other signals may be the result of relatively recent convergence. Their separation for a considerable period of time, i.e., *parallel evolution,* has also culminated in many different signals that are neither similar in function or origin.

The origin and evolution of communication signals have been studied for some time in animal behavior. *Communication* is defined biologically (Wilson, 1975) as an action on the part of one animal that alters the probability of behaviors in another animal in a fashion adaptive to either one or both. Communication is regarded as neither the signal of the sender nor the response of the receiver, but rather the interaction between the two. Biological signals may be classified into two conceptual categories,—discrete and graded. *Discrete signals* are likened to a light switch in which the signal is either on or off, present or absent. Discrete signals evolve such that the intensity and duration of the signaling behavior becomes less variable, no matter how weak or strong the invoking stimulus may be. High risk signals are usually discrete so that misinterpretation is minimal. The predator warning call of some primates may be of this sort where the duration and intensity of the alarm is fixed. However, other primate species may use *graded signals* to indicate not only the presence of a possibly less dangerous predator but also whether it is terrestrial or avian, near or far. The evolution of graded signals results in increased behavioral flexibility, subtlety of signaling and conservation of energy. Often the greater the motivation of the animal, the more intense and prolonged the signal given. For example, the threat behaviors of a primate species can usually be classified on a continuum of graded intensities. If a simple threat-face is sufficient to alter the behavior of the other animal, then a more energy-consuming threat-chase can be reserved for situations where there is less compliance. It is analogous in humans to the difference between a simple "no" and a spanking.

One of the more lasting principles of communication was proposed as early as 1872 by Charles Darwin in his book, *The Expressions of the Emotions in Man and Animals.* It was called the *Principle of Antithesis,* which suggested that the evolution of one behavior assured the *preadaptation* of its opposite. Specifically, if an animal is signaling aggression but for some reason its intentions are reversed, then its behavior will follow, with the opposite signal being conveyed. Darwin's classic example was that of a dog approaching what it thought to be a strange man, who later turned out to be its master. Instead of the dog walking assertively upright as it had been, its body sank downward into a crouched position with its tail lowered and wagging. The essence of the example was to indicate that the antithesis of the original emotional state can manifest signals, conveying the opposite information.

An equally important concept in the study of social signals is called *ritualization*. This is a process whereby an essentially neutral behavior changes to become an increasingly more effective signal. The initial behavior is often some movement or anatomical feature that may arise originally in a context quite unrelated to its eventual message. During the ritualization process, these movements evolve to make their communicative functions still more effective. Often additional morphological changes or vocalizations are acquired that enhance the conspicuousness of the movements. The behavior becomes simplified, stereotyped and exaggerated such that its final form is referred to as a *display*.

Ritualization often begins in situations of conflict, for instance, if an animal intends to leave but does not want to depart alone, or wishes to approach a potential mate but is fearful to do so. These hesitations in behavior, of first repeatedly approaching and then turning away, become ritualized into signaling to conspecifics intended courses of action and are termed *intention movements*. For example, migratory birds intending to fly away, but not alone, typically crouch, raise their tails and spread their wings slightly just before taking off. In a stereotyped form, the signal serves to coordinate the movement of flocked members. Not all signals that have evolved from conflict situations have relevance to the particular context in which the animal finds itself. In the case of an animal approaching an intimidating mate, fear-reducing behavior may occur, such as preening in birds. The preening has nothing to do with the particular situation but becomes ritualized as a signal of courtship. In response to that *displacement behavior*, the mate's intentions may become ambivalent, taking the form of a *redirected aggression* such as pecking at a nearby pebble. The pecking may in turn become ritualized, and so forth, resulting in an evolved courtship display.

Another unifying principle in animal communication is the idea of *composite signals*, with the combination resulting in still a different message from that of each of its components. Dominant signaling (Nickelson and Lockard, 1978) and play invitations (Heestand et al., 1980) are two examples of composite signals in nonhuman primates. In the former, a dominant male monkey can be recognized by his erect posture and confident stride. In the latter, although invitation signals may take many different forms depending upon the particular species, feigned wrestling such as gazing at playmates with the head upside down, or stiff, stilted locomotion of mock chasing and fighting are usually unambiguous solicitations of play.

Another important communication concept is the *context* in which the signal occurs. An animal with a relatively limited signal repertoire can increase the information transmitted by presenting its signal in a different context. The meaning of the signal would then be modulated by the situation simultaneously impinging on the receiver. For example, in primate play many of the component behaviors could be misinterpreted out of context as real aggression.

All of these communication concepts and many of the observational techniques and procedures employed in animal communication are directly applicable to the study of human social signals. However, in this endeavor several not intuitively obvious assumptions must be made: (a) human social signals are consistent and do not happen by chance; (b) whereas human social interactions may be intricate, the signals of which they are composed are often not; (c) it is the function served by a signal (rather than its exact form) which is of cardinal importance to its understanding; and (d) if two signals serve the same function, the one requiring less energy expenditure will be more frequently manifested. These assumptions were derived empirically by observing the interactions of humans as you would other mammals. The problem is not in finding consistent human displays once you begin looking, but in perceiving what it is you are seeing. To segment the display into meaningful parts that can be reliably observed is the difficult task. To accomplish this objective, the tried techniques employed in the study of animal communication can be used. *Ethological methodology*, i.e., the description and quantification of the behavior of an animal in its usual environment are particularly helpful in the reduction of complex interactions to essential—and not necessarily easily detected components.

Therefore, the study of human signals is not a formidable task if certain guidelines are used. One looks for consistencies in signaling and uses quantitative methods to assess these consistencies. Helpful correlaries of these guidelines stem directly from the theoretical foundation and principles of communication discussed above: (a) that there are essential signals which are predisposed to occur reliably in particular situations if the individual is to survive; (b) to the extent that selective pressures have been extensive in the evolution of these signals, their forms have become ritualized; (c) in minimizing energy expenditure and maximizing efficiency of information conveyed, these signals may occur as *fragments* of the original communication, providing graded signals; (d) that the antithesis of these signals provide opposite signals; and (e) that antithetical behaviors that have become efficiently fragmented provide opposite graded signals. With these guidelines and correlaries one may now meaningfully ask questions or make predictions about human social signals and proceed systematically to answer empirically these questions or to test these predictions.

The most likely starting point is to look at those human social signals that have evolved to ensure individual survival. In terms of Mayr's classification (1974) of opened and closed evolutionary programs, these behavioral signals would be mixed, where certain essential components are genetically encoded but some flexibility in expression and interpretation occurs, depending on the situation and the individuals involved. Given our social mammalian

heritage, there are at least four categories of signals that undoubtedly have genetic predispositions to occur, namely, those occurring in breeding, in parental offspring relations, in play episodes
and in peer interactions. The first category guarantees reproduction and, when pair bonding occurs, favors predator defense and
the division of labor between the sexes for a more efficient
exploitation of available resources. The second category is a direct
consequence of an extended infancy (since many mammals have
altricial offspring) where survival of the infant necessitates parental
care for a period of time. The third category, play, is the practicing
at young ages behaviors necessary for survival and reproduction at
older ages. The fourth category stems from the simple fact that
humans are social animals whose individual survival at times
depends upon minimizing agonistic encounters and facilitating
affiliative interactions among peers. In the nomenclature of animal
behavior, the latter exchanges would be regarded, at least in part,
as dominant and submissive signals within a very sensitive period
during adolescence when the juvenile is approaching adulthood
and potential reproduction.

The foregoing classification implies that it is the total reproductive life of an individual as well as those of its relatives, i.e., *kin
selection* (Hamilton, 1964) that determines its ultimate reproductive
success. This assumption, termed *inclusive fitness* by Hamilton,
encompasses the first of two global categories of natural selection
that provide some understanding as to how social signals evolve.
The second mechanism, suggested by Trivers (1971), to handle
selection among individuals who are not related, is termed *reciprocal altruism*. The latter, simply stated, is a means whereby an
individual increases his own inclusive fitness by assisting, at little
personal risk, another individual who returns the favor simultaneously (e.g., cooperative behavior) or at a later time. The most
blatant example of reciprocal altruism is conception between unrelated mates. Their offspring is mutually beneficial in terms of
reproductive success. The distinction between these two
mechanisms will be more clearly seen when they are used to
explain the data of the illustrative studies cited below.

**Study
Methods
and Data**   Six studies will be presented to demonstrate the applicability of
evolutionary theory, ethological methodology and principles of
communication, to the understanding of human social signals. The
first research project illustrates the importance of demographic
data, particularly with respect to conservative behaviors (in the
anthropological sense)—such as how individuals group themselves in public. It uses a primate model to study the composition
of human subgroups such as subadult males. The second study
addresses the evolution of smiling and laughter, where it is
assumed that the signals have separate origins but are *homologous*
(i.e., by common ancestry) with displays in several other primate

species. A third study on departure signals is representative of *analogous* behaviors (i.e., of common function but not ancestry) in other species. A fourth study on begging gestures is more difficult to categorize but considers some of the signals in the sharing of resources among hominids. The fifth study exemplifies composite signals and considers communication at a distance in a hitchhiking setting. The final study involves parent–infant communication, showing an interesting interplay of infant and maternal behaviors. The first five research projects include signals primarily classified as peer exchanges and, in some, potential mating interactions. The last study involves parental caregiving and infant feedback signals and to some degree evolved differences in adult female and male roles. In all six cases, the emphasis will be placed on an interpretation of the data in terms of *distal causation* (or ultimate causation), that is, evolutionary, ontogenetic or cultural explanations. Acculturated signals, i.e., widespread learned signals which have been passed on from one generation to the next, etc., are considered under this category of causation since explanations of their manifestations are not found in immediate physiological or situational antecedents, i.e., *proximal causation*. Moreover, culture has been an evolutionary strategy in the primate order where versatility in behavior to changing environmental and social contexts has been at a premium.

Considering the first study (Lockard and Adams, 1980), a primate model for a human subgroup was employed. In several nonhuman primate species, subadult males have been observed to exhibit a developmental stage not shared by females (Schaller, 1963; Hall and DeVore, 1965; Itorgawa, 1975; Hrdy, 1977). While females appear to be gradually integrated into the adult structure on reaching reproductive age, subadult males seem to remain apart for a time (i.e., at the periphery of the group), associating largely with other same-age males. An analogous stage in the development of human males (18–20 year olds) was assessed by an analysis of the relative frequencies of various age–sex groupings in public.

The hypothesis tested was whether subadult males, 18–20 year olds, would be seen in all-male groups of three or more members in greater than expected frequencies. Data gathering was located where a demographic cross section of a metropolitan area was likely to be observed and at times of the day where there were no rigid constraints on group composition, namely, 7–9 p.m. weekdays and 1–5 p.m. weekends. Over 10,000 groups (from 1 to 6 members) were observed as they exited along well-defined pathways from large, enclosed shopping malls. The sex and estimated age of each group member were recorded. Prior to the conduct of the study, the observers were well trained to estimate ages within a mean directional variance of $1\frac{1}{2}$ years for the age range of research interest (12–26 year olds). The data were subjected to computer collation and observed frequencies of specified age–sex groupings were compared by chi-square statistics to expected frequencies based on a binomial distribution, where the probability of either a male or female singleton was assumed to be $\frac{1}{2}$ and the probability of any combination of individuals was the product of their respective probabilities.

As shown in Figure 1 for the percentage comparisons of triads and quadrads, groups of three or four subadult males are out in public in much greater frequency than would be expected and in greater frequency than comparable-age, same-sex females ($\chi^2 = 40.93$, df = 6, $p < .001$). Since a strong same-sex peer orientation is evident for both female and male juveniles age 15–17 years, why is it that female triads age 18–20 years are not as prevalent as those of males? It is possible, as has been suggested for other species of primates (Devore, 1971; Fox, 1972) that although human subadult males are sexually mature, they are not sufficiently developed, either physically or experiencially, to compete with older males for either females or essential resources of their society. It is likely at this age that groupings of two friends—

Figure 1
Percentage of male and female groups of three or four individuals, for five age categories, observed in public. The focal category is subadult, 18–20 years old, where a significantly greater number ($p < .001$) than expected same-sex male groups are seen than either all-female or mixed-sex (not shown) groups.

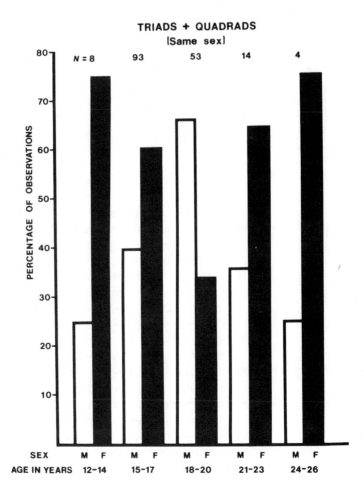

be it male, female or mixed-sex dyads—represent a transition to adulthood more than do triadic or greater groupings. The "extra" individuals may reflect and therefore signal a message of "youth-fulness" rather than one of cultural assimilation. In other words, many 18–20 year old males may still be practicing to become adult males by testing their abilities against similar-age males. The fact that they are seen in groups of three to four in shopping malls at all may be indicative of an "overflow" from their possibly even more numerous peripheral "play groups."

The findings of this study suggest not only that subgroup status for subadult males is a viable concept for future research but the importance of a demographic approach in establishing a social phenomenon for further study. The hypothesis tested was specific enough to be either supported, as in the present case, or refuted if the findings had been different, indicating the fruitfulness of an analogous primate model when applied appropriately.

The idea for the second study to be reviewed (Lockard et al., 1977) developed from two separate observations on what superficially appeared to be similar facial expressions. The first, by van Hooff (1967), culminated in a series of studies on nonhuman primates from which he categorized two different mouth grimaces, the *silent bared-teeth* and the *relaxed open-mouth* display. He postulated that these signals evolved separately and served different functions and that they were homologous, respectively, in many Old World primate species. The second observation was by the present author in which it was casually noted that whereas human smiling was appropriate in most affiliative situations, laughter was more restricted. In fact, laughter rarely commenced a social exchange and if it were manifested it was usually later in the interaction after the situation had become more familiar. The one exception seemed to be greeting exchanges among close relatives or good friends.

Therefore, using the two primate mouth displays described by van Hooff as models, the question was posed as to whether the mouth expression accompanying human laughter is simply a more intense form of smiling or whether the former display is of different phyletic origin. The earlier consensus in the literature placed smiling and laughter on a single continuum of graded intensities (Andrew, 1963). More recently (van Hooff, 1967, 1971; Hinde, 1974) it was suggested that smiling and laughter were more adequately described in terms of two dimensions; one indicating the amount of teeth exposure (i.e., affiliativeness) and the other the degree of mouth opening (i.e., playfulness). In other words, it was proposed that the smile and the laughter mouth were originally two different displays in nonhuman primates but have converged in humans. However, it was hypothesized in the present study (based on preliminary observations) that the convergence is incomplete and that smiling and laughter still serve separate functions. Moreover, it is suggested that smiling originated from the

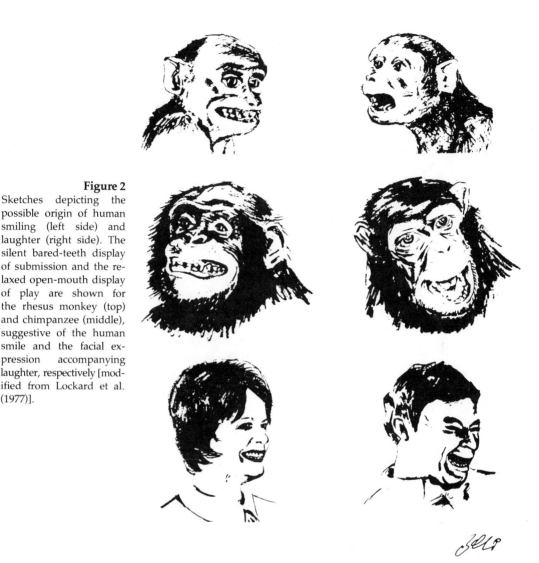

Figure 2
Sketches depicting the possible origin of human smiling (left side) and laughter (right side). The silent bared-teeth display of submission and the relaxed open-mouth display of play are shown for the rhesus monkey (top) and chimpanzee (middle), suggestive of the human smile and the facial expression accompanying laughter, respectively [modified from Lockard et al. (1977)].

silent bared-teeth submissive grimace and now signals affiliative intentions (Figure 2, left side) and that laughter evolved from the relaxed open-mouth display of mock threat and has come to indicate a playful or recreational intent (Figure 2, right side). The intent of this study was to discern the differences in both form and context that adult smiling and the mouth expression accompanying laughter may take. It was reasoned that if such displays were initially different in origin and still serve to some extent their original functions, then they should be either temporally distinct (i.e., occurring at different times of the same situation) or mutually exclusive (i.e., occurring frequently in different situations) in certain types of social exchanges.

The two mouth expressions in question are distinguishable primarily by the extent of teeth exposure, degree of lip retraction and the curvature of the corners of the mouth. Smiling ranges from closed lips with slightly turned-up mouth corners to front teeth exposure (mouth sometimes open) with sharp upturned mouth corners. The laughter grimace is an opened mouth, teeth biting edges showing (particularly lower jaw) and rounded lip corners. Laughter vocalizations vary from a barely audible grunt or mild chuckle with vertical chest movements to an intense guffaw with both head and chest movements and sometimes eye closure. In intense laughter the head moves backward and then forward and the chest movements are quite exaggerated.

The form, frequency and temporal occurrence of the smile and the laughter mouth of one member of a pair were observed and recorded in over 140 dyads in four social situations. The first situation was goal-oriented, such as buying a meal or purchasing a ticket. The individuals involved were task-oriented and expected the interchange to be brief. The second situation consisted of work breaks among friends at college or on the job, while having coffee or at lunch time. The third category was chance encounters between acquaintances, such as exchanges in hallways at work or between college classes. The fourth category of interactions was leisure episodes such as dining out, parties or social gatherings.

Although individual differences and cultural shaping of adult expressions tended to mask consistencies, the findings affirmed that front-teeth smiling and the more open-mouth expression associated with laughter still serve relatively separate functions. Most forms of smiling were evident in greeting and departure interactions (Figure 3, sharp mouth corners). The facial expression

Figure 3
The percent of individuals smiling (mouth corners 1 and 2) or manifesting the facial mouth of laughter (corners 3 and 4) in the first two 5-sec intervals of dyadic interactions in four social contexts (goal oriented, work break, chance encounter and leisure situation). Smiles are evident in all four contexts whereas laughter mouths are rarely manifested in the initial exchanges in other than leisure situations [modified from Lockard et al. (1977)].

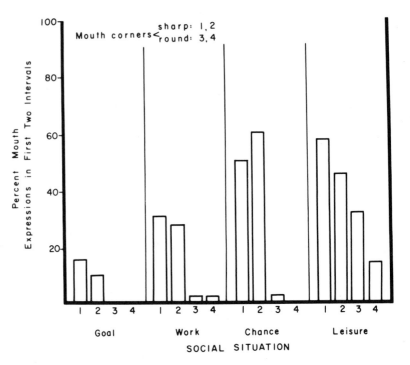

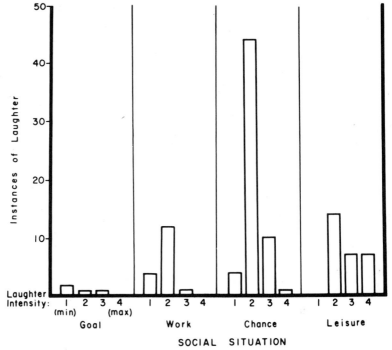

Figure 4
Instances of laughter, in terms of laughter intensity, in four social contexts (goal-oriented, $N = 38$ individuals; work break, $N = 29$; chance encounter, $N = 32$; leisure episode, $N = 42$). Laughing was generally rare in the goal-oriented context and laughter intensity 4 was prevalent only in leisure interactions [modified from Lockard et al. (1977)].

of frank laughter was seen almost exclusively in a recreational context (Figure 3, round mouth corners). If frank laughter did occur in the other social situations it was usually during the later stages when the exchanges were more relaxed and less formal (Figure 4).

However, some degree of convergence of the two displays was indicated by the data since there was some difficulty in detecting the facial differences between smiling and laughter *in the milder form of each*. The process by which the convergence could have occurred is relatively straightforward. For example, if an initially submissive display such as the silent bared-teeth expression prevented agonistic encounters, it might well have come (through natural selection) to stand for affiliative intentions. Signals of friendliness have been of considerable importance in the survival of hominids and, certainly, would have been subject to ritualization. Exaggeration of affiliative smiling could have taken the form of auditory accentuation, as in laughter vocalization or play-face simulation, such as that approximating the relaxed open-mouth display. The latter possibility is supported by chimpanzee data in which one of three variants of the silent bared-teeth display is reciprocally manifested in an affiliative intention between two animals (van Hooff, 1971). In humans as well, smiling has been reported to sometimes serve as an invitation to approach in mother–infant interactions (Vine, 1973).

The interchange of smiling and laughter could also be a learned phenomenon. If the two displays tend to occur in different contexts, both of which signal friendly intentions, it is conceivable that adults learn to mix the two displays in the same context. For example, in highly affiliative situations such as social reception lines and amicable interactions between superiors and subordinates, forced laughter often accompanies a broad smile with front teeth showing and mouth corners turned up. It seems, therefore, quite likely that these variations in form and occurrence of smiling and the laughter mouth either through some degree of convergence or learning, or both, have created the appearance of a continuum of graded signals masking originally discreet displays of different phyletic origins.

The third study to be considered addresses the importance of intention movements in social communication (Lockard et al., 1978). Since survival in most social vertebrates is dependent on group cohesion, individual members often coordinate their activities. This coordination in the flight of some passerine birds is accomplished by ritualized preparatory movements of flight, the exaggeration of which functionally synchronizes flock movement. Savannah baboons exhibit a similar behavior in the restless movements of peripheral males (away from and back to the group), signaling alternative directions of troop departure. Since humans are social primates, postural movements may serve an analogous function. For example, when an individual is anxious to leave, traditional departure vocalizations such as, "It is getting late; I'll see you later." etc., are often augmented by rapid postural changes. This phenomenon is particularly noticeable in children whose stationary postures are difficult to maintain. Whenever an adult detains a child, the child often oscillates back and forth intending to leave but somewhat afraid to do so. The present study was concerned with the investigation of these postural changes in adults as signals of imminent departure.

Four different kinds of postural stances, the number of shifts from one stance to another, and whether the shifts were toward or away from another individual were studied in pairs of adults from the beginning to the end of an interaction. The stances were classified as either (a) equal weight, closed stance (i.e., the legs bearing equal body weight and approximately 6–12 inches distance from toe to toe); (b) equal weight, open stance (greater than 12 inches toe to toe); (c) unequal weight, crossed-leg stance; or (d) unequal weight, uncrossed stance (i.e., one leg bearing more body weight than the other). Only those individuals who were stationery for 45 seconds to five minutes before departure were included as subjects; the behavior of only one member of each pair was recorded in any given interaction; and the sex of the individuals involved and whether they left separately or together were noted.

Data of about 200 pairs of individuals implicated both stance and weight shift as departure signals. At the onset of a dyadic interaction, the equal weight, closed stance was the most common, whereas in the terminal stages of the interaction, the unequal weight, uncrossed stance predominated. The open and crossed-leg stances were infrequent at any time. As for weight shifts, they too were not distributed equally during a dyadic exchange but were noticeably more numerous at the beginning of an interaction and especially just prior to departure for most subjects. There were no significant sex differences in stance or in weight shifts.

In addition to observations of pairs of individuals in a variety of public areas (zoo, airport, shopping centers and recreational centers) the stances and weight shifts of single individuals who were stationary (either sightseeing, window-shopping or waiting at a stoplight) were also recorded. Preadaptations of social signals are often seen in solitary behavior. As shown in Figure 5, the data on single individuals were in the same direction as for dyads. Just prior to locomotion, singletons gave more weight shifts than during the middle portion of their stationary, standing posture (Figure 5, left side). In dyadic interactions in which the members of the pairs departed separately, the increase in weight shifts from the middle to the last portion of the interaction was more exaggerated (Figure 5, right side) than in singletons (Figure 5, left side). Communication among pairs requires that each member of the pair be able to send and receive signals. Increased frequency of weight shifts of individuals in dyads departing separately over that of singletons suggests that weight shifts were functioning as a social signal. Support was given this hypothesis in the finding that there were no significant differences between short-duration interactions and longer-duration interactions in any of the variables studied. Therefore, the results cannot be interpreted in terms of restlessness alone.

Weight shifts away from the other member of the dyad also increased in the last portion of the dyadic interactions. Since data were taken on only one member of each pair, assuming that the

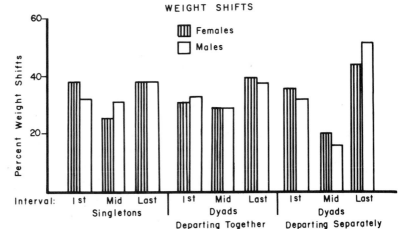

Figure 5
Percent weight-shifts in stance in terms of the first, middle and last 10-sec intervals of a stationary position. Female and male singletons are compared to dyads, the members of which either left together or separately. Dyads departing separately frequently shifted their weight from one leg to the other prior to leavetaking [modified from Lockard et al. (1978)].

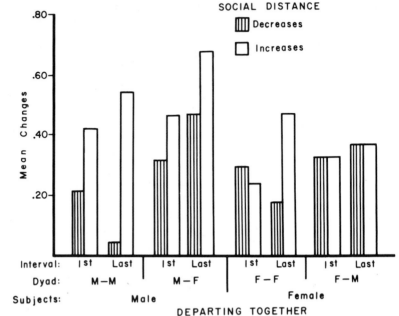

Figure 6
Mean changes in social distance with weight-shifts in stance of dyadic members for the first and last 10-sec interval of a stationary position. Females of female–male (F–M) dyads do not increase their social distance prior to departing together with males as do the members of all other dyads [modified from Lockard et al. (1978)].

subject is the first member of the pair, there were four possible dyadic combinations: male–male, male–female, female–female and female–male. As seen in Figure 6, the data for male subjects revealed increases in social distance (i.e., increases in the frequency of weight shifts away from the other member of the pair) for both male–male or male–female dyads regardless of whether they left separately or together. Female subjects also increased their social distance just prior to departure in all dyadic combinations except female–male pairs in which the members departed together.

The results indicated that increased frequency of unequal weight stances, weight shifts in general and, particularly, weight shifts away from other individuals (i.e., increased social distance) may alone, but especially in combination, signal imminent departure. Members of a pair who departed separately gave more exaggerated postural changes than singletons who were about to locomote. This exaggeration did not occur in dyads departing together as no separation signal was required. Moreover, the social distance changes preceding departure were consistent with the intention of the dyads; except for females leaving with males, most individuals of all other dyadic combinations increased their social distance upon departure. This finding suggested that if individuals of a dyad depart together a female has a closer mean social distance to a male than to a female member of a pair. In contrast, males consistently increased their social distance just prior to locomoting, regardless of the sex of the other member.

The ethological study of postural changes permits the comparison of signals among species in terms of signal function and probable origin. Postures and locomotion are characteristic of individual animals and, therefore, available to selective pressures. For instance, those behaviors that synchronize group movement may have reproductive, protective and food-foraging advantages. The adaptive significance of these processes would, in turn, enhance the social characteristics of the intention movement, providing important signal components for social animals.

Since stationary bipedal postures of humans are difficult to maintain for any length of time, the standing individual adjusts his weight to optimize postural comfort. This phenomena becomes exaggerated during departure when it functions as a social signal of leave-taking. Signaling readiness to depart prepares interacting individuals for a social transition. A smooth change in the social situation facilitates the continuance of affiliative ties. Abrupt verbal signals on departure (e.g., "good-bye," "must be going" or "see you later") appear to be buffered by nonverbal cues such as stance changes and weight shifts. Although not researched in the present study, it is quite likely that other behavioral changes, such as the breaking of eye contact and hand gesturing, also function as intentional signals to depart.

A begging hand gesture was investigated in the fourth study on food sharing (Lockard et al., 1976; Lockard, 1977). Food sharing among nonhuman primates is rare, documented only in chimpanzees *(Pan troglodytes)*. Submissive behaviors and begging gestures are essential displays in the sharing of food among these animals. Food sharing between related chimpanzees, such as mother–offspring or siblings (Figure 7), and the sharing of captured prey among the adult animals involved (Figure 8) and other familiar conspecifics indicate that there are "rules-of-the-game" as well. These rules may be influenced by kin selection and reciprocal altruism. In the case of the former, sharing food with relatives could increase the fitness of individuals with common genes. With respect to the latter, sharing food with individuals who are not relatives, but which at some other time would benefit the giver or the giver's relatives, could also be adaptive.

Sharing of food and other resources is an established practice among humans, but the behaviors, contexts and rules thought to be important in its manifestation have not been studied in detail. The present research attempted to do so, employing panhandling as a model, to explore some aspects of the voluntary sharing of resources among adults. In panhandling the supposedly "needy" individual requests or begs for money from a potentially helpful stranger. Although the observation of several actual panhandlers indicated some of the important variables to study, it was inefficient in that considerable research time was spent in locating the panhandlers to watch. Therefore a more expeditious procedure was employed whereby several college students served as panhandlers.

Figure 7
Line drawing illustrating a potential food sharing episode between related chimpanzees. Note the extended arm of the younger animal. Sharing food with relatives may increase one's inclusive fitness (i.e., by perpetuating those genes held in common with other individuals) through kin selection.

Two female and two male students approached separately over 500 target groupings of individuals. A target was either a single male, a single female, two males, two females, a male and a female together or a family grouping of one adult female and male plus at least one child. Each panhandler approached an approximately equal number of targets and requested 10¢ without explanation. The submissive approach consisted of head down, stooped shoulders, no eye contact, and an extended right arm begging-hand gesture. The dominant approach consisted of upright stance, head erect, eye contact—with no begging gesture. Target individuals both eating and not eating were approached on sunny and overcast days during spring and autumn when the panhandler was dressed either casually, shabbily or handsomely.

The data indicate that females were generally more successful panhandlers than males, dress and weather showing no consistent trend. The panhandlers were more successful in approaching target individuals who were consuming food than those who were not. With all conditions, a dominant approach tended to be more advantageous than a submissive approach although that comparison did not reach statistical significance. Success rate of the panhandlers in spring was 53% and in autumn, 34%.

In looking at the more specific findings of the study (Figure 9), it was found that male panhandlers were comparatively successful only when they approached, in a submissive posture, females who were eating. Females were particularly more successful than male panhandlers when they approached, in a submissive posture, males who were eating, or when they approached, in a dominant posture, a single female or single male who was not eating. Targets of more than one individual, especially a family or a male and a female together, were resistant to panhandling.

The results are striking in view of the fact that the male and female panhandlers were requesting a small amount of money (10¢) and were most successful when approaching, in a submissive posture, target individuals who were consuming food. In fact, the most potent variable of the study was whether the

Figure 8
Line drawing depicting a potential food-sharing situation between adult male chimpanzees after a successful spontaneous "hunting" episode. Note the extended arm and the facial grimace of the begging chimpanzee. Food sharing among "cooperative hunters" is possibly mediated by reciprocal altruism which increases the fitness of the receiver now and the giver later when the "favor" is returned.

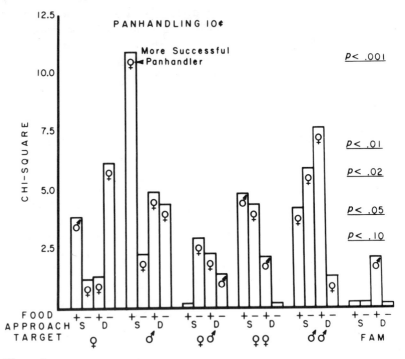

Figure 9

Chi-square values (statistical tests) and probability levels of significance
($p < .10 - .001$) of the success rate of female and male panhandlers. Each
panhandler approached either submissively (S) or dominantly (D) individuals who were either consuming food ($+$) or not ($-$). The target groups
were either one or two females or males, a female and male together, or a
family with at least one child. The sex of the more successful panhandler is
shown at the top of the histogram bars or not at all if neither sex had an
advantage. For example, a female panhandler approaching submissively a
single male (who is eating) is quite successful in achieving 10¢ ($\chi^2 = 10.81$,
$p < .001$) as compared to a male panhandler approaching in like manner a
similar target category.

target individuals were engaged in food consumption. Moreover,
in addition to giving 10¢, target individuals who were eating often
offered some of their food to the panhandler. The common practice
among humans of trading resources may have its origins in
primitive food-sharing tendencies. In the past, hominids may well
have had to engage in reciprocal food sharing to survive.

The results also suggested that there may be appropriate behaviors (i.e., submissive postures and begging gestures) and
specific rules (e.g., a female approaching a male but not a family)
for achieving one's share of food. If food consumption was not in
evidence, a dominant female panhandler was relatively successful
in obtaining 10¢ only when approaching a single male or another
single female. The potential sexual connotations of the former and
the dominant–submissive implications of the latter are interesting.
However, a target grouping of at least two individuals (either two

females, a male and a female together, or a family) was sufficient to reduce the dominant advantage. This result is consistent with findings that groups are generally less willing to come to someone's assistance than single individuals (Latané and Darley, 1969).

Whereas sharing among individuals of a family is very common, a family unit *per se* may be a "natural barrier" to more general food distribution. The economics of modern society (i.e., trading resources either directly or indirectly via money) may overcome through reciprocal altruism a resistance to share only among relatives favored by kin selection. Kin selection may be the more basic rule, however, as evidenced here by the resistance of families to share resources with strangers with whom reciprocal altruism is unlikely. Moreover, the occurrence of reciprocal altruism may require some familiarity among the parties concerned since a nicely dressed panhandler (indicative of the potential to reciprocate) was no more successful than a shabbily dressed panhandler when either was a stranger to the target individuals.

The fact that $\frac{1}{3}$ (autumn) to over $\frac{1}{2}$ (spring) of the people approached by the panhandlers did share, irrespective of conditions, suggests that sharing is a likely evolutionary strategy of human survival. The probability of a begging individual acquiring a handout would undoubtedly increase to the extent that the panhandler could appear to be a relative or at least a peer member of the target group. A handout would almost assuredly occur if the begging individual also submissively approached during spring a single target individual who was consuming food. Knowing the rules and displaying the appropriate behaviors in the proper context may be as adaptive for humans as it is for chimpanzees.

In the fifth study conducted (Morgan et al., 1975), social signals at a distance were investigated. Although some research has been done on short-range communication, very little is known about more long-range signals. Hitchhiking was the situation under study as it is a dyadic interaction at a distance, which lends itself to observation and quantification. In a sequence of nonverbal behaviors the hitchhiker solicits assistance from a motorist who, in turn, either stops or drives on. The driver must make a rapid decision based upon his response set and the signals of the hitchhiker. Preliminary observations of actual hitchhikers indicated that visibility, gestures, facial expressions, sex, age, dress and climate might influence the driver's decision.

During 18 hours of observation, rides were solicited by two female and two male college students individually from drivers of well over 4,000 cars. Data were collected by the hitchhiker (who did not accept rides) and by an inconspicuous observer. The recorded data include the number of cars passing the hitchhiker in a 15-minute interval, the number of motorists offering rides, demographic information on the apparent age and sex of the driver, number and ages of passengers and the type of vehicle. Sex, secondary sexual characteristics, eye contact, hand gestures and food, all playing a signaling role in anthropoid social interactions, were experimentally manipulated. With fixed facial expression, eye contact was directed either at the driver or along the side of the road. Two hand gestures were utilized, either the traditional extended-arm, thumb-up hitchhiking gesture or a palm-up, "begging" gesture with extended arm and flexed fingers. The secondary sex characteristics that were studied were bust size in females and beard growth in males. A portion of the time the hitchhikers were also eating fruit. All of these variables were arranged in a counterbalanced experimental design.

As shown in Figure 10, sex and eye contact were the variables with the strongest effects. Females received approximately three times as many rides as males. Within each sex, eye contact essentially doubled the hitchhiker's rate of success. There was a statistically nonsignificant positive trend for the secondary sex characteristics. When these data were analyzed more specifically, an augmented bust alone did improve ride offerings for the females; however, the results for bearded males were ambiguous. Whereas the begging hand gestures regardless of condition showed a statistically nonsignificant inverse trend, males in the bearded, eye-contact condition were offered significantly fewer rides when begging than when using the traditional gesture. An

Figure 10
Percent success in hitching a ride in terms of the variable(s) manipulated. Most successful hitchhikers were big-busted females making eye-contact with drivers. Least successful hitchhikers were males making no eye-contact with drivers and using a begging gesture [modified from Morgan et al. (1975)].

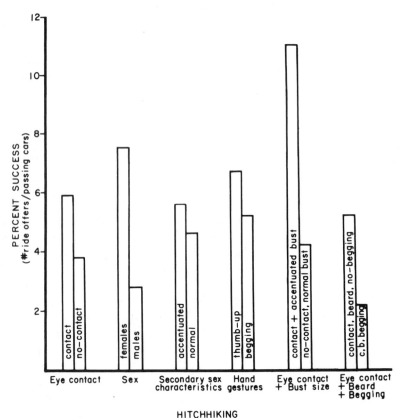

interesting negative correlation was manifested between taller hitchhikers (regardless of sex) and the begging gesture. As predicted, female hitchhikers and the augmented bust, eye-contact condition received the greatest number of ride offerings: approximately one in 10 motorists stopped as compared to the overall rate of one in 20.

When the demographic data were analyzed it was found that hitchhikers are most likely to receive ride offers during spring (8.3%) in contrast to fall (6.9%) and winter (5.0%) from males (88.5%), drivers in the age range 20–30 years (55.8%), motorists *without* passengers (79.8%) especially children under 10 (2.9%), drivers of sedans (81.3%), and drivers of vehicles three to four years old (48.1%). Male motorists offered significantly more rides to hitchhikers who were female rather than male. Few female motorists offered rides and showed no sex preference for hitchhikers.

The results of this study indicated that motorists are sometimes willing to pick up hitchhikers, and the attempt to make eye contact with the driver markedly improves the rate of ride offers, but the overall rate is low. Females have a much better chance than males of being offered a ride, and females who accentuate bust size improve their rate of rides from male drivers in the same general age range as the hitchhiker. Some signals, in particular beards, height, the begging gesture and eating produced variable results depending in part upon other signals with which they were paired. This outcome demonstrated that *appropriateness* is an essential component of an effective long-range signal. Although a signal may be easily perceived at a distance it must also be understood in the particular context in which it was employed. To the extent that a signal is ambiguous (e.g., a tall or bearded hitchhiker engaged in incongruous behaviors such as begging or eating) it becomes less effective.

The understanding of a signal requires either a common evolutionary, cultural or a situational history of the participants. Eye contact, sexual characteristics and hand gestures are highly effective displays in hitchhiking—in part, because they are not unique to this situation. Body communication is well rooted in primate evolution and the selective pressures of survival in the past may well be the basis for nonverbal communication in the present. As was shown by the hitchhiking model, the effective long-range signals were those that maximized interests (sexuality, eye contact and height) and safety (femaleness) and minimized danger (maleness).

The last study to be discussed considers some of the first social signals in an individual's life, namely, those between mother and infant (Lockard et al., 1979). If evolutionarily the care of infants has rested primarily with the female, then early attachments between mother and infant would be advantageous to the survival of the infant. It has been suggested in several other studies that mother–

infant bonds are formed very soon after birth (Klaus and Kennell, 1976). It was reported that this bonding is weaker among mothers separated from their premature babies for long periods immediately after birth than among those closely in contact with their babies after delivery. It was also suggested that there is a disproportionally high percentage of premature babies among "battered children" or among those infants who fail to thrive where no organic cause for poor weight gain was indicated. It was found that early skin-to-skin contact between mother and infant led to better infant care, prolonged breast feeding, improved weight gain and decreased infection as compared to a control group of mothers and infants who had later skin-to-skin contact.

The present study investigated a possible bonding signal between mother and infant having to do with heartbeat imprinting. It was reported by Salk (1973) that heartbeat recordings at normal rate (60–70 cycles per minute) soothed infants, while other rhythmic sounds played at the same rate had an upsetting effect. It was shown by Ambrose (1969) that newborn infants who were rocked at approximately a heartbeat rate were much quieter than infants the same age who were rocked at faster or slower speeds. Munn (1965) established the fact that the infant is capable of hearing loud, sharp noises while still *in utero*. Then Morris (1971) suggested that the fetus becomes imprinted to the constant pulsating of the mother's heart.

In a preliminary investigation by the present author of family groupings in public, it was found that the majority of the observed mothers carried infants of less than one-year old on the left side. A second, more extensive study was conducted to determine the reliability of such observations and to ascertain what percentage of left-side carriages involved older infants or were manifested by adult males. A third study was conducted in Senegal, Africa, where the infants are carried in soft-cloth backpacks. The intent of that research was to ascertain whether the infant itself chooses by head placement to be nearer its mother's heart on the left side.

Over 4,000 adult–child groupings in a variety of public places were observed in terms of sex and age of adults accompanying children, sex and age of infant or child, the side (right or left) on which (and the way in which) the adult was carrying the child. Family groupings of more than one child were also recorded. The data indicated that sex and age of infant, sex of parent and whether the infant was accompanied by both its parents are important parameters in the way infants are carried.

The findings are illustrated in Figures 11 and 12. In Dakar, Senegal, young infants (less than one-year old) who are carried dorsally in backpacks showed a left-side head placement with respect to their mother's back (near the heart). Older infants (one year or older) showed no such preference. Adult Dakar males rarely carried children in public. In Seattle, Washington (U.S.A.), adult females who carried young infants ventrally did so predomi-

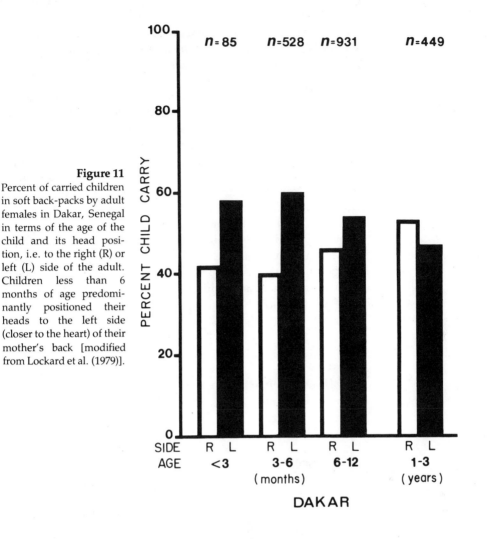

Figure 11
Percent of carried children in soft back-packs by adult females in Dakar, Senegal in terms of the age of the child and its head position, i.e. to the right (R) or left (L) side of the adult. Children less than 6 months of age predominantly positioned their heads to the left side (closer to the heart) of their mother's back [modified from Lockard et al. (1979)].

nantly on the left side. The strongest left-side bias was with male infants 0–3 months old. There was a tendency for adult females to carry older infants on the right side. Although single adult females carried young infants more than did single adult males, young infants were carried equally often by either sex when adult males were accompanying adult females. Adult males showed no consistently predominant left-side bias when carrying young infants. Adult males carried older infants more frequently than did adult females and predominantly on the right side.

If by primate heritage, the primary responsibility for offspring survival during its first few months was that of the female, then a signal that facilitated the mother–infant bond would be adaptive. Since maternity can be ascertained with nearly 100% certainty, i.e., the female knows from birth who her infant is, and if the infant knows its mother initially by her heartbeat, then the basis for initiating the mother–infant bond is available at birth. If, on the other hand, paternity is only suspected and adult male protection of the infant is not essential until the infant is mobile apart from the mother, then paternal-care behaviors need not be given until the infant is older. This interpretation is compatible with the hypothesis of conservation of maternal energy. When the infant is altricial and the female is lactating, a considerable amount of maternal investment is required. With the development of the infant and consumption of solid foods, the male may then assume an increasingly larger role in infant care so that the female is partially freed to invest in a second offspring. If this were the case, it would be predicted that a considerable amount of paternal care would be evident in the transition of offspring from infancy to childhood, especially in families with more than one child.

Although the adult male did do his share of infant carry when he was accompanying an adult female, that finding may speak more to pair bonding than to paternal care. Assisting the female in infant carry may accrue reciprocally certain sexual favors and attention for the male at a later time. To account for the strong

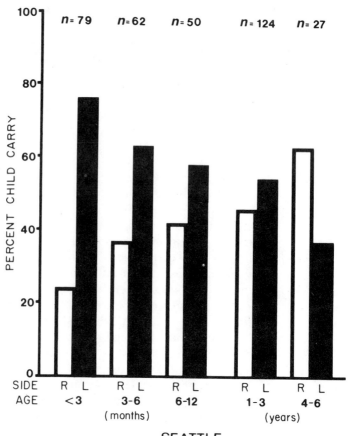

Figure 12
Percent of carried children by adult females in Seattle, Washington, in terms of the age of the child and the right (R) or left (L) side of the adult on which it is carried. Children less than 1 year of age are carried predominantly on the left side (near the heart) of their mothers [modified from Lockard et al. (1979)].

left-side bias in the carry of infant males, several variables in the differential development of males and females could be proposed. For instance, the male infant could be regarded as a more immature organism than the female for the same chronological age, since males usually reach puberty at an older age than females. Extrapolating further it would then be essential that the mother–infant bond be relatively stronger for male infants than for female infants if the former were to survive. However, a more parsimonious explanation for which there are some data (Tanner, 1973) is to suggest that a male is a more active organism initially than the female and requires for its pacification, in the ventral position, a greater frequency of left-side carriages than the female. (In the dorsal position used in Senegal, it is assumed that infant activity is not a function of the mother's behavior since heartbeat pacification is under the direct control of the infant). If this interpretation is correct, one would then predict that adult females in the U.S.A. would carry ill or injured infants ventrally on the left side more than well infants of the same chronological age, since irritability in the form of activity often increases with illness. More conventional hypotheses in terms of strength of hand grip (Spottswood and Burghardt, 1976), weight of infant (Tanner, 1973) and handedness (Hanaway and Burghardt, 1976) to account for the present findings are either ambiguous or not supported by the existing data in the literature.

Generating Hypotheses

Maternal-care behaviors, in general, are particularly illustrative of the fruitfulness of the theoretical and methodological approach expounded here. Some of the least subtle and first-appearing signals in maternal care are proximity, body contact, extended eye contact, facial grimaces, rhythmic movements and soft vocalizations between mother and infant. Interestingly enough, these classes of signals are typical of courtship as well and may provide a possible evolutionary root for the elaboration of primitive primate breeding behaviors into pair bonding. In maternal care the most intimate contact occurs initially, diminishing into fragments as the infant matures, i.e., from a full embrace and engulfment of the newborn to partial embraces of arm around the shoulder and hand clasp as the child develops. In courtship the reverse seems to be the case, i.e., with the least intimate elements appearing at the beginning of courtship, e.g., hand clasp initially and embracing later. However, in both situations it is decidedly more complex than these descriptions would indicate. For example, to the extent that maternal care and pair-bonding signals at any point in the interactions are not meant to be obvious (e.g., as in public), only fragments of the full intensity signals will be apparent. This is again the idea that an attenuated behavior or the antithesis of a behavior can function as a different (i.e., graded) or opposite signal. Moreover, to the extent that a fragment serves equally well the same function as the total signal, the former is more likely to occur as it takes less effort (i.e., energy conservation).

Carrying the above line of reasoning further, let us assume for the purpose of theoretical parsimony that an evolved behavioral signal takes the route of least resistance, i.e., arises from one or more preadaptations which are already a part of an organism's behavioral repertoire. For instance, primate allogrooming behavior originally evolved to remove ectoparasites from areas of the body not easily reached by self-grooming (e.g., the middle of the back). Once allogrooming was part of the behavioral repertoire of primates, it became a preadaptation for affiliative interactions among individual animals of a group (Hutchins and Barash, 1976) and evolved to serve this function as well. In similar fashion, then, the four basic categories of human behavioral signals suggested earlier (reproduction, parental-care, play behavior and affiliative peer signals) would be likely sources for preadaptations of additional signals, e.g., courtship signals in pair bonding. As shown in the schematic of Table I, it is hypothesized that there are four possible sources of preadaptation from which male courtship signals could evolve and four different sources for females. Adult males have developed from male infants into male peers and eventually into potential male breeding partners and fathers; whereas adult females have been female infants, female peers, potential female mates and subsequently potential mothers. The origins of courtship signals for males and females, therefore, could be quite disparate. Moreover, for either sex, some preadaptations may be more amenable to selective pressures of courtship than other preadaptations. When these alternatives are considered, there may

Table I
Possible Origins of Courtship Behaviors

Developmental Phase	Males (M or m)[a] Interactions Ego Other	Females (F or f)[a] Interactions Ego Other
Infancy	$m_i - F_{MO}$[b]	$f_i - F_{MO}$[b]
Childhood	$m_{pp} - M_{FA}$	$f_{pp} - M_{FA}$
Adolescence	$m_j - m_j$	$f_j - f_j$
	$m_j - f_j$	$f_j - m_j$
	$M_b - M_B$	$F_b - F_B$
	$M_b - F_b$	$F_b - M_b$
	$M_b - F_B$	$F_b - M_B$
Adulthood	$M_{fa} - f_{pp}$	$F_{mo} - f_i$
	$M_{fa} - m_{pp}$	$F_{mo} - m_i$

[a]Lower case letter = subadult. Upper case letter = adult. Subscripts: i = infant, pp = prepuberty, j = juvenile, b = potential breeder, fa = potential father, mo = potential mother, B = breeder, FA = father, MO = mother.

[b]Early phase interactions may continue into later phases.

be certain logical and quantifiable priorities to the manifestation of adaptive courtship signals of males and females as well as to other kinds of signals.

The productivity of the above approach to the understanding of human social signals is most vividly illustrated when answers or predictions concerning origin or mechanism of signals can be empirically tested. Some of the predictions in maternal-care signaling that are amenable to such evaluation are as follows: (a) With the maturation of the infant, *fragments* of mother–infant signals will occur more frequently than the composite behaviors, i.e., the full intensity behaviors will be seen less and less. The adaptive significance of such an outcome, from the point of view of the mother, would be conservation of maternal energy to then devote to younger, more immature siblings and, from the point of view of the growing infant, greater maternal independence in preparation for adulthood. (b) Distantly related female adults (e.g., a third cousin of the mother) to the infant will manifest fewer maternal-care signals or elements of these behaviors toward the infant than will closely related female adults (e.g., the mother's sister). The explanation here lies with the concentration of care-giving energy on infants with whom you share more genes. (c) To the extent that female courtship or pair-bonding signals as embellishments of breeding signals arose, in part, from maternal–infant preadaptations, many of the signal fragments of maternal care will be common to the female part of courtship as well. (d) To the extent that male courtship signals developed to some extent from paternal-care preadaptations, those signals will be common to the latter category and different from female courtship signals. (e) If, however, male courtship signals developed mainly from affiliative-peer preadaptations, fragments of the latter category will be more common to male courtship than paternal-care behaviors, and so forth.

As represented by these exemplary predictions, there remains only the enormous work to actually conduct the observational studies to test the hypotheses, and to reject or modify the models in order to have eventually a greater understanding of human social signals. Although the six studies already discussed indicate indirectly how such predictions are evaluated, for purposes of clarity, an experimental design for hypotheses (c) and (d) will be briefly outlined. First, parental–infant and courtship behaviors for both female and male adults would have to be observed, defined and quantified. Female courtship signals or their fragments would be compared to the signals of mothers of male infants, and male courtship signals or their fragments would be compared with those of fathers of female infants, as well as female courtship signals. Videotape procedures or movie film would undoubtedly have to be utilized to slow down the signals for detailed observations and comparisons. If in courtship the female "mothers" the male, and the male in turn "protects" the female in terms of very specific behaviors or fragments from the behavioral categories of assumed origin, then these hypotheses would tend to be supported. For example, mothers of newborns give a very specific facial gaze (Klaus and Kennell, 1976), called an *en face* to their infants in which the mother aligns her face in the same plane as that of the infant's face and looks at the infant for extended periods of time. This behavior correlates with certain hormonal changes and is thought to facilitate the bond between mother and infant. Perhaps adult females in courtship exhibit *en face* to their mates in bonding their relationship with them. On the other hand, paternal behavior involves the carrying of mobile infants (over one year of age) when both parents are together (Lockard et al., 1979). If courting males symbolically carry their mates in a manner similar to carrying an infant (as ritualized in the "over the threshold" in newlywed couples), perhaps the messages in the two different contexts are the same. However, if these hypotheses are not supported by objective data, then the model in question should be rejected or modified accordingly. Only when human ethologists are willing to relinquish refuted models and generate others in accordance with the evidence will a science of human social behavior exist.

It would seem that the ethological approach utilized to study animal behavior can be appropriately applied to human social behavior. Moreover, we are the only species in which conspecifics can knowingly act as stooges to elicit the signals under study (e.g., playing the part of a panhandler or hitchhiker). If waiting to observe "the real" situations is either very time consuming or does not allow the rigorous control necessary to test predictions, then employing experimental situations may warrant some *limited* deception. However, as in the study of animal communication, observations and descriptions of actual interactions are invaluable preliminary data, at the very least, for the designing of research and the interpretation of the findings in studies of human social signals.

References

Ambrose, J.A. 1969. Cited in Bowlby, J. *Attachment and Loss.* New York: Basic Books, pp. 291–295.

Andrew, R. J. 1963. Evolution of facial expression. *Science* 142:1034–1041.

Darwin, Charles. 1872. *The Expressions of the Emotions in Man and Animals.* Chicago: University of Chicago Press; reprinted 1965; Fourth Impression 1970, pp. 50–65.

DeVore, I. 1971. The evaluation of human society. In J.F. Eisenberg and W.S. Dillon (eds.) *Man and Beast: Comparative Social Behavior.* Washington, DC: Smithsonian Institution Press, pp. 297–311.

Fox, R. 1972. Alliance and constraint: Sexual selection in the evolution of human kinship systems. In B. Campbell (ed.) *Sexual Selection and the Descent of Man* (1871–1971). Chicago: Aldine, pp. 282–331.

Hall, K.R.L., and DeVore, I. 1965. Baboon social behavior. In I. DeVore (ed.) *Primate Behavior: Field Studies of Monkeys and Apes.* New York: Holt, Rinehart and Winston, pp. 53–110.

Hamilton, W.D. 1964. The genetical evolution of social behavior. I. *International Journal of Theoretical Biology* 7:1–16.

Hanaway, T.P., and Burghardt, G.M. 1976. The development of sexually dimorphic book-carrying behavior. *Bulletin of the Psychonomic Society* 7:267–270.

Heestand, J.E., Begert, S.P., and Lockard, J.S. 1980. Play behavior in slow loris *(Nycticebus coucang)*. Submitted, *Applied Animal Ethology*.

Hinde, R.A. 1974. *Biological Bases of Human Social Behaviour*. New York: McGraw-Hill, pp. 127–132.

Hrdy, S.B. 1977. *The Langurs of Abu: Female and Male Strategies of Reproduction*. Cambridge, MA: Harvard University Press.

Hutchins, M., and Barash, D. 1976. Grooming in primates: Implications for its utilitarian function. *Primates* 17:145–150.

Itorgawa, N. 1975. Variables in male leaving a group of Japanese macaques. In S. Kondo, M. Kawai, A. Ehara and S. Kawamura (eds.) *Proceedings from the Symposium of the Fifth Congress of the International Primatological Society* (Nagoya, Japan, August, 1974). Tokyo: Japanese Science Press, pp. 233–245.

Klaus, M.H., and Kennell, J.H. 1976. *Maternal–Infant Bonding: The Impact of Early Separation or Loss on Family Development*. St. Louis: C.V. Mosby Co.

Latané, B., and Darley, J.M. 1969. Bystander "apathy." *American Scientist* 57:244–268.

Lockard, J.S. 1977. Panhandling as an example of the sharing of resources. *Science* 198:858.

Lockard, J.S., and Adams, R.M. 1980. Peripheral males: A primate model for a human subgroup. Submitted, *Ethology and Sociobiology*.

Lockard, J.S., McDonald, L.L., Clifford, D.A., and Martinez, R. 1976. Panhandling: Sharing of resources (reciprocal altruism or kinship selection). *Science* 191:406–408.

Lockard, J.S., Fahrenbruch, C.E., Smith, J.L., and Morgan, C.J. 1977. Smiling and laughter: Different phyletic origins? *Bulletin of the Psychonomic Society* 10:183–186.

Lockard, J.S., Schiele, B.J., Allen, D.L., and Wiemer, M.J. 1978. Human postural signals: Stance, weight shifts, and social distance as intention movements to depart. *Animal Behaviour* 26:219–224.

Lockard, J.S., Daley, P.C., and Gunderson, V. M. 1979. Maternal and paternal differences in infant carry: U.S. and African data. *American Naturalist* 113:235–246.

Mayr, E. 1974. Behavior programs and evolutionary strategies. *American Scientist* 62:650–659.

Morgan, C.J., Lockard, J.S., Fahrenbruch, C.E., and Smith, J.L. 1975. Hitchhiking: Social signals at a distance. *Psychonomic Science* 5:459–461.

Morris, D. 1971. *Intimate Behavior*. New York: Random House, pp. 1–11.

Munn, N.L. 1965. *The Evolution and Growth of Human Behavior*. Boston: Houghton Mifflin Co., pp. 181–182.

Nickelson, S.A., and Lockard, J.S. 1978. Ethogram of Celebes monkeys *(Macaca nigra)* in two captive habitats. *Primates* 19:437–447.

Salk, L. 1973. The role of the heartbeat in relations between mother and infant. *Scientific American* 228:24–29.

Schaller, G. 1963. *The Mountain Gorilla: Ecology and Behavior*. Chicago: University of Chicago Press.

Spottswood, P.J., and Burghardt, G.M. 1976. The effects of sex, book weight, and grip strength on book carrying styles. *Bulletin of the Psychonomic Society* 8:150–152.

Tanner, J.M. 1973. Variability of growth and maturity in newborn infants. In M. Lewis and L.A. Rosenblum (eds.) *The Effect of the Infant on Its Caregiver.* New York: Wiley, pp. 77–103.

Trivers, R.L. 1971. The evolution of reciprocal altruism. *O. Rev. Biol.* 46:35–57.

van Hooff, J.A.R.A.M. 1967. The facial displays of the Catarrhine moneys and apes. In Morris, D. (ed.) *Primate Ethology.* London: Widenfeld and Nicolson, pp. 7–67.

van Hooff, J.A.R.A.M. 1971. *Aspects of the Social Behaviour and Communication in Human and Higher Non-Human Primates.* Rotterdam: Bronder-Offset, pp. 17–187.

Vine, I. 1973. The role of facial visual signalling in early social development. In M. von Cranach and Vine, I. (eds.) *Social Communication and Movement: Studies of Men and Chimpanzees.* London: Academic Press, pp. 195–298.

Wilson, E.O. 1975. Communication: Basic principles. In Wilson, E.O. (ed.) *Sociobiology: The New Synthesis.* Cambridge, MA: Belknap/Harvard University Press, pp. 176–200.

A Synopsis of Primate Phylogeny

Daris R. Swindler

2

Man belongs to the genus *Homo* and is placed in the order Primates along with all other prosimians, monkeys and apes. Additionally, he is a member of the family Hominidae and together with the anthropoid apes constitutes the superfamily Hominoidea. The history of the diversified members of this order is a fascinating story that has been told many times. It is a long history, perhaps as much as 65 to 70 million years. New fossil material and frequently new interpretations appear annually, which adds to the excitement of paleoanthropology. There is not the space here to consider all of these discoveries but rather I shall attempt to unravel the emergence and evolution of some of the more important primate fossils and how they relate to the evolution of ourselves, *Homo sapiens sapiens*.

Time is an essential ingredient in any evolutionary theory and to better understand this temporal component I shall use the United States as a yardstick for measuring the age of the earth.

To begin with, let us travel by train from Union Square in San Francisco to Grand Central Station in New York City. The total distance is approximately 2,460 miles. If we suppose that a mile represents 2,000,000 years then the 2,460 miles become approximately 5 billion years, which fits the most recent estimates of the age of the earth. From San Francisco to Nebraska is a solitary journey since there is no life on earth as yet. Indeed, we must reach Ames, Iowa, before the first single-cell organisms are observed. Near Cleveland, Ohio, some marine invertebrates are seen in the shallow inland seas, while in western Pennsylvania primitive fish and the first land plants are making an appearance. Just west of the small town of Glen Union we get a glimpse of the first land animals, the amphibians. The reptiles appear at Williamsport, Pennsylvania, and it is another 25 miles to Millville before we see the first mammal-like reptiles and modern varieties of insects. It is 12 more miles before we see the beginnings of the egg-laying mammals and dinosaurs. For the next 30 miles we see the evolution of the large dinosaurs, toothed birds and insect-eating marsupials. When we reach the Pennsylvania–New Jersey line, the dinosaurs have disappeared. In western New Jersey we see carnivores and hoofed animals and in addition, the first primates (prosimians). As we cross the Passaic River we notice for the first time monkeys and apes, and by the time we reach the Hudson River some of the apes resemble man. On the other side of the Hudson River these apelike-man creatures are truly man and they walk erect. Between the east bank of the Hudson River and midtown Manhattan, fire, agriculture and society become a part of man's life. Approximately five feet from the entrance to Grand Central Station Christ is born, and the Declaration of Independence is signed just six inches from the terminal. On this scale, man as a producer of culture is merely the final one-half mile of the journey and an average lifetime is only two inches.[1] Hopefully this yardstick will assist the reader to better understand and appreciate the temporal perspective as we review the history of the primates.

The age of the earth, then, is approximately 5,000,000,000 (5 billion) years. Of this enormous amount of time, primates have been on earth only about 65,000,000 (Table I). Their humble beginnings are represented by many fossil teeth and a few jaws from Montana. The earliest primate (prosimian) from the late Cretaceous is called *Purgatorius* (Figure 1). The genus survived into the Paleocene and was closely related to the insectivores. Indeed, many of these early mammals were very similar, adding to the difficulty of separating them into different taxa; nevertheless, identification is vitally important if one is looking for the *beginning* radiations of an animal group. Teeth are extremely valuable in taxonomy and, fortunately for the paleontologist, they are more frequently preserved than many other body parts. The teeth of *Purgatorius* have been examined by several authorities and the consensus is that they are primate (Van Valen and Sloan, 1965; Clemens, 1974). Whether *Purgatorius* gave rise to any of the Paleocene prosimians is not yet known.

The prosimians of the Paleocene represent a wide variety of forms ranging in size from a common house mouse to an animal as large as a modern cat. Of the many Paleocene genera only one (*Plesiadapis*) has been found in both North America and Europe (France), suggesting that the group utilized the land bridges connecting North America with Northern Europe at that time. *Plesiadapis* was an interesting animal, possessing slightly flattened claws and large, procumbent incisors. In addition, it has been suggested that the animal's mode of locomotion was hopping or jumping, a type of locomotion still practiced by some modern prosimians.

These earliest primates possessed long snouts and undoubtedly a well-developed sense of smell. However, they are arboreal,

---

[1]The data in this paragraph were taken from Kraus (1964).

Table I
Geological Time

Era	Period	Epoch	Life
Cenozoic	Quaternary	Holocene Recent (Began 25,000 years ago)	Living races
		Pleistocene (Began 1,000,000 years ago)	Homo sapiens Homo erectus Homo habilis
	Tertiary	Pliocene (Began 12,000,000 years ago)	Australopithecus Modern anthropoid ape
		Miocene (Began 26,000,000 years ago)	Divergence of anthropoid apes
		Oligocene (Began 38,000,000 years ago)	Divergence of gibbons
		Eocene (Began 58,000,000 years ago)	Divergence of primates from generalized mammalian stock
		Paleocene (Began 68,000,000 years ago)	Notharctus or lemur
Mesozoic	Cretaceous Jurassic Triassic	(Began 127,000,000 years ago) (Began 152,000,000 years ago) (Began 182,000,000 years ago)	Placental insectivores Nonplacental mammals
Paleozoic	Permian Carboniferous Devonian Silurian Ordovician Cambrian	(Began 203,000,000 years ago) (Began 500,000,000 years ago)	Insects Fishes Sea urchins Corals Brachiapods Cephalopods Bivalves
Archean	Pre-Cambrian (First life perhaps 3–4,000,000,000 years ago) Age of the earth 4–5,000,000,000 years		Occasional fossils Carboniferous shales

perhaps having prehensile hands and feet. Binocular vision had not yet evolved and, indeed, the living prosimians do not have the well-developed binocular vision of the more advanced primates.

If there is some suspicion about the primate affinities of these late Cretaceous and Paleocene forms, the onset of the Eocene removes all doubt, for here we find fossils resembling modern primates in their total morphology (Table I). The Eocene saw the development and deployment of several prosimian primate families and, quite possibly, one anthropoid group (Figure 1). The Eocene prosimians possessed several anatomical features not found in the Paleocene forms; for example, they had larger eyes and brains, somewhat shorter muzzles, the large opening (foramen magnum) at the base of the skull was located more forward, and

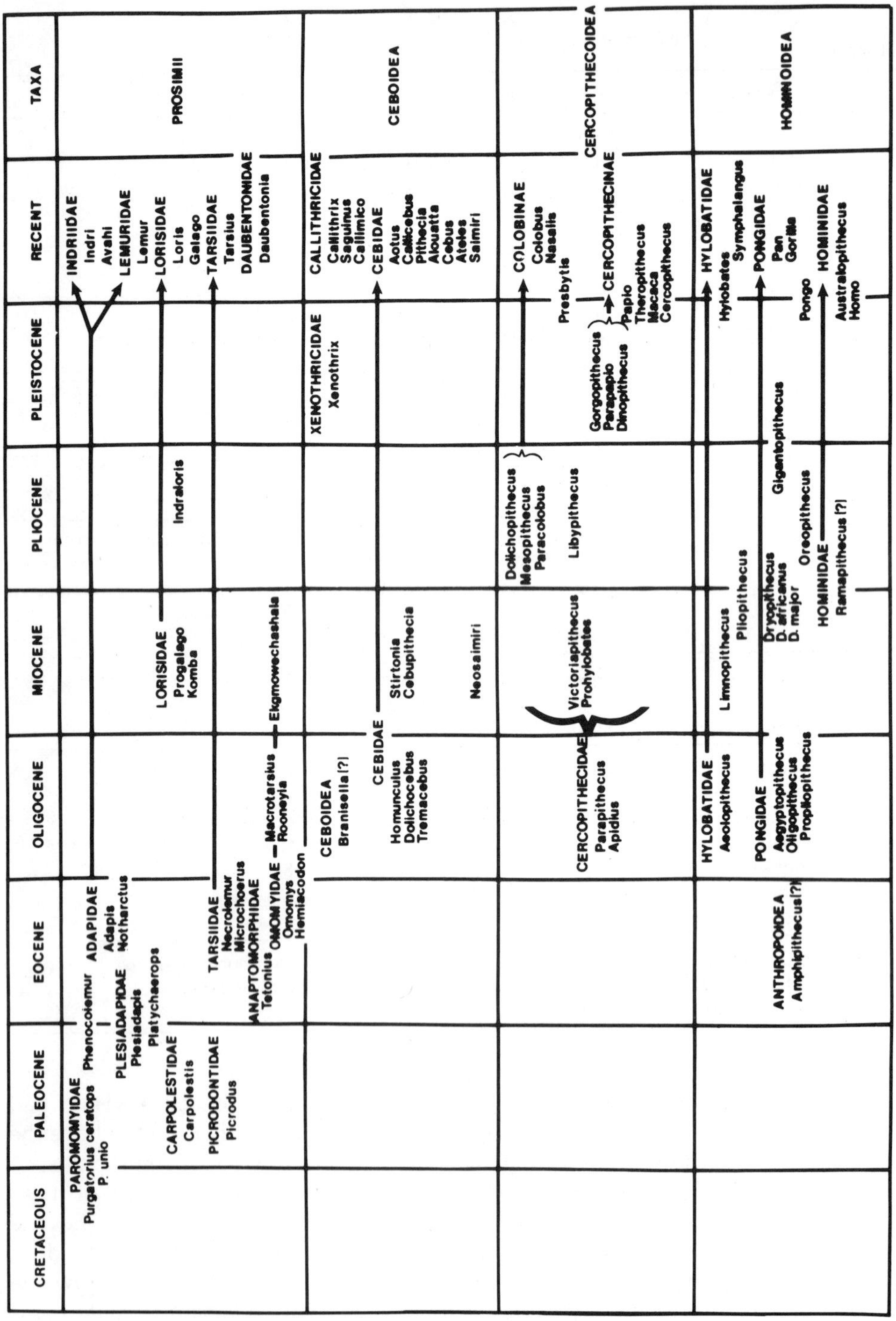

Figure 1
Tertiary history of the primates.

NOTE: species have lower case letters

CRETACEOUS	PALEOCENE	EOCENE	OLIGOCENE	MIOCENE	PLIOCENE	PLEISTOCENE	RECENT	TAXA
	PAROMOMYIDAE Purgatorius ceratops P. unio						INDRIIDAE Indri Avahi	
	Phenacolemur	ADAPIDAE Adapis Notharctus					LEMURIDAE Lemur	
	PLESIADAPIDAE Plesiadapis Platychaerops			LORISIDAE Progalago Komba	Indraloris		LORISIDAE Loris Galago	PROSIMII
	CARPOLESTIDAE Carpolestis						TARSIIDAE Tarsius	
	PICRODONTIDAE Picrodus	TARSIIDAE Necrolemur Microchoerus					DAUBENTONIIDAE Daubentonia	
		ANAPTOMORPHIDAE Tetonius OMOMYIDAE — Macrotarsius — Ekgmowechashala Omomys Rooneyia Hemiacodon						
			CEBOIDEA Branisella (?)			XENOTHRICIDAE Xenothrix	CALLITHRICIDAE Callithrix Saguinus Callimico	
			CEBIDAE Homunculus Dolichocebus Tremacebus	Stirtonia Cebupithecia			CEBIDAE Aotus Callicebus Pithecia Alouatta Cebus Ateles Saimiri	CEBOIDEA
				Neosaimiri				
			CERCOPITHECIDAE Parapithecus Apidium	Victoriapithecus Prohylobates	Dolichopithecus Mesopithecus Paracolobus Libypithecus		COLOBINAE Colobus Nasalis Presbytis	
						Gorgopithecus Parapapio Dinopithecus	CERCOPITHECINAE Papio Theropithecus Macaca Cercopithecus	CERCOPITHECOIDEA
			HYLOBATIDAE Aeolopithecus	Limnopithecus Pliopithecus			HYLOBATIDAE Hylobates Symphalangus	
			PONGIDAE Aegyptopithecus Oligopithecus Propliopithecus	Dryopithecus D. africanus D. major	Gigantopithecus		PONGIDAE Pongo Pan Gorilla	HOMINOIDEA
		ANTHROPOIDEA Amphipithecus (?)		HOMINIDAE Ramapithecus (?)	Oreopithecus		HOMINIDAE Australopithecus Homo	

the limb-bone proportions (where known) were unequal. These features all represent changes from the Paleocene forms which suggest important behavior correlates. For example, the eyes were not only larger but they were shifting from a lateral position to a more frontal orientation, resulting in stereoscopic vision. Certainly this change in the visual system was associated with arboreal life and the locomotor habit of jumping from branch to branch. This mode of locomotion requires the animal to make distance judgments continually, since miscalculations can result in fatal falls. Commensurate with this change was a reduction of the snout, which in turn was correlated with a reduction of the olfactory sense. The more forward position of the foramen magnum strongly suggests that these little creatures were erect while sitting and hopping. The shorter upper branches were undoubtedly used to explore the immediate environment while sitting in an upright position.

The Omomyidae (Figure 1) represent a diverse group of prosimians that many students believe gave rise to the higher primates. They have been found in North America, Asia and Europe. There were many genera, some quite specialized while others were rather generalized. Whatever the ultimate fate of the omomyines they certainly represent an intriguing puzzle for the paleontologist.

Another engrossing but to-date unsolved enigma are the two fossils *Amphipithecus* and *Pondaungia* from the Eocene of Burma (Figure 1). They have been considered everything from prosimians to pongids and certainly some of the ambiguity results from the fact that both specimens are known only from three or four fragmentary jaws containing a few worn teeth.

The Eocene witnessed the adaptive radiation of the prosimian primates and their geographic deployment in North America, Asia and Europe. Specific Eocene ancestors of more advanced primates have not been definitely identified but it is becoming clearer that this geologic period represents an explosive datum in primate history and may well have ushered in the Ceboidea, Cercopithecoidea and Hominoidea.

In the Oligocene, primates are scarce, being found mainly in Africa, albeit, a couple of forms have been located in North and South America: *Rooneyia* and *Branisella* (Figure 1). To date, none has been found in Europe. One site in Africa known as the Fayum is near Cairo, Egypt, yielding all the Oligocene fossil primates from the Old World. Such forms as *Parapithecus*, *Aeolopithecus* and *Aegyptopithecus* may represent forerunners of the cercopithecoids, gibbons and great apes (Simons, 1967). If the current opinion is correct, it implies that the gibbons separated from the great apes long before the latter parted from the hominids. Moreover, it now seems likely that *Aegyptopithecus* (ca 29 million B.P.) may be near the common ancestry of both the great apes and man (Figure 2). Here we see fossil evidence for the initial radiation of the higher primates and, thus, these early forms adumbrate the subsequent

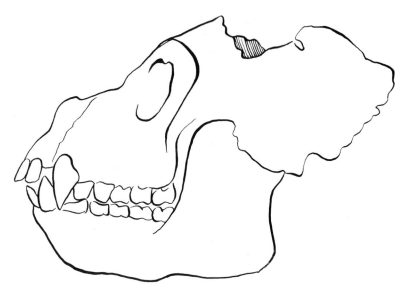

Figure 2
Skull of *Aegyptopithecus zeuxis* [modified from Pilbeam (1972)].

primates that have played such a notable role in human phylogeny.

During the next period, the Miocene, the primates expanded into what are approximately the geographic regions they occupy today. As a matter of fact, there were Miocene apes in Europe and parts of Asia where they are absent today. By now the gibbons were represented by such forms as *Pliopithecus* and *Limnopithecus* (Figure 1). These gibbonlike creatures possessed long canines and arm bones that were longer relative to the leg bones. Certainly, these were not gibbons as we know them today; however, they did display the necessary anatomic prerequisites for evolving into them.

The majority of other Miocene apes constitute a single genus, *Dryopithecus* (Figure 1). The dryopithecines emblazon a wide variety of forms that inhabited Europe, Africa and Asia. Today, it is thought that the living great apes, gorilla, chimpanzee and orang evolved from this widely distributed group of Miocene apes. They are known mostly from jaws and teeth and the dental evidence strongly implies a subsistence based on fruits and leaves which is the most common diet of their descendents today. Postcranial material is scanty but where it does exist it points to a rather generalized quadrupedal animal that probably ran on all fours and when the occasion demanded, the creature could hop or spring (Napier and Davis, 1959). There is no indication at this time of brachiation (swinging from branch to branch with the body suspended from the forelimbs), which is the mode of arboreal locomotion employed by the modern apes.

In the Pliocene, two hominoids deserve consideration. They are *Gigantopithecus* and *Ramapithecus* (Figure 1). *Gigantopithecus* was known for over 25 years from several isolated teeth discovered in

Chinese drugstores. Then in the late 1950s three mandibular fragments with teeth were found in Kwangsi Province, southern China (Figure 3). This Chinese material is relatively recent, dating perhaps from one million to one-half million years ago. Indeed, there is good evidence that *Gigantopithecus* was coeval with Peking man *(Homo erectus)*. Almost 10 years after this discovery, a mandibular fragment was uncovered in northern India from deposits dating between 3 and 7 million years B.P. (Simons and Ettel, 1972). Together this material suggests that a large primate, much more massive than the living gorilla, existed for several million years and perhaps its extinction can be attributed to the lapidating proclivities of the genus *Homo*. At present, *Gigantopithecus* is placed in the superfamily Hominoidea and usually in the family Pongidae, although some students maintain its position is with the hominids.

The other form, *Ramapithecus* (Figure 4), lived some 12 to 14 million years ago and according to some students represents the ancestor of the Hominidae (Simons, 1964). It has been found in India, Africa and more recently in Hungary. To date, only teeth, maxillae and fragments of the lower jaw have been found. The snout is short and the palate is somewhat parabolic and the upper canine is said to be small while the molars are worn in a pattern somewhat similar to that in humans. Collectively, these features

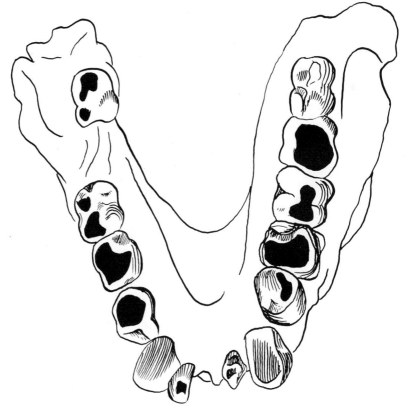

Figure 3
Mandible of *Giganto-pithecus blacki* (drawn from cast).

Figure 4
Occlusal view of maxillary
teeth of *Ramapithecus pun-
jabicus* (drawn from cast).

1 cm

would seem to suggest a hominid. However, work, begun with
Yulish (1970), followed by Andrews (1971) and most recently
Frayer (1974), has led to some doubt regarding the hominid status
of *Ramapithecus*. Frayer (1974) in particular, has presented the most
cogent arguments against accepting any close hominid relationships for *Ramapithecus*. In total morphology, *Ramapithecus* is beginning to appear more and more like a fossil ape *(Dryopithecus)* which
means that the hominid ancestor is yet to be found.

The major hominid trends, as represented by *Ramapithecus*,
involved mainly reduction of the snout and the anterior teeth
(incisors and canines). Indeed, some students have argued that
since *Ramapithecus* possessed reduced canines they must have used
tools and may also have been terrestrial bipeds. The fragmentary
jaws and teeth available for study do not permit such inferences: in
truth, we do not know if *Ramapithecus* was arboreal or ground-
living, or whether it was a brachiating, bipedal or quadrupedal
creature.

The traditional idea that reduced canines are correlated with tool
use is open to suspicion today. Other selective forces could have
been operating on this region of the oral cavity according to Every
(1970) and Tattersall (1972). These students suggest that the

reduced hominid canine could have resulted during the general reduction of the incisors in order to effect a more efficient biting arrangement of the front teeth. Because of the complex nature of this problem it remains unresolved at the present time.

The end of the Tertiary is marked by a change in climate from warm to cool (Table II). The transition in climate did not occur at the same time throughout the world but rather, there were fluctuations of temperature for a long time. Gradually the cooler climates prevailed and with the lowering temperatures appeared a different faunal assemblage that is called the Villafranchian. The Villafranchian can be identified for at least three million years. The boundary between the Pliocene and Pleistocene is a hotly disputed issue at the present time, and it is difficult to find a consensus among geologists. Fossil hominids were present during these times and now let us consider them. Whatever the ultimate decision regarding the Pliocene–Pleistocene border may be, it now seems clear that the genus *Homo* has been adaptively radiating for at least two to three million years.

Before turning to the fossils themselves, several basic trends in hominid evolution will be examined. In addition to the reduced snout and canine observed in *Ramapithecus*, the true hominids of two to three million years ago were undergoing morphologic changes that allowed several important behavioral adaptations.

The hominid pelvis is quite different from the pongid pelvis and many of these differences were present in the Early Pleistocene hominids. With the rearrangement of pelvic anatomy, the bones of

Table II
Pleistocene Chronology of Early Man

Age	Pleistocene Glaciation	Fossils
10,000	Holocene	
20,000		Cro-Magnon
30,000		Combe-Capelle
		Skhul
50,000		Tabun
70,000		
90,000	Wurm	Classic Neanderthal
100,000	Riss–Wurm Interglacial	Fontechevade
200,000	Riss	
300,000	Mindel–Riss Interglacial	Arago, Swanscombe, Steinheim
400,000	Mindel	*H. erectus*, Peking Man
500,000	Gunz–Mindel Interglacial	Maur Jaw
600,000	Gunz	Lantian
800,000		*H. erectus* Europe
		H. erectus Java
1 million		*A. robustus, A. africanus, A. boisei*
1.5 million	Villafranchian	
2 million		
Pliocene		Skull 1470

the lower limbs and foot assumed more of the body weight, the spinal column became more S-shaped and the head shifted more forward. At the same time, the upper limbs became free from weight bearing and the hands were at last able to pick up and examine objects. This erect cursorial biped could now explore a new world with new stimuli, resulting in a marked increase in brain size. Our hominid ancestors were fully bipedal before there was any appreciable expansion of the brain, although throughout the hominid fossil record there is a trend toward increasing brain size. During the Australopithecine phase of hominid evolution the brain increased very slowly, whereas there was a rapid increase during the Middle Pleistocene. This "explosion" in brain size was undoubtedly associated with tool-making, increasing social contacts and ever-increasing hunting organization. During this time the selective pressures for manipulation of objects and the development of motor skills must have been intense. In other words, survival of the group became the ultimate goal of these early hunters. For, as noted by Washburn and Lancaster (1968), if we wish to "understand the origin and the nature of human behavior, there is no choice but to try to understand man, the hunter."

The australopithecines were found in South Africa in 1924. One year later Dart (1925) reported the discovery and alluded to the likeness to human skulls (Figure 5). Since then, australopithecines have been found in other parts of Africa, notably in the Olduvai Gorge in Tanzania, the Omo Valley of Southern Ethiopia and Lake

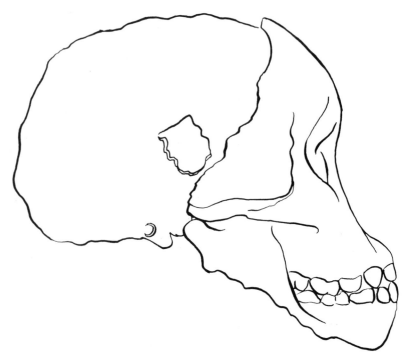

Figure 5
Skull of *Australopithecus africanus*, the taung's child [modified from Pilbeam (1972)].

Turkana, formerly known as Lake Rudolf, in Kenya. There is a great amount of material and many scientists have studied the specimens through the years. Debate continues but there is no doubt about the hominid status of the australopithecines. They were erect bipedal animals ranging in stature from about four and one-half feet to well over five and one-half feet. Their cranial capacities varied from 494 cc in *Australopithecus africanus* to 530 cc in *Australopithecus boisei* (Tobias, 1971). This range overlaps that for living gorillas and is somewhat larger than for living chimpanzees. Incidentally, the normal adult range in modern man is from about 1,000 to 2,000 cc. Crude stone tools (choppers) have been found associated with the Lake Turkana australopithecines dating from about 2.6 million years ago (Leakey et al., 1972). Assorted stone tools have also been found associated with Olduvai Hominid 5, *Australopithecus boisei* from Bed I, which is dated at about 1.8 million years. The hand bones of the australopithecines indicate that they were capable of manufacturing and using these tools known as the Oldowan culture. This tool complex was made of chert and tuff and consisted of a variety of forms ranging from choppers to discoids to spheroids. Indeed, it has been suggested that the spheroids indicate the use of the bolas for hunting birds and running animals as still employed in many regions of the world today. This cultural complexity strongly suggests that these early hominids possessed the rudiments of language no matter how crude it may have been.

Modern human groups display little sexual dimorphism in tooth and body size, while in terrestrial nonhuman primates the male is larger and more muscular than the female. For example, male baboons may be nearly twice as heavy and possess canines an inch longer than the female. The integrity and defense of the baboon troup depends on the ability of the male to defend it against predators, so size has been selected for during the evolution of these animals. The australopithecines are more sexually dimorphic than modern human populations but do not attain the degree of differences displayed by living terrestrial nonhuman primates. This should not be surprising when one considers the stage of morphological and cultural development of the australopithecines.

In 1972 a badly fragmented skull was discovered on the eastern shore of Lake Turkana and given the number "1470" (Leakey, 1973a). Leakey (1973b) has attributed this specimen to the genus *Homo* (Figure 6). The fossil is dated from approximately 2.6 million years B.P. The cranium is very humanlike, possessing no sagittal cresting, little postorbital constriction and an endocranial volume of 770–775 cc (Day et al., 1975). Only time and the discovery of more fossils will solve the problem raised by "1470," namely, did the genus *Homo* exist nearly three million years ago alongside of the australopithecines? If true, this will mean that the genus *Homo* is much older than previously thought and that these two hominid genera are quite ancient, perhaps as much as four or five million

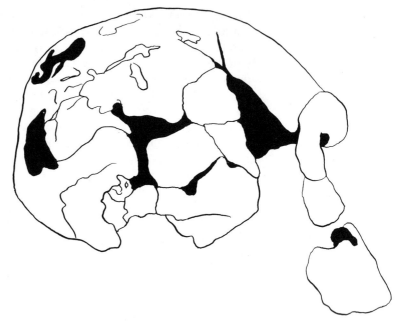

Figure 6
Skull of ER 1470 from Lake
Turkana, Kenya [modified
from Lasker (1976)].

years B.P. Thus. it is beginning to appear that the common
ancestor of *Australopithecus* and *Homo* will be found during these
critical evolutionary times and that the two genera ran a parallel
course for several million years which would deny the australopithecines any direct place in human phylogeny (Leakey,
1973b; Oxnard, 1975). Not all students accept this hypothesis, since
many still see the australopithecines as the immediate ancestors of
Homo. Perhaps the studies of C.D. Johanson in the Afar region of
Ethiopia will help clarify this problem. Johanson and co-workers
have found numerous hominid skeletal fragments dating over
three million years B.P.; however to date, no descriptions have
been published.

Fossil bones attributable to *Homo erectus* have been known since
1890, when Eugene Dubois discovered a skull cap and femur in the
Trinil beds of Java. These were originally known as *Pithecanthropus
erectus*. Other material has been uncovered from a deeper horizon
(Djetis beds) but all are assigned to *Homo erectus*. The time span for
all of these fossils is between 500,000 and 1,900,000 years B.P. Their
cranial volumes ranged from 800 to 1000 cc and they may have
been on the average somewhat taller than the Australopithecines.
No stone implements have been found with the Java *Homo erectus*.

There is a famous cave known as Choukoutien near Peking,
China that has yielded *Homo erectus* material since the mid-1920s
(Figure 7). There is a total of 40 individuals represented. In contrast
to Java, stone tools (flakes and choppers) were associated with the
Chinese *Homo erectus* specimens. Additionally, the first use of fire
is credited to these creatures as well as what may well be the first

evidence of cannibalism. In total morphological pattern, the Chinese *Homo erectus* was similar to the ones from Java, although the average endocranial capacity of approximately 1040 cc was larger than that ascribed to the Java specimens (Straus, 1967). This material has not been dated chronometrically but most students agree that the Choukoutien cave deposits probably range from 500,000 to 400,000 years B.P. This would place them at about the beginning of the Mindel (2nd) glaciation in Europe (Table II).

A slightly older site (about 600,000 years B.P.) at Lantian, Shensi Province, China has produced another *Homo erectus*. Perhaps its most notable feature is the absence of the third molar, a condition usually considered "advanced" today.

In Europe there are several specimens of *Homo erectus* and one or two that may represent a transitional phase between *Homo erectus* and *Homo sapiens neanderthalensis*. They range in time from the Mauer jaw of Germany (about 450,000 years B.P.), to the Arago material from France (about 200,000 years B.P.). The latter fossil has large eyebrow ridges, a flat forehead and probably possessed a relatively small brain (de Lumley and de Lumley, 1971). There is also a skull from Petralona, Greece that is apparently *Homo erectus* but to date there is no detailed description (Lasker, 1976).

When *Homo erectus* is compared with the australopithecines, two anatomical differences are immediately apparent. One, *H. erectus*, has a larger brain than the australopithecines, while the body size is approximately the same. Two, the face and teeth of *H. erectus*, are smaller than in the australopithecines; indeed, the teeth of the former fall within the upper limits of the range in some living human populations. This increase in brain size was undoubtedly related to increasing cultural modifications, which resulted in more selective pressure for larger brains. Although some of the tools

Figure 7
Skull of *Homo erectus*, "Peking Man" [modified from Le Gros Clark (1964)].

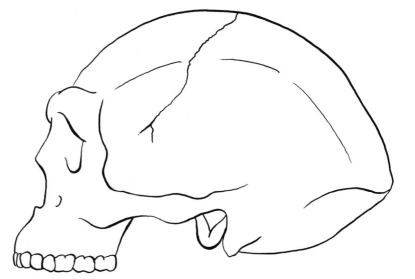

were not greatly different between the two groups, there was one cultural item that was new—fire. The first evidence of fire was at Choukoutien, near Peking, China. There are fire hearths there that were reused many times, suggesting that the inhabitants gathered around them to distribute food, eat and keep warm. Fire, of course, benefits its possessors in many ways and it now appears that these Middle Pleistocene hominids had fire at many of their campsites in Europe. Hunting and gathering was well established and one can conjecture that some sort of division of labor between the sexes was present.

Neanderthal man appeared about 100,000 years ago, distributed throughout Europe, Africa and Central Asia. They persisted up to about the last phases of the Wurm glaciation, some 40,000 years ago. There is some evidence that the earlier forms gave rise to the later *Homo sapiens* while the later varieties became extinct. The later or classic Neanderthals were limited geographically to Western Europe and displayed a large supraorbital torus (browridge), a sloping or reclining forehead, a bun-shaped configuration to the back end of the skull and a long, narrow and prognathous face (Figure 8). On the other hand, the earlier or progressive varieties (Figure 9) came from a much more extensive area, but it should be understood that there is a certain amount of geographical overlap between the two forms.

Morphologically, the progressive types had more vertically oriented foreheads; the supraorbital torus was smaller and not complete above the orbits; and the occipital portion of the skull was

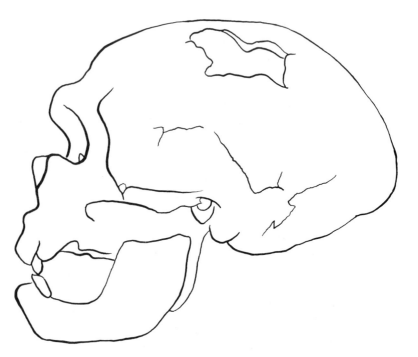

Figure 8
Skull of *Homo sapiens neanderthalensis*, La Chapelle aux-Saints [modified from Le Gros Clark (1964)].

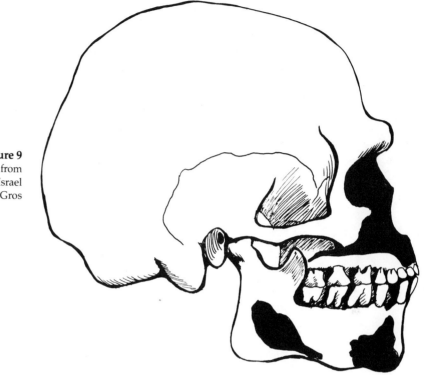

Figure 9
Skull of Skhūl V from Mount Carmel, Israel [modified from Le Gros Clark (1964)].

enlarged rather than bun-shaped. Both forms were fully erect, with endocranial capacities ranging from 1200 to well over 1600 cc. Incidentally, endocranial casts suggest a brain not inferior to that of modern man.

The fate of Neanderthal man has been debated for several decades and is still in dispute. Did classic forms become extinct while their closely related progressive cousins evolved into modern man, *Homo sapiens sapiens?* Many students believe this thesis while others maintain the opposite, that classic Neanderthals were the immediate antecedents of modern man. There are certain Neanderthaloid fossils that seem to substantiate both theories. Some of these more taxonomically troublesome but at the same time, more intriguing specimens are Tabūn and Skhūl from Israel, Steinheim and Ehringsdorf from Germany, Swanscombe from England and Fontéchevade from France. All of these specimens show a mixture of Neanderthal and modern features. Some, for example, the Skhūl specimens, have relatively round, high foreheads with large, discontinuous brow ridges. The facial skeleton is less robust than in Neanderthaloids and there is a definite chin, while the back of the skull is rounded. Skhūl, although showing a mixture of features, appears to be more like modern man than some of the other specimens.

The morphologic lists could be drawn for each specimen; however, we would probably be no closer to the answer to the fate of Neanderthal man. Modern hominids evolved some 30,000 to 35,000 years ago with the transition occurring during the Wurm glaciation and such fossils as Combe-Capelle and Cro-Magnon, both from the Dordogne region of France, ushered in the first members of our subspecies, *Homo sapiens sapiens* (Figure 10). They possessed an Upper Paleolithic culture, consisting of many stone and bone tools among which were blades, burins and scrapers. Cave art flourished in parts of southern Europe, often becoming quite sophisticated as exemplified by the paintings from the Altamira Cave in northern Spain. Obviously, these paintings served a magic or religious function since many animals were drawn with spears in them, thus hoping to ensure the success of the hunt. Finally, many semisubterranean pit houses have been found in parts of Eastern Europe. Collectively, these new cultural attributes strongly suggest that *Homo sapiens sapiens* of the Upper Paleolithic was well on his way to becoming the complex social animal we know today.

In summary, the early primates were arboreal creatures living in tropical rainforests, feeding mainly on leaves and fruits. They probably lived in small social groups that were more or less permanent throughout the year. They possessed binocular vision and were probably nocturnal, although some may have been diurnal. In the Oligocene and particularly in the early Miocene, our

Figure 10
Skull of *Homo sapiens sapiens*, Combe Capelle, France [modified from Le Gros Clark (1964)].

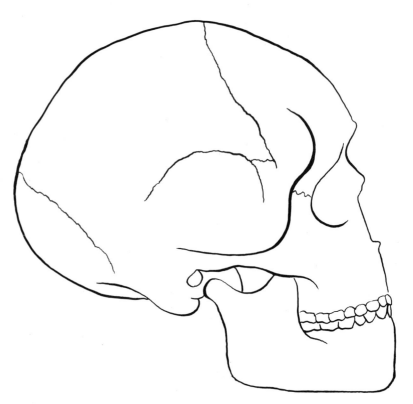

ancestors were very similar to the living Old World monkeys. Their brains were large when compared with other animals living at that time and they probably had an appreciable amount of learning as a part of their behavior. During this time group cohesion (dominance) became more stable and undoubtedly some sort of communication was developing among the members of a troop such as vocalizations and gestures. Somewhat later in the Miocene our immediate forebearers were morphologically more similar to the great apes, especially to the chimpanzee. They lived along the edges of forests and probably spent a great deal of time foraging on the ground for food while experimenting with upright walking. It was during this time, late Miocene or early Pliocene, that the Hominidae emerged in the form of *Ramapithecus*, or some equally "advanced" creature. A new ecological niche was being explored, one in which humankind would ultimately evolve. There is little question today that the period between 10 million and four million years ago was critical for the evolution of *Homo*. With more ground feeding came more meat eating, demanding planned hunting parties, food sharing, tools and undoubtedly a division of labor based upon sex. All of these behaviors require a more sophisticated system of communication (language). The skeletal evidence to support these cultural manifestations is found in the remains of the early hominids considered here. These hominids were erect, bipedal animals with expanding brains and changing diets; thus the last million years of human evolution have been spent mainly in remolding the cranial and facial skeleton.

Humankind has been a hunter and gatherer for more than 98% of its existence; the question now facing this relatively new addition to the planet is survival. Has our animal heritage prepared us to cope with the many complex problems confronting us today? Hopefully it has, but answers are urgently needed to a wide range of moral, ethical and ecological issues if our species is to survive.

References   Andrews, P. 1971. *Ramapithecus wickeri* mandible from Fort Ternan, Kenya. *Nature* 231: 192–194.

Clemens, W.A. 1974. *Purgatorius*, an early Paromomyid primate (Mammalia). *Science* 184: 903–905.

Dart, R.A. 1925. *Australopithecus africanus*: The man-ape of South Africa. *Nature* 115: 195–199.

Day, M.H., Leakey, R.E.F., Walker A.C., and Wood, B.A. 1975. New hominids from East Rudolf, Kenya. *Amer. J. Phys. Anthro.* 42: 461–475.

deLumley, H., and deLumley, M.A. 1971. Decouverte de restes humaines anteneandertaliens dates du debut du Riss a la Caune de l'Arago (Tautavel, Pyrenees Orientales). *Comptes Rendus de l'Academie des Sciences, Paris-Serie D* 272: 1739–1742.

Every, R. 1970. Sharpness of teeth in man and other primates. *Postilla* 143: 1.

Frayer, D.W. 1974. A reappraisal of *Ramapithecus*. *Yearbook of Phys. Anthropol.* 18: 19–30.

Kraus, B.S. 1964. *The Basis of Human Evolution*. New York: Harper and Row.

Lasker, G.L. 1976. *Physical Anthropology.* 2nd ed. New York: Holt, Rinehart and Winston.

Leakey, R.E.F. 1973a. Skull 1470, discovery in Kenya of the earliest suggestion of the genus *Homo* — nearly three million years old — compels a rethinking of mankind's pedigree. *National Geographic,* pp. 818–829.

――――. 1973b. Evidence for an advanced Plio-Pleistocene hominid from East Rudolf, Kenya. *Nature* 242: 447–450.

Leakey, R.E.F., Mungai, J.M., and Walker, A.C. 1972. New australopithecines from East Rudolph, Kenya. *Amer. J. Phys. Anthro.* 35: 175–186.

Napier, J.R., and Davis, P.R. 1959. The four limb skeleton and associated remains of *Proconsul africanus. Fossil Mamm. of Africa* 16: 1–69 (a publication of the British Museum of Natural History).

Oxnard, C.E. 1975. The place of the australopithecines in human evolution: Grounds for doubt? *Nature* 258: 389–395.

Simons, E.L. 1964. On the mandible of *Ramapithecus. Proc. Nat. Acad. Sci.* 51: 528–535.

――――. 1967. The earliest apes. *Scientific American* 217: 28–35.

Simons, E.L., and Ettel, P.C. 1972. *Gigantopithecus. Scientific American* 222: 76–85.

Straus, W.L., Jr. 1967. Nature of the problem and the evidence. In *Time and Stratigraphy in the Evolution of Man.* Washington, DC: NAS-NRC Publication No. 1469. pp. 1–17.

Tattersall, I. 1972. Of lemurs and men. *Natural History* 81: 32.

Tobias, P.V. 1971. *The Brain in Hominid Evolution.* New York: Columbia University Press.

Van Valen, L., and Sloan, R.E. 1965. The earliest primates. *Science* 150: 743–745.

Washburn, S., and Lancaster, C. 1968. The evaluation of hunting. In R. Lee and I. DeVore (eds) *Man, the Hunter.* Chicago: Aldine-Atherton.

Yulish, S. 1970. Anterior tooth reduction in *Ramapithecus. Primates* 11: 255–270.

Habitat Selection:
General Theory and
Applications to Human Behavior

Gordon H. Orians

3

The process of adaptation to physiological, biological and social components of the environment involves behavioral decisions concerning the kinds of activities in which to engage, where to perform them and toward whom they should be directed. Two distinct types of questions can be asked about these choices. First, how are they made? To answer this question requires knowing both the specific external stimuli that trigger the behavior and the internal physiological mechanisms by which external stimuli are perceived, transmitted, integrated with existing internal information and used as a basis for making decisions. This question is concerned with *proximate factors* responsible for the observed behavior (Lack, 1954).

Second, why have particular choice patterns evolved as opposed to others that might be imagined? An answer to this question is directed not toward physiological mechanisms but toward the *consequences* of the decisions as they influence the relative genetic contributions to subsequent generations of the individuals making the choices. The focus of research intended to answer this question is toward longer-term measurements of survival and reproduction and comparisons must be made among individuals who make the behavioral choices in different ways. It is important to be explicit about which question is the focus of a particular investigation and to recognize that both are legitimate and intrinsically interesting. Failure to do so leads to fruitless arguments of the form: "The animal chose that food because it was rewarding to eat it." "No, the animal chose that food because it was more nutritious and led to better health." Both statements may be correct (or incorrect). However, they are not mutually exclusive but rather answers to different questions. Here, I will be concerned primarily with the adaptive significance of habitat selection and will not deal in depth with physiological mechanisms by which choices are made.

For any study of evolutionary processes it is necessary to identify some variable that operates independently of the physiology of the organisms concerned. This external variable (or variables) constitutes the driving force(s) for the action of natural selection on the traits under consideration. I treat behavioral choice mechanisms as dependent variables that have been evolutionarily molded by one or more independent variables. The most likely independent variable is intrinsic variation in the suitability of environments in space and time. If there are such differences, then animals that prefer to settle in habitats where their survival and reproductive success is better contribute more genes to subsequent generations and tend to replace individuals that prefer less suitable habitats. The main theoretical problems are to specify the nature of habitat differences, to understand how they are modified by the presence of conspecific individuals and, from this information, to predict optimal patterns of habitat selection. First, I present a model that assumes that organisms have perfect knowledge about habitats and population densities and demonstrate the usefulness of making such manifestly untrue assumptions. Then I turn to a consideration of how organisms should behave when they possess less than perfect information, as they always do, and especially how much time and energy they should invest in increasing their knowledge about habitats. Finally, I consider these general theories in the light of human habitat selection behavior.

Although there is no convincing reason to believe that human habitat selection mechanisms have evolved by processes different from those affecting other species, the literature on human behavior related to habitats has been confused by uncritical use of analogies with behavior of other species and a failure to appreciate the subtle and complex ways in which animals respond to space and the presence of other individuals in it. Defense of exclusive space (territorial behavior in the classical sense) is less prevalent than might be imagined from some writing in this area (Ardrey, 1960, 1966; Lorenz, 1966).

Reactions to conspecifics in the same area can take on many forms, only some of which actually involve behavioral exclusion. The factors favoring defense of space have been adequately reviewed elsewhere (Brown, 1964; Brown and Orians, 1970; Hinde, 1956; Schoener, 1968; Wilson, 1975) and will not be treated in detail here. It suffices to point out that a general theory of habitat selection that incorporates effects of conspecifics (or individuals of competing species) can be used to illuminate situations when defense of space is to be expected and when it is not.

I will generally ignore the interesting and complex problem of how environments mold the perceptions of people living in them. A general review of that topic is provided by Tuan (1974). Rather my focus is on more universal aspects of human habitat selection, patterns that might be expected to reveal themselves despite the complexities of ontogenetically modified environmental perceptions.

Theory   For our purposes, a *habitat* is a piece of terrain large enough that the organism being considered is able to spend at least one breeding season there, meeting all of its resource needs within its confines. A habitat is considered to be a mosaic of *patches* differing from one another in ways that affect the fitness of the organism. Patches are small enough that the organism must use a number of them to satisfy its needs during a single breeding season. Depending on the particular activity involved, different patches have different values. For example, the patch with the best nest sites or the best protection against predators may not be the best for foraging. Since any organism has many needs during a breeding cycle, selection of a habitat should evolve in accordance with the ability of patches within the habitat to satisfy these needs weighted by the importance of each of the needs to total fitness.

It is useful to visualize the habitat selection process as a hierarchical one in which selection of a habitat commits the organism to a set of patches. Selection of a patch further limits the available options but the organism still may choose from among a number of different behavioral activities within the patch. The suitability of a patch for different activities should strongly influence the behaviors likely to be chosen. Finally, the organism makes decisions concerning its behavior toward the individual objects it encounters: predators, prey, mates, competitors, nest sites and so forth. This hierarchical scheme of behavioral decision is shown in Figure 1.

An important feature of this scheme is that higher level decisions constrain lower level decisions more than *the reverse*. Also, lower level decisions are generally made with much greater frequency than higher level decisions and, hence, the consequences to the organism of each individual decision are usually less. For example, a poor decision about a specific prey item will reduce fitness much less than a poor decision about a habitat since the latter strongly affects the options available at all lower levels and for longer time periods. However, some lower level decisions may be very important, such as a response to a hungry predator. In any case, the time and energy invested in a decision should be positively correlated with the importance of that decision to the

Figure 1

A hierarchical scheme of behavioral decisions related to space. Choices at higher levels, i.e., habitat and patch, constrain choices at lower levels more than *vice versa* [modified from Charnov (1973)].

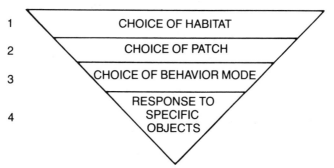

fitness of the individual. Not surprisingly, we invest more time when buying a house than when deciding on a restaurant for dinner.

It is useful to begin consideration of habitat selection with a model that makes two unreasonable assumptions which later will be relaxed. They are that the organism possesses perfect knowledge of the qualities of the available habitats and that choosing from among them carries no costs in terms of time and energy. If we further assume that increasing density of conspecific individuals lowers the quality of a habitat, whether this be due to resource depletion, attraction of predators and/or improved conditions for disease transmission, a pattern similar to that shown in Figure 2 is expected. It graphs fitness in three habitats of different intrinsic qualities together with the expected changes in fitness as a function of population density in each one. Given perfect knowledge and free choice, an organism should elect the best of the three until the density of individuals in that habitat type reaches D_2 at which point success is equal in both the first and second ranked habitats. At this time, individuals should begin to elect habitat 2 as well as habitat 1 and densities should increase in both until point D_3 at which time habitat 3 is equally good. In other words, each individual is assumed to select the best option from those available and the final result is that individuals will have settled in all three habitats at densities such that higher densities in the better habitats are sufficient to offset exactly the intrinsic superiority of those habitats. A hypothetical final distribution of individuals is indicated by the circles on Figure 2. Such a distribution, in which the expected fitnesses of all individuals are the same in all habitats, is appropriately referred to as an Ideal Free Distribution (Fretwell and Lucas, 1969). It is ideal because perfect no-cost knowledge is assumed and free because no time or social constraints are imposed on the decisions.

For several reasons choice of habitat is likely to be neither ideal nor free. First, there is some error associated with the assessment of any particular habitat. Since, by definition, a habitat contains resources sufficient for an entire breeding season or longer, the organism must not only assess the current status of a habitat but also predict its value throughout the breeding season. This may be difficult because key resources needed later in the season may not be present at the time the decision must be made. Presumably the assessment error can be reduced by investing more time in the decision, searching over the area more carefully for additional clues as to its current and probable future status, but this investment reduces the time available to visit and assess other habitats which may, in fact, be better. Also, for many species the total time available for breeding may be short and breeding success may be poorer if it is started later. In general, the first bits of knowledge about an area should reduce estimation errors more than additional bits of knowledge. If so, the contribution to fitness from invest-

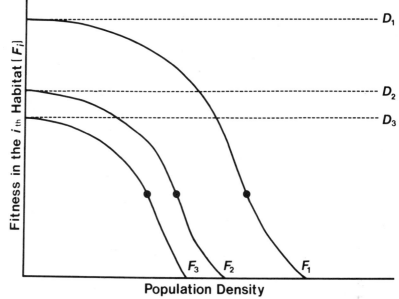

Figure 2
Fitness as a function of population density in habitats of different intrinsic qualities [modified from Fretwell and Lucas (1969)].See text for explanation.

ments in time to acquire information may drop rapidly to the point where the costs of additional information exceed the benefits to the individual of that information, setting a theoretical limit to information acquisition.

Second, organisms possess incomplete knowledge about alternative habitats, their intrinsic qualities and the existing densities of conspecifics in them. Increasing this knowledge requires more exploratory behavior, costly in time and energy. Should an organism accept a particular suboptimal habitat when it doesn't know if a better one really exists within its searching range or where it might be? Such decisions ought to be molded by the time constraints operating on the decision process (i.e., shortness of breeding season), the energy and time costs of searching and the rate of mortality while searching. Several qualitative generalizations emerge from a consideration of these factors. They can be stated as the following testable predictions:

a. The probability of accepting a given habitat should be positively correlated with its perceived quality.
b. Organisms with highly restricted searching times (short breeding seasons, few unoccupied sites) should be more willing to accept a lower quality habitat than ones with longer searching times.
c. Organisms with poor searching abilities should more readily accept poorer quality habitats.
d. The higher the risk while searching, the more willing an organism ought to be to accept a poorer habitat.

Thus, if the cost to the organism (total loss in fitness) from continuing to search is high, its standards of acceptance should be low. If the value of additional information is a declining function of the information the organism already possesses, as we have postulated, then optimal investment in a habitat decision is determined by the interaction of cost and benefit curves of the general form shown in Figure 3. If the environment is highly variable, the mean error of a habitat decision made on the basis of limited information will, on the average, be greater than if the environment is less variable. Therefore, habitat variability selects for increased investment in the selection process while increasing costs of delay select for quick decisions. Thus, the optimal investment is least for organisms in a constant, predictable environment where time is constrained and the risks while searching are high (I_a).

Figure 3
A cost–benefit model of investment of time and energy in habitat selection. Both costs and benefits are expressed in fitness units. It is assumed that the value of additional information is greater in variable than in constant environments. $\hat{I}_a$ = optimal investment in a constant environment under conditions of high risk, time constrained searching. $\hat{I}_b$ = optimal investment in a constant environment under conditions of low risk, time relaxed searching. $\hat{I}_c$ = optimal investment in a variable environment under conditions of high risk, time constrained searching. $\hat{I}_d$ = optimal investment in a variable environment under conditions of low risk, time relaxed searching. The exact positions of the curves are, of course, unknown and changes could reverse the relative positions of $\hat{I}_b$ and $\hat{I}_c$, but the general relationships are likely to hold over a broad range of organisms and environments.

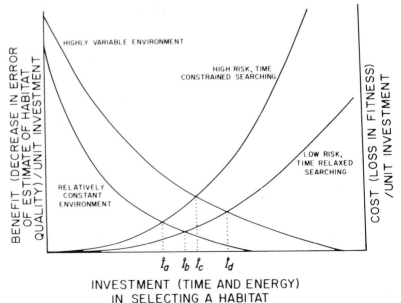

Habitat Selection Under Conditions of Ignorance

Given that investment in habitat selection depends on mobility, risk during search, time constraints on searching and unpredictability of the environment, what kinds of cues should be used to make estimates of habitat and patch quality?

One important piece of evidence is provided by the survival of the individual making the decision. If an individual has successfully reached maturity in a particular habitat, that fact constitutes *prima facie* evidence of its suitability. Therefore, it is not surprising that many animals develop strong behavioral attraction to the types of habitats and particular places where they were born and raised. These behavioral tendencies are strongly developed among humans. A second useful piece of evidence is provided by the presence of other individuals in a habitat. They indicate that others have made a positive assessment of the habitat and that they have survived there. Therefore, provided their density is not too great, it may be preferable to settle near them rather than searching for an empty habitat. This will be particularly valuable in species where the fitness of solitary pairs is lower than the fitness of individuals in larger groups, that is if the fitness–population density curves have humps at densities greater than zero rather than starting at a maximum as shown in Figure 2.

Emotions and Habitat Selection

To analyze habitat selection in species other than *Homo sapiens*, it is sufficient to consider the evolution of tendencies to exhibit preferences and to invest differentially in decisions concerning habitats, but to apply these ideas to human behavior, emotional aspects of responses to habitats should also be considered. Because we might ask other humans how they feel about different habitats, we have at our disposal information in addition to that available from measuring the particular choices made.

In all organisms habitat selection presumably involves emotional responses. If, as is likely, the strength of these responses is a key proximate factor in decisions, then the ability of a habitat to "turn on" an organism should be positively correlated with its expected fitness in it. Good habitats should evoke strong positive responses and poorer habitats should evoke weaker or negative responses. These responses should be modified by the presence or absence of other individuals in the habitats, because they influence fitness, and by the internal state of the organism. For example, a hungry animal may accept a second-rate site more readily than a well-fed one, since hunger is a signal that good habitats have not been encountered. Therefore, emotional responses are an unusually valuable source of information about the evolution of human habitat selection.

Components of the Value of Habitats to Man

Since the period of offspring dependency in humans is so long, either a habitat must provide resources on a more or less permanent basis or a human social group must move from one habitat to another within or between years. The many factors influencing intrinsic habitat quality can conveniently be divided into resource availability and protection from predators.

Resource availability. Habitats differ greatly in their production of food suitable for human consumption. For our purposes, it is most useful to restrict consideration to tropical and subtropical habitats since *Homo sapiens* evolved in the tropics and has only relatively recently invaded higher latitudes (Leakey, 1963; Robinson, 1963). The genetic basis of human habitat selection behavior has presumably been molded primarily in relation to tropical habitats and has been only weakly modified in the short interval in which we have lived in temperate environments. Ontogenetic components of habitat selection behavior are, of course, not similarly constrained.

The main differences among tropical habitats concern the duration and severity of the dry season. Most tropical regions have pronounced fluctuations in mean monthly precipitation. If the dry season is short and some rain falls throughout the season, dense evergreen forests are the natural vegetation. With increasing length of dry season, the vegetation changes to a seasonally deciduous forest, evergreen forests being confined to depressions and river valleys where subsurface moisture is always available. At still longer dry seasons the stature of the forests decreases while the period of leaflessness and the mean distance between trees increases. With increasing aridity intertree distances steadily increase until finally trees are not competitively viable and vegetation consists of a mixture of grass, forbs and small shrubs.

Primary productivity declines along such a moisture gradient (Bourliere and Hadley, 1970; Hopkins, 1967) but productivity of food suitable for human consumption does not. In closed forests most of the photosynthesis takes place high above the ground and canopy individuals are the most prolific producers of fruit. Not surprisingly, most herbivores and frugivores live in the trees (Eisenberg and Thorington, 1974; Elton, 1973; Harrison, 1962) and food resources for a terrestrial omnivore are low and intermittently available. In savannahs, however, trees are shorter and much of the photosynthesis is performed by grasses that lack wood, so that most photosynthetic products are in a form highly suitable for consumption by grazing mammals. The biomasses and production of meat by grazing mammals in tropical savannahs is much higher than in tropical forests (Bourliere, 1963; Dasman, 1964; Hopkins, 1967; Lamprey, 1964; Wiegert and Evans, 1967) and populations of carnivores are correspondingly denser. In addition, many species of plants in seasonally dry climates store energy in underground stems, roots and tubers which form a concentrated food source readily exploitable by an animal with modest digging abilities.

With still great aridity, however, total annual photosynthesis is so low, that though it all takes place at suitable heights, total annual production of useful plant tissues is lower than in more humid regions. Thus, resource availability per unit area for early man must have been highest in tropical savannahs and lower in both wetter and drier habitats.

A second important resource for human existence is water, both for drinking and other direct uses and because aquatic habitats are often rich producers of high-protein foods. The most abundant aquatic plants are usually microscopic and lack wood so that they are entirely consumable by small grazing animals, which in turn support high populations of larger arthropods and fish, excellent foods for man, often readily captured by simple methods. Thus, in the Amazon Basin, human settlements are generally located along rivers, and aquatic environments are a major source of proteins (Meggers, 1973). This was, however, apparently less true in Africa perhaps because the prevalence of aquatic-borne diseases forced people to settle away from the water even if they went to the rivers for hunting and fishing purposes (Miracle, 1973). It has even been suggested that a significant part of human evolution took place on seashores (Sauer, 1963).

Protection from predators. During much of our evolution we were exposed to attacks by large carnivores and some otherwise suitable habitats may not have been occupied because it was too risky to live there. An important component of predator protection is having a safe sleeping place. Early human settlements were often situated near caves, cliffs and trees to which the inhabitants retreated at night. An important early use of fire was to block entrances to caves in which people slept so that they would not be surprised in highly confined conditions by large predators.

Another component of risk to predation is being taken by surprise during the day. In a dense forest, predators cannot be seen at a distance and our capacity to detect them by other sensory modes is poor. Accordingly, the risk of being attacked in a closed forest was much higher than in more open country where we could use our good eyesight. Increased visibility is also of value in hunting because game can be located at great distances and an attack strategy planned that yields a higher probability of success. Savannahs are also favorable because the most common terrestrial predators are poor tree climbers in comparison with humans and a relatively safe retreat is always close at hand.

These arguments combine to yield a picture that tropical savannahs, particularly those with irregular relief providing cliffs and caves, should have been the optimal environment for early man. These conditions should have enhanced both resource availability and protection from predators. We expect human responses to habitats to have evolved in accordance with these intrinsic habitat qualities. The strength of our emotional responses to savannahlike environments has been pointed out by Dubos (1968, 1976) and a thorough, cross-cultural comparison of the roles of cliffs, water and trees in environmental perception is provided by Tuan (1974). The theory developed here is a formalized extension of their ideas.

Human Responses to Habitat Types

In terms of the general theory of habitat selection developed earlier, humans have low risk while searching, extended breeding seasons, and the need to make long term evaluations of a habitat if even a single offspring is to be raised to maturity. Therefore, we expect careful evaluations to be made prior to choosing a habitat and a great deal of emotion to be involved in the selection process. The simplest tests of this thesis are difficult to make, however, because seldom do humans invade empty environments where ideal, free choices can be made. Rather, choices are usually made in already occupied environments where choices are constrained by the locations and behavior of the people living there. Therefore, a number of indirect tests must be employed to infer habitat selection mechanisms.

One point in recent history where settling did occur in a more or less empty environment was in the North American West, where a technologically advanced culture began to occupy a region which was, from its perspective, essentially unutilized. Fortunately, there is a substantial literature recording the responses of early explorers and settlers to habitats in the West that can be used to infer something about preference rankings and, hence, settling patterns.

Habitat selection preferences in already inhabited areas can be inferred by a study of the willingness of people to evict already settled persons. Wars have historically been an important part of this process, but perhaps more can be learned from a study of a more ritualized pattern of eviction, namely offering a sufficiently high price for the land that the owner is willing to sell. The prices that land brings should reflect quite accurately our evolved habitat preference rankings, and since in most societies there is still a relatively free market in land, much can be learned from a study of real estate prices.

Finally, it is useful to study the structure of "esthetic vegetation," that is, vegetation manipulated simply for the enjoyment we receive from it. Many of our modifications of vegetation have a highly utilitarian purpose, such as raising food or driving motorized vehicles over them. These are in general not highly esthetic patches and their basic design is determined by other yield characteristics. However, parks and yards (and sometimes roadsides) are generally designed purely for the pleasure they give and, therefore, these man-made environments should reflect our evolutionarily based preferences.

Emotional responses to habitats. Since it is now regarded as inappropriate to record emotional responses in scientific writings, recent scientific literature is a poor source of information on this component of habitat selection. It is, however, entirely appropriate, indeed desirable, to record these impressions vividly in literary essays, poems and journals. In Western literature, closed forests are normally associated with depressed emotional states and fears. They are regarded as homes of witches, gnomes, gremlins, trolls and devils, not to mention natural predators, such as wolves, which are most likely to intercept unsuspecting children taking a short-cut through the woods rather than the longer, safer, more open route to grandmother's house, in spite of the fact that wolves are more characteristic of open country than they are of forests! Conversely, open plains without trees are regarded as desolate. When traveling across prairies, people long for the sight of trees. When settling in grasslands we invariably plant trees and invest heavily in tending them in that inhospitable environment.

Some of the responses to vegetation by early explorers in the American Great Plains are illustrative of these reactions. In 1849 and 1854, Captain R. B. Marcy led expeditions for the United States Government through little-explored territory in the southern plains. The quotations from Captain Marcy (below) were taken from Malin (1956). On September 12, 1849, the group approached the headwaters of the Clear Fork of the Brazos River, traveling

over as beautiful a country for eight miles as I ever beheld. It was a perfectly level grassy glade, and covered with a growth of large mesquite trees at uniform distances, standing with great regularity, and presenting more the appearance of an immense peach orchard than a wilderness. The grass is of the short buffalo variety, and as uniform and even as new mown meadow, and the soil is as rich, and very similar to that in the Red River bottoms.

The words of W. P. Parker who traveled on the same expedition were even more vivid:

The view was the most extensive and glowing in the sunset, the most striking that we had enjoyed during the whole trip, combining the grandeur of immense space—the plain extending to the horizon on every side from our point of view—with the beauty of the contrast between the golden carpet of buffalo grass and the pale green of the mesquite trees dotting its surface.

In 1854, while overlooking the treeless valley of the Big Wichita River, Marcy wrote in a very different vein:

It is in almost every respect, the most uninteresting and forbidding land I have ever visited. A barren and parsimonious soil, affording little but weeds and coarse unwholesome grass, with an admixture of cacti, of most uncomely and grotesque shapes, studded with a formidable armour [sic] of thorns which defies the approach of man or beast, added to the fact already alluded to, of the scarcity of wood or good water, would seem to render it probable that this section was not designed by the Creator for

occupation, and I question if the next century will see it populated by civilized man. Even the Indians shun this country.
[Notes taken during the expedition through unexplored Texas, in the summer and fall of 1854. Philadelphia, 1896.]

Both these men were typical of early explorers of the American West in that they responded positively, often strongly so, to open savannah environments with scattered trees and abundant grass, while they reacted negatively to treeless plains, especially if they were flat. It is true that the savannahs had richer grass for horses and shade from the sun, but recognizing that does not explain the strength of the emotional responses recorded in such accounts.

The emotional appeal of savannah environments is also apparent in the literature on landscape architecture. Actually landscape design is a relatively recent art in Western civilization, not really developing until the 18th century. Several influences combined to create an interest in designing landscapes, one of which was the availability of more leisure time. Another was the need for timber that was felt acutely throughout the 17th and 18th centuries in England because of the threat of war (Colvin, 1970, p. 59).

In creating environments in which it is pleasant to relax, designers have come to recognize the value of a mixture of trees and open places. The admonitions of Colvin (1970, p. 124), if followed, have the effect of creating savannah environments for esthetic purposes:

Trees when suitably spaced in relation to the ground plan, have the effect of multiplying the two-dimensional area by their height, so increasing the volume of cubic space contained within their height as do walls and ceilings in the case of buildings. The absence of this effect, resulting from open spaces very large by comparison to the height of their trees, is a defect in the case of parks or gardens intended for rest or leisurely movement, but may be desirable in other cases, where the use is different; as in agricultural landscape, or where the speed of movement is greater (as in the case of playing-fields), or on slopes or undulating ground where the vertical dimension does not depend on trees alone.

Flat sites, however, offer tempting opportunity for lavish and grandiose design, and the human factor is all too often forgotten. Recent town-planning schemes in more than one country have included vistas and squares of such majestic proportions that the courage of the mere pedestrian quails at the thought of crossing from one side to the other. Ponderous monuments, vast civic buildings and gigantic spaces surrounding them are a means by which powerful rulers seek to immortalize themselves at the expense of posterity. The use of such scale, so far as open spaces are concerned, can be justified only on the assumption of complete mechanization of the populace.

Flatness is usually regarded as boring and depressing to humans and we try to escape from flat areas if we can. Cliffs and bluffs attract us and this attraction is often associated with strong desires to climb to the top. Such behavior is probably valuable in terms of detecting game and potential enemies, but it is also intrinsically rewarding and is engaged in enthusiastically as recreation by well-fed, unthreatened persons with no intentions of hunting then or in the future. It suffices to climb and look out to stimulate a level of physical effort that is normally shunned. Valleys of modest size have exerted powerful attraction for humans for ages (Tuan, 1974, p. 117).

The esthetic value of water is also very familiar. We are willing to spend vast sums of money to create bodies of water where they don't exist or to enhance the recreational value of a body of water even when that use conflicts with, say, resource harvesting. The city of Seattle is situated on a narrow strip of land between Puget Sound and Lake Washington, a large fresh-water lake about 20 miles long. Lake Washington is naturally oligotrophic and, due to the high precipitation in the region, the residence time for a molecule of water in the lake is very short, averaging about three years (Edmondson, 1961). Extensive use is made of the lake for recreational purposes throughout the year. When levels of algae began to rise as a result of enrichment of the lake by effluent from a number of waste disposal plants, responses to changes in lake color, smell and the decaying algae on the shores were sufficient that voters enacted legislation to create a municipal sewage disposal system that diverted all sewage to Puget Sound at a cost of $120,000,000 (Edmondson, 1968). The stimulus was apparently entirely recreational and the effort successful in returning the lake to its previous state.

The emotional pleasures associated with being around water are truly remarkable. Otherwise impatient people are willing to spend hours watching waves crash onto a beach or water flow over a falls. Sailboaters are a group of fanatics matched in their enthusiasm only by those engaged in forms of displacement hunting, such as bird watching.

These emotional responses are so familiar that we take them for granted; it never occurs to us to ask why we feel that way about lakes, rivers, cliffs and savannahs. Why don't other environments have the same effects on us? Our responses are exactly as would be predicted from the previous analysis of habitat quality combined with the assumption that positive responses to habitats are a major proximate factor in making decisions about settling.

The Values of Habitats as Reflected in Prices Paid to Live in Them

In the United States there is a relatively open market in real estate and private property has generally been allowed to be bought and sold in accordance with the willingness of people to pay for it. Therefore, the prices paid for land of different characteristics should be a valuable index of our responses to habitats. It is most useful to consider residential lots since the uses made of them are primarily esthetic. Purchase of, say, farmland or land for a factory is strongly influenced by other considerations which may override intrinsic emotional responses to the habitat. Besides, when one is in a factory one cannot normally see outside.

Two comparisons of special interest to the student of human habitat selection are those between lots with and without views and between lots with and without waterfront, other aspects of the real estate being held as constant as possible. Views and waterfronts enter into appraisals of real estate in all parts of the country but the manner in which they do so is very complex. Real estate agents in Seattle have an unofficial complex classification of views, ranging from "pigeon-hole views" that permit a small section of the mountains to be seen, to "sweeping views" which can encompass the entire Olympic Mountains or an extensive stretch of the Cascade Mountains. The more extensive the view, the greater the increment to the value of the property. If a view of Puget Sound or Lake Washington is also included in the foreground, the value of the property is even greater.

Although all real estate agents and appraisers are in agreement that views enhance the value of property, there appear to be no recognizable rules of thumb employed by any of the persons that I have contacted that permit rough values to be assigned to views of different breadths and quality. In the case of waterfront, however, it is easier to assess values. Lots are commonly sold on the basis of linear footage of waterfront irrespective of the depth of the lot, indicating that the value of the waterfront strongly dominates that of the remainder of the land.

The structure of esthetic vegetation. People everywhere mold vegetation for purely esthetic purposes. Outdoor relaxation times are spent in some kind of vegetation and, not surprisingly, we structure that vegetation to maximize the pleasure it gives. If the theory espoused here is generally correct, this esthetic vegetation should resemble tropical savannahs, with dense grasses on the ground and with short, laterally spreading trees sufficiently separated that their canopies do not touch. The type of esthetic vegetation that can most readily assume a savannah form is the park. Parks are usually large enough to create a savannah atmosphere and, even if there are specialized use sections, such as tennis courts, swimming pools, etc., considerable areas are devoted to places for people to walk or sit and do nothing.

As the accompanying photographs illustrate, parks in all parts of the world show remarkable similarities to savannahs (Figure 4). The spacing of the trees is appropriate: they are usually selected to be of the correct savannah stature, and we are especially fond of mowed lawns. Most revealing are Japanese gardens, which are based on shapes of trees and shrubs rather than flowers and for which a number of woody plants have been genetically selected for their shapes. These cultivated varieties are invariably of shorter

a

b

c

d

Figure 4

Representative natural savannahs and parks. (a) Blue Oak *(Quercus douglasii)* parkland in the Coast Ranges, Colusa County, California. Some of the hills in the distance are covered with chaparral. (b) Valley Oak *(Quercus lobata)* savannah in the Sacramento Valley, California. (c) Ponderosa Pine *(Pinus ponderosa)* savannah in Spokane County, Washington. (d) City park in Geneva, Switzerland in early spring prior to leafing of the deciduous trees. (e) Japanese Garden in the University of Washington Arboretum, Seattle, Washington.

e

stature than the wild types from which they were derived and they show strong tendencies to grow laterally and have flat tops like the African acacias. Manicuring enhances an open, layered canopy effect and many also have the small leaves and open sprays characteristic of tropical savannah trees. These varieties have been selected for purely esthetic purposes since they do not yield useful food products or wood.

Discussion   All three lines of evidence strongly suggest that we enjoy being in savannah vegetation, prefer to avoid both closed forests and open plains, will pay more for land giving us the impression of being a savannah, mold recreational environments to be more like savannahs, and develop varieties of ornamental plants that converge on the shapes typical of tropical savannahs of Africa, the probable site of our evolutionary origins. These behavioral tendencies are all well known but they are so obvious that it has not seemed worthwhile to ask questions about them. Yet it is precisely those aspects of our behavior that seem so obvious so as to not require any explanations that are the most likely to reveal the imprint of selective forces that have molded us. As anthropologists have long known, the values of a society that nobody questions reveal most about a culture.

There are several compelling reasons for believing that evolutionarily molded behavioral responses should often be ones of which we are not aware. Evolutionarily programmed responses are made without "conscious effort," that is, they are made while leaving the brain free to attend to those aspects of behavior which *do* require attention. It is advantageous to handle many decisions unconsciously since there is a strict limit to the number of events to which attention can be directed at any one time. In the case of habitat selection, the basic choices are handled emotionally without reflection, while the details of sites are evaluated carefully, with particular attention being paid to specific features that would make one site better than another. The consequence of the initial emotional response is to greatly limit the potential sites requiring closer scrutiny.

The tests of the "savannah theory" presented here are general and preliminary. It is, however, possible to develop the theory in much greater detail to predict finer features of our emotional responses to landscapes. For example, we should be able to predict in some detail the features that make one park more beautiful than another. These features should involve shape and spacing of trees, luxuriance of the grass growth and possibly the presence of denser clumps of trees indicating, perhaps, a source of water (Colvin, 1970). It should be possible to obtain consistent rankings of the scenic qualities of different parks that relate to these and other features of the vegetation. In similar manner, lots should be orderable according to the degree to which the views, etc., match with the savannah ideal.

The theory, if further substantiated, can also be used as a guide in the design of landscapes. Creative and experienced manipulators of landscapes have always had a deep intuitive feeling for the esthetic qualities of landscapes and they are unlikely to be helped much by an evolutionary theory. But there are many landscapes being modified by committees and by persons of lesser creative abilities. The quality of, say, the average city park may be upgraded by a better understanding of the ways in which we respond emotionally to vegetation and why these responses have evolved.

References

Ardrey, R. 1960. *African Genesis.* New York: Dell.

————. 1966. *The Territorial Imperative.* New York: Atheneum.

Bourliere, F. 1963. Observations on the ecology of some African mammals. In F. C. Howell and F. Bourliere (eds.) *African Ecology and Human Evolution.* Chicago: Aldine.

Bourliere, F., and Hadley, M. 1970. The ecology of tropical savannahs. *Ann. Rev. Ecology & Systematics.* 1:125–152.

Brown, J. L. 1964. The evolution of diversity in avian territorial systems. *Wilson Bull.* 76:160–169

Brown, J. L., and Orians, G. H. 1970. Spacing patterns in mobile animals. *Ann. Rev. Ecology & Systematics.* 1:239–262.

Charnov, E. R. 1973. Optimal foraging: Some theoretical explorations. Ph. D. thesis, University of Washington.

Colvin, B. 1970. *Land and Landscape: Evolution, Design and Control.* London: John Murray.

Dasmann, R. F. 1964. *African Game Ranching.* Oxford: Pergammon.

Dubos, R. 1968. *So Human an Animal.* New York: Scribner.

————. 1976. Symbiosis between the earth and humankind. *Science* 193:459–462.

Edmondson, W. T. 1961. Changes in Lake Washington following an increase in the nutrient income. *Verh. Internat. Verein. Limnol.* 14:167–175.

————. 1968. Water-quality management and eutrophication; The Lake Washington case. In T. H. Campbell and R. O. Sylvester (eds.) *Water Resource Management and Public Policy.* Seattle: University of Washington Press.

Eisenberg, J. F., and Thorington, Jr., R. W. 1974. A preliminary analysis of a neotropical mammal fauna. *Biotropica.* 5:150–161.

Elton, C. S. 1973. The structure of invertebrate populations inside neotropical rain forest. *J. Anim. Ecol.* 42:55–104.

Fittkau, E. J., and Klinge, H. 1973. On biomass and trophic structure of the central Amazonian rain forest ecosystem. *Biotropica* 5:2–14.

Fretwell, S. D., and Lucas, H. L. 1969. On territorial behavior and other factors influencing distribution in birds. I. Theoretical development. *Acta Biotheoretica.* 19:16–36.

Harrison, J. L. 1962. The distribution of feeding habits among animals in a tropical rain forest. *J. Anim. Ecol.* 31:53–63.

Hinde, R. A. 1956. The biological significance of the territories of birds. *Ibis* 98: 340–369.

Hopkins, B. 1967. A comparison between productivity in forest and savannah in Africa. *J. Ecol.* 55:19–20.

Lack, D. 1954. *The Natural Regulation of Animal Numbers.* Oxford: Clarendon Press.

Lamprey, H. F. 1964. Estimation of the large mammal densities, biomass and energy exchange in the Tarangire Game Reserve and the Masai Steppe, in Tanganyika. *E. Afr. Wildlife J.* 2:1–46.

Leakey, L. S. B. 1963. Very early East African Hominidae, and their ecological setting. In F. C. Howell and F. Bourliere (eds.) *African Ecology and Human Evolution.* Chicago: Aldine.

Lorenz, K. 1966. *On Aggression.* London: Methuen.

Malin, J .C. 1956. *The Grassland of North America. Prolegomena to Its History, with Addenda*. Lawrence, KS: James Malin.

Marcy, Captain R. B. 1849. Report on exploration and survey of route from Fort Smith, Arkansas, to Santa Fé, New Mexico, made in 1849. House ex. doc., 45: 31st Congress, First session, Public Document 577.

———. 1854. Message of the President of the United States communicating . . . a copy of the report and maps of Captain Marcy of his explorations of the Big Wichita and the headwaters of the Brazos Rivers, 1854. Senate ex. doc., 60: 35th Congress, First Session, Public Document 821.

Meggers, B. J. 1973. Some problems of cultural adaptation in Amazonia with emphasis on the Pre-European period. In B. J. Meggers, E. S. Ayensu and W. D. Duckwork (eds.) *Tropical Forest Ecosystems in Africa and South America: A Comparative Review*. Washington, D C: Smithsonian Institution Press.

Miracle, M. P. 1973. The Congo Basin as a habitat for man. In B. J. Meggers, E. S. Ayensu and W. D. Duckwork (eds.) *Tropical Forest Ecosystems in Africa and South America: A Comparative Review*. Washington, D C: Smithsonian Institution Press.

Robinson, J. T. 1963. Adaptive radiation in the Australopithecines and the origin of man. In F. C. Howell and F. Bourliere (eds.) *African Ecology and Human Evolution*. Chicago: Aldine.

Sauer, C. O. 1963. Seashore—Primitive Home of Man? In J. Leighly. (ed.) *Land and Life*. Berkeley: Univ. of Calif. Press.

Schoener, T. W. 1968. Sizes of feeding territories among birds. *Ecology* 49:123–141.

Talbot, L. M., and Talbot, M. H. 1962. Food preferences of some East African wild ungulates. *E. African Agric. For. J.* 27:131–138.

Tuan, Yi-Fu. 1974. *Topophilia. A Study of Environmental Perception, Attitudes and Values*. Englewood Cliffs, NJ: Prentice-Hall.

Van Zyle, J. H. M. 1965. The vegetation of the S.A. Lombard Nature Reserve and its utilization by certain antelopes. *Zoologica Africana* 1:55–71.

Wanner, H. 1970. Soil respiration, litter fall and productivity of tropical rain forest. *J. Ecol.* 58:543–547.

Wiegert, R. G., and Evans, F. C. 1967. Investigations of secondary productivity in grasslands. In K. Petrusevicz. (ed.) *Secondary Productivity of Terrestrial Ecosystems*, Vol. 2. Warsaw and Krakow: Institute of Ecology, Polish Academy of Sciences.

Wilson, E. O. 1975. *Sociobiology: The New Synthesis*. Cambridge, MA: Belknap/Harvard University Press.

The Human Family:
A Sociobiological Look

Pierre L. van den Berghe

4

Perhaps the safest statement that can be made about understanding human behavior is that one must examine it from at least three complementary points of view:

1. We are one biological species among many, and thus we share a phylogenesis that makes us a special kind of animal with a complex set of biological predispositions to act in certain ways and to learn certain things.
2. We live in a physical habitat, in symbiosis with many other species, and we are constantly adapting to that habitat, both biologically and culturally.
3. As a very special part of our biological heritage as brainy primates we have developed and transmitted a wide array of cultural traditions that have enormously increased our adaptive capabilities to a wide array of niches.

One of the main reasons why contemporary social science is hardly more advanced than that of Plato, Ibn Khaldun or Machiavelli is that social scientists have, by and large, ignored human biology and ecology. They have postulated that humans were so unique in their ability to communicate in symbolic language and to transmit complex cultures that our behavior did not bear comparison with that of other animals. They have also set up false antimonies between nature and nurture, heredity and environment, instinct and learning, and have promulgated for about half a century a credo of almost absolute cultural determinism: our behavior was proclaimed the product of our culture—our minds, *tabulae rasae* to be inscribed by fellow humans.

Such cultural determinism could only be sustained by refusing to compare our behavior with that of other species. To be sure, we are highly adaptable animals; our behavior is more labile than that of any other known species; we do have a remarkable ability to transmit what we have learned through a complex, symbolic language. In other words, our genetic programs for behavior tend to be "open" rather than "closed" (Mayr, 1974). Our behavioral repertoire is clearly distinct from that of other species, but, nevertheless, biologically predisposed. Unlike our "best friend," *Canis familiaris,* for instance, we do not routinely sniff the genitalia of our conspecifics before copulating, and we do not mark the boundaries of our gardens by scattering urine. Neither do we routinely and generally express our sociability by grooming the scalp of our visitors for dandruff, as do many other primates. Such behavior would be equally out of human character for a Zulu, a Papuan, an Eskimo or a Yankee. We do copulate, defend territories and express friendship, but we do so in distinctly human ways, irrespective of culture.

The model of human behavior presented here is one of *interaction* between the above three selective pressures. Biology, ecology and culture are so intertwined in our actual behavior that to treat them as discrete domains does not make any sense. Our biology shapes our ecology and our culture; our habitat modifies the other two; finally, our culture has now developed the capability of profoundly altering both our biology and our habitat. This feedback from culture to biology and ecology became dramatically more important since the development of agriculture 8,000 years ago and, at an ever accelerating pace, since the Industrial Revolution.

The vast sociological and anthropological literature on the human family generally takes the position that, while the family fulfills certain biological functions, notably sex and reproduction, it is to be understood overwhelmingly in cultural terms (Goode, 1963; Murdock, 1949; Lévi-Strauss, 1968; Parsons and Bales, 1954). Anthropologists in particular have stressed the diversity of family forms in different cultures. Without seeking to deny such diversity and the importance of culture in shaping such human institutions as marriage, filiation, incest and inheritance rules, I argue that

1. the human family has biologically evolved in a form which is, in some ways, analogous to family groups in other species, and in some important ways a uniquely human direction;
2. the human family, while showing considerable diversity of form across cultures, also exhibits certain important features that are universal to our species;
3. these "cultural universals," as anthropologists call them, can plausibly be hypothesized to have their origin in biological evolution as shaped by ecological adaptations.

What we call the mating and reproductive system of a species is simply a model set of behaviors that have evolved and become partly biologically predisposed because they are conducive to the fitness (i. e., reproductive success) of individual animals in a given set of environmental conditions and constraints (Emlen and Oring, 1977). There is no reason to exempt humans from that statement. It is true that humans show considerable individual and societal variability in their mating and reproductive behavior, but so do many other animal species, especially under different ecological conditions (Barash, 1977). Human societies that have adapted to a wider range of habitats than practically any other mammalian species can therefore be expected to show a considerable range of ecological responses. Indeed, much of what we call "culture" in humans is a set of ecologically induced responses. Much of human culture is incomprehensible without reference to both evolutionary biology and ecology.

To substantiate the biological evolution of human behavior is extremely difficult: behavior leaves no fossils, and we impose stringent ethical restrictions on experimentation with our own species. We are thus left with three main lines of evidence:

1. The generality of certain forms of behavior in a species is presumptive (but not conclusive) evidence of, at least, a partly biological predisposition (Mayr, 1974).[1]
2. If similar relationships between forms of behavior, habitat and somatic features are found in species that are either phylogenetically related or that have adapted to similar ecological conditions, or both, that too is presumptive evidence for biological selection for that behavior (Alexander, 1971, 1975; Campbell, 1972; Crook, 1972; DeVore and Washburn, 1963; Fox, 1975; Hamilton, 1975; Mazur, 1973; Tiger and Fox, 1971; Trivers, 1971, 1972; van den Berghe, 1973, 1974, 1975; Washburn and DeVore, 1961; West Eberhard, 1975; Wilson, 1975; Wynne-Edwards, 1962).
3. Research with other species, especially with primates, can suggest causal relationships in human behavior (Harlow and Harlow, 1965; Kummer, 1968, 1971).

Let us now examine some of the basic features of the human family and suggest a possible origin for them in biological evolution. Again, this is not to suggest that cultural evolution has not

---

[1]Most sociologists and anthropologists would probably still reject this argument, and explain universals in terms of cultural convergence on similar solutions to universal problems of the human condition, or in functionalist jargon, "universal structural prerequisites" of human societies. These phrases have always sounded singularly vacuous of empirical content; they merely hide an inability to account for species-wide uniformities in cultural terms. Given the relatively unspecialized adaptation of *Homo sapiens* to an extremely wide range of habitats, the cultural explanation of universals is even less convincing. If more specialized species are labile enough to modify certain features of their behavior profoundly and rapidly under different environmental conditions (as many mammals, and especially primates, do), then, why should the most behaviorally labile of mammals remain so consistently itself in certain features of its behavior while being so rapidly adaptable in others? If the cultural hypothesis were of such sweeping validity as most social scientists believe, then human cultures would presumably share practically nothing in common. To suggest that rain forest Pygmies and Arctic wasteland Eskimos, for instance, converged on similar cultural adaptations to "universal structural prerequisites" explains nothing.

been important, but rather that human culture is itself based on a set of generic capabilities and predispositions and, thus, that one should not treat biology and culture as two discrete categories— but as two interacting ones. Culture is itself an evolutionary strategy enabling our species to adapt to environmental changes, including changes of our own making, faster and more efficiently then we could by biological selection alone. Overriding the range of cultural variation in human family structure, certain important uniformities are generic to the species. In the following list (although not exhaustive) are features that might be interpreted in terms of biological evolution which will be discussed later.

1. The human family is based on a relatively stable pair bond between an adult male and one or more adult females. To be sure, humans are not as rigidly pair-bonded as some birds and mammals (e. g., foxes and gibbons) which are rigidly monogamous, but neither are we a promiscuous species, like chimpanzees and dogs, for example. Human groups that have experimented with promiscuity have not survived very long. It is true that many societies tolerate a period of premarital "try-outs" for youths in their teens, but all societies institutionalize a relatively stable pair bond in the form of marriage. Even where divorce is permitted and relatively unstigmatized, marriages typically last for periods of years rather than months. Those human females who make promiscuity a profession typically find the arrangement sexually unsatisfying, often seeking stable pair bond with a pimp—even at great financial cost.

   However, strict monogamy is not the rule either. Some three-fourths of human societies institutionalize polygyny, while only a handful tolerate polyandry and then only for very exceptional reasons (rules of hypergamy with polygyny in the upper strata and polyandry at the bottom, or female infanticide for population control purposes in marginal habitats) and under special conditions (fraternal polyandry, i.e., a woman marrying a set of brothers) (Murdock, 1949). In polygynous societies, most men are typically monogamously married because the sex ratio allows only a certain amount of polygyny (made possible largely through the differential age between husbands and wives), but polygyny is quite often the preferred arrangement.

   This common preference for polygyny in most societies and the nearly total absence of polyandry suggest that pair bonding is stricter for women than for men or, in biological terms, that human males and females have different reproductive strategies. Males seek to monopolize sexual access to "their" females, but also to inseminate as many as possible. Females seek a stable relationship with a male who will make a contribution to the survival of their offspring. In simpler terms, like most higher vertebrates where females make a far heavier investment per offspring than males, women are more interested in the quality of their progeny and men in their quantity. Such a suggestion is confirmed by the extremely widespread double standard of sexual morality in human societies. There are many societies that condone extramarital behavior for men much more than for women and, very few, if any, where the reverse is true.

2. Within the nuclear family, mating has been (again, with the exotic textbook exceptions of the Inca and the Egyptian royal families) restricted by "incest taboos" to the mated couple. That is, all societies have rules that parents may not mate with children, nor siblings with each other. Many anthropologists have followed Lévi-Strauss (1968) in considering the incest taboo as the major "passage from nature to culture," but such a purely cultural explanation is highly questionable.

3. Mated pairs (husbands and wives) typically share with their subadult offspring a common place of residence (home), which is a defended territory. Territoriality is defined here as the defense of fixed space against occupation by largely nonrelated conspecifics. In that sense, territoriality is a universal phenomenon in human societies, but the controversy as to whether it is cultural or biological still rages (Mazur, 1973; Tiger and Fox, 1971; van den Berghe, 1974). The most plausible conclusion at this stage is that it is both, and territorial behavior is also mediated by ecological conditions (such as population density), as indeed seems true of other species (Wilson, 1975). The evidence for a partly biological predisposition for territoriality in humans is that it is not only universal in the species, but takes very similar and ritualized forms in all societies. Also, men consistently seem to play a more aggressive role in territorial defense than women.

   Defense of the home is not the only expression of human territoriality, but it is perhaps the most universal and uniformly ritualized one. In almost all, if not all societies, the home is not a territory that can be casually entered by outsiders. The stranger must stop outside the boundary of the home, make his presence known, usually through some kind of a noise, wait for the occupant to recognize his presence, make a sign of harmless intent and await the occupant's invitation to proceed. Without knowing anything about a foreign culture, one can reliably avoid trouble by following this basic ritual (the specific details of which do vary culturally, of course) and, conversely, to violate this basic etiquette is to invite aggression, indeed, to risk one's life. Adult men are the main defenders of the home territory; intrusions by adult men seem to arouse more defensive behavior than by women or children.

4. The human family is strongly dominance-ordered on the basis of age and sex (van den Berghe, 1973). In all societies, adults are dominant over children, and men over women. Individual women may dominate individual men, but in all known societies the normal expectation is that a male is the head of the

family household. Jural family authority is almost invariably vested either in the husband-father (in patrilineal and bilateral descent societies), or in the brother-maternal uncle (in matrilineal societies) (Murdock, 1949). In addition, finer gradations of age quite commonly determine the dominance order between children and between adults. Older children are dominant over younger ones, women over subadolescent children of both sexes, men over women, older men over younger men and older women over younger ones. The relationship between age and dominance often reverses itself, however, beyond mature middle age. Very few societies (and families) are genuinely gerontocratic. Most societies and families are ruled by men in late middle age, not by patriarchs in their dotage. No society or family system anywhere in the world has ever been egalitarian or genuinely democratic. Some of the smaller and technologically simpler societies have come close to establishing a consensual democracy among *adult men*, but, even in those societies, the family has been clearly dominance ordered (van den Berghe, 1973).

5. The basic survival tasks of child-raising, defense and food production have been performed in all human societies by basically the same kind of division of labor based upon age and sex, both within and outside the family. Women have everywhere carried by far the greater burden of child-care, often with the help of subadult females and have, in addition, produced much or even most of the food that could be gathered or grown within the vicinity of the home. This is the pattern in nearly all hunting and gathering societies, and in most societies with swidden agriculture, although men have played an increasingly important role in food production in the complex agricultural societies. Men have typically monopolized war, hunting (and scavenging) and herding (D'Andrade, 1966; Goode, 1963; Lenski, 1966; Martin and Voorhies, 1975; van den Berghe, 1973).

There are a few textbook exceptions to these generalizations, such as the famous "Amazon" corps in the Dahomey army, recreational hunting in the European aristocracy, llama and alpaca herding in the high Andes and so on, but the basic pattern of the human division of labor by age and sex is remarkably uniform. Only in the complex agrarian and industrial societies, where production tasks became increasingly divorced from the family, where technology reduces the importance of physical strength and diminishes hazards to child raising, does consistency in the sexual division of labor begin to break down. Even in these complex societies, most families still conform to the basic human pattern: women stay at home to care for the children; men go out to "earn a living." If anything, the role of women in production has been *reduced* rather than enhanced in complex societies.

This brief survey of species-wide characteristics of the human family makes no claim to either exhaustiveness or originality. With the exception of territoriality that most social scientists have much ignored or denied in humans, the characteristics just mentioned are widely recognized by sociologists and anthropologists as "cultural universals," but their universality or near-universality is generally ascribed to cultural factors. All societies, we are told, had to face certain basic problems of survival and, therefore, converge on similar cultural solutions. This line of "explanation" is question-begging. Other species have developed other solutions to similar problems. Conversely, many human reformers have convincingly argued that traditional ways of doing things were inefficient, undesirable or both. Many Utopian groups of highly dedicated and self-selected members have made earnest attempts to practice free love, abolish the family, eliminate the sexual division of labor, raise children permissively, be egalitarian and nonpossessive and so on. Such groups as the Oneida community, countless contemporary communes, religious orders, Kibbutzim and many others have all foundered on the bedrock of the human family. Most fail altogether; the few that survive longer than a few months do so in one of two ways: either they abondon some of their Utopian goals and revert to something very close to a traditional family or they live in celibate, monosexual, nonreproductive, familyless communities that can only survive by recruitment— often, indeed, by economic parasitism on a larger society. Monastic orders represent the latter solution; Kibbutzim, the former (Spiro, 1956, 1958; Tiger and Shepher, 1975).

If dedicated attempts to change things based on highly rational premises fail so consistently to produce viable, self-reproducing alternatives to the human family as we have characterized it, we may at least advance the hypothesis that we are biologically predisposed to be the kind of animal we are, not, to be sure, in a narrow inflexible way as, say, social insects, but within broad flexible limits.

It is one thing to advance such a hypothesis and quite another to substantiate it. At this stage we can only make tentative suggestions whereby we induce phylogenesis from comparisons within and between contemporary species. Before I attempt to suggest possible clusters of causal relations between the behavioral features listed above, and certain features of human anatomy, physiology and ecology, I must sound an important *caveat*. Often such attempts are dismissed by cultural determinists as "mere analogies," wherein various species are conveniently picked to prove similarities. That, of course, is not sociobiology, but anthropomorphic fable writing. When two species exhibit a similar kind of behavior, one cannot jump to the conclusion that that behavior is the product of a common phylogenesis. The hypothesis that one deals with *homologous* behavior as a result of parallel evolution only becomes plausible to the extent that one deals with sizable numbers of closely related species and with a clearly defined, ritualized behavioral phenotype.

Conversely, when two even closely related species exhibit different behaviors, one cannot conclude that, therefore, these behaviors are *not* genetically predisposed. For instance, *Papio hamadryas*, and *Papio annubis* are so closely related that they produce hybrids in the wild, yet their mating behavior and their social organization are markedly different, and some of their differences have been convincingly demonstrated through field experiments not to be learned adaptations to different ecological niches (Kummer, 1971).

The main purpose of cross-specific comparisons is not to prove homologies, but rather to suggest that, if different species have biologically evolved clusters of interrelated traits similar to those found in humans, then a purely cultural explanation of these traits in humans is at least open to question. This is the case, even though the vast majority of these similarities are the result of convergent rather than parallel evolution and are, therefore, analogous rather than homologous to each other.

Let us return to the behavioral characteristics of the human family that were sketched earlier and try to interpret them sociobiologically. Many of the hypothesized relationships I am going to suggest are not novel, although some have not, to my knowledge, been applied specifically to humans. A number of paleontologists and primatologists have suggested a general evolutionary scenario of early hominids as terrestrial primates who gradually shifted from a predominantly vegetarian and insectivorous diet to a more omnivorous one that included the flesh of large mammals (DeVore and Washburn, 1963; Washburn and DeVore, 1961). Popularized by Ardrey (1961, 1966) and others as the "killer ape" theory of human evolution, this view has been widely attacked (Montagu, 1973), but not convincingly refuted. The paleontological evidence is clear: a few million years ago, our hominid ancestors on the open plains of Pleistocene Africa shifted from the kind of foraging economy that still largely characterizes contemporary baboons, to a mixed economy of foraging and hunting and scavenging of large mammals (Alcock, 1975). This significant ecological change almost certainly entailed a chain of adaptive changes in our behavior and social organization.

Whether early hominids were already pair-bonded or not, that is, whether anything like the modern human family already existed when that ecological shift took place, is an open question. A few contemporary terrestrial primates, such as the hamadryas baboon, the patas monkey and the gelada baboon, have polygynous one-male groups, and thus relatively stable pair bonds not unlike those of human families, but most primate species do not (Kummer, 1968, 1971). In any case, early man, as a primate, and thus a relatively unspecialized mammal, was a poorly equipped carnivore, giving birth to infants that were heavily dependent and remarkably unprecocious. Successful hunting of large mammals (and scavenging of carcasses from large felines and canines) implied two crucial social adaptations:

1. It took several cooperating men to make a kill or to steal one from large carnivores. (This adaptation took place long before the development of efficient and accurate projectiles such as boomerangs, blow guns, bows and arrows, spears and slingshots). The corollary of this cooperation meant the regular association of human groups larger than nuclear families. Indeed, such groups, ranging in size from around 20 to 60, may well have existed long before the hunting-and-scavenging adaptation, as groups of this order of magnitude are characteristic of many primates and nearly all predominantly terrestrial ones.
2. Pregnant and lactating females (i.e., the vast majority of adult females) and subadults would be a handicap rather than an asset in long-distance hunting and scavenging. There developed, therefore, a division of labor by age and sex, whereby adult males hunted and scavenged large prey and waged war with competing hominid bands; females stayed close to their home base with their young, collecting vegetable foods, insects, reptiles, eggs and other relatively immobile edibles. The corollary of that division of labor was *food sharing*, a trait singularly absent in most primates (except, to a limited extent, in the chimpanzee), but of paramount importance among humans.

Sociologists and anthropologists have long noted the importance of food sharing in our species, but they have usually interpreted it as an eminently cultural act, stressing the ritual aspects of it in religion, hospitality, the maintenance of hierarchical relations and so on. Of course, I do not dispute that specific forms of food sharing, such as taking communion in a Catholic Church or exchanging coca leaves between Andean Indians, are indeed learned, symbolic cultural acts; rather, I am suggesting that food sharing in humans may have a basis in biological evolution as well. The behavior is not only universal in the species, but its ritualization is basically similar in all cultures. Communion and commensality are indeed universal features of hospitality and of nearly every basic form of friendly, nonagonistic relationship between humans. The first impulse of humans seeking to establish such a nonagonistic relationship is to offer food, drink or other ingestible substances (such as tobacco), not out of physiological necessity, but to establish sociability. I know of no society in which casual eating in the presence of others without offering to share food is not considered bad manners and, indeed, many societies avoid situations where the sharing of food would be awkward, costly or inconvenient. (For example, one avoids visiting others at meal times, one refrains from eating in many public places, one eats secretively in periods of food shortages and so on.) Begging typically takes the form of a request for food (or to buy food) and restaurants are favorite targets of professional beggars. The impulse to share food is nearly irresistible (Lockard et al., 1976).

The evolution of food-sharing behavior in humans is probably relatively recent, because it is rare in the primate order. Other primates have fundamentally different ways of expressing their sociability, such as grooming. Other animals, however, have independently evolved other forms of food sharing between conspecifics. Many social insects, for instance, share food in noncultural ways. A number of social carnivores, such as African hunting dogs, regurgitate meat to pups and even to other adult dogs. If such forms of food sharing have been biologically evolved in other species, there is no *a priori* reason for rejecting a biological interpretation of food sharing in humans.

The relationship between the evolution of food sharing and that of the family is open to speculation since we do not know which behavior evolved first. It would be consistent with modern sociobiological notions of altruism (Hamilton, 1964, 1975; Trivers, 1971; Trivers and Hare, 1976; Wilson, 1975) to hypothesize that food sharing was either applied to already existing family groups, or that it served to establish the human family. In either case, kin selection, which seems such a widespread tendency in the altruistic behavior of so many social organisms, from insects to vertebrates, would in all likelihood have applied to food sharing. It would also be consistent with Trivers' notion of reciprocal altruism; the kin-selected food sharing would then have generalized to larger groups beyond the family (Trivers, 1971).

The "incest taboo," or, in biological terms, the fact that the human family group (at least in its nuclear form, and typically larger kin groups as well) is an outbreeding unit, has fascinated anthropologists for at least a century. While early anthropologists (Westermarck, 1921) advanced biological explanations for the incest taboo, it became fashionable for later generations of social scientists to reject such ideas. Perhaps the most widely advanced and the most plausible explanation for the universality of the incest taboo in humans is that outbreeding establishes ties between family groups, and thereby enlarges societies that would have a competitive edge over smaller, more endogamous ones. The argument is generally presented in terms of cultural evolution, but is not incompatible with a hypothesis of biological evolution. Inclusive fitness theory predicts that altruistic behavior is proportional to degree of biological relatedness (Hamilton, 1964, 1975; Trivers, 1971; Trivers and Hare, 1976; Wilson, 1975); thus, on biological evolutionary grounds, we would expect interrelated intermarrying family groups to behave cooperatively. Complex human systems of matrimonial exchanges and alliances are but another example of the way humans use a uniquely cultural medium to express relationships also present in noncultural ways in other species. Culture is not something fundamentally different from biological evolution; it grows out of it.

The most general biological explanation for outbreeding is simply that the adaptive advantage in producing genetically diverse offspring is such that evolutionary selection will be for sexual reproduction (as distinguished from parthenogenesis) and for outbreeding (Trivers and Hare, 1976). On the other hand, gregarious species also maximize altruistic behavior by maintaining, as we have just seen, biological relatedness between members of the interacting group. One would thus expect to find in gregarious species a balance between outbreeding and inbreeding. The selective advantage in having diverse offspring would be counterbalanced by the advantage in maintaining cohesive groups of related individuals. Outbreeding, among social vertebrates can, therefore, be expected to stop far short of being complete.[2]

This is precisely what happens in humans. All human societies show a tension between principles of exogamy and endogamy. All societies have groups *out of which* one must marry, and other groups *within which* one must marry (or a least within which it is preferred that one marry). Exogamy and endogamy are two sides of social reality: all societies have both. This leads us to the most fundamental problems of the social sciences, namely, the basis of human sociality itself. Here, too, it is suggested that instead of postulating a unique basis for human sociality, we may more parsimoniously account for it in terms of broader cross-specifically applicable concepts.

There is a remarkable consistency in the way human groups maintain boundaries between in-groups and out-groups. Territoriality plays an important role in this process and so does endogamy. If, following Wilson (1975) and, much before him, Radcliffe-Brown (1952), we define a *society* as a group of conspecifies bounded by a zone of much less frequent interactions than the rate which prevails between its members; and a *population* as a group bounded by a zone of much less frequent interbreeding than the prevailing rate within the group; then it is clear that human rules of exogamy and endogamy, cultural though they are in their form, play a key role in circumscribing both human societies and populations, and do so in ways which are directly analogous to the mating systems of other animals. Rules of endogamy and exogamy in human populations are thus at the very analytical core of sociology and, by

---

[2]The social insects are very different in this respect. They manage to have both outbreeding and cohesive societies of up to tens of thousands of closely related individuals by having a single or very few females lay all or nearly all the fertile eggs, and by having them lay thousands of such eggs. The gregariousness of social insects, especially of the social Hymenoptera is thus made possible both by worker sterility and by haplodiploidy, i. e., the fact that the females are diploid and the males haploid. For the consequences of haplodiploidy in the social insects, see Wilson (1975), and Trivers and Hare (1976).

extension, of sociobiology: they define the interplay between society and population. Far from marking the Lévi-Straussian "passage de la nature à la culture," marriage rules are merely the specifically human idiom of sociality and mating.

A common arrangement in scores of human societies is one where the unilineal descent groups (patrilineages or matrilineages) are exogamous, but where there is a preference for cross-cousin marriage. (Cross-cousins are children of mother's brothers or father's sisters, as distinguished from parallel-cousins who are children of a set of sisters or of brothers.)

In these societies, parallel-cousins (half of whom belong to ego's own lineage) are typically forbidden marriage partners, while cross-cousins are strongly preferred, even through the degree of biological relatedness between the two sets of cousins is identical (one-eight in both cases). In such societies, then, the culturally recognized descent groups (lineages and clans) are typically exogamous, thereby making for a measure of outbreeding (between siblings, and between parallel-cousins who are often terminologically identified with siblings). At the same time, a rule of cross-cousin marriage ensures establishment of a set of matriomonial alliances with other descent groups that are *socially distinct* but *biologically related*. A large measure of outbreeding is practiced while, at the same time, ties of cooperation are maintained between hundreds or even thousands of individuals who are biologically related to each other.

Some anthropologists, notably Lévi-Strauss (1968) and White (1959), have interpreted this arrangement as the most elementary form of human kinship structure, but have given a purely cultural explanation for it. The incest taboo, by forcing men to swap sisters for brides, establishes relations between wider social groups and, thus, marks the great "jump from nature to culture." As we have suggested here, the biological explanation is far more general and parsimonious. There is no need to invoke culture as the *deus ex machina* of evolution, as does Lévi-Strauss.

Indeed, outbreeding, and more especially sibling-avoidance in mating, is quite widespread in many nonhuman species (Bischof, 1972; Lorenz, 1970). The young of many mammals living in family units with pair-bonded adults disperse from the parental home before the onset of sexual maturation and, thus, are unlikely to mate. Such is the case, for instance, of the gibbon (*Hylobates lar*), a monogamous ape, living in small nuclear families. Here again, the interpretation of the human "incest taboo" as a unique cultural invention, indeed as the origin of culture, is gratuitous and therefore suspect as Parker (1976) rightly concludes in a recent survey of the evidence.

Strong evidence for a partly biogenic explanation of sibling avoidance in humans was recently collected in a study of marriage in Israeli Kibbutzim. Shepher (1971) discovered that out of 2769 marriages involving members of Kibbutzim, only 14 cases were between members of the *same* Kibbutz age group. Looking at these cases, he found that in only five of them had the spouses been raised together before the age of six, and then never for more than two out of those six years of early childhood. It should be added that there is *no* cultural rule of Kibbutz exogamy. Cultural norms are neutral or even slightly favorable to intermarriage between members of the same Kibbutz, yet it practically never occurs. The practice in Kibbutzim is to raise children communally from infancy, at least during their waking hours, and in some Kibbutzim around the clock. Kibbutz children are thus raised under conditions closely resembling those of siblings in normal human families. Shepher hypothesizes that humans are negatively imprinted not to develop pair bonds with individuals with whom they have been raised during a critical period of early childhood. Ethnographic data support Shepher's hypothesis, for, when asked whether they would marry each other, young people raised together on a Kibbutz typically reply that, though they feel very close, they could not develop an erotic relationship because they regard each other as siblings.

Shepher's extensive study merely confirmed what many had already observed and even reported about the Kibbutz (Spiro, 1958). Nor is the Kibbutz case the only one in support of the biogenic explanation of sibling incest (Fox, 1962). In China, for instance, there existed a custom of contracting child marriages wherein the infant bride would, in effect, become an adopted daughter-in-law in the household of her husband. The marriage would not be consummated until the onset of the girl's puberty, but the child spouses were raised together. This form of marriage was not considered desirable, but it was a way for a poor man to give away a daughter in infancy without incurring the costs of her upbringing and without having to give her a dowry. Wolf (1966) found that in a Taiwan village he studied there were 19 such cases of child marriages but that, in 17 of the cases, the young people concerned refused to consummate the marriage upon adolescence, despite parental pressure. In the two cases where the marriages were consummated, the child-brides had been separated from their husbands until the age of eight and 11, respectively.

The little we know about actual incest behavior also tends to support a negative imprinting hypothesis. Weinberg (1963) who studied cases of actual incest in America reports that out of 37 cases of sibling incest, 31 were transitory attachments, and that in all six cases of a stable bond, the siblings had been separated from early childhood.

Existing evidence thus suggests that the biologically predisposed mechanism for outbreeding is not avoidance of kin as such, but of those with whom one has been raised during a critical period in early childhood. Under normal conditions this would, of course, apply to members of the nuclear or even extended family. The hypothesis of negative imprinting fits the ethnographic data much better than any purely cultural explanation. It is also interesting to note that many cultures regularly marry people unknown or barely known to each other before the wedding. Some cultures even go through a pretense of the spouses not even seeing each other before the wedding (e.g., the ritual of the veiled bride in the Christian and Muslim tradition). Many cultures thus take it for granted that, within certain age limits, a pair bond routinely develops between almost any two strangers of opposite sex. Indeed, many cultures assume that it is better for spouses not to have known each other before the wedding.

So far, we have considered only rules of *marriage*, which are, as anthropologists are fond of repeating, a uniquely human tradition. We found that human rules of exogamy and endogamy, cultural though these are, nevertheless are fully compatible with a wider biological interpretation of outbreeding and sociality in many other species. If we look at human mating, as distinguished from marriage—and the two are obviously far from synonymous—we find that the fit to the biological interpretation remains good. Generally, mating rules in human societies do not conflict with marriage rules, but they are often less restrictive. More specifically, rules of outbreeding typically apply equally to marriage and mating, but rules of inbreeding are enforced more strictly in the case of marriage than of mating. There are many societies, in short, in which partners that would be regarded as unsuitable for marriage because of a rule of endogamy (such as class, ethnic or racial endogamy) are acceptable as mates. The slave societies established by various European powers, for instance, all had strict rules prohibiting (or at least strongly stigmatizing) marriage between freeman and slave and, indeed, often between white and black as well. Yet, mating between these groups was frequent, as we know.

It follows from the above that outbreeding in human populations is frequently (if not typically) greater than the sometimes restrictive rules of endogamy might suggest. *Exogamy* typically applies to mating as well as marriage, but endogamy often does not or, at least, not as strongly. *Endogamy* is a rule whereby socially recognized groups larger than family groups maintain some degree of biological relatedness and, hence, some basis for altruistic behavior. Rules of endogamy, therefore, are much less consequential for extramarital mating than for marriage, since the former, in contrast to the latter, typically does not establish permanent social groupings. On the other hand, rules of exogamy, which make for outbreeding, apply both to mating and marriage. The young bourgeois of the 19th century European novel, for instance, could marry neither his sister nor the parlor maid, but he was free to copulate with the maid and not with his sister. When the maid was put "in the family way," she was typically dismissed so that she and her child could make no claim on her seducer's family.

Let us now focus on the pair bond between spouses and its

consequences for the sexual division of labor in the raising of children. We have suggested that humans are by nature non-promiscuous animals leaning toward fairly (but not rigidly) stable monogamy or polygyny. Most societies show a preference for polygyny, though the polygyny is generally limited to a minority of the men having two to four wives, but seldom more. Most human families range from monogamous to small-scale polygynous. Husbands are fairly consistently older than their wives in nearly all societies, and this permits a limited degree of polygyny in many societies, but prolonged celibacy of most males is not found in any human society, as is the case with the all-bachelor groups of a number of bird and mammal species. The evolutionary factors that favored the development of pair bonding in humans are a matter of conjecture.

We already suggested that food sharing arising from the sexual division of labor in gathering and hunting may have been a contributing factor. Another may have been the disappearance of estrus in the human female—hence her continuous sexual accessibility. It is true that there are many estrous species that are also pair-bonding, including some primate ones, so, clearly, absence of estrus is not a necessary, nor presumably a sufficient, condition for pair bonding; however, lack of estrus may well have been a facilitating factor in the development of human pair bonding. Since the human female seems exceptional in not having a clear period of greatly heightened sexual receptivity, cross-species comparisons are not very useful in this respect.

There is however, a cluster of four characteristics which covary with great consistency in a wide range of birds and mammal species, including *Homo sapiens*. These characteristics are

1. sexual dimorphism in size, that is, the degree to which one sex of a species (generally the male in birds and mammals) is larger than the other;
2. sexual bimaturism, or the differential time span that it takes the males and the females of a species to attain sexual maturity (In most birds and mammals where there is sexual bimaturism, it takes males longer to be fully grown and sexually mature.);
3. parental investment, defined as the time and energy spent by parents on their offspring;
4. polygyny, defined as exclusive or near-exclusive mating of one male with more than one female.

In a wide gamut of higher vertebrates ranging from pinnipeds (LeBoeuf, 1974) to grouse (Wiley, 1974), the relationship between these four variables is clear. To the degree that the males of a species are bigger than the females, they also take longer to reach their full size, they tend to invest less in their young then females and they tend to be polygynous. Polygyny almost inevitably makes for differential parental investment for males and females. Since a polygynous male will, by definition, have more offspring than any one of his females, it follows that his investment in any given offspring will be less than that of the offspring's mother. Even if the father has a substantial investment in his children collectively (which is often *not* the case in highly polygynous species), he has to divide his attention between more of them than his females. The causal link between polygyny and sexual bimaturism is also clear. Holding other factors constant (notably sex ratio at birth, and sex-specific mortality before maturation), the longer it takes males to achieve maturity in relation to females, the fewer adult males there will be in relation to adult females and thus the easier polygyny is to maintain.

Finally, the linkage between bimaturism and dimorphism also seems close and direct. Differences in size, but also in many other secondary sexual characteristics (such as plumage, tooth size, musculature, pilosity and so on) between the males and females of a species tend to develop principally during the additional period that it takes the male to attain its full maturity. In other words, males and females look much alike until both reach the age of female maturity, but the dimorphism becomes increasingly accentuated in the interval between the female's and the male's full maturity.

Polygynous species are also often characterized by agonistic competition between males for females, another factor that selects males for strength and bigness, that is, for sexual dimorphism and bimaturism. Harem systems of mating favor bigger, stronger, older males, and force younger males to postpone reproduction; indeed, in extreme cases, most males may even be permanently excluded as among elephant seals *(Mirounga angustirostris)*, a highly polygynous species where males get to be three times as heavy as females and take two and a half to three times as long to reach full maturity (LeBoeuf, 1974).

The human data fit these cross-specific generalizations remarkably well. As a species, we are moderately polygynous, dimorphic and bimaturing. The asymmetry of parental investment is clear but not overwhelming: men, too, typically have some involvement in child-raising, much more than elephant seal bulls, for instance, whose main contribution to the pups is to smother them to death below their masses of blubber, but much less than the males of many birds who share equally with females the tasks of hatching the eggs and feeding the fledglings. We are, in short, just about where we belong on these four interrelated continua, and morphological and physiological features seem more predictive of some basic aspects of our behavior than any purely cultural explanation.

As is usually the case, the vast majority of human cultures go along with our biology rather than try to buck it. All or nearly all human cultures, for instance, recognize sexual bimaturism: men marry at a later age than women, and the average age difference of husbands and wives at first marriage fluctuates within relatively narrow limits from culture to culture. (In polygynous societies, the age difference between spouses tends to increase with each of the man's successive marriages; human polygyny is a privilege of age and high status, as in nonhuman societies.) Most human cultures openly prefer polygyny; the minority that are prescriptively monogamous have, for the most part, only become so in recent times, and continue to condone a double standard of marital fidelity for men and women. Most cultures take sexual dimorphism into account in their sexual division of labor. All cultures assign the main responsibility for raising young children to women.

To summarize the main line of argument here, the importance of culture is not denied in humans. Even the features of our social behavior and family organization, for which origins in biological evolution were suggested, are always expressed through a rich cultural medium. For instance, we institutionalize pair bonding in marriage, a uniquely human institution that incorporates many things besides pair bonding and reproduction. We recognize sexual dimorphism, but we institutionalize a sexual division of labor that goes well beyond the simple biologically evolved pattern. There are good biological reasons why women should raise children more than men, but there are no good reasons why women should not be airline pilots, or men typists.

My quarrel is only with social scientists who would continue to seek purely cultural explanations for practically all aspects of our behavior, even when cross-specific comparisons suggest intellectually more parsimonious explanations.

Surely, *ad hoc* cultural explanations for humans are weaker than biological explanations that apply to a wide range of species. It seems increasingly anachronistic that most social scientists should accept evolutionary concepts in anatomy and physiology, while rejecting evolutionary thinking when applied to behavior.

The great intellectual challenge of sociobiology is that, for the first time, it suggests the possibility of incorporating the study of the behavior of the species that happens to be our own in a theoretical framework of breathtakingly wider scope. True, psychological behaviorism also attempted to do so, but unlike sociobiology it did not make room for the enormous behavioral diversity between species. Behaviorism stressed ontogeny to the almost complete exclusion of phylogeny. It was static and nonevolutionary, and therefore quite limited in scope, although quite persuasive as far as it went. Behaviorism showed us how much like rats and pigeons we were, which was true enough, but only in a limited and rather unexciting sense. Sociobiology allows us to be as uniquely human as we really are. It only asks us to concede that every other species is also unique in some respects. It squarely puts us back in the evolutionary scheme of things where we belong; and it does so at the moment of our phylogeny where we can profoundly alter the evolution of our entire biosphere.

References   Alcock, J. 1975. *Animal Behavior: an Evolution Approach*. Sunderland MA: Sinauer Associates.

Alexander, R.D. 1971. The search for an evolutionary philosophy of man. *Proceedings of the Royal Society (Victoria)* 84: 99–120.

———. 1975. The search for a general theory of behavior. *Behavioral Science* 20: 77–100.

Ardrey, R. 1961. *African Genesis*. New York: Atheneum.

———. 1966. *The Territorial Imperative*. New York: Atheneum.

Austin, W. T., and Bates, F. L. 1974. Ethological indicators of dominance and territory in a human captive population. *Social Forces* 52: 447–455.

Barash, D. 1977. *Sociobiology and Behavior*. New York: Elsevier.

Bischof, N. 1972. The biological foundations of the incest taboo. *Social Science Information* 11: 7–36.

Campbell, B. G. (ed.) 1972. *Sexual Selection and the Descent of Man, 1871–1971*. Chicago: Aldine.

Crook, J. H. 1972. Sexual selection, dimorphism, and social organization in the primates. In B. G. Campbell (ed.) *Sexual Selection and the Descent of Man, 1871-1971*. Chicago: Aldine.

D'Andrade, R. G. 1966. Sex differences and cultural institutions. In Eleanor E. Maccoby (ed.) *The Development of Sex Differences*. Stanford: Stanford University Press.

DeVore, I. 1965. Male dominance and mating behavior in baboons. In Frank A. Beach (ed.) *Sex and Behavior*. New York: Wiley.

DeVore, I., and Washburn, S. L. 1963. Baboon ecology and human evolution. *Viking Fund Publications in Anthropology* 36: 333–367.

Emlen, S. T., and Oring, L. W. 1977. Ecology, sexual selection and the evolution of mating systems. *Science* 197: 215–223.

Fox, R. 1962. Sibling incest. *British Journal of Sociology* 13: 128–150.

———. 1972. Alliance and constraint. In B. G. Campbell (ed.) *Sexual Selection and the Descent of Man, 1871–1971*. Chicago: Aldine.

———. (ed.) 1975. *Biosocial Anthropology*. New York: Wiley.

Goode, W. J. 1963. *World Revolution and Family Patterns*. New York: The Free Press.

Hamilton, W. D. 1964. The genetical evolution of social behaviour. *Journal of Theoretical Biology* 7: 1–52.

———. 1975. Innate social aptitudes of man: An approach from evolutionary genetics. In Robin Fox (ed.) *Biosocial Anthropology*. New York: Wiley.

Harlow, H. F., and Harlow, M. K. 1965. The effect of rearing conditions on behavior. In John Money (ed.) *Sex Research: New Developments*. New York: Holt, Rinehart and Winston.

Hinde, R. A. 1974. *Biological Bases of Human Social Behaviour*. New York: McGraw-Hill.

Kummer, H. 1968. *Social Organization of Hamadryas Baboons*. Chicago: University of Chicago Press.

———. 1971. *Primate Societies*. Chicago: Aldine-Atherton.

LeBoeuf, B. J. 1974. Male–male competition and reproductive success in elephant seals. *American Zoologist* 14: 163–176.

Lenski, G. 1966. *Power and Privilege*. New York: McGraw-Hill.

Lévi-Strauss, C. 1968. *The Elementary Structures of Kinship*. Boston: Beacon Press.

Lockard, J. S., McDonald, L. L., Clifford, D. A., and Martinez, R. 1976. Panhandling: Sharing of resources. *Science* 191: 406–408.

Lorenz, K. 1970. *Studies in Animal and Human Behavior*. Cambridge, MA: Harvard University Press.

Martin, M. K., and Voorhies, B. 1975. *Female of the Species*. New York: Columbia University Press.

Mayr, E. 1974. Behavior programs and evolutionary strategies. *American Scientist* 62(6): 650–659.

Mazur, A. 1973. A cross-species comparison of status in small established groups. *American Sociological Review* 38: 513–530.

Montagu, A. (ed.) 1973. *Man and Aggression*. New York: Oxford University Press.

Murdock, G. P. 1949. *Social Structure*. New York: Macmillan.

Parker, S. 1976. The precultural basis of the incest taboo: Toward a biosocial theory. *American Anthropologist* 73(2): 285–305.

Parsons, T., and Bales, R. F. 1954. *Family, Socialization and Interaction Process*. Glencoe, IL: The Free Press.

Radcliffe-Brown, A. R. 1952. *Structure and Function in Primitive Society*. Glencoe, IL: The Free Press.

Shepher, J. 1971. Mate selection among second generation Kibbutz adolescents and adults. *Archives of Sexual Behavior* 1(4): 293–307.

Spiro, M. E. 1956. *Kibbutz: Venture in Utopia*. Cambridge, MA: Harvard University Press.

———. 1958. *Children of the Kibbutz*. Cambridge, MA: Harvard University Press.

Tiger, L., and Fox, R. 1971. *The Imperial Animal*. New York: Holt, Rinehart and Winston.

Tiger, L., and Shepher, J. 1975. *Women in the Kibbutz*. New York: Harcourt, Brace, Jovanovich.

Trivers, R. L. 1971. The evolution of reciprocal altruism. *Quarterly Review of Biology* 46: 35–57.

———. 1972. Parental investment and sexual selection. In B. G. Campbell (ed.) *Sexual Selection and the Descent of Man*. Chicago: Aldine.

Trivers, R. L., and Hare, H. 1976. Haplodiploidy and the evolution of the social insects. *Science* 191(4224): 249–263.

van den Berghe, P. L. 1973. *Age and Sex in Human Societies*. Belmont, CA: Wadsworth.

———. 1974. Bringing breasts back in. *American Sociological Review* 39: 777–788.

———. 1975. *Man in Society, A Biosocial View*. New York: Elsevier.

Washburn, S. L., and DeVore, I. 1961. Social behavior of baboons and early man. *Viking Fund Publications in Anthropology* 31: 91–105.

Weinberg, Kirson S. 1963. *Incest Behavior*. New York: Citadel Press.

West Eberhard, M. J. 1975. The evolution of social behavior by kin selection. *Quarterly Review of Biology* 50: 1–33.

Westermarck, E. 1921. *The History of Human Marriage*. London: Macmillan.

White, L. 1959. *The Evolution of Culture*. New York: McGraw-Hill.

Wiley, R. H. 1974. Evolution of social organization and life-history patterns among grouse. *The Quarterly Review of Biology* 49: 201–227.

Wilson, E. O. 1975. *Sociobiology: The New Synthesis*. Cambridge, MA: Belknap/Harvard University Press.

Wolf, Arthur P. 1966. Childhood association, sexual attraction and the incest taboo, a Chinese case. *American Anthropologist* 68(4): 883–898.

Wynne-Edwards, V. C. 1962. *Animal Dispersion in Relation to Social Behaviour*. Edinburgh: Oliver and Boyd.

The Desire to Bear Children

Halbert B. Robinson, Stephen C. Woods,
Allan E. Williams

5

This chapter attempts to review the theories concerning population trends in human and nonhuman groups from the two widely separated scientific disciplines of demography and ethology, and to present several hypotheses concerning the interaction of biological and cultural variables that may in part determine the motivation to bear and rear children. Of central concern is the marked discrepancy in birth rates between the more- and less-developed nations.

Both demographers, who concern themselves with human population patterns, and ethologists, who deal primarily with nonhuman populations, have analyzed population trends in terms of the relation between death and birth rates. With respect to death rates, both disciplines have considered such variables as climatic conditions, food supplies, natural longevity and disease, among a long list of contributing factors. In addition, demographers have emphasized various factors contributing to the health status of populations, such as sanitation projects, immunization programs and individualized medical care; and ethologists have stressed the importance of predators, including man. In considering birth rates, the two sciences have presented strongly divergent hypotheses. Demographers have tended to emphasize social and economic factors whereas ethologists have stressed genetically determined behavioral patterns. In only one respect have members of the two disciplines considered a common variable that is hypothesized to contribute to family size, namely, the existence of group members to assist the mother in caring for the young.

It is the contention here that the emphasis of demographers on social and economic factors on the one hand and the exclusive pursuit of genetic determinants by ethologists on the other have caused an equally important set of interactions to remain almost totally unexplored. It is proposed that the behaviors involved in reproductive and caretaking activities of many species result from a complex interweaving of genetic and environmental variables. Among most higher-order species, including human beings, it is suggested that the motivation to bear and rear children is, in part, a function of the experiences of potential parents with infants and toddlers during the formative years. It is tentatively proposed, then, that the decrease in the birth rate, which has characterized all of the industrialized and urbanized nations, may have resulted, in part, from a breakdown of age-old patterns of interaction between very young children and those who are entering child-bearing years. More specifically, it is suggested that age segregation in urbanized societies may have interfered with the firm establishment of motive systems dependent on endocrine system factors which are organized, in part, by interactions between preadolescents with babies and toddlers.

It is also proposed that the desire to bear and rear children may be influenced by the number of family members who will participate in child-care functions, but that this factor is more complex than has been recognized. Different family members play quite different roles. For example, it is hypothesized that fathers tend not to be strongly attracted to infants but become more positively oriented to their offspring after infancy, quite possibly through motivational patterns influenced by biological evolution. Children are not powerfully attracted to infants and young children but become so as they enter the adolescent period, females at this time becoming more strongly attracted to infants and males more strongly attracted to toddlers. These motivational changes may in large part be determined by changes in the organization of the endocrine system.

It is proposed, then, that among the most important determinants of family size are (1) the motivation to have children for their own sake (this desire being in part a function of biological systems organized during the formative years) and (2) the array of individuals available to assist the mother in caring for the children (the caretaking patterns among family members being in part a result of evolutionary processes).

In developing the hypotheses which are suggested above, a broad range of theoretical proposals and research evidence comparing both human and nonhuman species is examined.

1. A brief discussion of the recent world-wide population increase, which has occurred concomitant with the reduction of birth rates in the more industrialized and urbanized nations.
2. A brief consideration of the factors that determine human birth rates.
3. A discussion of the factors that have been proposed to play a part in human motivation to bear children.
4. A brief consideration of the factors that determine birth rates of nonhuman species.
5. A discussion of the factors that have been proposed as determinants of motive systems controlling reproductive and parenting behaviors of nonhuman species.

6. A tentative extension of the proposals concerning nonhuman species to human beings.
7. A discussion of the nature of parenting functions and the distribution of these functions among potential caretakers of the young.
8. A consideration of the potential role of endocrine systems in reproductive and parenting behaviors.
9. A list of specific hypotheses concerning reproductive and parenting behaviors in human beings.
10. Some suggestions for research.

Factors Affecting Human Population Trends

From 1960 to 1970, the population of human beings on the world grew almost 2% annually, a rate that implies a doubling of size every 35 years. As Table I indicates, the recent levels of population growth are more than twice those for the first half of the 20th century and four to five times greater than those for the 19th century.

The most important determinant of this dramatic increase in population has been declining mortality. Following the Industrial Revolution, mortality rates began to descend in some parts of Europe and are presently at a very low level in all developed countries (United Nations, 1973). More recently, mortality has been reduced to a low to moderate level in almost all regions of the world (United Nations, 1975).

During the period 1965–1970, there were only 14 deaths for every 1000 people in the world, an all-time low. In the more-developed countries there were an average of nine deaths per 1000 inhabitants, and in the less-developed nations an average of 16 per

Table I
Conjectures of Historical Population Growth[a]

Date	Population (millions)	Average annual increase (%)	Approximate no. of years for population to double
B.C.			
7000–6000	5–10		
A.D.			
1	200–400	0.0	
1650	470–545	0.0	
1750	629–961	0.4	173
1800	813–1,125	0.4	173
1850	1,128–1,402	0.5	139
1900	1,550–1,762	0.5	139
1950	2,486	0.8	86
1960	2,982	1.8	36
1965	3,289	2.0	35

[a]From United Nations (1973, p. 10).

1000. During the same period the world-wide birth rate was 33 per 1000 population. The figures for the more- and less-developed countries averaged 18 and 39 per 1000, respectively (United Nations, 1975).

Fortunately, most population groups produce fewer children than they are potentially capable of producing. Birth rates of more than 60 per 1000 population have been reported (Kuczynski, 1936; Raskin, 1956), but very few, if any, societies today record more than 48 births per 1000 (United Nations, 1975). As noted above, the birth rate in the more-developed nations is less than one-half the rate in the less-developed nations. There is, in fact, no overlap in the distributions of birth rates in the two groups of nations; rates from 1970 to 1975 in the more-developed nations ranged from 15 to 21 per 1000 inhabitants with an average of 17.2, while rates in the less-developed nations ranged from 23 to 48 per 1000 inhabitants with an average of 37.9 (United Nations, 1975). It is the fact that birth rates have decreased in a dramatic fashion in all those nations that have become industrialized and urbanized that is of central concern in this paper. How can we understand this important, potentially world-saving, demographic transition?

Factors Determining Birth Rates

A complex set of variables relate to birth rates. In a classic paper, Davis and Blake (1956) partitioned the factors determining fertility into those affecting intercourse, conception, gestation and parturition. Among the more important "intercourse" variables are those that govern the formation and dissolution of sexual unions, including age at marriage and disruption by separation, divorce and death; and those that govern exposure to intercourse within sexual unions, such as periods of voluntary or involuntary abstinence. Among these variables, age at marriage is probably most important (Hajnal, 1965). Agarwala (1967) has proposed, for example, that the Indian birth rate would be reduced by 30% by 1991–1992 if all Indian women waited until age 19 or older to marry.

Among the "conception" variables, levels of fecundity are affected by involuntary causes such as health status and lactation, and by voluntary causes such as sterilization and the use of contraceptive techniques. For our purposes here, involuntary causes will be ignored, although it should be noted that such variables as malnutrition and maternal disease can suppress conception and increase fetal and neonatal mortality. It is generally believed that contraception has become the principal means of controlling births and that it has been responsible for the shift from high to low fertility rates in many countries (United Nations, 1973). Contraception by *coitus interruptus* and *coitus reservatus* was documented in a wide range of societies as early as the 17th century (Meuvret, 1965; Wrigley, 1966, 1968). The ancient establishment of *coitus interruptus* is attested to by its mention in the Book of Genesis. [See also Himes (1936).]

Among the *gestation* and *parturition* variables are fetal and neonatal mortality from both involuntary and voluntary causes. Abortion, like various other methods of birth control, has been known and practiced since time immemorial (Landry, 1934). It has been an important factor in controlling birth rates in almost all of the more developed countries, particularly during their transition from high to low birth rates (Freedman, 1966a). A great many societies also have practiced infanticide at some period of their history (Carr-Saunders, 1922; Ford, 1945; Himes, 1936; Lévi-Strauss, 1955; Nag, 1962), but it probably is no longer an important method of controlling family size (Hawthorn, 1970). Abortion, though, "may well be the most widely used single method [to control family size] in the world today" (Freedman, 1966b, p. 817).

A number of conclusions are suggested by the foregoing data. The voluntary measures that have affected the size of families are numerous. They include a variety of customs that determine sexual unions, a large number of contraceptive techniques, abortion and infanticide. Most societies have used a combination of these measures for centuries. Since the beginnings of recorded history, then, adults have had the means to control family size (Dumond, 1974). As Hawthorn notes, "The question is not so much did they know how to control births, but why did they choose not to do so?" (1970, p. 48). Certainly, parents in the developed nations of the world have excellent control today over the number of children they produce. A study on the growth of American families found that only 17% of the families had conceived more children than they had originally wanted (Whelpton et al., 1966). If parents have in the past been able to, and can now even more effectively control the number of children they produce, it seems reasonable to assert that family size has been and certainly continues to a large extent to be a function of the desire to bear and care for children.

Factors Affecting the Desire to Bear Children

A wide range of variables has been proposed as determining family size. The themes that recur most frequently relate to cultural, economic and social factors which influence the functioning of the family unit. Cultural factors are those institutionalized norms and values of a society that guide parents in the number of children they produce. Such social norms and values have been described by Koslov in his analysis of the institution of the large family. They find their support, he asserts, in "public opinion, moral canons, the roles of marriage and lastly, the precepts of religion" (1967, p. 158). It is generally agreed, however, that the relationship between family size and social norms is far from clear (Freedman, 1961–1962). Attempts to relate birth rates to religious precepts, for example, have generally produced ambiguous or negative results (Aries, 1948; Bourgeois-Pichat, 1948, 1950).

Most population theorists have pointed to the central importance of a complex of economic factors and resulting changes in family structure as determinants of family size. The usual argument is that large families predominate in areas in which the utility of children is important because they provide productive labor to augment family income and are a source of security at the end of their parents' productive lives. In these areas, the extended family functions as an interdependent economic unit, roles within the kinship system are specific according to the needs of the family unit and social norms support the maintenance of strong family ties. Since childhood mortality in such areas is typically relatively high, there is an especially strong impetus to produce a large number of children (Sauvy, 1966; United Nations, 1973).

Small families are said to predominate in areas in which the utility of children is low and the cost of rearing them is high. In these regions, most families live in increasingly industrialized urban centers in which social norms prohibit child labor and force children to participate in an extended educational system. The families do not function as interdependent economic units, and kinship ties become diffuse as individual needs take precedence over family needs. As the costs of child-rearing become more burdensome and childhood mortality rates decline, there is an ever stronger need to limit the number of children born (Leibenstein, 1957; Ryder, 1959; United Nations, 1973).

The most striking fact from the demographic literature has been the dramatic reduction of the birth rate in every country that has become industrialized and urbanized. Any theory of birth rate must account for this transition from high to low rates that has inevitably accompanied modernization. The most popular explanations have pointed to the economic and social changes, discussed above, that transformed the functions of the family and children during the transition from preindustrial to urban–industrial society. While most theorists agree that a wide array of interacting factors have been involved in the economic and social transitions, all attempts to associate the decline of birth rates with one particular factor or complex factors have been disappointing. As Coale (1967, p. 208) pointed out:

Fertility fell in Spain, Bulgaria and other Southern and Eastern European countries when mortality was still very high; in many countries rural fertility declined as early and as much as urban fertility; in some countries industrialization was far advanced before marital fertility fell, in others a major decline preceded substantial industrialization. . . . In European national experience, the only factor apparently always changing at the same time that fertility declined was literacy, but the onset of fertility decline has no consistent relationship with the proportion literate at the time.

Curiously, the desire to have children for their own sake, apart from their ascribed economic or social utility, has not been studied. It has been tacitly assumed that this desire is constant within and among population groups and has remained stable over time. It seems probable, however, that there have always been important individual differences in attraction to children and the desire to bear and care for them. It seems probable, too, that the marked changes of lifestyle accompanying industrialization and urbanization have affected basic feelings and attitudes about children and the desire to bear and rear them. An inevitable consequence of modernization has been the disruption of age-old patterns of interaction within families and communities. The extended family has tended to be replaced by the nuclear family (Dumond, 1974). The traditional roles of mothers, fathers, other caretakers and children have been drastically altered. Segregation by age has become the norm, severely reducing opportunities for adolescents and young adults to interact with babies and young children. Intrafamilial sharing of the burdens and pleasures of childrearing has been reduced as extended families and community participation have been replaced by nuclear families and institutionalized child-care and educational programs (Aries, 1962).

Family Structure and Family Size

It has been proposed, of course, that the extended family system is favorable to high fertility (Davis, 1955a, 1955b; Davis and Blake, 1956; Lorimer, 1954). There have, however, been few empirical attempts to assess the specific effects of various family systems on birth rates (United Nations, 1973), and the few existing studies have produced ambiguous results (Burch and Gendell, 1970).

Several mechanisms by which family systems may influence birth rates have been proposed. Lorimer emphasized the influence of cultural and religious ideals concerning family strength and continuity which over time are incorporated into the personality structure. He insisted that the resulting "cultural inertia" which hampers "any rational adjustment of reproductive patterns to objective conditions . . . is the most powerful obstacle . . . to the rational ordering of personal behavior influencing population trends" (1954, p. 251). Most writers give greater weight to structural features of family systems that determine such behaviors as age at marriage. Davis (1955a) argues, for example, that the economic solidarity of the extended family encourages early marriage because the children need not support themselves and that young parents are encouraged to have many children to strengthen the family line.

A few theorists have proposed that there is no inherent relationship between family system and family size. They argue that the decision to have children is a function of the needs of the parents alone and not those of the wider kinship group. In some instances the need for children is high, as on the American frontier. In others it is low, as in an industrial city. Burch and Gendall conclude that "the widespread conviction that extended family structure is (statistically) *associated* with—let alone a contributing *cause* of—high fertility is not yet empirically warranted" (1970, p. 232). No one has looked at the contribution of the larger number of caretakers possible in extended families as a determinant of family size. It seems probable that it is not merely the presence of potential caretakers but rather the manner in which they share the tasks of caretaking that is important.

Biological Factors and "Desire" to Bear Children

Man is not the only animal whose population has aroused scientific interest and speculation. Birth and death rates and their determinants and interrelationships have been studied in a wide range of species (Wilson, 1975). Indeed, reproductive rates and the factors influencing survival rates are basic variables in all theories of evolution and have been of central concern in the study of most species.

Determinants of Population Density

Various environmental factors such as the availability of food, climatic conditions and the presence of predators and disease have been responsible for determining survival rates of species. Each distinct population group has adapted over time to its own set of circumstances. One aspect of this adaptation is the number of offspring produced by the typical mother. Reproduction rates are, of course, ultimately determined by survival rates, which are in turn controlled by such selective pressures as availability of food and predation. Food supplies, number of predators and other important regulating factors can and do vary over time, resulting in variations of population density. It has been demonstrated, however, that population control is more complicated than this in some species, and that some animals possess biological mechanisms that decrease fertility in response to social factors such as crowding and aggression (Christian, 1959, 1960, 1963, 1970). The biological mechanisms are often found in endocrine feedback systems "which can regulate and limit population growth in response to increases in overall social pressure" (Christian and Davis, 1964, p. 1553).

Attempts to demonstrate such biological mechanisms in human beings have been negative (Lawrence, 1974). Indeed, it is difficult to argue persuasively that such mechanisms should be found in man. All species in which the mechanisms have been demonstrated have experienced the consequences of overpopulation countless times over centuries, thus setting up the required circumstances for the evolution of mechanisms responsive to the relevant social stimuli. Man has rarely experienced overpopulation. The balance between birth and death rates has been fairly stable until the past few decades, and when any group has grown too large it has almost always been possible for some members to migrate to uninhabited or underpopulated locations.

Determinants of Reproductive and Parenting Behaviors

There are a variety of ways, however, in which social factors influence population growth within different species. A wide range of social stimuli are intimately involved with the development of reproductive and parenting behaviors and with the eliciting of these behaviors in mature animals.

Classical ethologists have been inclined to explain the behaviors involved in reproduction and parenting by positing appetites that push the animal to fulfill certain needs (e.g., needs for sexual release or for nurturing offspring) and fixed action patterns that are consumatory behaviors (e.g., copulating or retrieving infants) elicited by a releasing stimulus when the appetites are above threshold level (Lorenz, 1958; Lorenz and Tinbergen, 1938). The strong emphasis on the genetic determination of behavior by the classical European ethologists has been criticized by many psychologists and ethologists in the United States (Lehrman, 1953; Moltz, 1965; Schneirla, 1946, 1956, 1957; Schneirla & Rosenblatt, 1961), who tend to see genetic and environmental factors acting in concert to produce behaviors that, although more-or-less typical within species, reflect individual differences in genetic endowment and the physical and social environment. All theorists agree, however, that there are species-typical behaviors that are strongly influenced, if not totally determined, by species-specific genetic factors. Among the behaviors most likely to have strong genetic components are reproductive and parenting behaviors, because these are most central to the process of biological evolution and species survival.

Certainly pairing, mating and parenting behaviors have in many animals definite ceremonial qualities which often require complicated symbolic actions—supported by stimulus cues or objects in the environment [see, e.g., Lorenz (1940, 1941) and Tinbergen (1939)]. Hediger points out that "the foundation of a family, or preparation for it, is often regularly dependent on a fixed ceremonial (display), a fixed time (rut), and . . . a fixed place (mating ground) . . ." (1950, p. 26). Disruption of any component of the species-typical system is likely to interfere with the bearing and rearing of offspring. The mating and parenting behaviors of many animals are seriously disrupted by removal from their natural habitat. Most wild species, for example, have difficulty reproducing in captivity and those who do successfully bear young often do not care for them (Hediger, 1950).[1]

There are two relatively distinct ways in which the interaction of genetic and environmental factors can affect reproductive and

---

[1]It is perhaps interesting to note in this context that slaves introduced into America were reported to have had a very low birth rate for several generations and were said to be very poor parents and that a large percentage of women in concentration camps during World War II were reported to have amenorrhea.

parenting behavior systems. First, disruptions of the normal sequence of interaction among genetic and environmental components during the process of development can produce a mature animal who will fail to mate or care for its young. Second, mature animals who have experienced a normal developmental sequence may meet situations lacking the normal environmental supports to reproduction and parenting, with consequent disruption of these processes.

There are myriad examples in various species of potential disruptions in the normal course of development which drastically affect later reproductive and parenting behaviors. The goslings and turtle doves that "imprinted" on Konrad Lorenz attempted to mate with him and would not mate with members of their own species (Lorenz, 1931). A number of studies [e.g., Harlow (1962)] suggest that if some primates are restricted from social contact with their peers during infancy, they are impaired in their adult sexual functioning. Rhesus monkeys raised with inanimate "mothers" are poor mothers as adults. They refuse to nurse their young, allow them to be removed without protest and often physically mistreat them (Harlow and Harlow, 1962a, b).

Examples of the importance of environmental factors that support reproductive and parenting behaviors in adult animals are also numerous. In all mammals, there are a variety of more-or-less species-typical stimuli that tend to arouse sexual interest and activity and others which elicit caretaking behaviors (Eibl-Eibesfeldt, 1975). In the absence of appropriate stimuli, these behaviors are eliminated. The courtship songs of various birds and the red coloring of the anogenital areas of various monkeys during estrus are examples of stimuli eliciting sexual behavior. In the absence of such stimuli, the normal reproductive patterns are disrupted. Parenting behavior may similarly be disrupted by small alterations of the stimulus situation. Mother goats establish an individual bond with their offspring only during a five-minute period following birth. If the young are removed for as little as two hours, their mothers will attack them upon return (Klopfer, 1971).

In fact, most studies in this area have concentrated on disruptions of socialization during infancy, although it is clear that in most of the higher-order species, reproductive and parenting behaviors come into prominence during the preadolescent and adolescent periods (Nash, 1970). There are, indeed, many reasons to argue that it is during the extended adolescent period that the interaction of the maturing biological systems with species-typical environmental events should determine motivational systems concerned with reproductive and parenting behavioral systems. During this period, endocrine and other changes occur which bring these systems into prominence, and there are typically marked changes in social expectations and roles.

This position is supported by studies of primate behavior at both the nonhuman and human levels. Among squirrel monkeys, baboons, macaques, vervets and chimpanzees, the nonhuman primates with which adequate studies have been accomplished, it is the preadolescent and adolescent females who are most likely to vie for opportunities to care for the young (Rowell, 1972). Among human beings, Fullard et al. (1975) reported that preference for pictures of infants, as opposed to adults, whether of human or nonhuman animals, increased sharply at 11 or 12 years of age. The increase occurred for both males and females but was more dramatic for the latter.

No one has as yet compared the attraction of male and female children, adolescents and adults to babies, toddlers and preschool children. It seems reasonable to expect that females should be more attracted to young infants and males more attracted to toddlers. During human evolution, with subsequent offspring born before previous offspring were mature, it was necessary that some of the burden of care of older children be shifted from the mother in order that she be able to devote adequate energy to the care of the vulnerable newborn infant. It seems reasonable to propose, therefore, that female responsivity to infants and male responsivity to toddlers, who do not require such specialized maternal care, might constitute the most adaptive behavior patterns. There is suggestive evidence from nonhuman primate groups to support this hypothesis. Female langurs, baboons and chimpanzees, for example, are highly interested in newborn infants but this interest decreases as the infant matures (DeVore, 1963; Jay, 1963; Rowell, 1972), while adult males more frequently interact with older infants (Rowell, 1972).

Caretaking Patterns and Number and Fitness of Offspring

The energy devoted to reproduction is distributed very differently among different species (Smith and Fretwell, 1974). Many produce large numbers of offspring and expend minimal or no energy at all nurturing them. Others produce very few offspring but devote substantial energy to caring for and protecting them. In most species which nurture their young, the mother is the sole caretaker. In some, the father is significantly involved in caretaking, and in a few species, other members of the social unit also help with the care of the young. The number and fitness of offspring are intimately related to caretaking patterns. All but a few of the offspring who are left to fend for themselves die before they reach maturity, as is the case with most insects and reptiles. Many more of those who are nurtured until they reach maturity live to reproduce, as is the case with most mammals. In general, the fewer the offspring produced, the greater the investment in caring for them after birth and the greater the proportion who survive to reproduce.

In most species that care for their young, each set of offspring is more-or-less capable of self-care before the next set is born. As has been indicated, in a few mammalian species such as the primates, including man, new offspring are born before those born previously reach maturity. These species usually live in social units and there are often members of the group who assist the mothers in caring for the young. The importance of nonmaternal care increases as the children develop past the infant period.

The presence of help for the mother is in some cases clearly a determinant of the number of offspring born. The male bobolink, a bird inhabiting the American prairie, mates with several females during each season but helps with the offspring of only his first mate. The average number of eggs produced by these primary females is 5.5, while the average produced by secondary females is 4.8 (Martin, 1974). It seems probable that the number of offspring born in nonhuman primate groups is regulated, in part, by the availability of potential caretakers other than the mother. As has been suggested, this may well also be the case in human families.

Hormones, Mating and Parenting Behaviors

Appropriate experiences with other members of the species during the course of development and appropriate environmental supports are surely important in reproductive and parenting behaviors. The role of biological mechanisms in these behaviors is not clear, though the role of the endocrine system is probably of great importance. Rosenzweig notes, for example, that "male rats reared for 15 weeks alone (or with other males) showed retarded development of the reproductive system as compared with those with heterosexual contact; the latter animals appeared to have the greater androgen production" (1973, p. 712). According to Nash, "When humans are experimentally injected with the same-sex hormones, they report a feeling of sexual tension" (1970, p. 176).

It has been noted that mother goats establish a bond with their offspring during a five-minute period following birth. It is interesting in this respect that the oxytocin level is very high in the mother goat following birth, but drops to a very low level after about five minutes (Folley and Kraggs, 1965). Some women report feelings of "maternal arousal" in the presence of infants. These women often describe their feelings as consisting of a fullness in the breasts, a tingling sensation along the spine and a sensation of warmth, all of which can result from hormonal activity (Robinson, 1974). While it must be reiterated that the role of endocrine factors is far from clear in reproductive and parenting behaviors, a number of thoughtful ethologists and psychologists see their role as decisive (Eibl-Eibesfeldt, 1975; Nash, 1970).

Although it is not clear which hormones are actually involved with interactions between individuals at different stages of development and under various environmental conditions, there are several likely candidates. These can be subdivided into those hormones whose major activity concerns reproduction and those hormones whose major function concerns arousal. The following is a brief summary of some of the relevant actions of the more likely hormones. Reviews can be found in Levine (1972), Williams (1974) and in the newly published series by the American Physiological Association on the endocrine system (Geiger, 1977).

Reproductive hormones. Steroid hormones—the androgens, estrogens, and progesterone—are all intimately involved with the development, morphology and functioning of the primary and secondary sex organs. In the appropriate concentrations, they determine sexual and parenting behaviors in most vertebrates. They are also crucial to the development of the fetus in human beings. Secretions of these hormones are mainly influenced by the presence or absence of a developing fetus and the secretion of two hormones from the anterior pituitary. The two anterior pituitary hormones are luteinizing hormone (LH) and follicle-stimulating hormone (FSH), and their secretion in turn appears to be determined entirely by various releasing hormones secreted by the brain. Normally, the various secretions of this system are influenced mainly by the internal rhythms that control the menstrual and pregnancy cycles. It is well documented, however, that this normal balance may also be influenced by cognitive factors, particularly emotional ones.

Prolactin is another hormone secreted by the anterior pituitary that is a possible controller of human behaviors relating to the desire to have offspring. As with LH and FSH, the secretion of prolactin is itself controlled by the brain through releasing hormones. Prolactin is responsible for many parenting reflexes in a variety of mammals. In humans, it is responsible for proper milk formation within the breasts and is secreted in the mother in relatively large quantities after delivery. One of its normal functions is the suppression of normal reproductive cycling during the period that an infant is nursing and the decline of nursing inhibits its continued secretion.

Oxytocin is a hormone secreted by the posterior pituitary. One of its major functions is the release of stored milk within the breasts into compartments where it is readily attainable by the suckling infant. Stimulation of the nipple is the primary releasing stimulus for its secretion. There is also evidence that stimuli associated with an infant (i.e., sight or sound) will cause a milk "letdown" in mothers, this reflex presumably being due to the secretion of oxytocin. Oxytocin also causes contractions of the uterus during copulation and delivery.

Arousal hormones. The first system here is analogous to the LH–FSH/steroids system discussed above. The group of steroids known as glucocorticoids (the best known of which is cortisol) are secreted from the adrenal cortex in response to the presence of a hormone from the anterior pituitary. The anterior pituitary hormone is called adrenocorticotrophic hormone or ACTH, and its secretion is in turn controlled by the presence of appropriate releasing hormones from the brain. The glucocorticoids function to protect the body any time that it is aroused, whether physically or emotionally. Appropriately, the glucocorticoids enhance the integrity of the cardiovascular system, provide excess fuels within the blood in case of emergency and so on. This system can easily be activated by stimuli external to the body and may be involved in parent–offspring interactions.

The final likely set of hormones are the catecholamines, adrenalin being the major member of this set. Adrenalin is secreted from the adrenal medulla during any kind of arousal, physical or cognitive. Like the glucocorticoids, the ability of the body to function well given an emergency is enhanced with adrenalin. The cells of the body that secrete catecholamines are themselves a branch of the nervous system, so that any stimuli reaching the brain could potentially activate the system.

Conclusions and Hypotheses

The point of the foregoing analysis is, of course, that changes in living patterns can dramatically affect the most basic of the biologically organized motivation systems. It seems reasonable to suppose, for example, that the radical environmental changes that have resulted from industrialization and urbanization may have altered, in affected human populations, basic feelings and attitudes concerning the bearing and rearing of children. Such a hypothesis is certainly consistent with the existing demographic data.

It is not proposed that the development of reproductive and parenting behaviors in human beings is in all particulars homologous with the development of such behaviors in nonhuman species. In the first place, the motivations and behaviors that define mating patterns in man have been for centuries separated from those involved in the motivations to produce children and to care for them. The understanding that the mating act produces offspring has probably been available to almost all human populations for centuries. Hawthorn notes that "if the famous Tully River blacks of Australia did not connect sexual intercourse with conception and pregnancy (Leach, 1967; Spiro, 1968), they are probably almost alone among recorded human societies" (1970, p. 38).

It seems certain, however, that some behaviors of human beings are determined in part by biological mechanisms that have been selected during the process of evolution. It is also clear that among the most important biological mechanisms, there should be those involved in reproduction and parenting. Further, biological mechanisms have been selected in the context of particular physical and social environmental structures. It is reasonable to postulate, therefore, that significant changes of social environmental conditions involved in reproductive and parenting behavioral patterns in man may disrupt coordinations between biological mechanisms and supporting environmental factors, resulting in new behavior patterns.

It is not postulated that the only determinants of decisions to bear and rear children are those involved with the kind of biological–environmental interactions proposed, nor is it contended that man is a totally irrational animal whose decisions are uninfluenced by interpretations of economic conditions, social norms, religious principles and so forth. It is proposed, however, that the behavior of human beings is strongly influenced by biological heritage just as it is by cultural heritage. It is also proposed that biological and cultural evolution have proceeded in concert and that significant changes of culture, which occur over a very short period, can strongly affect the harmony of that concert. More specifically, it is suggested that the dramatic changes resulting from modernization have affected age-old coordinations of biological and environmental systems involved in reproduction and parenting behaviors.

While it has been proposed before that the family structure is a determinant of family size, no one has demonstrated that the actual contribution to child-care of the larger number of potential caretakers in extended families is associated with the number of children. As in many nonhuman species, the number of offspring in human families is related to the energy available for child-care. Family size is, then, determined in part by the number of family members who actually contribute to child-care.

The position we have taken generates several important hypotheses which could be evaluated empirically for, essentially, the first time:

1. The desire of human beings to bear and rear children is, in part, a function of specific experiences with infants and young children during biologically sensitive periods.
2. The desire to bear and rear children is, in part, a function of specific stimuli that influence biologically organized motivational systems of mature human beings.
3. Different family structures and community organization patterns tend to present different experiences to developing and mature human beings, which in turn strongly affect their desire to produce children.
4. The motivation to produce children is, in part, a function of an hormonally organized system.
5. There are specific stimuli that interact during sensitive periods with specific hormones and hormone receptor sites to determine the strength of the motivation to have children.
6. There are specific stimuli that act to release specific hormones in mature human beings and thereby to elicit specific feelings, attitudes and behavioral repertoires concerned with young children.
7. Human females have evolved to be more attracted by and responsive to infants, whereas human males have evolved to be more responsive to toddlers and preschool-age children.

8. The desire to bear children interacts with expectations concerning the energy that will be required to rear them. Sharing of the burdens of child-care by husband, relatives, older children and others will, therefore, increase the probability that a mother will act to satisfy her desire for another child.

Both correlational and experimental studies might be employed to test these predictions. For example, the degree of attraction of women and men to young children could be ascertained and then correlated with the number of children they have and with particular experiences they may have had during developmentally sensitive periods. Hormonal levels could be assessed and quantified separately for developing and adult individuals at different ages to determine the influence of the endocrine profile on the motivation to bear and rear children. Finally, the desire for children for their own sake could be analyzed in terms of cultural, community and family traditions and the differential experiences of nuclear and extended families that may influence this desire. Such research would compare and evaluate the interaction of biologically and experiencially mediated individual motivation to expend energy in child rearing. Most importantly, it would substitute interpretable data for speculation as to the major determinants of human population trends.

References   Agarwala, S. N. 1967. Effect of a rise in female marriage age on birth rate in India. In *United Nations, World Population Conference 1965, 2.* New York: United Nations.

Aries, P. 1948. *Histoire des populations francaises et de leurs attitudes devant la vie depuis le XVIII ͤ siècle.* Paris: Editions Self.

———. 1962. *Centuries of Childhood: A Social History of Family Life* (translated by R. Baldick). New York: Vintage.

Bourgeois-Pichat, J. 1948. Un nouvel indice de mesure de la fécondité. *Population* (Paris) 3(2): 293–312.

———. 1950. Analyse de la mortalité infantile. *Revue de l'Institut International de Statistique* (Netherlands) 18 (1 & 2).

Burch, T. K., and Gendell, M. 1970. Extended family structure and fertility: Some conceptual and methodological issues. *Journal of Marriage and the Family* 32: 227–236.

Carr-Saunders, A. 1922. *The Population Problem: A Study in Human Evolution.* Oxford: Clarendan Press.

Christian, J. J. 1959. The roles of endocrine and behavioral factors in the growth of mammalian populations. In *Comparative Endocrinology.* New York: Wiley, pp. 71–97.

———. 1960. Factors in mass mortality of a herd of sika deer (cervus hippon). *Chesapeake Science* No. 1, pp. 79–95.

———. 1963. Endocrine adaptive mechanisms and the physiologic regulation of population growth. In M. V. Meyer and I. Gelder (eds.) *Physiological Mammology.* New York: Academic Press, pp. 189–353.

———. 1970. Social subordination, population density, and mammalian evolution. *Science* 168: 84–90.

Christian, J. J., and Davis, D. E. 1964. Endocrines, behavior, and population. *Science* 146: 1550–1560.

Coale, A. J. 1967. Factors associated with the development of low fertility: An historic summary. In *United Nations, World Population Conference 1965, 2.* New York: United Nations.

Davis, K. 1955a. Institutional patterns favouring high fertility in underdeveloped areas. *Eugenics Quarterly* No. 2.

――――. 1955b. Malthus and the theory of population. In P. F. Lazarsfeld and M. Rosenberg (eds.) *The Language of Social Research.* Glencoe, IL: Free Press.

Davis, K., and Blake, J. 1956. Social structure and fertility: An analytic framework. *Economic Development and Cultural Change* 4: 211–235.

DeVore, I. 1963. Mother–infant relations in free-ranging baboons. In H. L. Rheingold (ed.) *Maternal Behavior in Mammals.* New York: Wiley.

Dumond, D. E. 1975. The limitations of human population: A natural history. *Science* 187: 713–721.

Eibl-Eibesfeldt, I. 1975. *Ethology: The Biology of Behavior,* 2nd ed. (translated by E. Klinghammer). New York: Holt, Rinehart and Winston.

Folley, S. J., and Kraggs, G. S. 1965. Levels of oxytocin in the jugular vein blood of goats during parturition. *J. Endocrinol.* 33: 301–315.

Ford, C. S. 1945. *A Comparative Study of Human Reproduction.* New Haven: Yale University Press.

Freedman, R. 1961–1962. The sociology of human fertility. *Current Sociology* 10/11 (2): 35–121.

――――. 1966a. Fertility: Statement by the moderator. In B. Berelson et al. (eds.) *Family Planning and Population Programmes.* Chicago and London: University of Chicago Press, pp. 37–38.

――――. 1966b. Family planning programmes today: Major themes of the conference. In B. Berelson et al. (eds.) *Family Planning and Population Programmes.* Chicago and London: University of Chicago Press, pp. 811–825.

Fullard, W., Reiling, A., Love, C., and Shaw, F. (Temple University). 1975. An investigation of Lorenz's babyness hypothesis. Paper presented at meetings of the Society for Research in Child Development, Denver, CO, April.

Geiger, S. R. (ed.). 1977. *Handbook of Physiology.* Washington, DC: American Physiological Society.

Hajnal, J. 1965. European marriage patterns in perspective. In D. V. Glass and D. E. C. Eversley (eds.) *Population in history: Essays in historical demography.* London: E. Arnold and Co.

Harlow, H. F. 1962. The heterosexual affectional system in monkeys. *Amer. Psychol.* 17: 1–9.

Harlow, H. F., and Harlow, M. K. 1962a. The effect of rearing conditions on behavior. *Bull. Menninger Clin.* 26: 213–224.

Harlow, H. F., and Harlow, M. K. 1962b. Social deprivation in monkeys. *Sci. Amer.* 207: 137–146.

Hawthorn, G. *The Sociology of Fertility.* 1970. London: Collier-Macmillan.

Hediger, H. 1950. *Wildtiere in Gefangenschaft—Ein Grundriss des Tiergartenbiologie.* Basel, Switzerland: Benno Schwabe. (Translated by G. Sircom as *Wild Animals in Captivity.* New York: Dover Publications, 1964.)

Himes, N. E. 1936. *A Medical History of Contraception.* Baltimore: Williams & Wilkins.

Jay, P. C. 1963. Mother–infant relations in langurs. In H. L. Rheingold (ed.) *Maternal Behavior in Mammals.* New York: Wiley.

Klopfer, P. H. 1971. Mother love: What turns it on? *Am. Sci.* 59: 404–407.

Kozlov, V. I. 1965. Some causes of high fertility of the population of developing countries. Cited in United Nations, *The Determinants and Consequences of Population Trends,* Series A/50, 1: 77. 1973.

Kuczynski, R. R. 1936. The measurement of population growth: Methods and results. New York: Oxford University Press.

Landry, A. 1934. La Révolution Démographique: *Études et Essais sur les Problèmes de la Population*. Paris: Sirey.

Lawrence, J. E. S. 1974. Science and sentiment: Overview of research on crowding and human behavior. *Psychol. Bull.* 81: 712–720.

Leach, E. R. 1966. Virgin birth. *Proceedings of the Royal Anthropological Institute* (London). pp. 39–50.

Lehrman, D. S. 1953. A critique of Konrad Lorenz's theory of instructive behavior. *Quart. Rev. Biol.* 28: 337–363.

Leibenstein, H. 1957. *Economic Backwardness and Economic Growth*. New York: Wiley.

Lévi-Strauss, C. 1955. *Tristes tropiques*. Paris: Plon. (Translated by John Russell as *World on the Wane*. London: Hutchinson, 1961.)

Levine, S. 1972. *Hormones and Behavior*. New York: Academic Press.

Lorenz, K. 1931. Beiträge zur ethologic sozialer corviden. *J. Ornithol.* 79: 67–127.

———. 1940. Durch domestikation verusachte störungen arteigenen verhaltens. *Z. Angew. Psychol.*, Charakt. Kde. 59: 2–81.

———. 1941. Vergleichende bewegungsstudien bei anatiden. *J. Ornithol.* 89: 194–294.

———. 1958. The evolution of behaviour. *Sci. Amer.* 199: 67–78.

Lorenz, K., and Tinbergen, N. 1938. Taxis und instinkthandlung in der eirollbewegung der graugans. *Z. Tierpsychol.* 2: 1–29.

Lorimer, F. 1954. *Culture and Human Fertility*. Paris: UNESCO.

Martin, S. G. 1974. Adaptations for polygamous breeding in the bobolink *(Dolinchonyx oryzivorus)*. *American Zoologist* 14: 109–120.

Meuvret, J. 1965. Demographic crisis in France from the sixteenth to the eighteenth century. In D. V. Glass and D. E. C. Eversley (eds.) *Population in History: Essays in Historical Demography*. London: E. Arnold and Co.

Moltz, N. 1965. Contemporary instinct theory and the fixed action pattern. *Psychol. Rev.* 72: 22–47.

Nag, M. 1962. Factors affecting human fertility in nonindustrial societies: A cross-cultural study. *Yale University Publications in Anthropology*, No. 66. New Haven: Yale University Press.

Nash, J. 1970. *Developmental Psychology: A Psychobiological Approach*. Englewood Cliffs, NJ: Prentice Hall.

Raskin, A. 1956. Naselenie Rossii za 100 let. Cited in United Nations, *The Determinants and Consequences of Population Trends*, Series A/50, 1: 73. 1973.

Robinson, H. B. 1974. Maternal arousal and the endocrine system. Paper presented for the Child Development Research Group, University of Washington.

Rosenzweig, M. R. 1973. Biological psychology. In P. Mussen and M. R. Rosenzweig (eds.) *Psychology: An Introduction*. Lexington, MA: D. C. Heath & Co.

Rowell, T. 1972. *The Social Behaviour of Monkeys*. Middlesex, England: Penguin Books.

Ryder, N. B. 1959. Fertility. In P. M. Hauser and O. D. Duncan (eds.) *The Study of Population: An Inventory and Appraisal*. Chicago: University of Chicago Press.

Sauvy, A. 1966. *Théorie générale de la population, I: Economic et population; II: Biologie sociale*. Paris: Presses Universitaires de France.

Schneirla, T. C. 1946. Problems in the biopsychology of social organization. *J. Abnorm. Soc. Psychol.* 41: 385–402.

———. 1956. Interrelationships of the "innate" and the "acquired" in instinctive behavior. In P. P. Grassé (ed.) *L'instinct dans le comportement des animaux*. Paris: Masson. pp. 387–452.

Schneirla, T. C. 1957. The concept of development in comparative physiology. In D. B. Harris (ed.) *The Concept of Development.* Minneapolis: University of Minnesota Press.

Schneirla, T. C., and Rosenblatt, J. S. 1961. Animal research panel, 1960. *Amer. J. Orthopsychiat.* 31: 223–291.

Smith, C. C., and Fretwell, S. D. 1974. The optimal balance between size and number of offspring. *Amer. Naturalist* 108: 499–506.

Spiro, N. E. 1968. Virgin birth, parthenogenesis and physiological paternity: An essay in cultural interpretation. *Man* 3: 242–261.

Tinbergen, N. 1939. On the analysis of social organization among vertebrates, with special reference to birds. *Amer. Midl. Nat.* 21.

———. 1951. *The Study of Instinct.* London and New York: Oxford University Press.

United Nations. 1973. *The Determinants and Consequences of Population Trends.* ST/SOA/Series A/50, 1.

United Nations. 1975. *The Population Debate: Dimensions and Perspectives.* ST/ESA/ Series A/54, 1.

Whelpton, P. K., Campbell, A. A., and Patterson, J. E. 1966. *Fertility and Family Planning in the United States.* Princeton: Princeton University Press.

Williams, R. H. 1974. *Textbook of Endocrinology.* Philadelphia: W. B. Saunders Co.

Wilson, E. O. 1975. *Sociobiology: The New Synthesis.* Cambridge, MA: Belknap/ Harvard University Press.

Wrigley, E. A. 1966. Family limitation in pre-industrial England. *Economic History Review,* 2nd ser. 18: 82–109.

———. 1968. Mortality in pre-industrial England: The example of Colyton, Devon, over three centuries. *Proceedings of the Amer. Acad. of Arts and Sciences* 97: 546–580.

Toward an Ontogenetic Monkey Model of Behavioral Development

Jonathan K. Lewis, Gene P. Sackett

6 Twenty years of developmental studies have been conducted on nonhuman primates who spent their infancy under various laboratory-rearing conditions. Here we will review a number of these studies, most of which used rhesus monkeys *(M. mulatta)* as subjects. We will also attempt to evaluate the data in terms of their impact on some ideas concerning primate development suggesting some avenues for future primate developmental research. As our literature review will be brief, we suggest that interested readers consult other sources for more detailed presentations [e.g., Harlow and Harlow (1965) and Sackett (1972)].

The laboratory study of varied rearing experiences in primates began with a series of experiments by Harry F. Harlow (1958) and his co-workers. These studies assessed the developmental consequences of raising rhesus monkeys without real monkey mothers. The work was stimulated by Harlow's initial observations of monkeys reared without mothers in order to study the development of their basic learning abilities uncontaminated by maternal influences. Early in infancy these nursery-raised animals exhibited excessive amounts of grasping, clinging and sucking on parts of their own bodies (Figure 1). As these monkeys grew older, they appeared to be markedly attached to the diapers that were kept in their cages—showing extreme disturbance whenever these diapers were removed. When placed together with more normal animals, these maternally-deprived infants failed to participate in normal social interactions. They showed excessive fear, withdrawal and self-directed activities—totally lacking playful behaviors.

The study of infants reared with inanimate cloth and wire surrogate mothers arose from these preliminary observations (Harlow and Zimmerman, 1959; Harlow and Harlow, 1962). These studies suggested to Harlow the important concept of primate affectional drives. Harlow proposed that infant primates had a contact comfort drive that was independent of nutritional support provided by the mother. The drive-reduction hypotheses prevalent at that time, including Sigmund Freud's psychoanalytic ideas, suggested that mothers become objects of infant emotional attachments due to learning established when the mother fulfills an infant's needs such as food when hungry and relief from pain when hurt. Harlow demonstrated that even when monkey infants are fed by a cold and uncomfortable wire mesh surrogate, they prefer and cling to a soft terry cloth surrogate who does not provide them with any food. This clinging to a cloth surrogate was especially strong when the infant faced a fear-inducing object (Figure 1).

These studies demonstrated that baby monkey behavior reflects needs for what Harlow called contact comfort—something to which the animal can cling. Infants reared with a soft object, whether a cloth surrogate or a plain cloth diaper, not only derive what appears to be emotional support from that object, but also gain weight faster than infants reared without such an object. However, further research showed that much more than a soft object is required for normal monkey development. For instance, Hansen (1966) studied monkeys reared alone in single wire cages containing a cloth surrogate mother. These animals had more disturbed behavior in the first 90 days of life, spent more time in contact with their cloth mothers after 90 days, and were slower to develop normal play patterns than laboratory infants reared by wild-born real monkey mothers (Figure 2).

Classification of Laboratory Rearing Conditions

The studies following Harlow's pioneering investigations imposed a number of different rearing experiences on developing rhesus monkey infants. These experiences can be classified in terms of their departure from the social conditions present in the natural environments of macaque monkeys. In nature these monkeys live in troops composed of a number of adult males, subsets of adult females related to each other on the maternal side, and juvenile and infant offspring of these related females. Both infants and juveniles spend much of their day in association with their mother and her relatives. Reproductively mature adult males do not all have the opportunity to mate with females. Some of them, especially younger ones from four to seven or eight years old, live in groups of peripheral males who do not have much contact with the central core of breeding males and females with offspring. The remaining, more dominant, adult males associate together and perform almost all of a troop's copulation during a yearly breeding season.

Infancy in most macaque monkey species covers the first year of life. During this time the monkey is at least partially dependent on the mother for protection, spends much of the 24-hour day in near proximity to her, but is decreasingly dependent on her as a food source after about 6–9 months of age. In most species, female macaques are reproductively mature by three and a half to four years of age, while males lag about a half-year behind. Full social

Figure 1
(a) Digital sucking and self-directed genital stimulation by monkeys raised in partial isolation. (b) Attachment behavior of infant rhesus monkey with its diaper. (c) Withdrawal reaction of infant following 9 months of total social isolation. (d) Infant nursing from wire surrogate mother yet spending most of its time on a cloth surrogate.

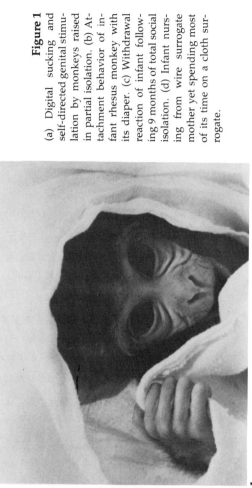

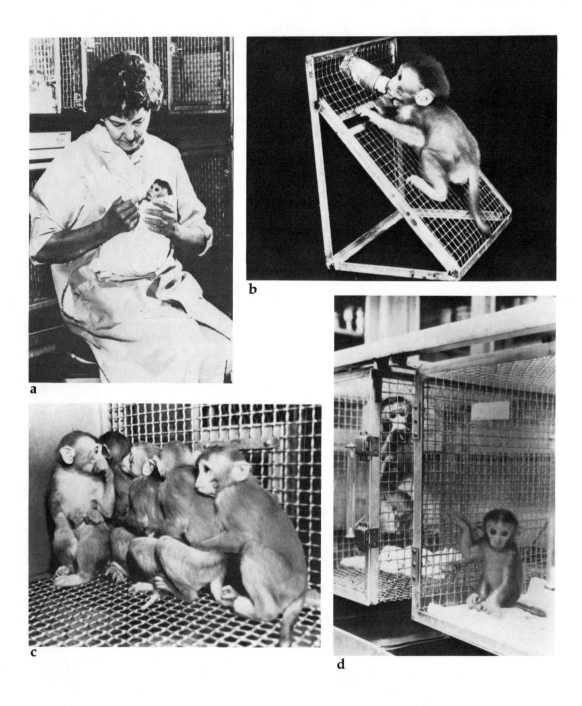

maturity may not be attained until animals are seven to 10 years old.

The situation deviating most markedly from natural conditions is total isolation (Figure 2). Here the newborn monkey is placed into a completely enclosed chamber. The animal can see itself and the cage interior, but has no visual or physical contact with any

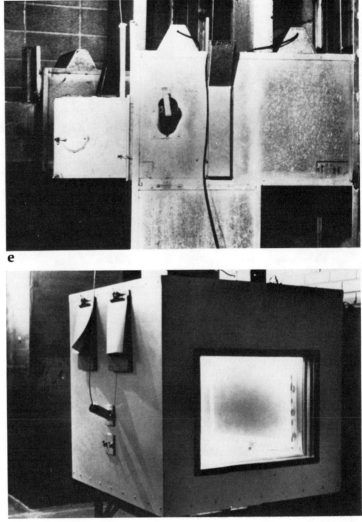

Figure 2
Basic rearing conditions for rhesus monkeys raised without mothers. (a) Human hand feeding of newborns. (b) 1-week-old infant that has achieved the ability to self-feed from a bottle on a wire rack. (c) Monkeys reared together in a 5-animal group. (d) Monkeys reared in partial social isolation. (e) and (f) Two examples of total social isolation chambers.

animate or inanimate objects outside its chamber (Harlow and Harlow, 1965). The only sources of varied stimulation for the total social isolate are feeding by a human during the first three to four weeks of life, introduction of food into its chamber thereafter, and feedback from its own behaviors as it moves about its barren but lit home.

Single-cage rearing, sometimes called partial social isolation, is a condition involving less social and sensory privation (Figure 2). Here the infant lives in a wire mesh cage. It can see and hear, but not touch, other animals living in nearby cages. Again, as newborns these animals require feeding by humans, but thereafter can locate and ingest food from a bottle without human intervention (Figure 2). Rearing with a surrogate mother (Figure 1) is somewhat

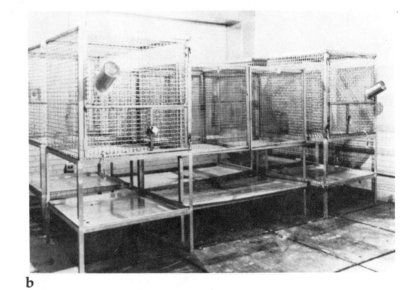

a   b

Figure 3
(a) Monkey mother with her newborn infant. (b) One apparatus, called the "Playpen" by Harlow, for rearing with mother and peer experience. Each large outer cage contains the mother and her infant. A small hole allows the infant to go into the central area of smaller cages where it can interact with other infants. The mothers are confined to the outer cages as the play area hole is too small for them to go through.

more stimulating, as the infant can climb on and cling to a large object. However, surrogate-raised infants also do not have physical contact with other monkeys.

Peer rearing (Figure 2) starts out like the single-cage situation. For the first several weeks of life the newborn lives alone in a cage and is fed by a human. After attaining self-feeding abilities, these animals are placed into groups of two to six other infants in a wire mesh cage. Here they have complete physical access to agemates, but they do not receive contact with mother monkeys or older animals.

A different rearing situation (Figure 3), initially more complex than peer rearing, concerns infants placed with their mothers in a single cage during infancy (Alexander and Harlow, 1965; Jensen et al., 1968). Here the infant receives a great deal of maternal contact but is deprived of the play experiences with agemates that occupy a great deal of an infant's time under natural conditions. A more natural rearing experience occurs when infants are reared with their mothers and are allowed access to agemates (Figure 3) for daily play periods (Hansen, 1966). In terms of laboratory experiments, the closest approximation to natural conditions are situations in which the infant has associations with both its mother, an adult male, younger and older monkeys, and agemates (Hinde et al., 1964; M. Harlow, 1971).

These laboratory situations form a ranking from severe social and environmental restriction and privation through complex social stimulation in environments containing many opportunities for nonsocial stimulation. Paralleling this ranking is a continuum of normality of social and nonsocial behavioral functioning. However, there have been a number of important exceptions to this correlation between degree of rearing privation and degree of later abnormal behavior. Next, we will describe some of the major behavioral effects of privation rearing experiences and some of the factors known to produce greater or lesser degrees of abnormality following socially deficient rearing.

Early Life Privation and Later Behavioral Functioning

Sexual behavior. The ability to participate in normal preadult (two to three years of age) and adult (three to four years on) heterosexual behavior is clearly affected by deprived rearing experiences. Deficiencies in sexual activities were shown by total and partial isolates, by monkeys raised on surrogate mothers, and by monkeys following rearing by a real mother but without access to agemates (Alexander and Harlow, 1965; Harlow, 1965; Senko, 1966). Males especially were affected, uniformly failing to show normal mounting, intromission and ejaculation behaviors even after months or years of pairings with sexually sophisticated and receptive breeding females. However, many socially deprived females eventually became pregnant following pairings with breeding males. Normal sexual performance was seen in females raised with peer contact during infancy, regardless of presence or absence of real or surrogate mothers. Most males reared with peers during infancy also exhibited normal sex behavior, although some showed quantitative deficits compared with wild-born breeding males. In general, these studies show that sexual behavior of males deprived of peer contact in infancy is devastated, while many females manage to develop biologically effective sexual behavior with mating experience.

Maternal behavior. A number of studies have assessed female rhesus monkeys reared under social deprivation conditions for their ability to perform species-typical maternal behaviors. These animals, dubbed "motherless mothers" by Harlow, fall into three qualitative mothering categories (Harlow et al., 1966). Some are adequate in that they do nurse, hold and groom their newborn offspring. Others are indifferent in that they do not harm their offspring, but they do fail to hold and nurse their baby during the early weeks of life. These newborns require handfeeding from humans during the first two to four weeks. The third groups are abusive in that they injure and even kill their offspring by directing violent aggression to them. This abuse usually occurs during the first week of life and surviving neonates must be permanently removed from the mother at that time. One especially interesting outcome in these studies suggests that abuse is much more likely to be directed toward male than female offspring of motherless mothers, while adequate maternal behavior is most often shown toward female babies (Ruppenthal et al., 1976). Another finding of merit is that indifferent mothering of the firstborn baby is often followed by adequate mothering of laterborn offspring. Abuse toward the firstborn, on the other hand, is usually followed by inadequate or abusive behavior with laterborn infants. This suggests that maternal behavior in monkeys is affected by rearing experiences, and, for at least some animals, learning that occurs with the firstborn can yield quite adequate later maternal behavior. Thus, a "maternal instinct" does not appear to be of sole importance as a determinant of macaque monkey maternal behaviors.

Fear and aggression. Normal expression of fear and aggression in rhesus monkeys appears to be very dependent on early life experiences. In this species aggressive behavior is frequent and occurs at very high levels when strangers are introduced to each other or to a group of animals that are familiar with one another. The amount and strength of aggression and fear are normally regulated by the expression of appropriate fear signals at the correct time during an encounter. These signals indicate that the animal losing an aggressive encounter yields to that aggressor, with the aggressor then usually terminating its physical attack. Under laboratory conditions, monkeys raised with mother and peer interaction develop the ability to express appropriate fear and submissive signals and to terminate attacks when such signals are given. Monkeys reared with peer contact also seem to develop normal aggressive behaviors, but may be somewhat more fearful under mild stress than either mother–peer or wild-born animals tested under laboratory conditions (Chamove, 1966). However, animals deprived of peer contact in infancy usually show deficiencies or abnormalities in these behaviors.

Monkeys raised by real mothers without peer contact show normal fear behavior but appear to be hyperaggressive as juveniles and adults (Joslyn, 1967; Alexander, 1966). Surrogate-reared and partial isolate monkeys, who are deprived of both real mother and agemate contact during infancy, show inappropriate or self-directed aggression (Figure 4) with great frequency (Cross and Harlow, 1965; Suomi et al., 1971). Self-directed attacks may be intensive enough to draw blood or to break a bone in the monkey's own body. As juveniles and adults, these monkeys are among the only ones to show aggression to young infants, a rare and highly inappropriate rhesus monkey behavior (Mitchell et al., 1966). Partial isolate and surrogate-raised monkeys also exhibit a syndrome of inappropriate fear in both social and nonsocial situations. At the extreme (Figure 1), this syndrome consists of intense withdrawal with self-clutching and body rocking—so-called "autistic" behavior—and a general unwillingness to explore novel stimuli. Total social isolates also exhibit this fear-withdrawal syn-

Figure 4
Self-abusive behavior by an adult male that had been raised in total social isolation as an infant.

drome and for them, it may constitute 50–90% of their activity in both social and nonsocial testing situations. Total isolates also exhibit self-aggression, but unlike partial isolates do not exhibit high levels of aggression toward other animals.

The most elegant demonstration that these emotional abnormalities result from a failure to learn appropriate communication behaviors is seen in work by Miller and his colleagues (Miller et al., 1967; Miller, 1971). Their initial experiment studied fully mature (seven to 10 years old) rhesus monkeys who were either wild-born or raised in total social isolation during infancy. In testing, the monkey subject observed another animal on a television screen. The TV monkey periodically showed a fear grimace, elicited by a tone that signaled the possible onset of an electric shock. The subject could not hear the tone but could see the demonstrator animal's face. If the subject pressed a lever during the "fear face" period, it avoided receiving an electric shock to its foot. Isolates and wild-born animals served as both demonstrators and subjects in all combinations. When both subject and demonstrator were wild-born, the subject avoided shock on over 90% of the trials— indicating that it perceived the "fear face" correctly and could use that stimulus as a discrimination cue. When the subject was wild-born and the demonstrator was an isolate, shock avoidance was reduced below 50%, indicating that isolates did not send clear facial cues. With isolates as subjects, regardless of the type of demonstrator, shock avoidance occurred on fewer than 25% of the trials. This indicated that isolates neither receive nor send facial communicative information with any useful accuracy.

Self-directed behavior. The most characteristic behavior produced by social privation during infancy in rhesus monkeys is heightened self-directed and stereotyped-repetitive actions. Normal adult monkeys do engage in some self-directed grooming and mouthing activities. However, monkeys raised without mothers—even though peer contact may be available—show levels of self-directed activity many times higher than that found in mother-raised animals. For total and partial isolates, these activities are seen at high levels even when the monkey is alone in its home cage or social pen housing situation (Sackett, 1972). As just mentioned, in social situations, self-directed behavior replaces virtually all social activity when total isolates and some partial isolates are placed into social groups with unfamiliar monkeys.

Social play. Rhesus monkeys raised with mothers and peer interaction show a characteristic pattern in the development of play behaviors during infancy. Parallel or object play gives way to mild social contact play during the first months of life. This is followed, in males, by "rough-and-tumble" play, lasting about four-to-five months. Play in both sexes reaches its highest values from six to 12 months of age, with approach–avoidance play being especially predominant, although more characteristic of females than of males (Harlow and Lauersdorf, 1974). Animals reared in peer groups of two to four monkeys show a delayed onset of these play behaviors, but have play patterns indistinguishable from mother–peer monkeys by two years of age (Chamove, 1966; Suomi et al., 1970; Harlow and Harlow, 1969). Monkeys raised by real mothers, but deprived by peer contact early in infancy, appear to have both delayed play onset and subnormal quantitative levels (Joslyn, 1967). The degree of abnormality in play behavior appears to be related to duration of peer deprivation early in life (Alexander, 1966). Longer periods of peer deprivation in infancy yield correspondingly greater play deficits, with most total social isolates seemingly incapable of normal play behavior during their entire life.

Summary of Social Deprivation Effects in Rhesus Monkeys

Broadly speaking, the degree to which rearing departs from situations in which mothers and peers are freely available to the developing rhesus monkey predicts the degree to which that monkey will be abnormal or deviant in most behaviors as a juvenile and adult. Isolate and wire cage reared animals are abnormal in all areas of behavior, except for the ability to perform on standard monkey learning tests. In fact, learning performance does not appear to differ between rearing conditions ranging from wild-born to total isolate. Thus, early rearing experiences involving social privation appear not to influence basic "intellectual abilities." However, the deprivation-raised animal's *willingness to perform* on learning tasks is markedly deviant (Harlow et al., 1969).

Deprivation of maternal contact during infancy yields rhesus monkeys that show heightened self-orality and fear behaviors, although play and aggression are fairly normal, as are sexual and maternal behaviors. Thus, peer contact appears to be a sufficient condition for development of typical rhesus monkey behavior, regardless of the presence or absence of a real monkey mother.

Rearing monkeys with mothers but with no peer contact produces animals that shy away from physical contact with other monkeys, showing hyperaggression toward others when touched but apparently normal sexual and maternal behavior. Thus, although the mother may provide sufficient stimulation for the development of some normal adult behavior, maternal stimulation alone is inadequate to produce fully normal behavioral development under laboratory conditions.

A demonstration by Sackett (1974) addressed the question of "ecological validity" and generality of these laboratory findings. Fully adult, six-to-10-year-old, rhesus monkeys reared in the laboratory were released on Guayacón Island off the southwest coast of Puerto Rico. This island contained about 80 "native" rhesus monkeys, living in three social groups. Among the 16 animals released were (i) wild-born monkeys who had lived in the laboratory from one to two years of age, (ii) mother–peer animals, (iii) partial social isolates and (iv) total social isolates.

Survival on the island occurred in direct correspondence with the laboratory behaviors of these animals. All wild-born subjects lived and joined a local social group. Female mother–peer animals joined a local group and produced offspring in their group. A male mother–peer monkey eventually became a dominant breeding male in the largest of the native groups. Several female partial isolates and one female total isolate also survived and joined the smaller native groups. However, these monkeys did not produce any offspring. All male partial and social isolates died within one to two weeks after release. One death occurred when a total isolate male fell from a high cliff. The other three were attacked and mortally wounded by dominant males of the largest native group.

This study demonstrated that socially deprived females could survive and become members of social groups. Mother–peer laboratory reared subjects had all of the behaviors necessary to become active, reproducing, members of a free ranging social group. Thus, laboratory data closely predicted the behavior of laboratory raised monkeys subjected to seminatural free ranging conditions.

Limitations in Generality of Rhesus Monkey Rearing Effects

Sex differences. Throughout the discussion above we pointed out that male and female rhesus monkeys were not responding in exactly the same way to deprivation-rearing experiences. In fact, on all measures of importance, rhesus monkey female total and partial isolates appear to be less affected by their poor infancy environments than males (Sackett, 1974; Mitchell, 1979). These sex differences appeared in personal, exploratory-curiosity and social behaviors. This suggests that all monkeys do not begin postnatal life on an equal footing with respect to vulnerability for abnormal development.

Sex differentiation occurs in primates during prenatal life. Embryos and early fetuses are physically undifferentiated by sex except for their chromosomes (XX for females, XY for males). About one-fourth of the way through gestation as yet unknown events trigger the process of male differentiation. Males develop testicular tissues and begin secreting the male hormone testosterone (Resko, 1970). Studies of rodents suggest that the fetal mammalian brain also begins to differentiate between sexes at this time (Levine, 1966). Thus, the process of becoming a male or remaining an anatomical female occurs prenatally, well after conception. Finding sex differences in effects of rearing conditions imposed immediately after birth therefore suggests that one major aspect of vulnerability to develop abnormal behavior involves prenatal mechanisms. At this time we know literally nothing about the actual prenatal mechanisms that might produce such differential vulnerability.

Reversibility. Until about 1972, we believed that the effects of isolation rearing in rhesus monkeys were permanent. A number of attempts to provide therapy for isolation-induced abnormalities had failed (Sackett, 1968). These involved experiments designed specifically to condition isolates to perform socially acceptable behaviors (a sort of simian behavior modification program) and also various studies housing juvenile and adult isolates with more normal animals. The composite results for about 75 animals were uniformly negative. Once an isolate reached the age of 12 to 15 months without showing signs of normal behavior, it continued to exhibit abnormal behavior into adulthood, irrespective of any therapy attempts.

In 1972, Suomi and Harlow reported that abnormal behaviors produced by six months of isolation could be reversed if the isolates were forced to interact with much younger immature animals. In fact, these three-month old "therapists" made repeated attempts to cling to their older isolate partners. Eventually the isolates accepted the younger monkeys and both received and initiated play with them. Three years later, Novak and Harlow (1975) reported essentially the same finding for rhesus monkeys that were isolated during the whole of the first year of life. This study revealed that even severe effects of deprivation-rearing could be reversed if therapy with a younger animal was initiated sufficiently early following the end of the isolation period. Further, this successful therapy also suggested that there was no "critical period" in infancy for socialization of rhesus monkeys. Even though isolation-rearing had clearly induced an asocial monkey, this therapy technique brought about a reversal toward normal behavior.

Species differences. In 1970, we initiated a program at the University of Washington Regional Primate Research Center with the goal of replicating rhesus *(Macaca mulatta)* isolation rearing effects in pigtail monkeys *(M. nemestrina).* Pigtails are phylogenetically very close to rhesus macaques. They are almost the same size; brain anatomy is highly similar; and they exhibit very similar development under laboratory rearing by real mothers. We raised over 60 pigtail monkeys in total social isolation and compared their post-rearing behavior with that of animals reared with mothers and peers (Sackett et al., 1976). We found that pigtails, like rhesus, developed self-directed and stereotyped behaviors while in the total social isolation situation.

After isolation, social behavior was studied from nine to 12 months of age during daily groupings in a playroom. Pigtail isolates recovered normal exploratory responses and many social behaviors without any special form of therapy. Unlike rhesus, as juveniles and young adults our pigtails were largely indistinguishable from mother–peer controls. They played, showed normal aggression and fear, explored novel objects and environments, and even engaged in relatively normal heterosexual behavior. They did continue to show some self-directed clutching and body rocking, but this usually occurred only under high-stress conditions and lasted for only short periods of time. In sum, like rhesus monkey females, pigtail macaques as a species appeared to be relatively buffered against the development of abnormal behavior following social deprivation rearing.

What Does It All Mean?

One of the principal uses of the rhesus monkey rearing data presented here has been as a model for problems of human abnormal behavior. There are two basic goals for such a model: (1) showing that factors underlying abnormal development in monkeys are also important determinants of human abnormal behavior and (2) using therapy procedures that work with abnormal monkeys to develop more effective therapy for human abnormalities. The finding of sex and species differences in monkey vulnerability to develop abnormal behavior following deficient rearing suggests that an appropriate monkey model will have to be more complex than we thought previously.

It is clear that environmental deprivation in infancy almost universally produces abnormalities that are at least temporary components of a monkey's behavioral repertoire. However, sex differences suggest that as yet unknown prenatal factors are of great importance in determining the extent, and possibly the degree, of reversibility of rearing-induced abnormalities. Although it seems likely that prenatal hormonal conditions are related to such "prenatal buffering" of abnormal behavior development, no direct or even indirect evidence exists for this hypothesis. Species differences in extent and reversibility of rearing-induced abnormalities also suggest that genetic factors are important. Again, little is known concerning specific genetic mechanisms that may determine risk for development of abnormal behavior.

Our interpretation of the research findings reviewed here leads us to believe that a comprehensive methodology is needed to understand the bases of behavioral development in primates and to achieve useful nonhuman primate models of abnormal human development. This experimental approach must be capable of studying variation in genetic factors and prenatal conditions, as well as postnatal environmental–social circumstances. To date, only field studies of primates provide useful information toward this goal, although we have initiated a series of laboratory investigations to develop a genetic–prenatal–postnatal model (Sackett and Holm, 1979).

Our pigtail monkey breeding colony contains 600 breeding animals. Of these, about 250 breeding females have had three or more conceptions during their colony tenure. We used a 15-year computerized history of the colony breeding records to generate a mathematical equation to predict the risk of a bad pregnancy outcome. Bad pregnancy outcomes include abortion, stillbirth, premature delivery, low birth weight of offspring and death of offspring from natural causes within the first 30 days after birth. The regression equation that we utilized identified 35 females at high risk for bad outcomes and 30 other females at low risk. Also, three males were found to be at high risk for bad outcomes, although the females involved with them were not at high risk. Three other males were selected for their low rate of bad outcomes.

In a three-year study these animals were interbred so as to predict either high- or low-risk outcomes. Sixty conceptions were achieved in which the mother and father were at low risk. For approximately half of the conceptions of each risk group, the pregnant female was exposed to high environmental stress. The stress was induced by daily hand-capture and confinement in a small cage. All pregnancies resulted from timed matings, so true gestational age was known for each conception. The purpose of this study was to determine whether (1) high- and low-risk females would maintain their risk characteristics under a controlled breeding program while living in single cages rather than a harem social group; (2) prenatal stress would increase the rate of bad pregnancy outcome for high- or low-risk females; (3) offspring would manifest any abnormalities of the central nervous system or endocrine problems at birth; and (4) surviving offspring would be deviant in growth, physiology or behavior.

The objective of this work was to yield a breeding population in which parents produced offspring at high or low risk for developmental abnormalities, and where risk would relate to either parental characteristics or to prenatal variables. When such a population was identified and validated, then we would vary parental (genetic?), prenatal and postnatal environmental factors in experiments that could localize the sources of behavioral abnormalities with respect to these factors and their combinations.

Our results showed that high-risk breeders did indeed produce an excess of bad pregnancy outcomes, but stress during pregnancy did not produce an even higher rate of bad outcomes. Low-risk breeders had almost uniformly excellent pregnancy outcomes, although stress during pregnancy may have increased their chances of abortion. However, this abortion effect did not quite reach acceptable levels of statistical significance.

Offspring of high-risk breeders were lower in birthweight and of shorter gestation than offspring of low-risk breeders. Growth was also slower for high-risk offspring. These effects were especially strong in offspring of high-risk females who were stressed during pregnancy. Behaviorally, offspring of high-risk breeders who were stressed during pregnancy were slower to develop through the neonatal reflex stage and exhibited at least some important differences from low-risk offspring on tests for learning performance and simple cognitive abilities. These differences suggest that there is at least some behavioral retardation during infancy in offspring of high-risk breeders. Thus, our general model for studying the ways in which parental, prenatal and postnatal factors come together to produce normal or deviant development appears to have validity. In our future work we will study the development of infants who are reared in good or bad environments and who came from high- or low-risk parents that received high or low levels of environmental or physiological stress during pregnancy.

It seems likely that progress in understanding abnormal behavior of primates will come largely from laboratory rather than field studies. Abnormal individuals have a high probability of dying in natural environments and so will fail to leave behind genes perpetuating any genetic factors underlying their behavioral maladies. Therefore, we suggest that investigators using laboratory primates consider the possibilities of combining either genetic or prenatal variation in their studies of postnatal factors affecting development. A promising direction for such work might lie in hybridization studies. Pigtail and rhesus monkeys can interbreed and produce viable offspring that are themselves often fertile. Such hybrids could provide data on heritability of risk factors, sex linkage of such risk factors and other related genetic issues. In sum, much more needs to be accomplished in the development of adequate experimental subjects and techniques before we can attain considerable progress in discovering fundamental principals concerning both normal and abnormal primate development.

References

Alexander, B.K. 1966. The effects of early peer deprivation on juvenile behavior of rhesus monkeys. Unpublished doctoral dissertaion, University of Wisconsin.

Alexander, B.K., and Harlow. H.F. 1965. Social behavior of juvenile rhesus monkeys subjected to different rearing conditions during the first 6 months of life. *Zoologishe Jahrbucher Physiologie* 71: 489–508.

Chamove, A.S. 1966. The effects of varying infant peer experience on social behavior in the rhesus monkey. Unpublished masters thesis, University of Wisconsin.

Cross, H.A., and Harlow, H.F. 1965. Prolonged and progressive effects of partial isolation on the behavior of macaque monkeys. *Journal of Experimental Research in Personality* 1: 39–49.

Hansen, E.W. 1966. The development of maternal and infant behavior in the rhesus monkey. *Behaviour* 27: 107–149.

Harlow, H.F. 1958. The nature of love. *American Psychologist* 13: 673–685.

———. 1965. Sexual behavior in the rhesus monkey. In F.A. Beach (ed.) *Sex and Behavior*. New York: Wiley, pp. 234–265.

Harlow, H.F., and Harlow, M.K. 1962. The effect of rearing conditions on behavior. *Bulletin of the Menninger Clinic* 26: 213–224.

Harlow, H.F., and Harlow, M.K. 1965. The affectional systems. In A.M. Schrier, H.F. Harlow and F. Stollnitz (eds.) *Behavior of Nonhuman Primates*, Vol. 2. New York: Academic Press, pp. 287–334.

Harlow, H.F., and Harlow, M.K. 1969. Effects of various mother–infant relationships on rhesus monkey behaviors. In B.M. Foss (Ed.) *Determinants of Infant Behavior*, Vol. 4. London: Methuen, pp. 1–35.

Harlow, H.F., and Lauersdorf, H.E. 1974. Sex differences in passion and play. *Perspectives in Biology and Medicine* 17: 348–360.

Harlow, H.F., and Zimmermann, R.R. 1959. Affectional responses in the infant monkey. *Science* 130: 421–432.

Harlow, H.F., Harlow, M.K., Dodsworth, R.O., and Arling, G.L. 1966. Maternal behavior of rhesus monkeys deprived of mothering and peer associations in infancy. *Proceedings of American Philosophical Society* 110: 58–66.

Harlow, H.F., Schiltz, K.A., and Harlow, M.K. 1969. Effects of social isolation on the learning performance of rhesus monkeys. In C.R. Carpenter (ed.) *Proceedings of 2nd International Congress of Primatology*, Vol. 1. New York: Karger, pp. 178–185.

Harlow, M.K. 1971. Nuclear family apparatus. *Behavior Research Methods and Instrumentation* 3: 301–304.

Hinde, R.A., Rowell, T.E., and Spencer-Boothe, Y. 1964. Behavior of socially living rhesus monkeys in their first six months. *Proceedings Zoological Society of London* 143: 609–649.

Jensen, G.D., Bobbitt, R.A., and Gordon, B.N. 1968. Effects of environment on the relationship between mother and infant pigtailed monkeys *(Macaca nemestrina)*. *J. Comp. and Phys. Psych.* 66: 259–263.

Joslyn, W.D. 1967. Behavior of socially experienced juvenile rhesus monkeys after eight months of late isolation and maternal–offspring relations and maternal separation in juvenile rhesus monkeys. Unpublished doctoral dissertation, University of Wisconsin.

Levine, S. 1966. Sex differences in the brain. *Scientific American* 214: 76–81.

Miller, R.E. 1971. Experimental studies of communication in the monkey. In L.A. Rosenblum (ed.) *Primate Behavior*, Vo. 2. New York: Academic Press, pp. 139–175.

Miller, R.E., Caul, W.F., and Mirsky, I.A. 1967. The communication of affects between feral and socially isolated monkeys. *Journal Personality and Social Psychology* 7: 231–239.

Mitchell, G.D. 1979. Sex differences in response to early social deprivation and separation. In *Behavioral Sex Differences in Nonhuman Priamtes*. New York: Van Nostrand-Reinhold.

Mitchell, G.D., Raymond, E.J., Ruppenthal, G.C., and Harlow, H.F. 1966. Longterm effects of total social isolation upon behavior of rhesus monkeys. *Psychological Reports* 18: 567–580.

Novak, M.A., and Harlow, H.F. 1975. Social recovery of monkeys isolated for the first year of life: I. Rehabilitation and therapy. *Developmental Psychology* 11: 453–465.

Resko, J.A. 1970. Androgen secretion by the fetal and neonatal rhesus monkey. *Endocrinology* 87: 680–687.

Ruppenthal, G.C., Arling, G.L., Harlow, H.F., Sackett, G.P., and Suomi, S.J. 1976. A 10-year perspective of motherless-mother monkey behavior. *Journal Abnormal Psychology* 85: 341–349.

Sackett, G.P. 1968. The persistence of abnormal behavior in monkeys following isolation rearing. In Porter R. (ed.) *The Role of Learning in Psychotherapy.* London:Churchill pp. 3–25.

———. 1972. Isolation rearing in monkeys: Diffuse and specific effects on later behavior. In Chauvin, R. (Ed.), *Animal Models of Human Behavior.* Paris: Collogues internationaux du C.N.R.S., pp. 61–110.

———. 1974. Sex differences in rhesus monkeys following varied rearing experiences. In R.C. Friedman, R.M. Richart and R.L. Vande Wiele (eds.) *Sex Differences in Behavior.* New York: Wiley, pp. 99–122.

Sackett, G.P., and Holm, R.A. 1979. Effects of parental characteristics and prenatal factors on pregnancy outcomes of pigtail macaques. In R.W. Bell and W.P. Smotherman (eds.) *Maternal Influences and Early Behavior.* Jamaica, NY: Spectrum.

Sackett, G.P., Holm, R.A., and Ruppenthal, G.C. 1976. Social isolation rearing: Species differences in behavior of macaque monkeys. *Developmental Psychology,* 12: 283–288.

Senko, M.G. 1966. The effects of early, intermediate, and late experience upon adult macaque sexual behavior. Unpublished masters thesis, University of Wisconsin.

Suomi, S.J., and Harlow, H.F. 1972. Social rehabilitation of isolation-reared monkeys. *Developmental Psychology* 6: 487–496.

Suomi, S.J., Harlow, H.F., and Domek, C.J. 1970. Effect of repetitive infant–infant separation of young monkeys. *Journal Abnormal Psychology* 76: 161–172.

Suomi, S.J., Harlow, H.F., and Kimbal, S.D. 1971. Behavioral effects of prolonged partial isolation in the rhesus monkey. *Psychological Reports* 29: 1171–1177.

The Evolution of Human Sexual Behavior

Bruce Ullock, Nathaniel N. Wagner

7

The evolution of human sexual behavior is most understandably viewed in terms of both its distal and proximal causation. Sexual behavior's distal function is the preservation of the species through biological reproduction. The proximate manifestations of human sexual behavior are dyadic interactions at various levels of intimacy in an emotional and physiological sense.

Hominids have moved as nomadic primates from the grassy plains of Africa to other regions of the world, existing first as hunter–gatherers, then as agriculturalists and technologists. Behavior generally, and sexual behavior specifically, is a result of the effects of human genetic constitution interacting with the environment. Konrad Lorenz in his introduction to *The Sexual Code* (Wickler, 1972) suggests that every species of animal and plant has adapted itself to its enviroment in a process of adjustment lasting eons; in a sense each species is the image of its environment. Alcock (1979) notes four considerations concerning the interaction between genes and the environment in an attempt to understand the origins of diversity in human behavior. First, there is no question that many elements of our behavior are relatively plastic and susceptible to cultural influences. Natural selection in the past has favored individuals who possess a range of learning abilities that underlie the capacity to become a highly cultural animal. Since reproductive survival depends on succeeding in the culture in which one is born, humans must possess substantial behavioral flexibility.

Second, it also seems probable that there is a set of major and minor traits that represents part of an ancestral set of adaptations that evolved during the two to four million years when our hominid ancestors were strictly hunter–gatherers. In other words, many of the traits that were an integral part of the hunter–gatherer way of life could have been retained as humans made the transition to agricultural and then industrial cultures. Alexander (1971) speaks to Alcock's position by suggesting that many aspects of our own behavior may seem to be mere perversions or products of civilization when in fact they are a great deal older and more complex than this, and perfectly reasonable or understandable in terms of our evolutionary history.

Third, there is theoretical evidence that in only 300 years a major allele could totally replace another in a human population. The point to be made is that people in one culture may have been selected for biological predispositions to behave in ways that help them survive and reproduce within their culture (Durham, 1976). This argument provides an alternative approach to phenomena that have been interpreted in an environmentalistic fashion. For example, Margaret Mead's famous hypothesis that sexual temperament is purely a matter of the culture into which one is born is oversimplified. She found (1949) in three New Guinean cultures three totally different modes of accepted male and female behavior. In the Mundugumor, both men and women exhibited highly aggressive, frequently violent sexual behavior of a very extreme sort. In the Arapesh, sex roles could hardly have been more different; both men and women behaved in a gentle and passive manner. Tchambuli males behaved in what we would consider an excitable, artistic, effeminate manner, while women were calm and masculine by our standards.

Fourth, another possible contributor to the diversity of human behavior may lie in the repression or accentuation of specified behavioral traits by the culture. To what extent these do or do not interact is conjecture at this time, but it is important to recognize their potential contributions. Unger and Denmark (1975) emphasize that perhaps the greatest problem addressing such issues is that experimental manipulation is nearly impossible; and according to Christiansen (1977) unethical. Weithorn (1975) also points to other aspects that confound the interpretation of cross cultural data, and in our opinion historical data as well. For example, the lack of "conceptual equivalences" may lead to biases in the gathering and treatment of information by researchers.

Wickler (1972) quite succinctly states that humans are different from other animals. Their behavior is that of a thinking being, so it cannot be assessed in terms of biology alone; but neither can it be assessed without biology. Findings on one species are best not extrapolated directly to other species but more realistically regarded as working hypotheses. Their applicability should be checked anew in each case. Generalities are especially precarious when culturally based norms of human social behavior are in question. The rapid alteration of the environment that humans effect with their culture and technology can place traditional norms in jeopardy. More recently acquired modes of behavior, which previously had little adaptive significance, may then become essential to the survival of the individual and the community. Wickler (1972) offers an example of what may be judged as atypical sexual behavior that becomes adaptive in a special context. In the course of initiation rites of gangs of young people in France, members of the gang submit to anal coition by their chief as a gesture of their seeking support and affection from their leader.

Hominid sexual behavior has changed over time, and the changes have not been at a constant rate. Alcock (1979) suggests that the evolution of human reproductive and sexual behavior was a function of the unique ecological pressures operating on humans, rather than predominantly a consequence of our primate heritage. Whereas hunting and gathering favored stable pair bonding, Trivers (1972) suggests that sexual selection favored different male and female reproductive strategies and that even when ostensibly cooperating in a joint task male and female interests were rarely identical. Reproduction became intimately linked with a division of labor between the sexes. The evolution of intelligence was also involved. These factors influenced the nature of human courtship and copulation to serve not only the production of offspring but pair formation and the prolonged child care necessary for survival of the helpless, big-brained progeny of our ancestors.

In order to better understand contemporary sexuality and its proximal causation, the concern here is with the historical antecedents that have molded the "plastic" components of our sexual behavior. In terms of Western civilization there have been four major traditions: Hebrew, Greek, Roman and Christian. The common threads and major shifts of emphasis will become obvious and provide tantalizing material for closing speculation as to distal mechanisms. The psychological and biological components of human sexual behavior could be viewed as complementary parts of a singular objective. Reproductive success in a species with altricial young obligates parental care for an extended period and becomes more than simply procreation. Pair bonding may be one means to that end.

Hebrew Tradition   The ancient Hebrew civilization, as recorded in the Old Testament and the Talmud, is one of the most important sources of our traditional sexual standards and an important source of knowledge about sexual behavior. The Jewish culture, which had its beginnings some 35 or 40 centuries ago in one of the many wandering Semitic tribes of the Middle East, did not come into full flower until after the Hebrew exodus from Egypt and their entrance into agriculture, sometime between 1450 and 1200 B.C. Hebraic society was male-dominated and had a double-standard sexual ethic. The seventh commandment, "Thou shalt not commit adultery," in theory applied to all but in practice applied only to females. At the time Moses came down from Mount Sinai with the commandments, Hebrew males kept slaves; it is a universal truth of male behavior in history that whenever males have access to females as slaves they use them sexually. The wife was considered the husband's property, as reflected in the 10th commandment, "Thou shalt not covet thy neighbor's house, thou shalt not covet thy neighbor's wife, nor his maidservant, nor his ox, nor his ass, nor anything that is thy neighbor's." Not only did the Hebrew male have intercourse regularly with his female slaves, but many rich Hebrew males had concubines too. When the married Hebrew male had sexual relations with his slave and with his concubine, he was not punished for adultery. If his wife had sexual relations with anyone else, she was severely punished. Consistent with the logic of the time, if the Jewish male had sexual relations with another man's wife, they were punished for adultery. The concept of females as property was the key to interpretation of the laws against adultery rather than our current interpretations that involve concepts such as fidelity and mutuality.

The ancient Hebrew tradition of the religion of the child being determined by the religion of the mother probably stems from these same circumstances. That is, the slave and the concubine usually were not Jewish and by having the children of these liaisons not Jewish, the Hebrew male was relieved of much of the responsibility for his bastard illegitimate offspring. These words, bastard and illegitimate, suggest the ambivalence and moral hostility that society felt and still feels to some degree toward extramarital relations.

Marriage and the family, the legitimate family, were important to the Hebrews. Marriages were arranged by one's parents—an almost universal phenomenon and constituted as much a bond between the two families as between the individual bride and groom. The legal age for marriage was twelve for girls, thirteen for boys. Virginity was strictly required of girls at the time of marriage. Virginity assumed that children born to the wife were her husband's and thus to be provided for and enjoy all the rights of inheritance. Large families were favored and male children especially valued. The woman's place was in the home, caring for the house and children. Activities outside the house were forbidden unless in relation to her husband's activities. The father held considerable power over his children and wife. Only men could initiate divorce proceedings. The Hebrew wife, however, had much more freedom than the Greek or Roman wife and participated more fully in her husband's life and in the society in general.

Greek Tradition   The city-state of Athens was the intellectual center of the world in the fourth and fifth centuries B.C., when Socrates, Plato and Aristotle were developing Western philosophy and history. They were interested in and commented on the position of women, the family and sexual behavior idealistically and realistically. Aristotle probably reflected the common attitude of the influential Greeks when in *Politics* he stated emphatically that women are naturally inferior to men. He felt, therefore, that women should obey men and strive only to perform well their family functions. Xenophone, a Greek Historian, wrote a small handbook called *The Economist* written in the form of a dialog between Socrates (under whom Xenophone had studied) and a young man, Ischomachus. The handbook deals with management of a household, servants, farming and training a wife. Ischomachus proceeds to explain to his wife that the gods had made man and woman to be different so as to be of the greatest use to each other. By their union, man and woman produce offspring and keep the race alive, but even more important, they profit by a division of labor. There are two general kinds of work—outdoor and indoor—of which man is for the former, woman for the latter; man is fitted to travel, to work in the field, to fight and to be active in public places; the woman is equipped to care for the children, train and watch over the servants, store and guard the household goods and perform other stay-at-home tasks. It seems to be a provision of nature that it is easier for a well-disposed woman to take care of her children than to neglect them, so it is more pleasing for a right-minded woman to attend to, rather than neglect her property which, being her own, affords her gratification. He assured his wife on philosophic grounds that the human body is most beautiful in its natural state and it is not useful to try to deceive for the husband knows her true appearance. To maintain her beauty a woman should not sit idle in her room but preside over the loom, move constantly about the house to watch the servants and trouble herself to do some of the kneading of dough and the shaking out and folding of linen. If she would thus exercise herself, she would take her food with a better appetite, would enjoy better health and would assume a more truly excellent complexion.

The Greeks during their "Golden Age" also had a double standard of sexual behavior. The relationship between the sexes was expressed concisely by Demosthenes: "Man has the hataera for erotic enjoyments, concubines for daily use and wives of equal rank to bring up children and to be faithful housewives". Extramarital sex was expected of husbands but strictly forbidden for wives. An upper-class woman had basically two alternatives in life. She could become a wife, which entailed a life consisting of those duties mentioned above, seldom seeing a man other than her husband. Her other alternative was to become a hataera, a mistress or a prostitute of learning and high social position. Some hataera were associated with religious sects and their prostitution was a vital part of the religious beliefs and practices. The hataera were often highly educated—much more so than most wives—and were expert at making themselves attractive and pleasing for men. Some became quite famous and influential through their association with great men. Hataera ranked lower than wives in societal esteem (as reflected in Demosthenes' famous utterance), but had more freedom than wives. Both wives and hataera were excluded from direct participation in public life; the Greek ideal of the full development of all human functions seems to have applied only to men.

Greek men also practiced *homosexuality*. Anal and oral intercourse bore no stigma, and many of the Greek philosophers had young male lovers. According to Hunt (1959) the symptoms of the enamored lover were not inventions of homosexual men but cultural traditions; fittingly enough, they first appeared in Greek literature in poems of a homosexual woman. She was Sappho, who caused the geographical label "Lesbian" to become a sexual one. Sappho lived in the sixth century B.C. at Mytilene on the Greek island of Lesbos and ran a sort of finishing school where she taught girls poetry, music and dancing. She fell madly in love with one after another of them and expressed her love in delicate but richly sensuous poems that won her, among later Greeks, the title of "The Tenth Muse." Her sexual preference did not prevent her from having a husband and rearing a daughter. Her poems had immense effect on life and erotic literature. In essence Sappho institutionalized the infatuatory component of sexual behavior; this is the beginning of that aspect of sexual behavior called "Western Love." The Greeks had coined two words for love: eros for *carnal love* and agape for *spiritual love*. Love as manifested in sexual behavior has never divested itself of the Greek influence. Sappho drew up a formal symptomatology of lovesickness which has been fully adhered to for 25 centuries; *Platonic love,* that long discussed and marvelously misapplied term originated with Plato's own attempts to build incorporeal metaphysics out of desires of the flesh. Yet for all its familiar aspects, love and its incumbent sexual behavior in classic Greece was peculiarly different in character from later Western behavior. It was considered not so much an enobling and transforming goal of life, but an amusing pastime and distraction, or sometimes a Godsent affliction. And its heartfelt expressions were poured forth not by young men and women who desired each other as mates but by married men serenading courtesans and by homosexuals wooing others of their kind (Hunt, 1959).

Roman Tradition   *Pagan love* existed in Rome, giving sexual behavior a fun loving no-holds-barred kind of lechery. The Roman patriarchy, circa 400 B.C. was probably the most extreme of the four great traditions. The patriarch held absolute power over his family. The role of the woman at that time was as a perpetual minor, with few "adult-type" obligations. The courtesan existed in Rome as it had in Athens, but its members were not as well educated or respected as the hataera. Whereas the Greeks made sexual pleasure a companion of the arts, the less refined Romans replaced the esthetic element for the most part with more earthy pursuits such as the gladatorial shows. The Roman wife had one advantage over her Greek counterpart—she was allowed to go to public places accompanied by her husband and to sit at banquets with him.

Female virginity, as in all double-standard societies, was highly valued by the Romans and they had many myths about it. For example, the sanctity of female purity was believed to hold sway over all nature and therefore virgins could tame wild animals. Sophisticated Romans scoffed at such folk tales, but they were cherished by the commonpeople.

Around the time of the Punic Wars (150 B.C.) Roman culture underwent some drastic changes, including great improvements in the legal status of women. The power of death was taken away from the husband. Women could inherit property freely. The divorce laws were equalized, making divorce by mutual agreement possible, and common law marriage became legally recognized. Upper-class women were allowed more and more participation in life outside the home and a wife could now relax with her husband instead of sitting while he relaxed. The double sexual standard was not abolished, as evidenced by the fact that adultery by the wife entitled the husband to kill her without a trial, while there was essentially no penalty for the adulterous husband. The family structure was considerably weakened by the fast growing middle class and upper class.

It is noteworthy that the changes taking place were resisted by conservative factions within the Roman citizenry. As the Roman Empire grew and Greece was conquered, changes continued in the Roman sexual behavior. Adultery became fashionable and excusable. Pederasty was also practiced by many. Divorce laws became liberalized to the point that all one spouse had to do was send the other a written notice to leave. Abortion and contraception became very common, as children were not needed to the extent they once were. The poor that could not afford abortion or contraception deposited the unwanted offspring in the garbage or somewhere else. The hedonistic Romans were to a great extent exemplified by their famous leader, the great Julius Caesar, who was at the same time a "fop, dandy and perfumed homosexual" [Hunt (1959) based on writings of ancient historians Suetonius and Plutarch]. Plutarch also tells us that Caesar's avenger, Mark Anthony, kept a harem of male and female concubines in his house. Octavian, who defeated Mark Anthony in 30 B.C. in the battle for the Roman Empire, was farsighted enough to see the danger to the Roman Empire that the low birth rate and lack of family solidarity presented. Augustus (Octavian) tried to legislate a return to morality but was almost entirely unsuccessful, although history does give some indication that his laws and good example were respected by a few. In addition to trying to legislate morality, Augustus exiled several morally offensive people including Ovid (a bisexual) who wrote *Ars Amatoria (The Art of Love)*, which amounted to a "cookbook" on attracting and consummating sexual affairs.

Christian Tradition   The disdain that Augustus held for the hedonistic sexuality of Rome was also shared by the emerging Christians of that era. The early Christians were unique in the ancient Western world in their recommendation of chastity for both sexes and their devaluation of marriage, sexual relations and family life. Their counterculture movement was antisex and antiwomen's liberation. They opposed the emancipation of women and the easier divorce laws which had developed since the Punic Wars and demanded a return to older, stricter Greek, Roman and Hebrew ideas. The Christians believed that Christ's coming was imminent and therefore that man should spend his time contemplating God and cleansing his soul rather than raising families and participating in sensual pleasures. Marriage was a second-rate choice, a concession to human weakness—an attitude emphatically stated by St. Paul,

It is good for man not to touch woman. Yet for fear of fornication, let each man have his own wife, and let woman have her own husband. . . . But this I say by way of concession, not by way of commandment. But I say to the unmarried and to widows it is good for them if they so remain, even as I. But if they do not have self-control, let them marry, for it is better to marry than to burn. . . . The virgin thinks about the things of the Lord, that she may be holy in body and in spirit. Whereas she who is married thinks about the things of the world, how she may please her husband. . . . He who gives his virgin in marriage does well, and he who does not give her does better (I Corinthians 7).

It is appropriate at this juncture to make a disclaimer regarding the reporting of historical facts in general and on interpreting the meaning of the Hebraic–Christian tradition in particular. The interpretations of the effects of Hebraic–Christian religious philosophies on sexual behavior are really based to a large degree on the interpretative writings of others, including the Bible, and reflect no omniscience on our part. By way of explanation two examples are given. The first example concerns I Corinthians 7:2–4. Paul defends marital intercourse as both a right and a duty, which is somewhat incongruous with our previous notion. Further, more explicitly than anywhere else in the Bible, it is affirmed that partners are equally obligated to surrender their bodies to one another for mutual enjoyment. An ascetic scribe, evidently finding Paul's position embarrassing, doctored the text of I Corinthians 7:3 so that it read: "The husband should give to his wife the good will (euonia) she is due." The King James version perpetuated that erroneous addition of euonia. The generalizations of many people about Paul's ascetic beliefs may have been poorly founded. The probability that many Christian lives have been profoundly influenced by the erroneous generalization seems to us quite substantial.

The second example concerns the "sin of Onan." In a Bible published by the Jewish Publications Society of North America in 1917, Genesis 38:6 reads,

And Judah took a wife for Urr his firstborn, and her name was Tamara . . . and Urr, Judah's firstborn was wicked in the sight of the Lord and the Lord slew him. And Judah said unto Onan, go into thy brother's wife and perform the duty of a husband's brother unto her and raise up seed to thy brother. And Onan knew that the seed would be his and it came to pass that when he went into his brother's wife that he spilt it on the ground, lest he should give seed to his brother. And the *thing* [the book does not say what "thing" is defined to be] which he did was evil in the sight of the Lord and he slew him also.

Now the King James version is exactly the same, except where it says, ". . . and Judah said unto Onan, go in unto thy brother's wife and marry her. . . ." The Dartmouth Bible, 2nd edition revised and enlarged, contains Genesis 37 and Genesis 39 but no Genesis 38.

In addition to the above points, the story of Onan illustrates how a Biblical tale may be generalized to affect Western thought in enormously important ways. For instance, in German, Swedish and a variety of other languages, the word for *masturbation* is a form of onanism. Masturbation is a particularly interesting phenomenon that occurs in nonhuman primates as well as humans. The extent to which a Biblical generalization has influenced common Western thought is depicted in two illustrations. The first is in a book by Mary Wood Allen (1897),

Every organ of the body is sacred and should be protected and this is just as true of the sexual organs as it is of the ears and the eyes. You should never handle them or allow anyone else to handle them. Girls sometimes form a habit they know is wrong, but usually they are ashamed of it, and it's called the habit of solitary vice. I was reading what a certain wise physician had to say about the effects of this habit; he is convinced that it causes a great many backaches and sideaches and other aches, tenderness of the spine, nervousness, indolence, pale cheeks, hollow eyes, languid manner. He says we can tell when a girl begins this habit of self abuse; she will suddenly decline in health and have a changed disposition. She will become peevish, morose, disobedient, lose her memory and love of study. She may become bold in manner, instead of being modest as a little girl should be. She will manifest an unnatural appetite, sometimes desiring mustard, pepper, vinegar, spices, cloves, clay, salt, chalk, charcoal, etc. Sometimes there is an ulceration about the root of the nails and the eyes look blank.

Now, so the gentlemen will not feel left out, here is a quote from the respected writer, Iwan Block (1908): "Treatment and Care for Masturbation: the diet should be light and unstimulating. The clothing and bedding light and cool." Also, from the American Educational Society (1918):

I would talk just as simply as I know how to that boy, without a bit of self-consciousness or affection, "in a certain part of your reproductive organs, in the testes which are in the scrotum which hangs down, there are two small glands which manufacture and secrete a fluid which we call the reproductive fluid. We will use the word which you will learn later on, semen. Now that fluid is not for the purpose of reproduction now in a boy's life, but it will be later on when you come to your full growth as a man, 21 or 24. As physicians now understand and have for the last few years, they know that the fluid which is being continually secreted and manufactured in your body by these glands in the testes is continuously being carried up to two small reservoirs provided for that fluid, and, then, if you do not waste it from the system, the blood comes and carries that vital fluid into the nerve centers of your spine and to the brain cells in your head so that you can have more energy, more vitality and more punch, and be a finer man in every way. Do you want to play football someday? Do you want to be captain of the team when you get there, boy? But if you want it to be all that you can be, you must save your semen in the body. Do not allow anyone to teach you to waste it from your body. It is your future punch and vitality and pep." (p. 2)

It is clear from the above passages that masturbation is a sin and it is obvious that it is a generalization from the Onan story in the Bible. There is a considerable debate in current theology about what the sin of Onan was. The tradition has been that the sin of Onan was to spill his seed on the ground, and spilling his seed on the ground, coitus interruptus, easily generalizes to masturbation because when you masturbate you spill your seed on the ground. Current biblical scholars say that the sin of Onan was not spilling his seed on the ground, but was the sin of pride, that he would not impregnate his sister-in-law in order to have sons that would be his brother's heirs and that he refused God's injunction in that regard. Regardless of which is the correct interpretation, the sin of Onan has essentially made people feel extraordinarily guilty, wrong, dirty for engaging in sex that is not reproductive.

Phipps (1970) points out that moral dualism has been pervasive, causing Western man to try to separate his Godly spirit from his devilish flesh. Ascetic renunciation of those sensual impulses that give pleasure when gratified has been considered essential for those who exemplify pure spirituality. The Protestant monk, Max Thurian, employs Matthew 5:28, "But I say to you that everyone who looks at a woman lustfully has already committed adultery with her . . .," to fortify his assertion that Christians must follow Christ in aiming at the pure love that renounces life. Tertullian influenced the interpretation of that verse when he used it as the basis for castigating sexual desire expressed either by a man for his fiancé or by a husband for his wife. Either expression he maintained is the essence of fornication. However, in the Old Testament licit qualification of sexual passion was encouraged and remarriage was a religious duty that every man took seriously. Further, there was virtually no moral contamination associated with marital intercourse and there are no instances of lifelong voluntary celibacy in the entire Old Testament.

The ascetic view of life was a harsh change for most people of that time and ran counter to Roman law, which favored large families and levied a fine on bachelors. For the first three centuries, Christianity was considered a radical movement and largely despised; its proponents, mostly poor people, were frequently persecuted and its influence was small.

The status of women suffered in many respects under Christianity. In one sense, they were afforded more equality in that all men as well as women were expected to be virginal at marriage and abstain from extramarital sex. As Jerome wrote in 399 A.D.: "A command that is given to men applies logically also to women. It cannot be that an adulterous wife should be put away and an unfaithful husband retained. . . . Among the Romans, men's unchastity goes unchecked; seduction and adultery are condemned, but free permission is given to lust to range the brothels and to have slave girls, as though it were a person's rank and not the sensual pleasures that constituted the offense. With us it is what is unlawful for women is equally unlawful for men, and as both sexes serve God they are bound by the same conditions". But, such equal treatment the Graeco-Roman world would not accept and in time the church informally modified its stand.

Celibacy began to be imposed on priests after the fourth century and along with the contempt for sexual pleasures (which some of the early Church fathers demonstrated by castrating themselves) they developed a contempt for women as Eve-like temptresses who were at the root of sinfulness [Hunt (1959) referring to Origen as the most famous case]. Tertullian's attack epitomizes this view: "You are the devil's gateway; you are the unsealer of that forbidden tree; you are the first deserter of the divine law; you are she who persuaded him who the devil was not valiant enough to attack. You destroyed so easily God's image, man. On account of your desert—that is death—even the son of God had to die." Being the source of sin, it was consistent that women were not allowed to own or inherit property. The Christian woman had the alternative of marriage or a nunnery—a much different choice than that offered the Greek and Roman women. Celibate females, however, were respected in Christian society since they were not temptresses; thus the traditional value of female virginity was raised to an extreme.

By the fifth century it was widely held that marriage was a sacrament, a holy indissoluble act, although it was not authoritatively defined as such until the Middle Ages by the Council of Trent. Some confusion did exist in Christian doctrine concerning divorce. In Matthew 19:9, Christ recognized fornication (adultery) as grounds for divorce but in Mark 10:11–12 He recognized no grounds whatever. Christianity, as Hunt (1959) puts it, affected marriage in two seemingly irreconcilable ways: It enobled it; it debased it.

During the sixth century, Western Christianity had to amalgamate itself with the barbarous Teutonic Tribes since it was then cut off from Imperial Roman influence. However, Christianity continued to affect human sexual behavior. Jerome, circa 500 A.D., argued, "Let a [married] man govern his voluptuous impulses and not rush headlong into intercourse. . . . He who too ardently loves his own wife is an adulterer." He further went on to argue that neither prayer nor communion were possible after husband and wife had intercourse. Abstinence the night before a Church festival was a prerequisite for attendance for married people. Augustine, a prolific theologian whose writings became enormously important, argued that the earlier in life a married couple begins to refrain from intercourse with each other the better they would seem in God's eyes, and he repeatedly maintained that the evil of lust—even married lust—was justified only when it had the sole and immediate aim of begetting children. In brief, Augustine set up a permanent barrier between personal affection and sexual expression and gave formal theological structure to the confused ideal of continent marriage and a sexual love. The Oedipal conflict had at last been enshrined in a religion and enlarged into a lifelong struggle for salvation.

After the Dark Ages (the early part of the Middle Ages) when Europe was in the barbaric doldrums, women's position in society suffered, the arts and sciences suffered and the Church became very sensuous. The eleventh century saw the advent of a new aspect to human sexual relations. The new aspect that started in France was called *courtly love:* courtly love introduced tenderness and gentleness within an adulterous framework. It preached fidelity and also introduced the notion that the loving aspect of sexual behavior must be a genuinely mutual relationship. Semi-erotic emotions began to be wedded to moral achievement. The female's status began to be enhanced. However, even the Renaissance was affected by the legacy of St. Augustine, particularly in terms of how women were viewed—either lady or witch. Inquisitors produced a huge compilation of information on witchcraft, most of the concern being dominated by sexual problems caused by witches such as: infertility, impotence, nocturnal emissions, painful coitus, nymphomania, satyriasis.

In spite of the negative legacy left by St. Augustine, by 1550 *marriage for love* was created. Mainly, as with other trends that have been discussed, the civilized aristocracy was the principal proponent. However, by this time there was an emerging middle class, and while the bourgeoisie could not afford courtly love, they certainly could take up this latest fad with a passion. This was also the first time that young marrieds lived apart from the family.

Out of the Renaissance came the Reformation. The Protestants devalued celibacy, praised marriage without qualification and argued that marital sex was wholesome and free of taint; nevertheless, they continued to examine, condemn and execute witches very much as the inquisitors had, often exhibiting the same morbid sexual fantasies (Hunt, 1959). Hunt goes on to say that conceivably the ascetic and repressive features that mark Puritanism at its unloveliest and have given it a bad name owe as much to one man's glandular shortcomings as to the social goals of the bourgeoisie. Calvin, the leader, was small, thin, dyspeptic, ailing, intense and unhumorous. Calvin spoke of marriage as having two main functions: the production of offspring and the remedying of incontinence. Few men were so stern and severe a character, but surprisingly enough, Calvin's ideas took hold. Seventeenth-century Puritanism was tightlipped, severe and pious, but it was simultaneously frank, strong-sexed and somewhat romantic. The frigidity and neuroses associated with Puritanism belong to a much later date: hellfire-and-brimstone sermons reached their zenith in the middle of the 18th century and the suffocating prudishness of the Victorians came in the middle of the 19th century.

Much of the distaste people today hold for Puritanism actually should be directed at the Victorian era. The Victorian approach to sexual behavior centered in England but existed as a model for America and Northern Europe. Here again we see the status of women elevated, since women were not needed as workmates for the men of the burgeoning middle and upper classes. These socioeconomic classes became more "romantic" in the sense that they elevated women by emphasizing the pure, motherlike, delicate and modest qualities. The Victorian male concentrated on the woman's value as an ideal. This was a very difficult situation as we have come to understand today. We have in the history of the Puget Sound in Washington State an excellent example of the Victorian era mentality in the deeds and mind of Asa Mercer who brought young unmarried females from the eastern United States because ". . . practically all the goodness in the world came from the influence of pure minded women." Another person of enormous impact from the Victorian era was Sigmund Freud: his herculean effort to coalesce a theoretical framework, based on his clinical observations and armchair philosophical endeavors, opened up a respectable new period in the study of human sexual behavior. He described sex as a drive force and labeled some of the "unconscious" thought processes that may exist in man.

Western Thought Entering the 20th century, we still find a philosophical and behavioral continuum that ranges in one dimension from the "sexual-desire-is-pathological-in-women" to the sexual radicals. Hendrik Ruitenbeck (1974) argues that contemporary sexuality has only one slogan: freedom—the freedom to experience all aspects of sexuality without restrictions. The Dutch writer, J.J. Beljon (1974), has defined the situation in the following terms:

The change in eroticism which we experience today has been conditioned by the fall of Christian morality. The act of intercourse no longer carries with it the taste of the forbidden fruit, since the Peeping Tom of Nazareth on his cross no longer hangs above the marital bed. Freedom to love but also freedom to Schund (pornography, trash). Freedom for great passion but also freedom for Unfug (mischief). Freedom for fidelity but also freedom for promiscuity.

Havelock Ellis (1939) has argued that love is not necessarily permanent, so adultery is acceptable; but it is reported that Ellis could not tolerate an extramarital affair in his own life. Others had proffered similar ideas earlier in this century, such as Judge Ben Lindsey's "companionate marriage" (Lindsey and Evans, 1927) that was terminable at will as long as there were no children. Fannie Hurst (1929) advocated "visiting marriage" with separate households. D.H. Lawrence (1930), the tormented exponent of sexual freedom, declared in the very last year of his life that it was not really sex that man needed, "It is a great blow to our self-esteem that we simply need another human being; I do not mean a mistress, the sexual relationship in the French sense. It is in relationship to one another that [people] have their true individuality and distinct being. It is a living contract, give and take." Lawrence's thoughts bring us closer to the conservative end of our current philosophical and behavioral continuums, at least in a traditional sense.

We see man involved in the most ambitious undertaking ever contemplated in terms of his sexual behavior or pair bonding. Western man is attempting to combine physical sexual outlet, affectionate friendship and the procreative familial functions all in a single relationship. Romantic attraction is considered to be the adequate basis for choosing one's lifelong partner; the sexual desires deliberately aroused in courtship are supposed to be held in check until after marriage. The sexual drives of both partners are supposed to be completely and permanently satisfied within marriage even though there was no testing period beforehand. Tenderness, mystery and excitement are expected to coexist with household cares, child-rearing problems and the routine of 15,000 nights together (Hunt, 1959).

There are still other changes in progress, as a consequence of several people and events from the first half of the 20th century that are currently influencing sexual behavior. As early as 1918, Marie Stopes was arguing for women's right to orgasm. The Industrial and Technological Revolutions have concentrated Western populations in cities where children are not economically advantageous, wives are not assets to their husbands in the same way as in the past and wives are not challenged in the city home of convenience.

Overpopulation   Margaret Sanger, a visiting nurse in 1920, witnessed and was appalled by the results of ungoverned fertility among the poor in New York City slums. She saw health and happiness ruined in squalid slums largely due to excessive child-bearing. Mostly as a result of her work, 300 birth control clinics were established by the 1930s in the United States. Unfortunately, the effects of birth control on low-socioeconomic-status people have not been as noticeable as on upper-middle-class populations whose use of contraceptives has become pervasive.

Population is the number one socioeconomic problem today. It is central to almost every difficulty we face, from pollution to unemployment. The population of the world remained relatively stable during most of our past, increasing very slowly with occasional drastic setbacks in the form of plagues which swept across the continents, wiping out as much as 50% of the population in a given year. Around 1850 a great upsurge in the rate of population growth began, which has continued unabated to the present. Globally it is not just food that is scarce. The rate that the world is exhausting reserves of minerals, fuel and water may become catastrophic before food shortage is generally critical (Pincher, 1973). This situation alone seems to be a sufficient reason for a substantial restriction of population growth. Some idea of the rate of reproduction is appreciated by considering the time it has taken to increase the world's population by each billion. This figure was achieved for the first time in 1830. It took only 100 years to reach the second billion. The third billion was reached 30 years later in 1960. Four billion was reached 15 years later in 1975.

The two main reasons for our population explosion are, first, the improvement in sanitation and the development of awareness of and the ability to deal with public health problems; second, the intensive utilization of fossil fuels. These factors have resulted in a decrease in the death rate, not an increase in the birth rate. Acceptance of the germ concept of disease and resultant public health and sanitary measures have drastically reduced epidemic-caused deaths. Consumption of fossil fuels has supplied the energy to feed the expanding population. These fossil fuels, which are an accumulation of the food and organic matter of previous ages when there were fewer people on earth than there were resources available, are quickly being exhausted. Continued increase in the human population can only result in famine, universal misery and a return to a higher death rate. Copious reproduction is completely inappropriate to our time.

It is, in our estimation, a pervasive problem that is and will affect our sexual behavior directly and indirectly in striking ways. Zero Population Growth, an organization which began as an association of scientists, now has a membership from the general public and is effective in spreading its message in the United States and elsewhere. This influence includes pressure in favor of later marriages and alternative careers to childbearing for women.

China and India with over a billion and a half people (38% of the world total) clearly bear the major burden of overpopulation. Nartman (1977) cites "tenuous" evidence that China's birthrate is approaching the low level characteristic of Western society (17 per thousand population) and that India's birthrate, while still incredibly high, has declined to the mid-thirties per thousand. These new figures if accurate hold considerable promise. However, even if all couples reproduced only to replace themselves, the population would continue to grow. The high proportion of persons currently in or entering the reproductive ages would produce more births than a decrease in population from deaths would evince. The population will not stabilize until the age structure stabilizes.

Patterns in marriages are changing radically from other pressures, too. One of the most obvious effects of this convenience is the steadily increasing freedom of women as a result of machines that eliminate household drudgery and cut the advantage of man's physical strength in other forms of employment. With a much longer life expectancy, better health and a small family, the bride of 19 no longer need dedicate herself to a whole lifetime in the nursery and kitchen. She can look forward to 30 years of active life after her children have been reared and left home. The old concept that marriage and parenthood are synonymous no longer holds. Companionship has become important, especially in the later years, and if a wife does not get it from her husband she may seek it elsewhere. Marriage is no longer regarded as a static or permanent union. Psychologists now speak of a dynamics of marriage, expressing the obvious fact that each union is beset with forces that are in continual change (Pincher, 1973).

Human Sexuality

Contraception offers an important alternative to copious reproduction or abstention. Contraception essentially makes the separation of sexual pleasure from reproduction a reality. The female clitoris, the anatomical correlate of the male penis, has no direct physiologic function in reproduction, although it quite possibly serves to ensure human mating behavior through pleasurable reinforcement of the sex act. There is also reasonably good evidence to suggest that considerable numbers of females are most interested in sexual behavior not at mid-cycle nor at the ovulation time, which would be the period of maximum fertility, but rather immediately before or after menstruation, which is the time of minimal reproductive fertility. A study done in Scandinavia (Linner, 1972) addresses the separation of recreational and reproductive sex. It has shown that only about 2% of sexual activity was performed with the conscious purpose of procreation.

The Western world is evolving into a Scandinavian mentality. Some religious groups experience great difficulty regarding the explanation of the relevance of their traditional Hebraic–Christian reproductive sexual mentality when talking to their young people. However, changes in the theological positions are also happening. Some sense of this transition can be gleaned in a quotation from the Christian theologian, W. Norman Pittenger (1970):

Basically the sexual desire and drive is deeply instinctive to man. Indeed we might say that a human being without that sexuality would be much less human. For the vast majority of men and women, some expression of sexuality in physical ways is both natural and inevitable. Even if the sexual organs cannot be used in establishing some mode of union with another *member* of the race, they are almost certain to be used in some fashion—as for example in masturbatory activity in the adult. Not more important than but intimately associated with the physical aspect of human sexuality, we are aware of the emotional side. In man the biological purpose while it may be prior to anything else in terms of historical development in the species is by no means the main objective in sexual relationships. On the contrary, the main objective seems to be twofold: first it is the urge to experience the ecstacy which is felt when humans engage in sexual acts. In the second place the objective is the realization of the feeling of union with another human being. This union in the fullest sense is a relationship of mutuality, in which through a giving and receiving one from and with the other, two lives are felt to be one. If man is a creature "becoming" whose subjective aim is fulfillment of his potentialities with the ultimate end his communion with God, he is also one who finds his proximate end in communion with others of his own kind.

Adaptive Reproductive Strategies

In conclusion, this historical view of human sexuality reveals not only considerable variability in expounded practices as a function of relatively temporary social changes (proximal mechanisms) but hints at several general trends that may have more distant precursors. Perhaps the most evident thread is the strong degree to which evolved (in the natural selection sense) mating strategies of males and females (Trivers, 1972) have influenced cultural norms of the past.

It is a biological fact that one male can inseminate (with little expenditure of reproductive energy) several females and, therefore, produce more than one offspring simultaneously; whereas one female can bear (with considerable expenditure of reproductive energy) only one offspring at a time. For this reason male promiscuity has been tolerated, if not condoned, for four thousand years. Fortuitous male copulations, with uncertain outcomes as to either paternity or continued well-being of young, have complemented (in terms of reproductive success) marriages to "quality" females and paternal investment in assured offspring.

Females have been regarded at one time or another throughout history as either property of, or inferior to, males such that the fidelity of some females could be ascertained with reasonable certainty to guarantee males that they fathered particular offspring. Conversely, certainty of maternity and assured resources from males "of means" to faithful females may have optimized female reproductive success. It is likely that these, or similar strategies, were operating in the historical past, although cloaked to varying degrees in different cultural and religious settings.

Moreover, the current human condition of overpopulation (Nartman, 1977) and the resistance of individuals (particularly in nonindustrialized societies) to voluntarily curbing population growth are also symptomatic of strong biological motivation to procreate. This resistance is especially evident if the probability is high that not all offspring will survive to reproductive age. The evolution of human sexual behavior has involved more than procreation, however. In addition, human sociality requires peer affiliations and altricial offspring require care giving. Human sexuality can be regarded as a biological system of affiliation, procreation and parenting with considerable flexibility and plasticity but, of necessity, with some built-in givens to assure its fertility. As is evident from the present historical review, the givens most certainly are not rigid behavioral patterns but more likely functional processes shaped by natural selection.

References

Alcock, J. 1979. *Animal Behavior*. Sunderland, MA: Sinauer Assoc.

Allen, M. 1897. *What Every Young Girl Should Know*. London: Vir Publishing.

Alexander, R.D. 1971. The search for an evolutionary philosophy of man, *Proc. Royal Soc. Vict.* 84: 99–120.

Beljon, J.J. 1974. In H. Ruitenbeck (ed.) *The New Sexuality*. New York: New Viewpoints.

Block, I. 1908. *The Sexual Life of Our Time and Its Relation to Modern Civilization* (B.E. Paul, trans.). New York: Allied Book Co.

Christiansen, L.B. 1977. *Experimental Methodology*. Boston: Allyn & Bacon.

Durham, W.H. 1976. Resource competition and human aggression, Part I: A review of primitive war. *Quart. Rev. Biol.* 51: 385–416.

Ellis, H. 1928. *Studies in the Psychology of Sex, Vol. 7*. Philadelphia: F. A. Davis.

———. 1939. *My Life*. Boston: H. Mifflin Co.

Hunt, M. 1959. *The Natural History of Love*. New York: Alfred A. Knopf.

Hurst, F. 1929. *Five and Ten*. New York: Harper & Bros.

Lawrence, D.H. 1930. *We Need One Another, Scribner's Vol. 87*, pp. 479–481. New York: C. Scribner.

Lindsey, B., and W. Evans. 1927. *The Companionate Marriage*. New York: Boni & Liveright.

Linner, B. 1972. *Sex and Society in Sweden*. New York: Harper & Row.

Mead, M. 1949. *Male and Female, A Study of the Sexes in a Changing World*, New York: W. Morrow.

Money, J., and P. Tucker. 1975. *Sexual Signature*. Boston: Little, Brown & Co.

Nartman, D. 1977. *Changing Contraceptive Patterns: A Global Perspective*, Population Bulletin, Vol. 32, No. 3, pp. 26–33. Population Reference Bureau Inc.

Phipps, W. 1970. *Was Jesus Married?* New York: Harper & Row.

Pincher, C. 1973. *Sex in Our Time*. London: Weidenfield and Nicolson.

Pittenger, W.N. 1970. *Making Sexuality Human*. Philadelphia: Pilgrim Press.

Rougemont, D. 1940. *Love in the Western World*. New York: Pantheon.

Ruitenbeck, H. 1974. *The New Sexuality*. New York: New Viewpoints.

Simon, W., and Gagnon, J.H. 1973. *Sexual Conduct*. Chicago: Aldine.

Stopes, M. 1918. *Married Love*. London: A.C. Field.

Trivers, R.L. 1972. Parental investment and sexual selection. In B. Campbell (ed.) *Sexual Selection and the Descent of Man*. Chicago: Aldine.

Unger, R.K., and Denmark, F.L. (eds.) 1975. *Woman: Dependent or Independent Variable*. New York: Psychological Dimensions.

Weithorn, C. 1975. Women's Role in Cross Cultural Perspective. In Unger, R.K., Denmark, F.L. (eds.) *Woman: Dependent or Independent Variable*. New York: Psychological Dimensions.

Wickler, W. 1972. *The Sexual Code*. Garden City: Doubleday.

Human Reproductive Strategies:
A Sociobiologic Overview

David P. Barash

8

Animals exhibit an incredible diversity of shapes and behaviors, but there is one thing that all living things share: they all reproduce. On one level, reproduction is a paradox: it requires time and energy in finding suitable mates, locating and often constructing an appropriate breeding place, provisioning the young and so forth. In addition, reproduction makes substantial metabolic demands upon would-be parents, especially the female, and especially among mammals since the entire burden of pregnancy and lactation falls on the mother. There are other negative aspects to reproduction, including increased susceptibility to predators while loaded down with the extra weight of offspring, increased visibility while breeding, the need to make extra foraging trips to provision the young, as well as the very real possibility of having to defend the offspring against predators. These all contribute to making parenthood a "hassle." Indeed, there is good reason to suppose that animals that successfully reproduce have a shorter lifespan than do those that abstain. Yet, reproduction is universal and, at least among nonhuman animals, abstention occurs only when it is enforced by either natural or artificial prohibitions. Why?

Of course, the answer is actually very clear: all living things are the offspring of other living things that have themselves reproduced successfully. Let us imagine two alternative alleles, A and A', competing for a given locus in the gene pool of a population. Assume that A differs from A' in that it predisposes its carrier to be less reproductively inclined than does A'. What would be the fate of these two alleles? In many ways, the carriers of A (the less reproductive allele) may be healthier, happier and possibly even live longer. But A would quickly disappear from the population, to be replaced by A'. In other words, evolution by natural selection would ensure that populations would be composed of individuals, each of whom has the capability and inclination to reproduce. Insofar as living things experience any evolutionary imperative, it is the imperative of reproduction.

There is currently a revolution underway in the sciences dealing with behavior. It is a revolution sparked by recognition of a new paradigm for the study of behavior: evolution by natural selection. The term *sociobiology* has been used to describe this new approach (Wilson, 1975; Barash, 1977a). Since the sociobiologic view assumes that evolution by natural selection is a major factor influencing social behavior, it necessarily accords great importance to reproductive behaviors. Given that reproduction is at the very heart of the evolutionary process, we expect that behaviors related to reproduction should especially reflect the action of natural selection (Barash, 1976a).

Although even sociobiologists do not deny that human beings are very *special* animals, it is equally undeniable that we are perfectly "good" animals; i.e., we are mammals, we reproduce via copulations and pregnancy, nourish our offspring through lactation (or at least have the capability!), and participate in nature in ways that go far beyond mere metaphor. The field of human sociobiology is relatively new. When it matures it will most likely be successful in dealing with behaviors that are especially crucial to the evolutionary process. Thus, I would be rather pessimistic that sociobiology will offer cogent insights into the behavior of General Motors, whereas it should be more successful in dealing with the behavior of the Board Chairman. Similarly, it will likely have more to say about the intimate details of our personal lives than about the complex professional functions in which we might engage. And further yet, it will have less to say about the books we read or write, and more to say about our eating, sleeping, fighting and, especially, reproducing.

Sociobiology is not the only approach to behavior that has involved evolution. In particular, ethology has a long evolutionary history (Eibl-Eibesfeldt, 1975). But where ethology and sociobiology differ is that ethology treated evolution as a basically static process (studying the *results* of the evolutionary process), whereas sociobiology uses evolution in a dynamic manner, employing the active process of natural selection to interpret and predict behavior. Thus, it uses natural selection as a *tool*—a remarkably powerful one at that.

Many people find it easier to talk about evolution than to *use* it. This is understandable and leads to one of the greatest potential weaknesses in the application of evolutionary biology to behavior—reliance on *post hoc* interpretations. Thus, once a behavior pattern is observed, it is temptingly easy for any imaginative biologist to interpret it as "clearly adaptive," although this may reflect the imagination of the biologist more than the action of natural selection. However, natural selection can be employed, as a predictive model as well as a cogent analytic device. The key lies in application of what I have termed the *central theorem of sociobiology* (Barash, 1977a): Insofar as the behavior in question reflects some component of genotype, individuals should behave so as to

maximize their inclusive fitness. We can predict that given a
"choice" situation, individuals will "elect" to follow the path of
maximum inclusive fitness. This prediction can be tested against
reality and, thus, confirmed or refuted as with any other branch of
science.

The concept of Darwinian fitness should be familiar to any
student of biology and indeed, to any informed citizen. The *central
theorem* is novel in two respects: the attribution of a genetic
influence on even complex patterns of social behavior, and the
notion of *inclusive* rather than *Darwinian* fitness. Ultimately, both
these approaches are justified by the fact that they work (i.e., they
appear to reflect the way the natural world is put together). The
role of genetics in behavior is increasingly recognized (Ehrman and
Parson, 1976), and a major component of the synthesis between
ethology and psychology (Hinde, 1970) was the recognition that
neither genes nor experience, acting alone, determines behavior. It
is accordingly legitimate and, in fact, necessary to consider the role
of each, in producing any behavior. Sociobiology does not purport
to "explain" all human behavior in genetic terms. Similarly, social
science ought not to do so in experiential terms. The evidence is
overwhelming that evolutionary considerations provide substantial insight into animal social behavior, and we are fully justified in
asking evolution to reveal whatever it can regarding our own.
Again, this is not to deny the role of social learning, traditions or
early experience. Genes can operate in a variety of subtle, indirect
ways, including predispositions to learn (Hinde and Stevenson-
Hinde, 1973) and vague but nonetheless real inclinations to behave
one way rather than another. Recognition that genes *influence*
(although they do not *determine*) social behavior was one of the
most important epiphanies leading to the sociobiologic revolution.

Inclusive fitness was a concept first elaborated by the British
geneticist Hamilton (1964). Although originally applied to the
paradox of worker sterility in the social Hymenoptera (bees, wasps
and ants), this approach has illuminated much of vertebrate social
behavior as well (West Eberhard, 1975); for a recent and particularly detailed study, see Kurland (1977). In brief, inclusive fitness
relies on the notion that solicitude for others should occur in direct
proportion as those others share genes by common descent with
the initiator; i.e., greater altruism toward close relatives and
reduced altruism as those relatives become increasingly "distant."
In this sense, even parental behavior is revealed as merely a special
case of individuals behaving so as to maximize their inclusive
fitness—the sum of Darwinian fitness (successfully reproducing
offspring) and increments to fitness through the reproductive
success of other relatives, with the importance of each relative
devalued in proportion as each shares fewer genes with the
altruist. Finally, relatedness alone is not sufficient to predict
altruistic inclinations: the other considerations are the benefit
derived by the beneficiary and the cost to the altruist for each

behavior in question. Cost and benefits are measured here in terms of units of inclusive fitness, with altruism likely in direct proportion as the benefit to the recipient is high and inversely as the cost to the altruist is high.

Before proceeding with direct consideration of the sociobiology of human reproduction, some comments are necessary concerning the role of animal models and examples. Sociobiology was developed by biologists, employing evolutionary theory in the analysis of animal behavior. Much of the controversy surrounding the new discipline has concerned its potential applicability to human beings (Allen et al., 1976; Wilson, 1976). There is nothing in sociobiologic theory that necessarily restricts it to nonhumans; accordingly, human sociobiology is no more inappropriate an endeavor than is hippopotamus sociobiology or the sociobiology of hairy-nosed wombats. But it may well be more complicated. Here I shall make frequent use of animal examples to suggest the possible action of natural selection on our own behavior. This is not to claim that because a behavior occurs in mallard ducks or honeybees, it must therefore occur in human beings. Indeed, we must beware of gratuitous extrapolations from one species to another: one of the cogent insights of evolutionary biology is that each species is unique, specifically and wonderfully adapted to the niche it occupies and therefore necessarily distinct from any other. Nonetheless, we can employ animal studies to gain insight into the basic processes whereby evolution operates on behavior, and then attempt to apply these principles of evolution-behavior linkage to the behavior of one of the world's least-understood organisms, *Homo sapiens*.

Mate Selection Among the various strategic decisions facing any would-be reproducer, one of the most important is, "With whom?" An unbiased look at any modern society plus even a modicum of unbiased introspection will reveal that courtship and other male–female interactions are of major importance to our species—and they probably always have been. Again, given the special place of reproduction in the evolutionary scheme, this is to be expected. In general, I would predict that a positive correlation exists between characteristics of a potential mate perceived as "attractive" and the contribution of those characteristics to eventual successful reproduction. Regular features, absence of disfigurement, "good" character and even control of useful resources—all are likely to seem attractive to potential mates. It's a rather hard-headed view of love and perhaps "fools give you reasons, wise men never try!" But, like it or not, from an evolutionary perspective love is a behavioral mechanism leading to fitness maximization via optimal bonding with appropriate others.

Male strategies. There are three major arenas in which male reproductive strategies unfold: (1) direct male–male competition; (2) less
direct male–male competition for resources that lead ultimately to
reproductive success; and (3) indirect competition through independent appeals to female choice. Arenas 1 and 2 are especially
difficult to separate in practice and are considered here as *intrasexual competition*. (Indeed, there is no clear-cut division between all
three arenas, which are simply stated here for heuristic purposes.)
There are many biological differences between men and women,
beyond those directly associated with difference in reproductive
function, and these differences are almost certainly the result of
differences in intrasexual competition. Thus, men are larger, have
a higher ratio of muscle to total body weight and are more
aggressive. This would be the predicted outcome of an evolutionary history of male–male competition, in which the victor enjoyed
a reproductive advantage over the loser (i.e., the victors were more
"fit"—they experienced higher inclusive fitness, so that genes
coding for traits such as larger size, muscularity and aggressiveness spread in our ancestral populations at the expense of genes
influencing the traits of the "losers").

This is admittedly speculative, as with any hypotheses concerning evolutionary events that occurred in prehistory. Indeed, one
major competing possibility should also be mentioned: the sexual
and behavioral dimorphism of humans could be the result of
selection for defense against predators and/or increased success in
hunting. Thus, if we consider our Australopithecine ancestors
attempting to survive on the predator-rich African savannah, it
seems obvious that selection would favor those males who were
maximally able to defend their families (as well as their food)
against lions, hyenas and wild dogs, as well as those most likely to
bring home the bacon. Given that our ancestors almost certainly
lived in small groups within which genetic kinship was high,
altruistic defense could also be selected via benefits conferred on
kin beyond the immediate family.

In any case, because of the biological differences between male
and female, among most species, males should compete among
themselves for access to females. This follows directly from the
greater investment that females generally provide their offspring,
thereby rendering them a resource for which the males will be
selected to compete (Trivers, 1972). Dominance–subordinance
relationships are among the most obvious mechanisms for such
competition, although others also exist: forcing competitors out of
the group (inducing dispersal), excluding them from a territory or
nest or even inflicting direct physical injury or death. The vast
majority of human societies were polygynous (van den Berghe,
1975), and considering that our sex ratio is close to equal, this
reflects a high degree of male–male competition, such that some
are excluded from breeding altogether, while others maintain more

than one mating partner. Among animals, a consequence of this pattern is that males often become sexually mature later than do females, since they are more fit by delaying their entrance into intrasexual competition (Selander, 1965). It is doubtless no coincidence that human males become sexually mature later than do females.

Males of the acanthocephalan worm, *Moniliformis dubius*, even go so far as to engage in homosexual rape (Abele and Gilchrist, 1977). These parasitic worms copulate in the intestines of their vertebrate hosts. Following the transfer of sperm, the male also delivers to the female a cementlike genital secretion that hardens within the female's vagina. The resulting "copulatory cap" serves two apparent functions, both directly serving to maximize the male's fitness: it keeps the male's sperm from leaking out and it also keeps other males from getting their sperm in. Males also transfer their cement to the genital openings of other males and significantly, in such cases of homosexual rape, this is accomplished without prior transfer of sperm—thereby proving that such behavior is not a simple case of mistaken identity. In this way, the male victim's genital region is sealed off and the "assailant" has eliminated a possible reproductive competitor. I am *not* suggesting that human homosexuality is in any way similar to this system; however, the acanthocephalan worms provide a striking testimony to the force of male–male competition among living things.

Aggressive male–male competition is actually a proximate mechanism for contributing to the ultimate, evolutionary end of fitness maximization. Such competition is positively selected only insofar as it leads ultimately to reproductive success, which it usually does by eliminating competitors and/or directly facilitating access to mates. Similarly, competition for resources represents an arena of male–male competition that is less direct insofar as the males are concerned, but more immediately applicable to the ultimate end of attracting females. Orians (1969) has investigated among animals the circumstances that select for females choosing to mate polygynously, even when unmated males are present. This decision appears superficially paradoxical in that such females are foregoing the possible paternal investment that a bachelor could offer, in return for being simply one of the many mates of a polygynist. The answer seems fairly clear: females are fittest by rejecting a bachelor and joining a harem provided that the harem-master commands sufficient resources that the "decision" results in females having greater reproductive success than if they mated monogamously. Plush polygyny may be a fitter strategy than poverty-stricken monogamy, provided that the former involves such considerations as greater food, protection from predators, superior nest sites and so forth. Orians (1969) emphasized that polygyny would be especially likely when the environment is sufficiently heterogeneous that substantial differences occur between quality of resources defended by different males. Those with better territories will become polygynists; those with poorer will remain bachelors. More recently, Emlen and Oring (1977) have pointed out that habitats and species can be characterized by their "polygyny potential."

Insofar as Orians' model holds for human beings, we can predict that a positive correlation will exist between male resources and the number of wives per man. Such an arrangement is explicitly institutionalized among Moslems. In addition, we may predict that insofar as resource accrual is a preferred male strategy (ultimately because of its evolutionary advantages via female choice), males should devote primary attention to job-related activities and accomplishments. Females, on the other hand, should be focused primarily on domestic accomplishments. Indeed, this is the primary pattern in most human societies.

Closely related to resource *control* is resource *display*; i.e., it does little good to control reproductively relevant resources unless the women know this. Hence, males should be selected for advertisement. Once again, this derives ultimately from the fundamental difference between male and female, as a result of which females are selected to be the careful comparison shoppers and males, the aggressive advertisers (Williams, 1966). This may explain the near-universal phenomenon of male braggadocio, trophy hunting and the display of relics, both from war and the hunt (R. Eaton, personal communication). Indeed, much of human courtship could be interpreted as the display of male resources—financial, social, athletic and, indeed, even courtship feeding may have its place in this regard. Thus, among many animals it is common for courting individuals, especially the males, to present the females with food during the display. The nutritional value of this offering may be significant, and among certain insects, females may choose prospective mates by their ability to provide a nourishing meal. In some cases, this may go so far as to involve cannibalism of the male by the female (Thornhill, 1976)—a strategy that actually represents evolutionary agreement by both male and female, as to what maximizes the fitness of both.

The phenomenon of female choice has been called "epigamic selection" (Huxley, 1938). It is the traditional explanation for such bizarre male features as the plumage of peacocks and argus pheasants, and such elaborate behavior as the construction efforts of bowerbirds. There are no obvious parallels in human biology; at least to our biased eyes, men are not generally considered more bizarre than are women. However, man may well have been under selection for behavior that advertises behavioral inclinations as well as resources, especially insofar as that behavior would relate directly to the perceived ability of females (the targets of the display) to reproduce. Such perception by females would confer a reproductive advantage upon males who generated that perception, so that any genetically influenced tendency in that direction would rapidly spread in a population.

For example, consider the following analog of male beachside muscle flexing, derived from some of my own research during the spring and early summer of 1977. I observed the courtship displays of *Dascyllus albisella*, Hawaiian coral reef fishes of the Pomacentrid family. The Pomacentrids include the damselfishes and anemonefishes, and are especially interesting because of their consistent and somewhat unusual reproductive pattern: males maintain and defend small mating territories at which females are induced to spawn. The eggs are then fertilized by the courting male, who proceeds to defend the developing eggs, generally by himself. Defense of the nest site and the just-fertilized egg is vigorous, and necessarily so, as coral reefs teem with potential egg predators. In studying courtship in *D. albisella*, I made several predictions based on evolutionary theory, all of which are relevant here. First, I predicted that while defending these territories, both before and after eggs were present, males would be especially aggressive toward species that are potential egg predators (as opposed to plankton and algae-feeders, for example). Second, I predicted that male aggressiveness toward such egg-predators would be especially high when females are nearby, and finally, I predicted that females would preferentially mate with males that scored high on the first two predictions. All three of these predictions were verified. In designing this study, I asked myself: If I were a female *D. albisella*, what would I look for in a prospective mate? Given that predation is a major source of mortality among developing eggs, and defense of these eggs falls entirely on the males, it seemed reasonable that females should be especially alert to any indices of the potential effectiveness of different males as defenders of their eggs—i.e., to the "promise" of male investment. Accordingly, males should be selected to emphasize that promise—hence, the enhanced male aggressiveness when females are watching. Once again, the relevance of this to human behavior is anecdotal at present, but, I think, nonetheless suggestive.

Given space limitation, the present discussion cannot cover all possible strategic considerations for mate selection by males. But it should be stressed that male options do not end with male–male competition. Other concerns relate more directly to choice of females, such choice becoming increasingly important as the society in question is increasingly monogamous. Thus, I predict that male scrutiny of prospective mates will be greatest in monogamous societies, especially when male promiscuity is unlikely. Males should choose females that are reproductively competent, and hence, younger rather than older. In general, they should avoid females who are unlikely to remain reproductively faithful and should especially avoid females who are pregnant with another's child. In this regard, it is interesting that male ring doves are significantly less likely to court females that indicate by their behavior that they have been courted and possibly inseminated by another male (Erickson and Zenone, 1976).

In addition, mammal biology suggests that males should be available for copulations outside the pair bond, while proclaiming marital fidelity. Furthermore, if wives are to be "shared," then a particular evolutionary advantage would derive from such sharing between brothers, as in such cases a man is at most a father to the offspring produced—at least, he is an uncle. Such a system has been described for "wife-sharing in the Tasmanian native hen" (Maynard Smith and Ridpath, 1972) and, significantly, patterns of this sort appear in humans as well (van den Berghe and Barash, 1977).

Female strategies. Insofar as females are selected for large parental investment, as a result of which males are selected for male–male competition (Trivers, 1972) and the acquisition and display of reproductively relevant resources, females should be selected for a more passive mate-selection strategy. They should be sensitive and responsive to male displays and, like the female *D. albisella* that mates preferentially with aggressively antipredatory males, they should be alert to male behavior that signals a high likelihood of reproductive success. By opting for a high parental investment, females have impelled males to compete for them; having saddled males with such competition, evolution has accordingly produced females who are most fit if they carefully assess the results of the fray. Of course, females may also accrue reproductively relevant resources, but the goal is more directly concerned with parenting per se, rather than intrasexual competition. There may even be a genetic mechanism which predisposes female mammals to lesser intrasexual competition than is typically the case for males (Whitney, 1976).

Females should be selected not only to recognize and appreciate male characteristics insofar as they relate to fitness enhancement, they should also respond positively to such traits. Thus, *hypergamy* would be predicted ("marrying up"). Indeed, this should be true for males as well, but in a species with a substantial "polygyny potential" (Emlen and Oring, 1977) such as *Homo sapiens*, we expect hypergamy to be especially a female strategy. Indeed, this seems to be the case (Blake, 1974).

It seems reasonable that females would enhance their fitness by making the most informed judgment possible. This may be part of the adaptive advantage (from the female's viewpoint) of *leks*, areas at which males congregate to perform communal courtship displays. The typical pattern among sage grouse, for example (Wiley, 1973), is for females to arrive at the lek, survey the displaying males and then mate preferentially with the dominant. In other words, there is an adaptive advantage to going "Where the boys are" insofar as that offers greater opportunity for females to make an informed choice. Female elephant seals apparently carry this strategy even further, actually inciting competition among males (Cox and LeBoeuf, 1977). These females vocalize loudly when mounted; this serves to activate the dominance hierarchy among males, generating aggressive competition among them such that the most dominant males are likely to copulate successfully. In this manner, females ensure that they will be inseminated only by these individuals—who are likely to be carrying genes that make the female most fit. The system may be substantially less automatic among humans, but I suggest that a similar pattern often obtains.

Given that human beings produce offspring that are utterly helpless and dependent and who require a prolonged period of parental attention, we can expect natural selection—operating on human behavior—to have evolved devices that facilitate reproductive success in the face of these stringent demands. And given the enormous disparity in male versus female parental investment, we can expect these devices to be particularly reflected in female strategies. Let us assume that the presence of a male enhances the ultimate success of the female–offspring unit; this seems reasonable since males can share food and provide defense. One possible female strategy is to widen the period of her sexual receptivity, so as to keep the male at home—or at least, nearby. Indeed, humans are unique in the extent to which female sexual responsiveness is independent of seasonal fluctuations; we are the only animal that enjoys sex equally and persistently throughout the year. This may represent a remarkable biological deception and one that is strikingly successful: among animals that experience a predictable estrus (female receptivity), males can be confident that copulations will have a high likelihood of conception. And similarly, males can be confident that copulations outside of estrus will not be biologically functional. Thus, they can essentially abandon the females without fear that they will be cuckolded. However, by extending their sexual receptivity throughout the menstrual cycle, human females effectively prevent males from confidently assessing the female's reproductive state, thereby perhaps necessitating that the males stay near home to look after their evolutionary futures. On top of this, human females have perfected the female orgasm—another human specialty—which gives females greater personal incentive to be sexually active, thereby giving their males further incentive not to linger too long on the hunt or with their colleagues.

During ovulation, when conception is most likely to occur, women experience a dramatic increase in their sensitivity to odors (LeMagnen, 1953). Similarly, there is some increase in sexual desire and the actual frequency of copulations (Michael and Zumpe, 1970). At the end of this cycle, during the three days surrounding menstrual bleeding, women typically experience a variety of perceptual problems, including difficulty in separating "relevant cues from irrelevant" (Koppell et al., 1969). It would be interesting to see whether the inverse obtains, as sociobiology would predict: greater perceptual capacity and discriminative abilities during ovulation, when the important decision "whom to copulate with" must be made.

The present consideration of female sexual strategies would not be complete without mention of the more traditional explanation for female sexual liberation. Thus, we are apparently unique among animals in practicing nonreproductive sex. In other words, human sex has been liberated from its purely reproductive function and used for a somewhat different, but not entirely unrelated purpose—the furtherance of pair bonding. This interpretation is compatible with my speculations above. Thus, the ultimate goal is similar in both cases: ensuring a lasting association between male and female. Indeed, looking at pair bonding with eyes truly jaundiced by evolutionary thinking, it becomes suspect of having adaptive significance beyond the supposed contribution of the male to successful female reproduction: the primary advantage to pair bonding from the male's viewpoint may well be that by engaging in a social system with restrictive mating, he guarantees his own sexual access, with reduced fears of dalliance by his female.

We can expect individuals of either sex to make the best of any reproductive situation, insofar as they are selected to do so. In this regard, a recent account of "female–female pairing in Western gulls" is especially interesting (Hunt and Hunt, 1977). These homosexual pairs seem to occur when there is a shortage of males, thereby leaving some females unpaired. So, these unmated females pair up, not unlike girls dancing together at a discotheque. But there is a substantial difference: these gulls are directly interested in reproducing. In three cases, one female showed a repertoire of male behavior, including mounting, attempted copulations and some courtship feeding. Furthermore, some fertile eggs were found among those incubated by female–female pairs. This is apparently the result of copulations with already-paired males. Attempts at such extramarital copulations by males are normally rejected by heterosexually paired females, but by contrast, the homosexually mated females acquiesce. From the viewpoint of evolutionary strategy, such behavior makes perfectly good sense.

Responses to Behavior of the Mate   Even after courtship and mating have occurred, individuals should still be sensitive to strategic options insofar as their inclusive fitness is influenced. For example, among kittiwake gulls, nearly two-thirds retain their mates of the previous season. But "divorce" also occurs: pairs that were not reproductively successful the previous year are three times more likely to change partners than are those that bred successfully (Coulson, 1966). The operative strategy here seems to be to jettison a mate that is found to be reproductively incompetent. Natural selection would clearly favor such a strategy, and it would be interesting to see the historic and cross-cultural correlation between marital breakdown and perceived detrements to successful reproduction. Certainly, failure to "consummate" a marriage is traditionally sufficient for annulment, and let us not forget Henry VIII!

Among species in which the male mates with a limited number of females and invests relatively heavily in parenting, we can expect mechanisms to have evolved that ensure that the offspring being reared are in fact the genetic products of the parents in question. Since the female is guaranteed to be related to her offspring (next section), we can expect such mechanisms to be especially well-developed among males. My study, "Male response to apparent female adultery in the mountain bluebird" (Barash, 1976b) is interesting in this regard. I placed models of a male near the mated female, such that the foraging male discovered an apparently adulterous couple upon his return. As predicted, the male's response was aggressive toward the model. In addition, he was aggressive toward his own female as well, so much so that in one case she was driven away and replaced by another female, with whom he successfully reared a brood. Furthermore, when this experiment was repeated later in the season (when breeding normally does not occur), the males were not at all aggressive toward their females. This variation in male "tolerance" is cued to the likelihood that they are being cuckolded by their mates and, accordingly, it is clearly adaptive. In general, I would predict a comparable pattern among human beings: since women can be entirely confident of their genetic relatedness with their offspring, they should be significantly more tolerant of adultery by their males, so long as such behavior does not increase the likelihood of losing the male's parental investment. On the other hand, males *are* evolutionarily threatened by any adultery of their mates and, therefore, a more vigorous male response to such female behavior would be predicted. To some extent then, sociobiology predicts a biological basis for the "double standard." Certainly, it would be interesting to examine the historical and cross-cultural evidence for differential responses by each sex to adultery by the other.

It is also possible for individuals to force a copulation upon an unwilling victim. For obvious anatomical reasons, rapists are invariably males. One of the best known situations concerns mallard ducks, in which rape is a remarkably common occurrence. It is interesting that rapists are most commonly unmated males, who are accordingly unable to achieve reproductive success through the more traditional channels. Females typically fight vigorously against the rapist(s) and often engage in "repulsion" behavior: a characteristic, hunched posture, combined with loud and distinctive calls. This apparently signals that she is incubating and, therefore, unlikely to be carrying fertilizable eggs (McKinney, 1975). Males typically respond to rapes of their mate by intervening aggressively against the assailant(s). Such overt physical defense is most likely when there is only a single attacker and is unlikely in cases of "gang rape." When the mated male is too late to intervene, he frequently responds by raping the female himself. Thus, normal copulation among mallards is preceeded by extensive, species-specific courtship behaviors. When males force copulations with "their" females, these normal courtship patterns are not present and the female typically struggles. Of 39 such forced copulations observed during a recent study of mallard rape (Barash, 1977b), 30 occurred within 10 minutes of a rape of the female in question. Apparently, the optimum strategy for a male whose female is being raped is to defend her, provided there are not too many attackers and provided the female is fertile at the time. Optimum strategy when the female has just *been* raped is apparently to introduce sperm as quickly as possible, to compete with those of the rapist(s). Note that successful performance of this strategy does not require any conscious assessment by either males or females of the evolutionary consequences of the behaviors in question. They are simply selected for certain behavioral responses to certain situations; in this case, genes predisposing males to defend their females and to force a copulation under the circumstances described will leave more offspring than will those that do not. Accordingly, the genes in question will spread in the population and the observed strategy will occur.

Strategies of Parenting

For many animals, reproductive responsibilities cease with fertilization. For example, oysters simply squirt their eggs or sperm into the surrounding water, after which the developing zygotes are on their own. Not so with us. We have a prolonged period of childhood dependency, necessitating an equally prolonged period of adult responsibility. Among the many reproductive decisions faced by *Homo sapiens* during its evolutionary history, we may identify:

How many offspring should be produced and how much should be invested in each?

Should they be boys or girls?

Who should take care of the children?

How much should they be defended?

What about children that are not one's own offspring?

Under what circumstances should parents and offspring be selected to disagree?

Only incomplete answers can be given here to these complex questions and many other questions might also be asked. But fortunately, the central theorem brings a degree of conceptual order to what might otherwise be chaotic diversity: parenting strategies seem above all to be designed to maximize the inclusive fitness of the individuals concerned.

Compared to many species, we produce a small number of offspring, investing relatively heavily in each. We go for quality rather than quantity—hence are "K-selected" (Pianka, 1970). Presumably, this is because our human specialization is for intelligence and modifiability of behavior. The enormous amount of learning necessary for us to become ultimately successful (in evolutionary terms, *reproducing*) individuals, requires a large investment in each of us, thus rendering the oyster strategy inadequate. In this regard, it would be interesting to follow the developing patterns of birth rates as a function of the diffusion of increasingly complex technology in Third World countries. Thus, the "demographic transition" is a phenomenon that has long puzzled demographers and sociologists: a reduction in birth rates generally follows the diffusion of Western technology. Insofar as such technology requires yet further investment in each child in order for him or her to participate in the new society, the demographic transition may reflect our own (perhaps unconscious) appreciation of the optimum investment strategy as culture change.

Surprisingly, there is even room in evolutionary theory for predictions concerning optimum production of boys or girls. Among polygynous species (with which *Homo sapiens* should be counted, in terms of our biology, if not our current cultural practices), females experience a lower variance in reproductive success than do males. Females are likely to reproduce, regardless of status, whereas males are likely either to experience enormous reproductive success (the harem-master) or none at all (peripheral bachelors). Accordingly, the optimum strategy in such species is for females preferentially to produce female offspring when they are themselves subordinate or in relatively poor physical condition and to produce male offspring when they are dominant or in relatively good conditions (Trivers and Willard, 1973). The production of females represents a conservative strategy, always likely to be successful, but unlikely to be wildly so; the production of males is more risky and likely to be either an evolutionary failure or a raging success. Therefore, females would be fittest if they placed their bets in accord with the likelihood of success.

Anthropologists might have data bearing on this—obtained either by comparing the sex ratios of offspring of low and high status families or by examining cultural practices for evidence of consistent bias in sex-specific infanticide. Certainly, it is well known that male fetuses and infants suffer a higher natural mortality than do females. This has traditionally been attributed to the biological "weakness" of males, perhaps due to the presence of the relatively noncontributor Y chromosome. But is is also possible that the explanation lies in evolutionary strategy; jettisoning of male offspring would be appropriate when female nutrition is poor so that the fetus is unlikely to get the extra "jump" that contributes to reproductive success in a male–male competitive world (Trivers and Willard, 1973).

It is essentially a behavioral "universal" that women contribute significantly more to child care than do men. On one level, this is easy to explain: like all good mammals, mothers lactate—not fathers. But why? In other words, what predisposes women to a more parental role than men? (Given that women undergo the strenuous metabolic demands of pregnancy, it seems only fair that their mates assume the role of lactation following parturition.) The sociobiologic explanation for our female bias in parenting is twofold: the fact that offspring represent a greater reproductive expenditure by their mothers than by their fathers, and the asymmetry of confidence in genetic relatedness between mothers and fathers.

If a new father abandoned his offspring, he could recoup biologically with minimum parental investment (some easily re-placed sperm), assuming of course that he could find a mate. However, a new mother would have a much more difficult time. Repetitive pregnancies are physically debilitating and if continued often enough, actually dangerous to survival. Clearly, mothers are more fit by investing in the offspring they have already produced and, whereas this may also hold for males, the evolutionary pay-off for parenting is higher for females. The other major difference between men and women, predisposing women to greater parenting duties, is the asymmetry in confidence of genetic relatedness. In a sense, women (and females of most species) enjoy an enormous advantage over males: because of internal fertiliza-tion, they can be entirely confident that the offspring on whom they lavish care are, in fact, their own. Males have no such certainty. This also predisposes females particularly to care for their young.

Among hoary marmots (large, colonial, ground-dwelling, mountain-inhabiting rodents), males normally show the general disinterest in their offspring typical of most mammals. Instead, they busy themselves with aggressive interactions with other adult males, as well as sexual overtures toward females. However, in isolated family situations, where males lack the opportunity to advance their fitness via interactions with other adults, they busy themselves significantly with their offspring. Female parental involvement is comparable in the two situations (Barash, 1975a). The consistent pattern among mammals is apparently for females to be invariably concerned with parenting, whereas males by contrast are more opportunistic and less reliable.

There is considerable evidence that parenting is strongly biased by confidence of genetic relatedness. Thus, male mountain bluebirds that form "consortships" with females who have already produced young with another male do not participate in the normal parenting duties assumed by the biological father (Power, 1975). In some cases, the genetic bias in parenting goes beyond the simple withholding of parental aid; it may actually correlate with infanticide. The best-studied case is among Asian langurs, tree-dwelling monkeys who are occasionally terrestrial. Females and juveniles typically reside in social groups, dominated by a single adult male who monopolizes the breeding. Periodically, however, he is replaced by an outside male, who necessarily is not the father of the infants within the group at the time of his take-over. Significantly, these newly ascendent males will often go about killing the infants in whom they have no genetic interest (Hrdy, 1974). This behavior, although vicious and unappealing by modern human standards, is clearly adaptive for the males concerned. By eliminating the offspring of the previous harem-master, they suffer no selective detriment themselves and may even profit by reducing competition. Significantly, females deprived of their lactating young are also induced to come into estrus more quickly, so that the new male can reproduce with them. The Bible recounts numerous instances of infants being "put to the sword"— significantly, male infants are usually so treated. Presumably, the females are spared as possible future mates. The animal example described above has been confirmed for other species as well, and its adaptive nature seems clear. Any human parallels must be indirect at best but may nonetheless be real. For example, I predict that an objective analysis of human inheritance patterns, as through legal wills, would demonstrate a significant bias toward genetically related offspring.

Human adoption is interesting in this regard, in that it seems to run counter to sociobiological prediction. However, we must remember that human social organization, as we experience it today in the Western world, is a very recent phenomenon. Anthropologists are generally agreed that more than 99% of our evolutionary history was spent in small social groups, rarely numbering more than 100. Within such bands, genetic relatedness was undoubtedly very high, thereby selecting for inclinations to care for any orphaned infant, through unconscious appeals to our inclusive fitness. Adoption of unrelated infants may in fact be nonadaptive (which is not to say it is not "good"), but it persists today because we are responding to behavioral systems instilled within us during our formative years in small social groups. Our culture changes much more quickly than our biology.

A common, perplexing child-rearing pattern among nonindustrial societies is the "avunculate," in which the mother's brother has substantial institutionalized interest in and control over his nieces and nephews—often more than over his own offspring. Such systems may in fact be consistent with evolutionary expectation if sexual promiscuity is sufficiently common in the society. Thus, an uncle is guaranteed 25% genetic similarity with his sister (common ancestry through the mother, assuming even that the fathers are different), whereas he has no guarantee of any genetic relatedness whatever to his "own" children (Alexander, 1974). On the other hand, it is interesting that matrilineal societies are characteristically unstable, perhaps because they "buck biology" in requiring an uncle to value his nephews and nieces over his offspring (van den Berghe and Barash, 1977). Inclusive fitness theory may well go a long way in cutting through the confusing morass of anthropological data concerning human family systems, demonstrating structural and functional commonalities hardly appreciated before the sociobiologic revolution (van den Berghe and Barash, 1977).

An important evolutionary component of parenting is defense against predators. We can predict that parental inclination to run risks in defense of offspring will vary with several factors including future reproductive opportunities for the parent (more risks when the parent has little to gain from refraining, i.e., a low reproductive value), the value to the offspring of such defense (more defense when it contributes more to offspring, and hence parent, reproductive success) and the likelihood that the offspring represent a "good" investment (shows characteristics indicative of future reproductive success). I compared defense of offspring among two closely related subspecies of white-crowned sparrow, a relatively common bird throughout North America. *Zonotrichia leucophrys pugetensis* inhabits long growing season environments and commonly produces at least two clutches of eggs during a season; it replaces clutches lost to predators. By contrast, *Zonotrichia leucophrys gambelli* inhabits short growing environments and never produces more than one clutch per season. Thus, *gambelli* parents would be more persistent in defending their offspring against a predator than would *pugetensis* parents. This is what I found, using a plastic model great horned owl to simulate a predator.

Similarly, evolution predicts that parents would be more inclined to defend older offspring rather than younger, since the younger individual is more easily replaced. I found exactly this pattern among certain European ground-nesting birds (Barash, 1975b) and predict that a similar situation pertains to humans. For "predator defense," substitute any of a variety of measures of parental solicitude, care and indulgence. Certainly, we need time to "grow to love" our own offspring. Once again, I am taking the evolutionary hard-line that "love" is a mechanism for achieving fitness maximization.

Another area of parenting in which evolutionary theory has been making significant contributions to nonhuman animals (which may also be applicable to humans) concerns predicted parent–offspring conflict. Robert L. Trivers (1974) has clarified the evolutionary expectations of parent–offspring conflict by pointing out that a fundamental asymmetry exists between the reproductive interests of mothers and their offspring. Thus, mothers are equally interested in the ultimate reproductive success of each of their offspring (since they are equally related to each) whereas the offspring themselves are twice as interested in their own success as in their siblings. Hence, a period of conflict is expected, when offspring seek to induce their parents (usually mothers, for reasons seen above) to invest more in them than the parents are selected to do. At some point, parents would "prefer" investing in another offspring, while the child "prefers" further investment in itself. Trivers' theory of parent–offspring conflict also predicts cross-generational disagreements concerning the duration of parental investment, as well as behavioral inclinations among siblings toward each other and toward other relatives (e. g., cousins), so long as parents and offspring do not experience relatedness to the recipient of offspring altruism or selfishness equivalent to that of the offspring in question.

Zoologist Richard Alexander has suggested (1974) that parent–offspring conflict is typically resolved in favor of the parents, largely since any genetically influenced tendency for offspring to prevail would necessarily be expressed in the offspring of those successful offspring, once they reproduce. Hence, it will carry a built-in tendency to be self-defeating. Accordingly, he suggests that "parental manipulation" of offspring is a biologically sponsored phenomenon.

Finally, even a brief consideration of human parenting strategies should include the evolutionary interpretation of a unique human characteristic, the menopause. Very few animals experience a prolonged period of nonreproductive lifespan and none that I know actually undergo a clear-cut termination of reproductive competence. Our interest in humans suggests two related questions: Why does menopause occur and why is it characteristic of women and not men? Those species that do experience a distinct old age during which reproductive competence is often diminished if not extinguished, are typically those that are highly intelligent and live in social groups—e.g., primates, elephants and possibly whales. This suggests that the selective advantage for survival into old age may be the accumulated store of wisdom that the "elderly" can contribute to younger members. Among humans, this wisdom may especially concern child-rearing. With the increasing frailty of old age, the disadvantages of reproducing increase as well. And of course, these disadvantages fall almost entirely upon women.

Of Morality and the Future Sociobiology is a controversial field of research to some extent because of its perceived political implications. Thus, some elements have severely criticized it for being elitist, racist, sexist and so forth. I have treated these objections elsewhere (Barash, 1977a) and will not deal extensively with them here.

In summary, my response to sociobiology's political critics is the following: (1) Sociobiology posits genetic *influence* on behavior, not genetic *determinism;* there is an enormous difference (Dobzhansky, 1976). (2) Perhaps any approach that gives some credence to genetics insofar as behavior is concerned runs the risk of being misconstrued as racist; however, by emphasizing the possibilities for cross-cultural universals indicating the biological similarity of all *Homo sapiens,* sociobiology is instead a cogent *antidote* for racism. (3) Sociobiology does not deny the role of environmental factors in shaping human behavior—indeed, it is less guilty of tunnel vision than is social science, with its usual disregard of "human nature." (4) Sociobiology is indeed "sexist" if sexism implies consideration of male–female differences in behavior. However, it does not consider either type of behavior pattern as somehow "better"; both are making the most of the evolutionary opportunities open to them. (5) It does not imply support for the *status quo,* in fact quite the opposite. Although the existence of a phenotype is *de facto* evidence that it is at least minimally adaptive, such patterns need not be in any way the "best of all possible worlds." In fact, evolution is opportunistic (Dobzhansky, 1951), constantly preferring immediate, short-term success over long-term adaptation. Hence, extinction. There is no moral judgement implied in evolutionary thinking: what is, is. This is not to say that there could not be something better. (6) In seeking to describe and understand behavior in its unique way, sociobiology does not in any way endorse or legitimize what it finds—just as the epidemiologist does not advocate the virus under study.

Finally, concern with productive strategies in the context of the evolution of human social behavior demands some attention to our future as a species, insofar as our reproduction influences this future. And that it does. If there is any evolutionary imperative shared by all living things, it is the imperative: Thou Shalt Reproduce. And yet, the future of *Homo sapiens* is seriously imperiled by our growing numbers. We are the only species on Earth capable of making decisions based on our perception of the "good of the species." Contrary to what is commonly believed, evolution operates via the differential reproduction of *individuals,* with each selected to maximize his or her inclusive fitness. Genes are quintessentially selfish (Dawkins, 1976), exquisitely designed programs for their own perpetuation and promulgation. Hence, the Evolutionary Imperative. We experience it and we are endangering ourselves (and our fellow creatures) by virtue of it. And yet, we alone of all species are capable of consciously resisting it, of deciding to value other considerations over our genetically mediated needs, our world over our impulses. Possibly, we can escape from the biological tyranny to which all other species are subject. In fact, we are already escaping vis-à-vis modifications in our criteria for mate selection, role differentiation between men and women, and numerous other aspects of our increasingly liberated behavior. Should we say "NO" to excessive reproduction and defy biology by changing our focus from individual, genetically mediated selfishness to a perspective encompassing the group, species, ecosystem and planet? Much depends on the answer.

Postscript   Since this chapter was originally written, there have been numerous developments relating to the sociobiology of reproductive strategies. Following is a brief summary: An excellent new primer has appeared (Daly and Wilson, 1978). I have written a nontechnical treatment of human sociobiology (Barash, 1979a). My research described earlier concerning mate selection in damselfishes and parental defense in white-crowned sparrows has been published (Barash, 1979b) in book form along with many other relevant studies of both animals and humans. A major study relating altruistic behavior among Belding's ground squirrels to kin selection has also appeared (Sherman, 1977), along with an entire new journal devoted to human ethology and sociobiology (*Ethology and Sociobiology*, published by Elsevier). A new book by Pierre van den Berghe (1979) cogently interprets human family systems in sociobiologic perspective. And a recent volume edited by Chagnon and Irons (1979) provides a wealth of theory and data concerning human reproductive strategies, covering such varied topics as mate competition, the avunculate, the extent to which cultural success parallels biological success, sex-preferential infanticide in stratified societies, and correlations of polygyny with degree of sexual dimorphism. This is only a small sample; a lot has happened, is happening and seems certain to continue.

References   Abele, L. G., and Gilchrist, S. 1977. Homosexual rape and sexual selection in Acanthocephalan worms. *Science* 197: 81–83.

Alexander, R. D. 1974. The evolution of social behavior. *Annual Review of Ecology and Systematics* 5: 325–383.

Allen, L. et al. 1976. Sociobiology—another biological determinism. *BioScience* 26: 182–186.

Barash, D. P. 1975a. Evolutionary aspects of parental behavior: the distraction of behavior of the alpine accentor, *Preunella collaris. Wilson Bulletin* 87: 367–373.

——. 1975b. Ecology of paternal behavior in the hoary marmot (*Marmota caligata*): An evolutionary interpretation. *Journal of Mammalogy* 56: 612–615.

——. 1976a. Some evolutionary aspects of parental behavior in animals and man. *American Journal of Psychology* 89: 195–217.

——. 1976b. The male response to apparent female adultery in the mountain bluebird, *Sialia currocoides*: An evolutionary interpretation. *The American Naturalist* 110: 1097–1101.

——. 1977a. *Sociobiology and Behavior.* New York: Elsevier.

——. 1977b. Sociobiology of rape in mallards (*Anas platyrhynchos*): Responses of the mated male. *Science* 197: 788–789.

———. 1979a. *The Whisperings Within*. New York: Harper & Row.

———. 1979b. Predictive sociobiology: Mate selection in damselfishes and parental defense in white-crowned sparrows. In G. Barlow and J. Silverberg (eds.) *Sociobiology: Beyond Nature/Nurture?*. AAAS Special Publication #35, Boulder, CO: Westview Press.

Blake, J. 1974. The changing status of women in developed countries. *Scientific American* 231: 136–147.

Chagnon, N., and Irons, W. 1979. *Evolutionary Biology and Human Social Behavior: An Anthropological Perspective*. No. Scituate, MA: Duxbury.

Coulson, J. C. 1966. The influence of the pair-bond and age on the breeding biology of the kittiwake gull, *Rissa tridactyla*. *Journal of Animal Ecology* 35: 269–279.

Cox, C. R., and LeBoeuf, B. J. 1977. Female incitation of male competition: A mechanism in sexual selection. *The American Naturalist* 111: 317–335.

Daly, M., and Wilson, M. 1978. *Sex, Evolution and Behavior*. No. Scituate, MA: Duxbury.

Dawkins, R. 1976. *The Selfish Gene*. Oxford: Oxford University Press.

Dobzhansky, T. 1951. *Genetics and the Origin of Species*. New York: Columbia University Press.

———. 1976. The myths of genetic predestination and of *tabula rasa*. *Perspectives in Biology and Medicine* 19: 156–170.

Emlen, S. T., and Oring, L. W. 1977. Ecology, sexual selection, and evolution of mating systems. *Science* 197: 215–223.

Erhman, L., and Parson, P.A. 1976. *The Genetics of Behavior*. Sunderland, MA: Sinnauer Associates.

Eibl-Eibesfeldt, I. 1975. *Ethology, the Biology of Behaviour*. New York: Holt, Rinehart and Winston.

Erickson, C. J., and Zenone, P. G. 1976. Courtship differences in male ring doves: Avoidance of cuckoldry? *Science* 192: 1353–1354.

Hamilton, W. D. 1964. The genetical theory of social behaviour: I. and II. *Journal of Theoretical Biology* 7: 1–52.

Hinde, R. A. 1970. *Animal Behaviour: A Synthesis of Ethology and Comparative Psychology*. New York: McGraw-Hill.

Hinde, R. A., and Stevenson-Hinde, J. 1973. *Constraints on Learning*. New York: Academic Press.

Hrdy, S. B. 1974. Male–male competition and infanticide among the langurs (*Presbytis entellus*) of Abu, Rajasthan. *Folia Primatologica* 22: 19–58.

Hunt, G. L., and Hunt, M. W. 1977. Female–female pairing in Western gulls (*Larus occidentalis*) in southern California. *Science* 196: 1466–1467.

Huxley, J. S. 1938. The present standing of the theory of sexual selection. In G. de Beer (ed.) *Evolution: Essays of Aspects of Evolutionary Biology Presented to Professor E. S. Goodrich on His Seventieth Birthday*, pp. 11–42. Oxford: Clarendon Press.

Koppell, B. S., et al. 1969. Variations in some measures of arousal during the menstual cycle. *Journal of Nervous and Mental Disease* 148: 180–187.

Kurland, B. S. 1977. *Kin Selection in the Japanese Monkey*. New York: S. Karger.

LeMagnen, J. 1953. L'olfaction: le fonctionnement olfactive et son intervention dans les regulations psychophysiologiques. *Journal de Physiologie* (Paris) 45: 285–322.

Maynard Smith, J., and Ridpath, M. G. 1972. Wife-sharing in the Tasmanian native hen, Tribonyx mortierii: A case of kin selection? *The American Naturalist* 106: 447–452.

McKinney, F. 1975. The evolution of duck displays. In G. Baerends et al. (eds.) *Function and Evolution in Behaviour*, pp. 331–349. London: Oxford University Press.

Michael, R. P., and Zumpe, D. 1970. Rhythmic changes in the copulatory frequency of rhesus monkeys in relation to the menstrual cycle and a comparison with the human cycle. *Journal of Reproduction and Fertility* 21: 199–201.

Orians, G. H. 1969. On the evolution of mating systems in birds and mammals. *The American Naturalist* 103: 589–603.

Pianka, E. 1970. On *r*- and *K*-selection. *The American Naturalist* 104: 292–297.

Power, H. W. 1975. Mountain bluebirds: Experimental evidence against altruism. *Science* 189: 142–143.

Selander, R. K. 1965. On mating systems and sexual selection. *The American Naturalist* 99: 129–140.

Sherman, P. 1977. Nepotism and the evolution of alarm calls. *Science* 197: 1246–1253.

Thornhill, R. 1976. Sexual selection and paternal investment in insects. *The American Naturalist* 110: 153–163.

Trivers, R. L. 1972. Parental investment and sexual selection. In B. Campbell (ed.) *Sexual Selection and the Descent of Man*, pp. 136–179. Chicago: Aldine.

———. 1974. Parent–offspring conflict. *American Zoologist* 14: 249–264.

Trivers, R. L., and Willard, D. E. 1973. Natural selection of parental ability to vary the sex ratio of offspring. *Science* 179: 90–92.

van den Berghe, P. 1975. *Man in Society*. New York: Elsevier.

———. 1979. *Human Family Systems*. New York: Elsevier.

van den Berghe, P., and Barash, D. P. 1977. Inclusive fitness theory and human family structure. *American Anthropologist* 79: 809–823.

Whitney, G. 1976. Genetic substrates for the initial evolution of human sociality. I. Sex chromosome mechanisms. *The American Naturalist* 110: 867–875.

Wiley, R. H. 1973. Territoriality and nonrandom mating in sage grouse, *Centrocercus urophasianus*. *Animal Behavior Monographs* 6: 85–169.

West-Eberhard, M. J. 1975. The evolution of social behavior by kin selection. *Quarterly Review of Biology* 50: 1–33.

Williams, G. C. 1966. *Adaptation and Natural Selection*. Princeton: Princeton University Press.

Wilson, E. O. 1975. *Sociobiology: The New Synthesis*. Cambridge: Belknap/Harvard University Press.

———. 1976. Academic vigilantism and the political significance of sociobiology. *BioScience* 26: 183–190.

Human Aggression as a Biological Adaptation

Gerald Borgia

9

Controversy has surrounded the use of evolutionary theory to study human behavior since Darwin's time. Much of the interest in evolution waned with rejection of the social-Darwinist concept championed by Spencer (1910). Not long ago Lorenz (1966) and Ardrey (1966) attempted to revive interest in the important problem of how evolution influences human behavior with books that focused on human aggression. Among the highly controversial ideas these authors suggested was that strong genetically inherited tendencies exist which cause controlled aggression in man. Even though numerous prominent biologists and social behaviorists rejected their approach (Montagu, 1968), the absence of a comprehensive alternative has caused many, especially those outside biology, to view Lorenz and Ardrey's work as the biological view and, generally, to reject both this approach and more recent evolutionary models.

Current attempts of evolutionary biologists to use natural selection to understand human social behavior, labeled by Wilson (1975) as sociobiology, are based on real advances in our understanding of evolution, and hold great promise in providing answers to questions about how patterns of human behavior are determined. However, there has been relatively little interest in using these new techniques to study human aggression. This is unfortunate because the central role played by aggression in models of classical ethology makes this topic especially suitable to contrast these two approaches to the study of behavior.

For those unfamiliar with recent advances in evolutionary theory, such a comparison would help dispel the belief that new models of social behavior are renewed versions of refuted views that have undergone some minor cosmetic changes (Lewontin, 1977). It is my intention to provide such a comparison here but first I shall review some of the advances that have led to different predictions about human behavior.

Predictions About Human Behavior

Use of inclusive fitness theory to predict individual and group behavior. This new approach to the understanding of behavior focuses on the work of Hamilton (1964). In his inclusive fitness model Hamilton argues that natural selection has caused every organism to behave in ways that historically have tended to maximize the representation of its genes in subsequent generations. He concludes that individuals will attempt to enhance the production of their own offspring and those of relatives, with aid distributed according to the degree of genetic relatedness to the donor. This theory has been significant in resolving Darwin's (1871) long-standing problem of explaining the evolution of so-called altruistic behaviors.

Focus on the individual as the primary unit of selection. Lack (1954) and Williams (1966) contributed to our understanding of evolutionary theory by pointing out that selection, operating on individual differences, seems to form the basis for the bulk of biological adaptation. This insight suggests the relative unimportance of group selection as a creative force in the production of adaptations.

Their observation was vital in interpreting behavior because it implied that evolution of group-beneficial characters, although costly to individuals, is unlikely to happen because of the relatively low extinction rates of groups, and because intergroup movements tend to reduce differences between groups. However, there has been some disagreement about the significance of Williams' conclusions. Wilson (1975) refers to the William's "fallacy" and suggests that group selection may be an important force affecting the evolution of adaptations. While Wilson's emphasis seems largely in error [see below, and Alexander and Borgia (1978)] it is important to point out that evolutionary biologists differ in how they interpret theoretical developments and, as is expected from any science, this affects their predictions.

Individuals are assumed to be highly adapted in their natural environment. Behavioral variants are expected to occur with sufficient frequency, and the pressures of natural selection are strong enough to cause most organisms to execute that which they need to do within reasonable limits of their physical abilities. This selectionist approach was used by Fisher (1930) in models for the evolution of sex, and forms the basis for the notion of *evolutionary stable strategies* developed by Maynard Smith and Price (1973). Obviously this assumption is just a starting point for the formation of hypotheses. However, it provides a good estimate of the causes of individual action. This approach is commonly overlooked in many ethological models (see below) that emphasize behavior as acting to meet needs created by imprecise physiological mechanisms. For example, Eibl-Eibesfeldt (1971, p. 69) states that animals ". . . actively seek out a releasing stimulus situation which will permit them to work off the fighting drive."

The assumption of low levels of adaptation implied that these earlier models were due to an imprecise understanding of evolutionary theory and did not allow biologists to make valid predictions. However, with recent advances in theory such predictions should be more accurate and substantiated more often. Assuming a high level of adaptation suggests that behaviors will represent the real needs of individuals. Behaviors can then be predicted by anticipating the needs of the organism under study. This knowledge of the habits of an organism can lead to predictions of behaviors under a broad range of conditions of population density, resource availability (Verner, 1964) or other factors likely to affect its behavior.

Alexander (1975) argues that traditional evolutionary studies based on phylogenetic comparisons between species have limited value as organisms acquire different needs, even though they may retain similarity in the form of their behavior. By contrast, a model that assumes a high level of individual adaptation allows valid comparisons even among species with very different phylogenetic histories.

Predictions about behavior are derived from evolutionary theory. Comparisons among groups are used to validate a general theory that is derived from, and consistent with, assumptions of how natural selection operates. Although this is implicit in most recent evolutionary models, it is not often recognized by critics of these models (Lewontin, 1977; Gould, 1977), who appear unable to discern the distinction between this approach and those in which predictions are made without regard to how natural selection might produce adaptations.

Recent advances in our understanding of natural selection provide a robust theory that has produced important changes in how we view the process of adaptation. These important changes have led to the development of a variety of novel hypotheses to explain behaviors. The power of selection theory to enhance our understanding of adaptation has led some (Dawkins, 1976) to assume the correctness of certain explanations of behavior without adequate tests. As in any other scientific discipline, before such models can be accepted as correct, they must be evaluated. Consistency with modern selection theory provides an important criterion for reviewing explanations of behavior, but additional tests are necessary (especially when there are several hypotheses which show this consistency) before we can be reasonably confident that a particular hypothesis provides a correct interpretation of the adaptive value of a behavior.

At times evolutionary hypotheses are not amenable to unambiguous tests because of the absence of variants in existing species or the presence of high economic or social costs; but even in these cases, evolutionary hypotheses may be valuable. Requiring the criterion of consistency with the evolutionary paradigm allows us to eliminate a great number of hypotheses concerning the origins of specific behaviors. When there are few reasonable remaining explanations, it is more likely that one of these is correct. It should not be assumed that such an approach accepts a hypothesis as correct based on consistency and that further tests are not required; rather, the view is that a hypothesis has been established that may be valuable in designing future courses of action. For example, in human groups the desire for an immediate solution may prompt us to assume a particular course of social action, often with little evidence that it will produce the desired result. A well-considered evolutionary hypothesis, although not tested, may yield a more accurate description of the costs and the likelihood of achieving this or other possible outcomes.

A General Model of Aggressive Behavior

Lorenz (1966) provided no precise model of how natural selection produced biological adaptations such as aggression. His explanations of behavior often suggested species-level benefits from individual behavior with little regard for the necessity of effective reproductive competition of an individual with his conspecifics (Holloway, 1968). In terms of the advantage to the species, within-species aggression must have appeared to conflict with an ideal pattern of adaptation. He was then forced to resolve the paradox emanating from the apparent discrepancy between patterns of animal behavior and the prevailing theory. Perhaps this problem was instrumental in his emphasis on the study of intraspecific aggression—a set of behaviors that to him must have appeared an anomaly. Lorenz shared with others his inability to determine the level at which natural selection operates. Darwin's (1871) inability to resolve this problem led him to separate natural selection, in which individual gains are generally good for the species, from sexual selection, a process in which individual acts often appear detrimental to the species.

Development of the inclusive fitness model and resolution of the problem of levels of selection resolved the paradox that has stifled the effective application of evolutionary theory. This, in turn, removed much of the mystery and, consequently, much of the interest that was inherent in the study of aggression. The latter may also account for the obvious absence of emphasis on the study of aggression with the advent of sociobiology.

A model of aggression in which individuals are programmed to maximize what Hamilton (1964) called their *inclusive fitness*, predicts that individuals will use aggression to enhance their own fitness and, where appropriate, that of their relatives. Any group or species advantage, according to the version of the model used here, will be considered (unless otherwise noted) a by-product of reproductively selfish acts by individuals. Yet within this limitation, as we will see below, the model permits complex interactions among individuals either acting alone or in coalitions. As a result, it may yield what appear to be high levels of group cohesion even among nonrelatives.

In its common usage, aggression is a physical attack by one individual that is designed to cause harm to another (Berkowitz, 1962; Hinde, 1974). Though definitions vary to some extent, there is general agreement on the critical point that a specific act need not be harmful but, rather, that it may be a product of adaptive behavior designed to cause harm. Nonphysical attacks (e.g., verbal or written) have sometimes been included in the definition of aggression, but such behavior seems better categorized as part of a general class of behaviors related to overt competition.

According to a view based on the selective retention of heritable beneficial effects, aggressive attacks are initiated to resolve real or anticipated conflicts in favor of the attacker. Such attacks are used to gain access to scarce resources, e.g., food, foraging sites, mates and refugia (Brown and Orians, 1970). Harming the victim is rarely the ultimate interest of the attacker but, for most species, attacks are the most economical means of taking control of a scarce item. Presumably, without the attack the victim would fail to relinquish or would otherwise limit the aggressor's ability to use the resource in question or, at least, more expensive forms of coercion would be needed. For attacks to be effective, real or anticipated harm to the victim must represent an actual decrement in the reproductive value of a target individual. This decrease in fitness must be greater than that resulting from relinquishing the contested resource (Parker, 1974).

Aggression and Competition

Although physical acts of aggression have been closely studied for many years by behaviorists, the long-term consequences have been more fully considered by ecologists. Within this ecological scheme, aggression is closely related to competition which, with cooperation, represents one of the two fundamental forms of social interaction. Competition is commonly subdivided into two types: scramble and contest competition (Nicholson, 1957). *Scramble competition* involves collection of resources without overt attempts to interfere with another's ability to accrue them. *Contest competition* involves exclusion of potential competitors from a limited resource. When contest competition is possible, aggression is the primary means by which resource control is achieved. Brown (1964) and Borgia (1979a) point out that scramble competition is possible under any condition of resource distribution and that it is possible for overt competition to occur where conditions are suitable for either form of competition.

Resource control is achieved by aggression through direct physical harm to victims, or by indirect actions in which the intention to attack (by a dominant or well-armed individual) is advertised and the less-endowed flees or suffers the consequences. Intention movements and threats function to the advantage of both receiver and sender because the former is able to escape the cost of being attacked while the latter can control access to the resource without the expense of an attack. Such mechanisms are most effective when (1) relative strengths of individuals can be judged by inexpensive means such as visual assessment of physical characteristics (Maynard Smith and Price, 1973; Parker, 1974); and (2) past interactions allow individuals to predict the outcomes of future encounters. Without this type of information, where the advertiser's relative strength and willingness to attack are communicated, threats or intention signals are likely to be of little value.

Different types of aggression, discussed by Moyer (1976) and others, fit the category of attempts to influence conflicts between competitors to one's own advantage. Although such a definition may not apply to such acts as infanticide and predation, their relationships can be explained. With respect to infanticide, it is likely that parents and offspring, who have similar but nonidentical reproductive interests, are in conflict over the utility of that offspring's survival (Trivers, 1974). This lack of parental interest may be due to a birth defect in the child or closeness in age to another unweaned child (Dickeman, 1975) or even to the fact that the child is not of the desired sex (Borgia, 1979b; Divale, 1972). A conflict exists between the child who is programmed to survive and a parent whose overall reproduction will be raised if the child is killed. Being in a position of power, the parent is able to resolve the conflict in her own favor (Alexander, 1974). As for predation, it can be viewed as extreme interspecific competition, wherein the net result is the aggressor's gain at the expense of the target.

Success for the aggressor in resource-based contests rarely results in the death of the target. Even though the victim's death might benefit the aggressor, attacks of a more limited nature often represent the best strategy for maximizing access to resources while minimizing risks and energetic cost. This contrasts with the examples given above in which death of the target is the only result that gives a positive payoff for aggression. We might then assume that the rarity of intraspecific killing noted by Lorenz (1966) must be due to its high cost. Killing will only occur when it is inexpensive relative to other means of excluding competitors, and if it lowers the long-term net costs to the attacker. Obviously there are mitigating circumstances—for instance, when a potential target is a close relative. For humans, group-imposed sanctions against murder raise the cost of life-threatening attacks. Aggressors must weigh these added costs before initiating an attack.

Evidence for Aggression as an Adaptation

Rigorous application of the inclusive fitness model to the study of aggression is still new and many of the tests necessary to evaluate such interactions have not yet been developed. However, there are data available that suggest this approach is valid.

The predictions about human aggressive behavior discussed here are a simple extension of Hamilton's inclusive fitness model.

Therefore, evidence in support of his model, even if not related to aggression, gives some support to these predictions. This evidence is convincing and reviewed elsewhere (Barash, 1977; Hamilton, 1964; Wilson, 1975).

Direct support for our aggression hypothesis is, of course, more convincing. Relevant data testing this hypothesis has been obtained from animal and human studies. Among numerous species of animals, genetic relatives are commonly involved in group-defense of core areas. This has been most evident in social insects [reviewed in Wilson (1973)], but it is also common in mammals (Schaller, 1972) and birds [(Ritter, 1938; Woolfenden, 1975) and as reviewed by Brown (1978)]. Among lions (Schaller, 1972) and macaques (Massey, 1977) close relatives are also often associated in alliances for within-group contests. The tendency for individuals to be aggressive only in situations that are likely to aid in their survival and reproduction provides further evidence.

Aggression is most common in contests of defensible rare items. Among many temperate birds, for example, territories are established by aggressive encounters only during the breeding season when localized feeding areas are needed in caring for young. In cases in which territories are held through the nonbreeding season, there is good reason to expect that local control of resources is important. For instance, acorn woodpecker groups hold territories that contain stored supplies (Ritter, 1938). Even in situations in which aggression is not used in the direct control of resources, as in the case of breeding leks (Robel, 1966), males aggregate and fight at specific times of the year, apparently to gain mating positions favored by females. Reduction in the amount of available resources tends to change patterns of aggressive behavior, as shown in field observations (Sale, 1972) and experiments (Borgia, 1979a). Attacks are directed at individuals (of the same or different species) who threaten to use valuable resources. This suggests that the tendency to attack may be a function of the age of the intruding individual. Young immature animals, who are not sexual competitors, are rarely attacked by or attack adults. Aggression among sexually mature individuals appears to be more common (Howard, 1977).

General patterns of human behavior are also consistent with the inclusive fitness model, for example, as in the tendency for relatives to form alliances. Chagnon (1968) states that brothers support sisters in times of strife. Also, marriage alliances have been reported throughout history, as have specific attempts to control aid between relatives through laws against nepotism (Darlington, 1969).

A primary motivation for crime is selfish gain, and it is this fact that allows police investigators to be surprisingly effective in capturing criminals. In attempts to solve crimes one of the first steps is to identify individuals who would profit most among those able to carry out the crime. For white collar crime, companies that violate laws are most commonly among marginal and declining firms, i.e., those least likely to persist without law violations (Lane,

1953). Among individuals, those with low incomes, low access to jobs and who have had a minimal education (generally of a lower socioeconomic level) are involved more often in crime than those who, because of superior economic conditions, would gain relatively less. Numerous studies have measured socioeconomic differences and have related these to differences in crime rate (Fergusson et al., 1975; Meadnka and Hill, 1976; Vinson and Homel, 1975). Also, differences in crime rates among racial groups are likely to be a function of differences in economic well-being. Federal Bureau of Investigation crime reports [see Fergusson et al. (1975)] show significantly higher per capita ($\times 1000$) violent and property crime among blacks (6.28 and 17.65, respectively) and native Americans (3.95 and 13.8) than whites (.896 and 5.37).

Other patterns which suggest a selfish basis to relevant social behavior include the formulation of laws that coincide with the interests of those who formulate them—hence, the common desire for participation in the rule-making process. Also, punishment of law violators commonly involves aggression, even if in all other circumstances within-group aggression is forbidden.

Abuse of offspring appears to be more common when individuals caring for them are not relatives. For example, in animals, males taking over harems kill the young sired by other males [lions: Schaller (1972); langurs: Sugiyama (1967); Hrdy (1977)] and in humans, conquering warriors kill offspring of their enemies [the biblical description in Deuteronomy; Parsons (1906); Darlington (1969)]. Daly and Wilson (1980) report a higher incidence of battered children in homes with a foster parent than those in which both biological parents are present. Infanticide of deformed children—those most likely to be poor candidates for future investment—appears to be common in many societies (Alexander, 1974; Dickeman, 1975; Parsons, 1906). Female-preferential infanticide is common in groups that place a high value on males, who as warriors (Divale, 1972) provide all of the defense for their family (Borgia, 1979b).

Reanalysis of Other Behavioral Models

The common ethological concept of aggression implies that individuals are not well adapted for maximizing their own fitness. This conception may have resulted from the use of imprecise theory in building models of behavior. Confusion may have arisen as to the level (individual or group) at which the behavior should be adaptive and resulted in an inability to build general predictive models (Alexander, 1975). Therefore, biologists assumed that a low level of adaptation existed. Recent advances in theory contradict this assumption. The importance of these advances can be seen when analyzing the function of "ritualized" aggression in courtship displays. Wynne-Edwards (1962), among others, has noticed the frequent incorporation of what appears to be aggression in mating displays. Some ethologists speculate that aggressiveness in males is advantageous when directed at other males, but difficult to control in the presence of females. Thus, females supposedly have evolved ritualized displays to control the male's behavior and allow safe and successful mating. Problems with these control mechanisms may exist, but it is unlikely that these difficulties have affected significantly the patterns of male behavior. Assuming a higher level of adaptation, it is likely that the appearance of aggressive components in courtship displays is not simply a product of the compromise between a male's need to hold valued territories and to inseminate females successfully. Aggressive components of courtship may have been favored by natural selection as signals of general vigor and the ability to hold territory (Borgia, 1979a). For example, aggressive displays by a subordinate male would soon attract a dominant male; uninterrupted displays would indicate to the female that the courting male is dominant and not a pretender. Presumably females that can discriminate in this way have greater reproductive success and, as a result of this type of preference, aggressive displays have become part of male courtship behavior.

A similar type of analysis could be made for other relevant hypotheses concerning motivation, especially the frustration–aggression hypothesis (Dollard et al., 1939; Miller, 1941), the Lorenz–Tinbergen hydraulic model (Lorenz, 1950), and the numerous variations of those models [reviewed by Kaufmann, (1970)]. These concepts are some of the few attempts to describe the motivation of behavior and may be summarized in the following way: Motivational or action-specific energy causes individuals to carry out daily tasks required for normal life functions. When an individual is unable to function, or if frustrated, these energies build up, resulting in a high level of anxiety. For instance, anxiety might build up when a noxious stimulus dictates a response to remove the source of that stimulus but, for some reason, the organism is unable to do so. High levels of anxiety are considered not only uncomfortable but harmful. Cathartic behaviors allow a release of anxiety by expenditure of accumulated motivational energies.

The hydraulic model has been questioned for several reasons. These include the failure to find any physical analogues of the processes described, and the fact that cathartic events may sometimes increase the probability of future aggression rather than decrease the probability as predicted by the model (Scott, 1958; Kenny, 1953; DeCharms and Wilkins, 1963; Sipes, 1975). Moreover, this model assumes a surprisingly low level of adaptation. For example, it is not clear why action-specific energies should be released as aggression (assuming that they need to be released) instead of in a form less likely to bring harm to the bearer. Thus, because there is limited support for these highly mechanistic models, and because behaviors can be explained more simply by assuming high levels of adaptation, the hydraulic model and its derivatives are of little value. Nevertheless, even with the general inadequacy of the hydraulic model, its legacies remain. Low levels of adaptation are assumed and such notions as those of displacement behaviors (Tinbergen, 1952) remain widely accepted.

Displacement behaviors are those that are said to occur out of context with no apparent direct function and which are hypothesized to reduce the harmful accumulation of activation energies. A common example is an attack by an individual of intermediate rank on an inanimate object or on an individual of lower status. This occurs after the attacker himself has been attacked by a more dominant individual. Yet adaptive alternatives to displacement behaviors are rarely considered. For instance, the initial attack, in the pattern of interactions described above, might suggest to onlookers that the dominant male sensed vulnerability in the attackee, or even that the attackee was harmed and is now more susceptible to displacement from his position in a hierarchy. In either event, rapid attack on a nearby individual should signal that no such vulnerability exists, at least not at a level that would allow easy displacement. By initiating an attack of so-called displacement, the individual under scrutiny is able to choose when and whom he attacks, thereby minimizing the costs in a display of strength and discouraging potential aggressive acts by the onlookers.

Displacement has been described as a mechanism to allow an individual to restore self-esteem after attack (White and Lippitt, 1960). However, attacks for the primary function of restoring self-esteem seem to be an expensive method for simply altering a mental state. Self-esteem may really function as a proximate device allowing conscious individuals to recognize their limitations. Perhaps it causes them to avoid entering into costly behaviors when there is a low probability of success or, alternatively, to be aggressive and gain high self-esteem with success in attacks. Similar arguments may be developed for the role of other emotions as mechanisms for unconscious evaluation or as motivators of essential behaviors.

An adaptive explanation for displacement behavior would seem to be of little value if inanimate objects are attacked. Yet even such "misdirected" behaviors, if common, may represent signals of intent or strategic moves in contests. Yet, such alternative explanations are infrequently considered or tested.

In fields apart from ethology these exists a variety of other models of human behavior. Among these are Freud's model of death wish (Thanatos), the desire for self-destruction. This makes little sense because there is no obvious mechanism by which natural selection could favor the existence of a death wish within any organism if its only apparent function is to cause self-destruction. Such tendencies might arise as an artifact of selection for other behavior, but a lack of this evidence (or evidence for even the existence of such a behavioral tendency) suggests this model is false.

Freud's other noted contribution to the study of aggression, the Oedipal complex, can be summarized as follows: Aggression and warfare are products of sexual instincts frustrated during childhood. A father and son are in sexual competition for the mother, and the less powerful boy learns to direct aggression away from his father and accept substitutes for his mother. Girls are faced with another kind of childhood problem when they discover that they have no penis. This discovery is claimed to lead them to a love for men based on a desire to share a penis, and an envy of men because they want their own penises. Oedipal love and competition with the father for the mother's affections are believed to be the cause of boys' attachment to their mother; girls develop strong ties with their father because of penis envy and feel that their mother castrated them.

The Freudian approach is mechanistic and does not deal with the possible adaptive significance of supposed Oedipal relationships. These relationships are seen to be ends in themselves rather than to serve the genetic interests of their bearers. The almost universal incest restriction that functions among close relatives to reduce biological costs of inbreeding—the common desire for sons and the paternal desire to provide sons with inheritance and wives—obviates any serious suggestion of instinctive competition between fathers and sons, especially for the son's mother.

Freud wanted to explain human behavior, such as aggression by males, female desire for males, and male domination of women, so he developed his Oedipal hypothesis. It has no theoretical basis from which predictions of male and female behavior are derived. Yet the cross-cultural evidence that many proponents use to support this concept is based on the same empirical observations Freud used to develop his hypothesis, e.g., that males of different generations compete for females. For example, Walsh and Scandalis (1975) state:

The cultural institution of the "pusher" in Murgin society overtly exemplifies the hostility toward young males of the father figure, who actively "pushed" the boy into combat, and possible maiming and death. This behavior demonstrates the murderous hostility of the father generation for the son generation. The only acceptable and possible genetic explanation for this behavior is that it must have its origin in Oedipal rivalry.

However, this is not a real test of Oedipal rivalry because it only reaffirms Freud's observation that there is intergenerational conflict among males. There is no attempt to explain the ultimate cause of these conflicts and, quite contrary to these authors' suggestion, there is another more reasonable hypothesis. It is that men at the peak of their reproductive potential would rather have someone else fight their fights, thereby allowing them to avoid injury and death. Males of the younger generation are convenient to use as warriors, but they could be replaced by slaves or mercenaries. The older males are concerned primarily with how well these younger males will fight—not with a need to dominate their sons.

Behavioral theorists claim that much of human behavior can be defined in terms of the controls imposed by their social environment. Larsen (1976) claims that humans act to minimize "social cost." This view is similar to what Pettigrew (1958) calls "conformity to socio-cultural norms," i.e., individual behavior responding to norms developed by the group. Larsen suggests that within stable social groups individuals follow behavioral pathways that conform to the rules of the group and thereby avoid penalties. He does not, however, describe how social groups develop rules for individual behavior and how variations in individual behavior within a group come to exist. In addition, his hypothesis, like Kaufmann's (1970) aggression–altruism model and other utility models (Edwards, 1954; Siegel, 1960; Siegel and Foriaker, 1960) focuses on utility to the individual actor, but it only vaguely defines what is meant by utility.

Without an adequate definition of utility we cannot easily predict who is supposed to benefit from the actor's behavior—the actor, a small set of other individuals, or the group—or what the utilitarian objectives are and how to weigh the outcomes of different acts. Thus, unless utility is carefully defined, these models can be used to explain almost any behavior by merely assigning it to a utilitarian value. By restricting considerations of utility to the maximizing of inclusive fitness, as was proposed by Hamilton (1964), evolutionarily advantageous choices can be unambiguously specified and evaluated. Comparisons between behaviors can then be made on a common basis—the effects of a behavior on an organism's fitness.

Control of Aggression

Humans characteristically live in groups; thus any analysis of human aggression requires study of interactions within and among groups. Reasons for grouping include the need for family units to care for dependent offspring, enhanced protection from attacks by other individuals or groups, and economic dependence among group members. Typically, groups prohibit intragroup aggression but encourage advantageous attacks on other groups (Davie, 1929). This dichotomy appears to enhance the unity of the group and, simultaneously, to make it more effective as a unit operating against competitors. This behavior may arise either from selection favoring groups in which individuals refrain from intragroup hostility, or through the development of social controls within groups that make aggressive acts unprofitable.

Social Control of Aggression

Rules for behavior are in evidence in every social group and individuals found to violate these rules are generally punished. Aggression against other group members commonly results in punishment that may be carried out by a designated official, or left to the individual who is harmed, or left to those who represent him (Otterbein, 1970). In order to be effective, punishments must be harmful to the fitness of the violator and involve physical, economic or social costs.

The type of rules that are made are dependent on who makes and enforces them. In groups where leaders possess unrestricted power and are not in danger of replacement, it is expected that they would make rules to protect themselves and their holdings from less prosperous members. In groups where power is more evenly distributed, it would be predicted that rules would be made to be advantageous to a larger cross section of the group. Members should agree to prohibit acts that lower the average fitness of group members, i.e., acts where the victimized individual loses more fitness than is gained by the actor.

Laws defining the acceptability of actions also provide limits that define when other group members may intervene. Laws lessen the ambiguity involved in determining if a violation has occurred and they allow swift action to be taken against violators. The action taken may include aggression as punishment where otherwise it would be prohibited.

In terms of evolutionary theory, the primary function of punishment of rule violators is deterrence—assuming that individuals in power are not using the legal system as a pretext to eliminate competitors. Thus, within the social group the individual must not only consider the payoff from a successful aggressive act, and the likelihood of its success, but also the added cost and likelihood of punishment. For most social systems, punishment is designed to make within-group aggression unprofitable (Larsen, 1976; Pettigrew, 1958). Presumably a conscious individual is able to anticipate the likelihood of punishment and its magnitude and use this information to estimate the payoff from an aggressive or otherwise illegal act.

Justice and revenge are commonly cited as alternative motivations for punishment; however, both can be related to deterrence. Justice reflects the interests of the whole social group, and revenge reflects the interest of a part of the group, usually individuals who have similar interests and are closely related. Revenge may have functional significance in showing that a group which has been attacked is not weak and susceptible to further attack. Revengeful acts are a deterrent against further transgressions that may harm individuals of the group—in particular, kin of the individual initially harmed. The problem of revenge is that it often encourages reciprocal attacks by kin of the original transgressor and may lead to continuous warfare. Hence, a system of punishment that circumvents the need for revenge is highly beneficial. In large communities one remedy is to make the crime the interest of the entire community, thereby giving the support of the community to the offended set of kinsmen and, simultaneously, making revenge illegal. By following the law, kinsmen are able to avoid costs of a reciprocal attack, save respectability, and avoid a demonstration of weakness. The uselessness of attempting to confront the entire community forces kin of the transgressor to accept justice or leave the community.

Becker (1968) has analyzed group responses to crime in an economic model similar to the cost/benefit approach discussed here. He predicts that investment in crime prevention should be proportional to the cost of crime to group members, so as to minimize the social loss in income from offenses. However, a flaw is apparent in this economic analysis: severe penalties, including death, can be used to increase the average cost for committing a crime, with little or no increased cost to members of the group. Yet for most societies, severe penalties are reserved for major law violations and are rarely applied for minor infractions even though they would seem to increase deterrence and reduce recidivism.

There might be several reasons for Becker's correlation between the cost of crime and the severity of penalties. If the penalty for minor criminal violations is severe, then escalation to more severe crime is likely. For instance real need may dictate the stealing of food, but with high penalties for this minor crime, the criminal may be more inclined to carry a weapon and inflict harm if it enhances even minimally his likelihood of escape. Therefore, a system of penalties must represent an effort to limit and control crime. The point here is that if legal opportunities to meet perceived basic needs are severely limited, more severe penalties for minor crimes, contrary to common expectations, lead to a greater net cost to social groups from crime.

Another factor influencing reduction in severity of punishment of minor crimes is self-interest. Individuals are unlikely to ask for severe penalties for crimes that either they, a close relative, or an important constituent might commit. Distinctions between legal and illegal activities are often vague. Economic conditions may change, forcing usually honest individuals into illegal activities during bad times. Under these circumstances, less than maximum penalties would be predicted because the individuals who formulate the penalties may themselves be forced into prohibited behavior. Therefore, an individual in power should seek a balance between the need to discourage crime and the likelihood of participation (and subsequent capture) in such crime by ego or his relatives. It is the seeking of this balance that may correlate the severity of penalties with the harm caused by crime, i.e., making the punishment fit the crime.

Control of Aggression: Group Selection

If group selection has caused more frequent and rapid extinction of groups containing reproductively selfish individuals, then intragroup conflict may be at lower levels than would be predicted from theory maximizing individual inclusive fitness. There has been a resurgence of interest in the possibility of group selection as a factor influencing behavior of all species (D.S. Wilson, 1975; E.O. Wilson, 1973, 1975); in contrast, see Alexander and Borgia (1978). Even the most stalwart opponent of group selection as a basis for adaptation (Williams, 1966) admits that if group selection is effective, human populations are among the most likely candidates.

Williams points out that group selection is expected to be most effective under conditions of low migration, high genetic variability among groups and rapid group extinction. Rapid group extinction through warfare has been implicated in the latter as a factor leading to rapid evolution of human brain size (Alexander and Tinkle, 1968; Bigelow, 1969, 1971, 1972). Bigelow (1969) cites evidence showing that warfare has been common in human history and that occasional mass killing has occurred. Yet data showing consistent large-scale killing, necessary for successful group selection of altruistic traits, are lacking (Teft, 1975). Even if group extinction might have contributed to the evolution of human mental capacity, individual advantages gained from intragroup competition and from the conquest of other groups, would likely counteract tendencies toward altruistic behavior within groups. These individual gains could, themselves, account for most of the observed changes in characteristics such as brain size.

There is additional evidence to suggest that extensive competition for women, wealth and status occurs within most social groups (Murdock, 1949), thus implying that a high level of altruism within groups is rare or nonexistent. Moreover, the correlation of high levels of theft with warfare (Textor, 1967) implies that, in cases where the effects of group selection are expected to be the strongest, the greatest lack of harmony also occurs. It is, in fact, in nonwarring groups that internal harmony appears to be the highest. Therefore, warfare and extinction do not appear to be factors for promoting intragroup cooperation.

Unappreciated in models of group selection are the high rates of migration of human populations due to exogamous marriages (Textor, 1967). Migration is significant in reducing differences in the genetic variation between groups and, as Williams (1966) and Lewontin (1970) point out, high levels of variation *between* selective units is critical for evolutionary change. In completely exogamous groups, 50% of each generation moves between groups—a migration rate too high for any of the common models of group selection to be effective. Tendencies toward endogamy reduce this effect, but endogamy is common where groups are large (Textor, 1967) and altruistic traits are least likely to be fixed by groupwide extinction in large groups.

Learning and Social Control

The success of social control is often dependent on learning. Learning is a mechanism for helping organisms identify contexts in which particular behaviors are advantageous or disadvantageous.

It is critical to almost all social organisms whose needs (and relative abilities to fulfill needs) within social groups can rarely be predicted before birth. Social groups control individual actions by setting and enforcing penalties for behavior against the interests of those in control of the group. Thus, parents, able to teach their young the laws of the group, help them to avoid punishment and to make use of fitness-enhancing opportunities. Such teaching is important because rules are highly variable among groups and may change with regard to particular behavior within groups. Parental instruction may be one of the few reliable means of programming children to behave "properly" in new settings.

This discussion of the importance of learning in the control of aggression is based on the assumption that offspring who are taught prohibitions against aggressive acts increase their reproductive success relative to those who are not. However, teaching nonaggression is said to occur without reference to its net effect on offspring (Montagu, 1968)—i.e., the implication is that nonaggression can be taught even if it is ultimately disadvantageous to children.

Up to this point adaptations have been assumed to be individually advantageous. Yet in parent–offspring interactions if interests differ between them, both cannot win (Trivers, 1974). Parents are generally in a position of power, and even though the learning process developed because it helps offspring, occasionally parents misprogram them to further their own interests (Alexander, 1974). While offspring should evolve to evaluate for themselves the reliability of such instruction, their dependence on parents suggests that following parental instruction is the best available pathway for long-term success.

Cooperation of parents or others in charge of instruction is necessary for successful training of nonaggression, if it is not in the offspring's best interest. The parent is commonly in a better position than the offspring to recognize attempts at misinformation and, because of its genetic interest in the child, the parent is unlikely to help in efforts to deceive the child. Parental efforts might be circumvented by removing the child from the control of the parent. However, considering the main reason for attempting to teach nonaggression—i.e., the desire to develop a less punitive system for the control of aggression—the costs of such intervention may not justify the supposed benefits. Moreover, the notion that such teaching will lead to the desired nonaggressiveness assumes a particular patterning or programming of behavior, similar to Cloak's (1975) parental instruction model. If there are other means of programming, perhaps dependent on the individual's own assessment of the end effects on his fitness (Durham, 1976b), then such instruction will be unsuccessful. A successful program in teaching nonaggression would face the additional problem of possibly limiting motivation of group members to respond to attacks from outside the group. Reduced defensive capabilities may lead to replacement of the peace-loving group by others who are aggressive. Teaching nonaggression would then seem to require elimination of aggression—the result it is supposed to produce—before the benign behavior could be steadily maintained in a population.

Warfare No other organism approaches man in his ability to carry out coordinated aggression between groups. Evolution of our ability to carry out warfare, its effects on human evolution and its proximate causes are subjects of an extensive literature [see Nettleship et al. (1975)]. Serious study of the relationship between natural selection theory and various aspects of warfare has been made by Fisher (1930), Alexander (1971), Alexander and Tinkle (1968), Bigelow (1969, 1971, 1972), Wilson (1975, 1978), Corning (1975) and Durham (1976a,b). These authors agree that warfare occurs because members of one group perceive an opportunity to enhance their fitness at the expense of the group they attack. Durham (1976a) presented the most detailed discussion of the causes of warfare from a modern adaptive perspective and suggested that aggression between groups is ultimately related to the acquisition of scarce resources. According to this view, warfare occurs as a reaction to threats by nearby groups so as to secure resources that might otherwise be available to enemies. Even though this rationale appears correct as an explanation for evolved warfare as discussed by Davie (1929), Otterbein (1970) and others, utility derived from resource control is not a sufficient explanation for behaviors such as revenge and trophy hunting. It is my intent to use the evolutionary model not only as an aid in understanding causes of warfare but also the effect warfare has had on the structure of social systems.

Utility of Warfare

Durham (1976a) uses case studies to support his arguments concerning the importance of resources in intergroup aggression, but this approach is of very limited value in hypothesis testing. More extensive cross-cultural studies involving statistical comparisons are needed to compare the potential payoff from aggression in bellicose and peaceful groups. Correlation of warfare with the existence of fixed settlements [Textor (1967): $\chi^2 = 15.3$, $p < .001$] may indicate such tendencies assuming, as has Otterbein (1970), that such settlements more often are established near to, or contain, valuable resources.

Durham's discussion of the causes of warfare focuses on the need for individuals to acquire material resources, e.g., livestock, land and structures. However, restricting consideration to this type of resource may underestimate the value of warfare. Chagnon (1968) and Davie (1929) provide convincing evidence that the desire to capture women for wives is often instrumental in warfare. Women are an essential resource because only they can convert other resources controlled by males into offspring. Moreover, unlike many avian mating systems (Verner, 1964), in humans the control of females by males prevents other males from attracting females automatically in proportion to the amount of material resources they control. In most social groups, especially where warfare is common, women are a scarce commodity for males. Recognizing the almost universal need for wives may contribute to the ubiquitousness of aggression and the relative paucity of so-called peaceful societies (Lee and DeVore, 1968; Lesser, 1967). It may also explain Otterbein's (1970) results in which the only societies without collective aggression in his sample were those that had no easily accessible nearby groups.

Slaves provide another potential source of nonmaterial gain from aggression by converting raw resources into usable goods. Captured wives and slaves must cause a net increase in offspring produced by the capturing males in order for the former to be an important factor in warfare. Captured women are valuable for converting material resources collected by a male (in nondefended areas) into usable goods, or using items controlled by a male to produce his offspring. It appears that women will be valued in almost all cases, with the possible exception being where additional wives do not increase a male's reproduction as, for example, when male and female reproduction are limited by the amount of goods a male can control or collect. Similarly, slaves are only useful in cases where added labor is important. Slaves are less valuable than wives because each slave must produce items of worth in excess of what he needs to survive and reproduce, or is needed by others to guard him from escape and the threat he offers as an enemy. A captured wife requires less guarding because she is not trained to fight and, after bearing children, would be less likely to take risks which would endanger her children.

Correlation between warfare and polygamy suggests that warfare is advantageous where wives are valuable. Among groups which Slater (1964) characterized as bellicose, polygamy is common; monogamy is more common in nonbellicose groups [Textor (1967): $\chi^2 = 6.33$, $p = .012$]. The association of warfare with high bride prices suggests that when warfare is prevalent, women are an important item limiting male reproduction. Societies in which women are acquired through difficult means (i.e., significant bride price) are more bellicose than those in which wives are obtained without these considerations [Textor (1967): $\chi^2 = 4.30$, $p = .038$]. High bride price may be a function of both the male's need for female productive ability and a scarcity of females created by sex-biased infanticide (Divale, 1972), which occurs when fathers value sons as warriors (Borgia, 1979b).

Slavery shows a similar pattern in its correlation with warfare [Textor (1967): $\chi^2 = 54.43$, $p < .001$], bride price [Textor (1967): χ^2

= 30.3, $p < .001$] and polygamy [Textor (1967): $\chi = 14.92$, $p < .001$]. Also its correlation with presence of individual property rights [Textor (1967): $\chi^2 = 4.87$, $p = .027$] suggests that slaves are valued most when resources are available and require processing.

Facilitation of Group Aggression

I have argued here that aggressive acts by individuals can be predicted with a fair degree of accuracy simply by identifying situations in which attacks will lead to profit. However, predictions of aggressive behavior among groups are more complicated because actions of groups are less coordinated than those of individuals—as a consequence of reduced effectiveness in communication, a greater diversity of interests and a greater ability to express this diversity. Individuals form a coherent functional unit with special tissues and organs for intragroup communication. Even with the development of language and role specialization, the degree of precision in communication and the speed at which information is transferred is much slower among groups than individuals. Diversity of genetic interests among group members contributes to the lack of coordination between nonkin groups, relative to individuals who comprise groups that are more genetically similar. Such limitations make rapid response by a group relatively more difficult than by individuals and result in missed opportunities to exploit potentially profitable situations. Thus, the likelihood of group members initiating warfare will depend not only on the material gain from that aggression, but on the extent to which members of groups are able to coordinate activities to carry out attacks.

Kinship and Coordination

One means of enhancing the coordination of group activities involves delegating power to one or a few individuals. With centralized control, decisions can be made more quickly, thereby enhancing the response of the group to opportunities for profitable attack. Yet delegating authority raises problems in that those in decision-making roles may use their positions for personal enrichment at the expense of other group members. Presumably such losses are typically less than the gains from coordinated activity. The level of abuse of power tolerated by group members is proportional to the contributions the leader makes in comparison to others who might replace him.

Structure of the social group also affects the degree of coordination in the group. Highly organized units with specialized roles are likely to be more responsive to external threat and more successful in conquest of other groups than less rigidly structured units. For instance, Otterbein (1970) has shown that frequency of warfare is correlated with social complexity.

For small groups, association with kin should enhance the coordination of group activities. Mutual genetic interest has the effect of reducing the likelihood of abusive leadership. Also, members who anticipate treatment more in tune with their interests are expected to be less hesitant in carrying out the instructions of a leader. Groups made up of genetic relatives have the benefit of an inherent social hierarchy based on the family. The organization resulting from family structure appears to be valued in a great number of social groups, as shown by the tendency for offspring to live near parents of either the bride or groom (Murdock, 1949). Kin associations among males [no society employs females as warriors; see Davie (1929)] facilitate fighting by the groups. Murdock's (1949) data show that in the vast majority of social groups, males who fight together are close relatives—an automatic consequence of patrilocal residence. Even where matrilocality is common, males remain in and fight with their natal group, which also contains their wife's parents. Close relationships among males who fight minimize problems of cheating, both during combat and in the division of spoils, and essentially eliminate armed conflict between brothers.

Among primates, humans are the only species that is patrilocal with large families. We are also the only group with coordinated intraspecific aggression. One is tempted to conclude that the ability of men to develop patrilocal associations with kin—perhaps assisted by the appearance of highly coordinated group activities such as hunting and warfare among males—aided in the development of their ability to control women and negotiate with males in other groups for wives.

Genetic relationship among individuals in different groups has been suggested as an important factor in determining patterns of warfare. The role of royal marriages as a basis for the formation of alliances is well known (Darlington, 1969). More recently Durham (1976a) has assigned significance to *average* genetic relatedness between groups as a factor affecting patterns of aggression among potentially warring groups. He suggested that high average relatedness leads to "competitive tolerance." For support, Durham mentions the work of Bohannon (1954) and Sahlins (1961) stating that " . . . a local group that seeks to expand its territory *attacks the most distantly related* adjacent group." Although Durham's suggestion seems a reasonable extension of the inclusive fitness model, average relatedness may be relatively unimportant in affecting choice of targets. Except for groups that have recently fissioned or are involved in near-exclusive trades for wives, average relationship between groups is likely to be very low. The closest relative (of the same generation) a warrior confronts in battle shares, on the average, only $\frac{1}{8}$ of his genes through identity by descent. Averaging his relationship with others of lower relationship in that group would only lead (except if the groups are very small) to rare instances in which economic and strategic differences based on differences in *average* genetic relatedness among potential target groups could influence patterns of aggression. In cases where a group under attack comprise close kin, warriors take precautions not to harm them (Druker, 1951). Patterns of attack observed by Sahlins and Bohannan more likely result from effects correlated with average relationship, such as economic ties between groups or alliances due to genetic relationships among leaders.

Although centralized control of groups aids in the coordination of their activities, especially warfare, leaders may use delegated authority against the interest of members. The greatest disparities occur in large groups. Group members should attempt to avoid loss of control by resisting consolidation into large political units except when it is necessary for survival—as when small groups are likely to be attacked by other large groups. Evidence that large groups tend to be more militaristic (Otterbein, 1970; Textor, 1967) supports the notion that consolidation occurs in response to intergroup aggression. For example, the Yanomamö highland groups tend to be smaller and less warlike than individuals in lowland areas (Chagnon, 1968; Smole, 1976).

Otterbein has analyzed social organization of groups from what Caneiro in Otterbein (1970) called an evolutionary/functionalist perspective. While he recognized that the formation of structurally complex, large groups are likely adaptations to external pressures such as warfare, he viewed less complex groups as primitive. Evolutionary anthropologists (Tylor, 1871) have described these groups as remnants of a primitive stage in an evolutionary sequence and not a result of selection favoring individuals in small groups who, with lowered probabilities of attack, benefit from living in smaller groups.

Additional costs to members living in large groups result from the delegation of power to leaders who have little or no traceable genetic relationship to them, as well as from the necessity to interact with a larger number of individuals who have, on the average, a lower degree of genetic relationship to them. Attempts made to reduce the impact of these effects include the structuring of patron–client relationships (Amsbury, 1975) along the lines of kinship, the strategic use of marriage alliances and the encouragement of local grouping of kinsmen. For example, young married men are expected to take up residence near their parents.

Conflicts of interest and their effects on group actions make prediction of group behavior, especially entrance into warfare, difficult. Even though a leader may exert a disproportionate level of control within the group, his continued authority is dependent on satisfying those who influence his ability to retain power. Because of his need to satisfy clients, predictions based on knowledge of the leader's immediate interests will only allow limited success in predicting his behavior. His ability to pursue personal interests depends on the level of power he has within the group, which is determined by kinship, reciprocity (Alexander, 1974; Trivers, 1971) and the recognition of his value to the group. Some self-indulgence by a leader may be accepted as part of payment for his services and to make the leadership position attractive to competent individuals. Beyond these limits, however, group members are expected to remove greedy leaders, and the level of indiscretion tolerated is proportional to the cost of replacing the leader with someone else more suitable (Claessen, 1975).

Proximate Facilitation

Initiation of warfare often depends on special ceremonies and other mechanisms that encourage individual participation. Because warfare may entail great risks to the participant while offering only indirect payoffs, proximate facilitation of aggression is necessary. The individual warrior should be concerned about the contributions made by others in his group, the real need for war, the kinds of direct benefits he might accrue and the level of risk he should accept. Groups better able to guarantee rewards to warriors should be, on the average, at an advantage because their warriors would be more willing to fight. The opportunity to take plunder, women and slaves may certainly encourage participation in combat. Also, the taking of scalps and heads, or the counting of coup (touching the bodies of fallen enemies), which have little intrinsic value, may provide incentives for risk-taking because they demonstrate the individual's contribution to the group's military effort. Harris (1977) has suggested that coup counting must be considered a form of sport. However, it is a certain method of demonstrating that the fallen individual is dead or severely wounded. This practice might also serve as a means of unambiguously accrediting the deaths of enemies to warriors; i.e., it is not acceptable to take coup on a kill made by another warrior.

Willingness to take risks in combat is also encouraged if the family of a fallen warrior is subsequently cared for by other members of the group. Fisher (1930) used similar arguments to account for the evolution of heroism. In each case, a warrior's most successful strategy for risk-taking might involve estimating the value of his activities to the group and the group's response to his acts of bravery. Special ceremonies may allow warriors to gauge the level of support from noncombatants and the commitment of other warriors. If villagers demonstrate great emotional and material support for war in ceremonies, then the warriors may correctly assume that war is of value to the community and commensurate rewards will be made for success. Congregation of warriors may also function as a public statement by each man that he will participate in combat. In industrial countries, political rallies and parades may be useful in encouraging involvement in warfare.

Concluding Remarks I have applied advances in evolutionary theory to the study of aggressive behavior in man. These advances in the understanding of natural selection come from the recognition of the individual as the fundamental unit on which natural selection operates. Individuals are suggested to participate in aggression only when such acts enhance their fitness relative to other behaviors they are capable of performing.

Explanations of aggressive behavior used in various disciplines have been reviewed; many of these are not consistent with the current evolutionary model. The differences between the evolutionary model and these other approaches to the study of behavior result from failure to identify the ultimate interests of individuals as those of genetic fitness. Lack of consistency with evolutionary theory (the central theory of biology) suggests that these other models should be re-evaluated.

Man characteristically lives in groups and, because of the potential harm of aggression, groups commonly take action to control its expression. To profitably adjust to their environment individuals should use aggression only when the advantages it brings outweigh the prospects of being captured and the costs of the ensuing punishment, or when it specifically serves the interests of the group, as in warfare or in the punishment of violators of group rules.

Mechanisms that might affect the level of aggression expressed within groups include deterrence through punishment of violators, learning about nonaggression and possibly the reduction of aggressive tendencies by group selection. It is unlikely that group selection has had any important effects because of the high rates of genetic exchange between groups as a function of systematic trading and capturing of wives. Reactions to proscriptions against aggression and the punishment of violators seem the only important means to achieve the control of aggression; learning is useful in familiarizing individuals with these proscriptions, but not as an ultimate means of control.

Warfare differs from *intragroup* aggression in not being susceptible to the same kinds of control mechanisms. Commonly there is no system of rules and punishment to control *intergroup* aggression, i.e., the tendency to attack other groups is most likely determined by the relative strength of groups and the expected gain. Although warfare is commonly correlated with conditions that suggest gain for attackers, predicting the incidence of these attacks is complicated by different patterns of group structure and different individual interests. Conflicts of interest, in turn, lead to variable patterns of social control and to different degrees of power centralized within groups, all of which affect decisions to initiate warfare.

The need to understand how our behavior is programmed is the essential unresolved problem for understanding patterns of human aggression. The mechanisms involved might vary from genetic programs for specific behaviors to systems in which responses depend on adjustments to meet general needs—e.g., pleasure and success—or to systems which appraise the effect of behaviors on genetic fitness, thus allowing for compensating responses. The latter two mechanisms might operate in man with little or no direct genetic control. Elucidation of these possibilities helps to evaluate the correctness of the assumption of high levels of adaptation, and to determine our ability to adapt to novel circumstances.

References   Alexander, R. D. 1971. The search for an evolutionary philosophy of man. *Proceedings of the Royal Society of Victoria* 84: 99–120.

———. 1974. The evolution of social behavior. *Ann. Rev. Ecol. Syst.* 5: 325–383.

———. 1975. The search for a general theory of behavior. *Behavioral Science* 20: 77–100.

Alexander, R. D., and Borgia, G. 1978. Group selection, altruism, and the levels of organization of life. *Ann. Rev. Ecol. Syst.* 9: 449–474.

Alexander, R. D., and Tinkle, D. 1968. A comparative review of *On Aggression* and *The Territorial Imperative*. *BioScience* 18: 245–248.

Amsbury, C. 1975. Patron–client structures, world organization, and war. In M. Nettleship, R. Givens and A. Nettleship (eds.) *War, Its Causes and Correlates*. The Hague: Mouton.

Ardrey, R. 1966. *The Territorial Imperative*. New York: Atheneum.

Barash, D. P. 1977. *Sociobiology and Behavior*. New York: Elsevier.

Becker, G. 1968. Crime and punishment: An economic approach. *Journal of Political Economy* 76: 169–217.

Berkowitz, L. 1962. *Aggression: A social psychological analysis*. New York: McGraw-Hill.

Bigelow, R. 1969. *The Dawn Warriors: Man's Evolution Towards Peace*. Boston: Little, Brown.

———. 1971. Relevance of ethology to human aggressiveness. *International Social Sciences Journal* 23: 18–26.

———. 1972. The evolution of cooperation, aggression, and self-control. *Nebraska Symposium on Motivation* 20: 1–57.

Borgia, G. 1979a. Sexual selection and the evolution of mating systems. In M. Blum and N. Blum (eds). *Sexual Selection and Reproductive Competition in Insects*, pp. 19–80. New York: Academic Press.

———. 1979b. Fisher's investment model and the economics of marriage. Unpublished ms.

Bohannon, P. 1954. The migration and expansion of the Tiv. *Africa* 24: 2–16.

Brown, J. 1964. The evolution of diversity in avian territorial systems. *Wilson Bull.* 76: 161-169.

———. 1978. Avian communal breeding systems. *Ann. Rev. Ecol. Syst.* 9: 123–156.

Brown, J. L., and Orians, G. 1970. Spacing patterns in mobile animals. *Ann. Rev. Ecol. Syst.* 1: 239–262.

Chagnon, N. 1968. *Yanomamö: The Fierce People*. New York: Holt, Rinehart and Winston.

Claessen, H. 1975. Circumstances under which civil war comes into existence. In M. Nettleship, R. Givens and A. Nettleship (eds.) *War, Its Causes and Correlates*. The Hague: Mouton.

Cloak, F. 1975. Is cultural ethology possible? *Human Ecology* 3: 161–182.

Corning, P. 1975. An evolutionary paradigm for the study of human aggression. In M. Nettleship, R. Givens and A. Nettleship (eds.) *War, Its Causes and Correlates*. The Hague: Moulton.

Daly, M., and Wilson, M. 1980. Abuse and neglect of children in evolutionary perspective. In R. Alexander and D. Tinkle (eds.) *Natural Selection and Social Behavior: Recent Research and Theory*. New York: Chiron Press.

Darlington, C. D. 1969. *The Evolution of Man and Society*. New York: Simon and Schuster.

Darwin, C. 1871. *The Descent of Man and Selection in Relation to Sex*. London: J. Murray.

Davie, M. 1929. *The Evolution of War*. New Haven: Yale University Press.

Dawkins, R. 1976. *The Selfish Gene*. New York: Oxford University Press.

DeCharms, R., and E. J. Wilkins. 1963. Some effects of verbal expression of hostility. *J. of Abnormal Social Psychology* 66: 462–470.

Dickeman, M. 1975. Demographic consequences of infanticide in man. *Ann. Rev. Ecol. Syst.* 6: 100–137.

Divale, W. 1972. Systematic population control in the middle and upper paleolithic. *World Archaeology* 42: 222–241.

Dollard, J., Miller, N., Doob, L., Mower, O., and Sears, R. 1939. *Frustration and Aggression*. New Haven: Yale University Press.

Druker, P. 1951. *The Northern and Central Nootkan Tribes*. Bureau of American Ethnology Bulletin 144. Washington, DC: U.S. Government Printing Office.

Durham, W. 1976a. Resource competition and human aggression. Part I: A review of primitive war. *Quant. Rev. Biol.* 51: 385–415.

———. 1976b. The adaptive significance of cultural behavior. *Human Ecology* 4: 89–121.

Edwards, W. 1954. A theory of decision-making. *Psychological Bulletin* 51: 385–417.

Eibl-Eibesfeldt, I. 1971. *Love and Hate*. New York: Holt, Rinehart and Winston.

Fergusson, D.M., Donnell, A., and Slater, S.W. 1975. The effects of race and socioeconomic status on juvenile offending statistics. *Joint Committee On Young Offenders* (Wellington), Research Report No. 2 (31 pages).

Fisher, R. A. 1930. *The Genetical Theory of Natural Selection*. 2nd ed. New York: Dover.

Gould, S. 1977. *Ever Since Darwin*. New York: Norton.

Hamilton, W. D. 1964. The evolution of social behavior. *J. Theor. Biol.* 7: 1–52.

Harris, M. 1977. *Cannibals and Kings*. New York: Random House.

Hinde, R. A. 1970. *Animal Behavior*, 2nd ed. New York: McGraw-Hill.

———. 1974. *The Biological Basis of Human Social Behavior*. New York: McGraw-Hill.

Holloway, R. 1968. Territory and aggression in man: A look at Ardrey's *Territorial Imperative*. In A. Montagu (ed.) *Man and Aggression*, pp. 96–102. New York: Oxford University Press.

Howard, R. D. 1977. The evolution of mating strategies and resource utilization in bullfrogs, *Rana catesbeiana*. Ph. D. dissertation, University of Michigan.

Hrdy, S. 1977. *The Langurs of Abu*. Cambridge, MA: Harvard University Press.

Kaufmann, H. 1970. *Aggression and Altruism*. New York: Holt, Rinehart and Winston.

Kenny, D. T. 1953. *An Experimental Test of the Catharsis Theory of Aggression*. Ann Arbor, MI: University Microfilms.

Lack, D. 1954. *Natural Regulation of Animal Numbers*. New York: Oxford University Press.

Lane, R. E. 1953. Why businessmen violate the law. *J. Criminal Law, Criminology and Police Science* 44: 102–117.

Larsen, K. S. 1976. *Aggression: Myths and Models.* Chicago: Nelson-Hall.

Lee, R. B., and DeVore, I. 1968. *Man the Hunter.* Chicago: Aldine.

Lesser, A. 1967. War and the state. In M. Fried, M. Harris and R. Murphy (eds.) *War,* pp. 92–96. Garden City: Natural History Press.

Lewontin, R. C. 1970. The units of selection. *Ann. Rev. Ecol. Syst.* 1: 1–18.

———. 1977. Sociobiology—a caricature of Darwinism. *Proc. Philosophy of Science Association* (1976) 2:22–31.

Lorenz, K. 1950. The comparative method in studying innate behavior patterns. Symposium of the Society for Experimental Biology 4: 221–268.

———. 1966. *On Aggression.* New York: Harcourt Brace Jovanovich.

Maynard Smith, J., and Price, G. R. 1973. The logic of animal conflict. *Nature* 246: 15–18.

Massey, A. 1977. Agonistic aids and kinship in a group of pigtail macaques. *Behav. Ecol. Sociobiol.* 2:31–40.

Meadnka, K. R., and Hill, K. Q. 1976. Re-examination of the etiology of urban crime. *Criminology* 13:491–506.

Miller, N. E. 1941. The frustration–aggression hypothesis. *Psychological Review* 48: 337–342.

Montagu, M.F.A. 1968. *Man and Aggression.* New York: Oxford University Press.

Moyer, K. E. 1976. *The Psychobiology of Aggression.* New York: Harper and Row.

Murdock, G. 1949. *Social Structure.* New York: Macmillan.

Nettleship, M., Givens, R., and Nettleship, A., 1975. *War, Its Causes and Correlates.* The Hague: Mouton.

Nicholson, A. J. 1957. Self-adjustment of populations to change. *Cold Spring Harbor Symp. Quant. Biol.* 22: 153–173.

Otterbein, K. 1970. *The Evolution of War.* New Haven: Human Relations Area Files Press.

Parker, G. 1974. Assessment strategy and the evolution of fighting behavior. *J. Theor. Biol.* 47: 223–243.

Parsons, E. C. 1906. *The Family.* New York: G. P. Putnam's Sons.

Pettigrew, T. F. 1958. Personality and socio-cultural factors in intergroup attitudes: A cross-national comparison. *Journal of Conflict Resolution* 2: 29–42.

Robel, R. 1966. Booming territory size and mating success of the greater prairie chicken (Tympanuchus cupido pinnatus). *Anim. Behav.* 14: 328–331.

Ritter, W. E. 1938. *The California Woodpecker and I.* Berkeley: University of California Press.

Sahlins, M. 1961. The segmentary lineage: An organization of predatory expansion. In R. Cohen and J. Middleton (eds.) *Comparative Political Systems,* pp. 89–119. Garden City: Natural History Press.

Sale, P. F. 1972. Effect of cover on agonistic behavior of a reef fish: A possible spacing mechanism. *Ecology* 53: 753–758.

Schaller, G. B. 1972. *The Serengeti Lion.* Chicago: University of Chicago Press.

Scott, J. P. 1958. *Aggression.* Chicago: University of Chicago Press.

———. 1975. Comment. In M. Nettleship, R. Givens and A. Nettleship (eds.) *War, Its Causes and Correlates,* pp. 385–387. The Hague: Mouton.

Siegel, S. 1960. Individual decision making under risk. In H. Gulliksen and S. Messick (eds.) *Psychological Scaling: Theory and Applications.* New York: Wiley.

Siegel, S., and Foriaker, L. 1960. *Bargaining and Group Decision Making.* New York: McGraw-Hill.

Sipes, R. 1975. War, combative sports, and aggression: A preliminary causal model of cultural patterning. In M. Nettleship, R. Givens and A. Nettleship (eds.) *War, Its Causes and Correlates*, pp. 749–764. The Hague: Mouton.

Slater, P. E. 1964. Unpublished coding guide for the cross-cultural study of narcissism. In Robert B. Textor (ed.) *A Cross-Cultural Summary*. New Haven, CT: Human Relations Area Files Press (1967).

Smole, W. J. 1976. *The Yanomamö Indians: A Cultural Geography*. Austin: University of Texas Press.

Spencer, H. 1910. *The Principles of Sociology*, 3rd ed., 3 vols., Vol. 2. London: Appleton.

Sugiyama, Y. 1967. Social organization of hanuman langurs. In S. A. Altmann (ed.) *Social Communication Among Primates*. Chicago: University of Chicago Press.

Teft, S. 1975. Commentary. In M. Nettleship, R. Givens, and A. Nettleship (eds.) *War, Its Causes and Correlates*, p. 259. The Hague: Mouton.

Textor, R. 1967. *A Cross-Cultural Summary*. New Haven, CT. Human Relations Area Files Press.

Tinbergen, N. 1952. "Derived" activities; their causation, biological significance, origin, and emancipation during evolution. *Quant. Rev. Biol.* 27: 1–32.

Trivers, R. 1971. The evolution of recriprocal altruism. *Quart. Rev. Biol.* 46:35–57.

———. 1972. Parental investment and sexual selection. In B. Campbell (ed.) *Sexual Selection and the Descent of Man, 1871–1971*. Chicago: Aldine.

———. 1974. Parent–offspring conflict. *Amer. Zool.* 14: 249–264.

Tylor, E. B. 1871. *Primitive Culture*, 2 vols. New York: Harper Torchbooks (1958).

Verner, J. 1964. The evolution of polygamy in the long-billed marsh wren. *Evolution* 18: 252–261.

Vinson, T., and Homel, R. 1975. Crime and disadvantage. The coincidence of medical and social problems in an Australian city. *Brit. J. Criminol.* 15:21–31.

Walsh, M., and Scandalis, B. 1975. Institutionalized forms of intergenerational male aggression. In M. Nettleship, R. Givens, and A. Nettleship (eds.) *War, Its Causes and Correlates*, pp. 134–155. The Hague: Mouton.

White, R., and Lippitt, R. 1960. *Autocracy and Democracy: An Experimental Inquiry*. New York: Harper.

Williams, G. 1966. *Adaptation and Natural Selection*. Princeton: Princeton University Press.

Wilson, D. S. 1975. A new model for group selection. *Proc. Natl. Acad. Sci. USA* 72:143–146.

Wilson, E. O. 1973. Group selection and its significance for ecology. *Bioscience* 23: 631–638.

———. 1975. *Sociobiology: The New Synthesis*. Cambridge, MA: Belknap/Harvard University Press.

———. 1978. *On Human Nature*. Cambridge, MA: Harvard University Press.

Wynne-Edwards, V. 1962. *Animal Dispersion in Relation to Social Behavior*. Edinburgh: Oliver and Boyd.

Woolfenden, G. E. 1975. Florida scrub jay helpers at the nest. *Auk* 92: 1–15.

Hybrid Vigor:
Evolutionary Biology And Sociology

Penelope J. Greene, Charles J. Morgan, David P. Barash

10

In the beginning, with Comte and Spencer, there was evolutionary thought in sociology. These early formulations were confused, teleological and, at best, of limited predictive power. They were selected against. The frequency of evolutionary thought in sociology dropped to mutational equilibrium in undergraduate papers, where it often proved developmentally lethal.

Social scientists are again beginning to deal with issues suggested by evolution. Advances in evolutionary biology have facilitated this renewed interest. And yet, no concise introduction to evolutionary theory is available, and certainly an understanding of the underlying principles is essential for a critical and informative reading of the literature. Further, considerable controversy [see, for example, the report by Wade (1976)] has been generated over the appropriateness of evolutionary theory for human social behavior; some reputable evolutionary biologists are opposed to this approach. To develop a perspective, or even to understand the controversy, requires a relatively clear understanding of how evolution by natural selection "operates".

Having originated in ethology, population genetics and theoretical ecology, "sociobiology" is a new discipline that applies evolutionary biology to the analysis of social behavior (Wilson, 1975). Spencer, who formulated the main outline of his evolutionary theory prior to Darwin's publication of The Origin of Species (Coser, 1971), saw literally everything as evolving. In particular, he saw societies evolving as independent units. Further, he saw evolution as progressive, tending toward a final perfect state. The social Darwinists, for instance, opposed legislation to help the poor, because it would only slow the operation of natural selection, increasing the time lag between the present and the final perfect state toward which we were evolving. We emphasize that this position does not necessarily follow from contemporary understanding of evolution.

The new sociobiology sees selection as taking place overwhelmingly at the individual level, not at the societal level. Changes in societies result from changes in individual behavior. Further, there is no implication that evolutionary change is "good." It takes place because of some situational, reproductive advantage. Environmental change can alter the direction of evolutionary change. Cooperation and altruism are central in human social behavior, and rather than bemoaning them as slowing evolutionary progress, sociobiology incorporates them into the framework of a unified theory. Such concepts are explicitly defined in terms of their reproductive consequences and make no assumptions about the underlying motivational states of the organism. Altruism, for example, is defined as behavior that benefits another animal at some personal cost to the actor, where cost and benefit are measured in terms of reproductive success. Semantic misunderstandings have frequently obscured the more interesting issues [see Greene and Barash (1976)].

Like most important concepts, evolution is simple—deceptively so—and often misunderstood. We shall attempt to outline the fundamental process of evolution as it is understood by most biologists, clarify certain areas of misunderstanding, outline the relevance of evolutionary biology to the study of behavior (including human behavior) and, finally, elaborate on a particular facet of sociobiology that appears to hold special promise for the social sciences: the evolution of altruism.

Evolution as a Process

Natural selection. Darwin did not "discover" evolution. Indeed, the notion that all living things are linked by common ancestry is an ancient one. Darwin's enormous contribution was not the *fact* of evolution, but rather the elucidation of a *mechanism* by which it could operate. That mechanism is *natural selection* and it derives from a combination of natural history observations and logic. The basic points are as follows:

1. Living organisms possess an inherent capacity to overreproduce. The population of any sexually reproducing species, for example, will remain constant if and only if every pair of adults produces an average of two offspring who, in turn, likewise become reproductive adults. Production of an average of fewer than two successful offspring per adult results in extinction and production of an average of more than two generates exponential increase. This leads to the second basic natural history observation.
2. Natural populations tend to remain numerically stable. This is not to deny the occurrence of short-term fluctuations. Nevertheless, populations do not experience unchecked exponential growth. The "balance of nature" is real.
3. This balance derives from the competition of individuals, such that some are more successful than others. It follows that if many individuals are competing for scarce resources with respect to reproductive opportunity, then individuals will be

successful in proportion to the characteristics they possess which benefit them in the struggle for existence.

4. Accordingly, an essential addition to Darwin's reasoning is the recognition that individuals differ from each other in their competitive prowess and that to some extent, these differences are inherited by their offspring.

5. The ultimate consequence of all this is that the genetic makeup of any species tends to change with time, reflecting the greater reproductive contribution of certain individuals (the "better adapted" ones) than of others. This change is evolution by natural selection.

If we consider the distribution of any trait, in any species, evolutionary change occurs when that distribution is changed by virtue of differential reproductive success among species members from one generation to the next. It requires only differential reproduction among individuals and some correspondence between the overt manifestation of a particular trait (phenotype) and its underlying genetic representation (genotype).

There are three types of selection that are of particular importance in evolutionary change. For example, many traits have a normal distribution. If individuals removed from the mean (in one direction) are relatively more successful in producing offspring, then the distribution of the trait in question will shift in that direction, from the parental to the offspring generation. This is *directional selection*. Figure 1 shows graphically an example where selection favors "more" of some trait rather than less, e.g., visual acuity.

Directional selection corresponds to the usual conception of evolutionary change. For example, the progressive increase in

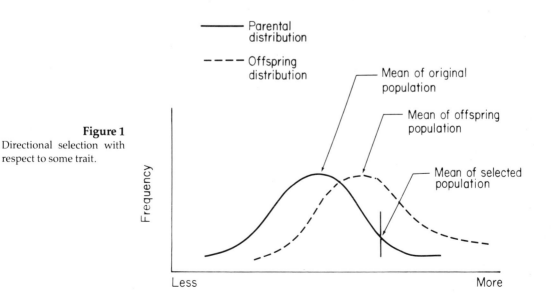

Figure 1
Directional selection with respect to some trait.

brain size among the ancestors of *Home sapiens* bespeaks directional selection. It occurred because individuals possessing larger brains produced and successfully raised more offspring (who were in turn differentially successful) than did individuals with smaller brains. This may have occurred because brain development conferred greater ability to procure and employ tools, communicate with and lead others, find food, avoid danger and so forth. Such an interpretation requires the (reasonable) assumption that brain size is to some degree inheritable, i.e., that largebrained individuals were more likely to produce largebrained offspring than were smallbrained individuals. In this example, largebrained individuals (or large brains *per se*) were "selected for," whereas smallbrained individuals (or small brains *per se*) were "selected against."

Alternatively, reproductive success (adaptation) may be inversely proportional to the distance from the mean, such that individuals are selected against in proportion as they deviate. Selection against the deviants is identified as *stabilizing selection* since it tends to stabilize the mean of a population from one generation to the next (Figure 2). While maintaining the mean, stabilizing selection decreases or maintains the genotypic and phenotypic variance within the population. However, the variance is not reduced entirely, as diversity is produced anew each generation by mutation and sexual recombination—the ultimate sources of the building blocks upon which evolution by natural selection can operate.

Stabilizing selection is probably the most frequent form of natural selection but it is rarely recognized because its effects are so undramatic. All directional selection leads ultimately to an equilibrium state where the mean of the distribution of the trait corresponds to the environmentally determined optimum for that trait. At that point, stabilizing selection occurs until such time as the

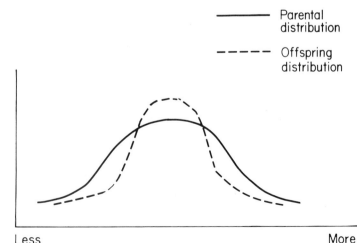

Figure 2
Stabilizing selection of a trait.

environment changes so as to render individuals on one side of the mean more successful reproductively than others, or a new mutation occurs which is selected for. Then, by definition, directional selection is again operating and the cycle continues.

There is a third form of selection which is multidirectional: *disruptive selection* (Figure 3). In this case, the population distribution shifts in two or more directions, resulting in a polymorphism. For example, the colors of certain insect pupae are characterized by a hue that is either green *or* brown; few individuals exist with intermediate colors.

Hardy–Weinberg Law. The modern "synthetic theory" of evolution (Huxley, 1942) commenced in the early 20th century from the rediscovery of Mendelian genetics and its amalgamation with Darwinian theory through the development of population genetics (Fisher, 1930; Haldane, 1932; Wright, 1931). The cornerstone of population genetics is the Hardy–Weinberg Law, which describes the relationship between frequencies of genes and genotypes in any population. For example, consider two alleles (alternate forms of the same gene) A and a, present in the population in proportion p and q, respectively, such that $p + q = 1$. The three possible genotypes in a sexually reproducing species (in which an individual receives an allele from each parent), AA, Aa and aa, will occur in proportion p^2, and $2pq$, and q^2, respectively. The Hardy–Weinberg Law describes a continuing equilibrium state for gene and genotype frequencies, i.e., a situation in which evolution is *not* occurring. However, Hardy–Weinberg equilibrium requires certain assumptions, specifically (a) the *absence* of emigration, immigration, and assortative (nonrandom) mating, (b) a sufficiently large population size to minimize sampling error (genetic drift) and (c) equal representation of each allele in succeeding generations (the absence of natural selection). The study of evolution, then, is essentially the study of those factors which disrupt Hardy–

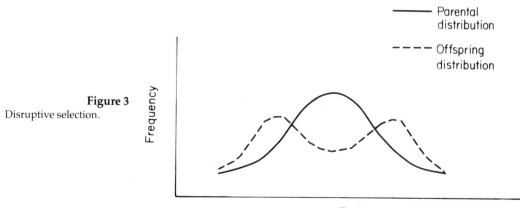

Figure 3
Disruptive selection.

Frequency

——— Parental distribution

– – – – Offspring distribution

Trait

Weinberg equilibrium; and the most important of these is natural selection.

Incorporating selection into a population in Hardy–Weinberg equilibrium, we need only recognize that each genotype frequency may be multiplied by a coefficient which reflects its particular reproductive success. Thus, the frequency of genotype AA in a nonequilibrium state may be found by evaluating p^2w_1, where w_1 represents the "relative fitness" of that genotype. The frequency of genotype Aa may similarly be represented as pqw_2 and that of aa by q^2w_3. The fitness of any genotype (or gene, or individual) is simply that number which, when multiplied by the frequency of that genotype (or gene, or individual) in one generation, gives its frequency in the next. Thus, genotypes (or genes, or individuals) that have a fitness greater than 1 will have increasing frequency in future generations, while those with fitness less than 1 will be reduced in frequency in future generations. Fitness is measured in terms of reproductive success and is only distantly related to "physical fitness." Any evolved characteristic that contributes to an organism's fitness is an *adaptation*. "Adaptation" is also employed in evolutionary biology to mean the process of achieving greater fitness through the acquisition of reproductively beneficial traits over time.

Genetic drift. Another mechanism that disrupts Hardy–Weinberg equilibrium is genetic drift (Wright, 1968) which Wilson (1975:64) has defined as "the alteration of gene frequencies through sampling error." The effects of sampling errors are, of course, most pronounced when the sample size is small. Thus, genetic drift is most likely to disturb a small population such that a particular allele may, by chance alone, not be passed from the parental to the offspring generation. Once this occurs, the change is irreversible, save through mutation or gene exchange with another group that has not lost the allele. The disappearance of an allele, coupled with mutations, may lead to new polymorphisms. The equivalent random process with respect to behavior and social organization has been labeled *social drift*. Just as all phenotypes derive from both a genetic and an environmental component, social drift can be attributed to a combination of genetics (genetic drift) and divergent experience [tradition drift: Wilson (1975:13)].

According to Sewell Wright (1968), the most rapid acquisition of adaptation is likely to occur in small, relatively isolated populations within which *both* natural selection and genetic drift are operating. Wright has developed an heuristic device called the "adaptive landscape" that is useful in considering this acquisition. For simplicity, we can consider a landscape based upon one trait, though the model clearly can be expanded to any number of traits. Briefly, the level of adaptation would be viewed as the height on the curve (Figure 4).

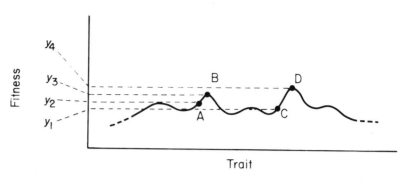

Figure 4
An adaptive landscape for one trait.

Suppose a set of individuals is currently characterized by a level of a trait with a fitness of y_2 in a particular environment (point A in Figure 4). If only natural selection is operating, then this set of individuals can increase its fitness (e.g., through directional selection) up to a limit of y_3, the local maximum of the curve. It *cannot* reach y_4 through natural selection alone because this would require a temporary decrease in fitness. However, if the population size is small enough, the random process of drift may operate such that a less fit trait temporarily predominates and these individuals may experience a temporary decrease in fitness (e.g., progress from point B to point C). It would be through a combination of random drift and natural selection, then, that other local maxima (e.g., D) could be reached.

This model is especially helpful in addressing one objection that is frequently directed at the sociobiological perspective, namely, that such a perspective supports the *status quo* by assuming that groups are optimally adapted. However, this is *not* implied by an evolutionary approach. That is, except for random drift or environmental change, a group may be approaching, or even "stranded" at, one level of adaptation (e.g., point B), with no hope of reaching a "better" (more fit, e.g., D) level. Notice that drift and/or environmental change, natural or artificial, can facilitate somewhat dramatic changes. Thus, the charge that sociobiology supports the notion that "the way things *are* is the way they must necessarily be" (Alper et al., 1976:426) is inappropriate. Mechanisms for change *do* exist. An understanding of these mechanisms is imperative for at least three sets of persons: those wishing to follow or contribute to the theoretical formulations of sociobiology, those wishing to apply the knowledge (e.g., to the study of genetic disorders) and those wishing to disagree.

Proximate and ultimate causation. Sociobiologists are concerned, of course, with one basic question: Why does animal x do behavior y? Answers to this question focus upon one or both of the two types of factors that influence behavior: proximate and ultimate factors. Proximate factors are the immediate mechanisms that "cause" a behavior. For example, consider the question of why redwinged blackbirds migrate. They may do so in response to climate changes, changes in day length, individual weight gain, and/or hormonal changes. The social sciences have traditionally dealt almost exclusively with proximate factors by studying internal mechanisms, external stimuli and the ontogeny of behavior within individuals. Consider again the question of why redwinged blackbirds migrate. Regardless of the hormonal or neural mechanisms, *why do they do it at all*? Ultimate factors are the evolutionary mechanisms that differentiated the comparative reproductive success of those who do or do not behave in a particular fashion. In this case, those birds that migrated were more successful reproductively, e.g., they did not die; they were better able to survive the winter in a warmer climate and so forth. The primary contribution that an evolutionary perspective may offer the social sciences is perhaps an understanding of the historical and environmental factors that have influenced behavior.

Analogy and homology. Another important duality in evolutionary biology involves the concepts of analogy and homology. Homologous structures are those that are similar because of common ancestry. Analogous structures are functionally similar structures appearing in unrelated animals. Analogies are based upon apparent resemblances, which may be superficial and hence misleading. For example, the wing of a bird and the wing of an insect are analogous—both contribute to flying. However, the similarities between the two are limited to their functional attributes and do not reflect common evolutionary descent: birds' wings consist of bones that are derived from the forearms of terrestrial reptiles from which they evolved, whereas an insect's wing develops as an outgrowth of its body wall. On the other hand, a bird's wing is homologous to the wing of a bat (with which it is also analogous) in that both structures derive from common ancestry. The point here is that any behavioral parallels between *Homo sapiens* and other animals are, by definition, analogies. They may or may not represent homologies as well.

The distinction between analogies and homologies suggests a strategy for making meaningful comparisons between humans and other animals. If we see behaviors similar to human behaviors in animals closely related to us, such as chimpanzees and gorillas, we may be looking at homologous behavior resting on a common genetic basis. This is the strategy most often employed [e.g., see Mazur (1973)]. We should also look to animals that have pursued an adaptive strategy similar to humans' and which have been subjected to similar selective pressures—i.e., the social carnivores (Schaller and Lowther, 1969). Well-studied social carnivores include wolves (Mech, 1970), lions (Schaller, 1972), hyenas (Kruuk, 1972) and wild dogs (van Lawick and van Lawick-Goodall, 1971).

They all live in intensely social groups, engage in highly coordinated, cooperative predatory behavior, and show apparent altruism on some occasions.

At the same time, there are important differences. Among lions, the females do almost all of the hunting; wild dogs hunt in packs composed of both males and females, and hyenas show "reverse" sexual dimorphism, with females larger than males. Clearly, then, we can learn nothing about human behavior by simply pointing at wolves or lions and comparing them with humans. But analogous selection pressures operating on both the social carnivores and our own ancestors may well have produced analogous adaptations. By contrast, given that nonhuman primates are often specialized for their unique ecological niche (e.g., tropical forests in the case of gorillas and orangutans), relevance to human behavior may be limited to "mere" homologies—common phylogenetic baggage shared between closely related species.

Evolutionary stable strategies. The notions of *divergent selection* and *frequency-dependent selection* together provide a basis for understanding interpersonal variability as something more than the raw material on which selection operates. The basic idea is that under given conditions either of two (or more) traits may be adaptive and the fitness conveyed by the traits is partly dependent on their frequency in the population. An example of frequency-dependent selection is seen when rarity confers an advantage, often because of preference by the opposite sex for individuals of rare phenotypes (Ehrman, 1966; Petit, 1958; Petit and Nouaud, 1975), or the tendency among predators to overlook rare types (Moment, 1962). Importantly, then, variability becomes something to be understood in evolutionary terms and not an argument against a genetic basis of behavior.

The South American cichlid fish *Cichlasoma citrinellum* occurs in either of two color morphs (varieties): a vertically striped camouflaged morph and a solid gold morph. The relative frequency of the two morphs varies from lake to lake. When raised separately in tanks, both morphs grow at the same rate, but when raised together, the gold variety is able to dominate the striped variety, get more food and grow faster. If this were the only thing that happened, one would expect the gold morph to replace the striped morph, but in the wild it is more conspicuous to predators. As the frequency of the gold morph increases, it becomes more subject to predation, which decreases its fitness. At some point a balance is struck, with the relative frequencies varying from lake to lake, presumably depending upon the local food and predator conditions (Barlow, 1973).

Maynard Smith and Price (1973) have used computer simulations to investigate the evolution of ritualized combat. Imagine a population of horned animals, each of which fights for mates and food. There are particular expected benefits and costs for any behavioral strategy. An animal that always fights to the death may eliminate its competitor, but risks injury or death. An animal that always runs away when attacked never wins anything. A third animal (bluffer) that attacks once and runs away if its opponent stands its ground will always lose to an animal pursuing the first strategy, and will always win against an animal pursuing the second. The fitness of each behavioral strategy varies with the distribution of different strategies. If there are a lot of cowards and bluffers, the fight-to-the-death strategist has an advantage; if there are a lot of fighters-to-the-death, the bluffer has an advantage, and so on. Under given conditions, the behavioral types will come to be distributed in relatively stable proportions, or the animals may play either strategy randomly but in those proportions. This is called an *evolutionarily stable strategy* and may be responsible for much of the variability present among natural populations. [See Maynard Smith (1976b) for a discussion of evolution and game theory, as well as a discussion of sex ratios.][1]

Heterosis. Another mechanism that could maintain genetic variation is heterozygote advantage or heterosis. Heterozygotes (with respect to a specific locus) are organisms that have two different alleles, for example, *Aa*. Homozygotes have identical alleles at the locus in question, i.e., *AA* or *aa*. If the heterozygote is more successful than either homozygote in a particular environment, both alleles will be maintained in the population. An illustrative example in humans is sickle cell anaemia. Individuals who have the disease are homozygous (let us call them *AA*), and they are characterized by severe and frequently lethal blood disorders. Those individuals who are homozygous for *not* having the trait (that is, *aa*) do in fact have more children in most environments. Thus one would expect the *A* allele to decrease in frequency through directional selection. However, in areas where malaria is prevalent, it turns out that individuals who are heterozygous with respect to sickle cell anaemia (that is, *Aa*) are more successful than *either* of the homozygotes. They do not suffer the debilitating effects of the disease, and they also happen to be not as susceptible to the effects of malaria as the *aa* individual. Thus, even if *all AA* and *aa* individuals died without reproducing (and this is certainly not the case), both the *A* and *a* alleles would be maintained in the population by the heterozygous individuals. That is, heterozygous couples will have offspring with the following genotypes: *AA*, *Aa*, *aA*, and *aa*. Half of these would be viable, and 50% of their offspring would, in turn, be viable heterozygotes.

---

[1]Limitations of space have made the preceding a rather cursory treatment. Good introductions of "how evolution works" can be found in Maynard Smith (1975), Stebbins (1971), and Dobzhansky (1970).

Understanding Natural Selection

Fitness. Darwin's phrase "survival of the fittest" (actually borrowed from Herbert Spencer) has had a grossly misleading influence upon subsequent interpretations of his work. Darwin himself used it correctly, equating fitness with reproductive success. Unfortunately, others have equated it with Tennyson's "nature red in tooth and claw," envisioning a world in which violence, brutality, dog-eat-dog and uncontrolled competition are "nature's way." Rather, natural selection is differential reproduction—no more, no less. Fighting prowess may certainly contribute to reproductive success in some circumstances and thus be selected because it increases fitness, but so do many other factors. In fact, a highly aggressive male lion may be selected against relative to his somewhat less aggressive counterpart who fights a bit less and copulates more. Furthermore, survival in intraspecific fighting often requires adherence to certain ritualized tournamentlike rules that dramatically reduce the likelihood of injury or bloodshed (Eibl-Eibesfeldt, 1961; Maynard Smith and Price, 1973). Among the other characteristics on which natural selection operates are the ability to choose an appropriate mate, adequate parenting, nest-building, foraging and self-maintenance behaviors, and resistance to cold, drought, famine, predators and so forth.

Randomness. Natural selection is sometimes considered to be only a random process and therefore inadequate to account for the evolution of complexity. Evolution does depend upon mutation and sexual recombination for the diversity upon which natural selection acts, and mutations and recombinations are essentially random events (although mutation and recombination *rates* are under the influence of natural selection). However, the mechanism of natural selection itself is not random. One can consider each living organism as a highly organized, nonrandom mass. R. A. Fisher (1930) specifically pointed to natural selection as the mechanism for this nonrandomness in nature. Living things provide an enormous array of genetic material, from which nature selects a very small, nonrandom sample. Furthermore, individuals in the atypical sample are likely to breed among themselves, producing new individuals whose genetic composition is yet more atypical. For example, consider a mutation occurring at a rate of 10^{-6}. The chances of finding a single individual with ten such mutations would be 10^{-60}. On the other hand, by differential reproduction of individuals possessing any such mutations, selection could produce the indicated type much sooner. Natural selection is uniquely equipped to produce such novel rearrangements. Whether it is a symphony, a poem or a human being, creativity is measured by the generation of nonrandom assemblages.

Group selection. Finally, a persistent misuse of evolutionary biology is the idea that evolution operates "for the benefit of the species." Since natural selection favors individuals in proportion as they are more fit, a frequent consequence of the evolutionary process is that species eventually tend to be composed of individuals each of which is well adapted. But these species adaptations are incidental by-products of natural selection operating by the differential reproduction of its constituent individuals. In general, when conflicts arise between individual and species benefit, selection favors the individual.

The suggestion that selection could possibly operate at the level of groups rather than individuals has been argued most cogently by Wynne-Edwards (1962), although it has been rejected by most ecologists and evolutionary biologists, largely because of the enormously greater power of individual selection (Crook, 1965; Weins, 1965). More recently, computer simulations have documented the theoretical feasibility of group selection (Boorman and Levitt, 1973; Gadgil, 1975; Levins, 1970). However, these models require such extreme conditions as to suggest that group selection is very unlikely in nature [see Lewontin (1970) for one purported example in a virus]. When originally proposed by Wynne-Edwards, group selection was used to explain the supposed evolution of reproductive restraint—a trait that may be advantageous to the group, although disadvantageous to the individual. In order for individually maladaptive traits to evolve via group selection, they would have to confer greater benefit upon the group than detriment to the individual. While this may not seem unreasonable, the problem is that for each trait of this sort to be maintained, differential reproduction of groups would have to exceed differential reproduction of individuals—a highly unlikely event, especially among vertebrates [e.g., see Maynard Smith (1976a) for a review of the controversy]. At this point, the power of individual selection is well-documented while group selection is problematic; therefore, it seems parsimonious to couch our thinking in terms of natural selection operating upon individuals rather than groups.

Relevance of Natural Selection to Behavior

In order for evolution to operate on any trait, there must be some correspondence—however slight—between that trait and the genetic make-up of the individuals involved. Social scientists in particular are inclined to reject this notion and indeed, sociology, anthropology and psychology are all strongly committed to environmental determinism of behavior. There can be no doubt that experiential factors are a major determinant of human behavior, but this does not necessitate rejection of genetic predispositions as well. It may be that one reason for the general social science attitude in this regard is the misimpression that somehow we must choose between either environmental or genetic determinants, thereby categorically rejecting the other. This is not the case.

Nature or nurture. One of the oldest and perhaps least productive controversies in science has concerned this genetics–environment issue, variously labeled nature–nurture or instinct–learning. However, it has since been recognized that both genetics and environment affect behavior: there can be no behavior without an organism to do the behaving, and the organism behaves within its environment. All behavior derives from the interaction of genotype and environment. [For a review of this synthesis, see especially Hinde (1970) and Lehrman (1970)].

It is clear that organisms differ in their relative reliance upon genotype and experience, and that for any single species, behaviors may differ insofar as the contribution of these factors is concerned. Human beings are highly susceptible to environmental factors, modifying their behavior dramatically as a result of experience. Some behaviors, such as the blink reflex, are quite unmodifiable by experience, while others, such as "personality," are relatively plastic. But just as reflexes require environmental inputs with regard to both normal development and actual elicitation of the behavior, even human personality is constrained within certain limits by our genotype.

Much of the resistance to the idea of genetic influences upon behavior derives from a misunderstanding of how genes operate. DNA provides merely a "blueprint" for subsequent construction. In some cases, it may specify precise effects, as with a reflex, but it may also specify rather vague and general propensities. Human behavior is not curled up within a gene, like the old conception of the tiny homunculus, waiting within sperm or egg, eventually to emerge fully developed and ready to perform. If we introduce a male European robin to a tuft of red feathers, it will invariably display its species-specific aggressive behaviors. Clearly we do not possess anything like this mouse-trap precision of response. But it has been too easy for students of human behavior to dismiss the animal models of ethology, thus denying the possibility of *any* human behavioral predispositions, just because we do not conform to these extreme examples.

In order for an evolutionary approach to be relevant to the study of human behavior, it is only necessary that we possess some genetically mediated tendencies to behave in particular fashions. For example, consider the response tendencies elicited by the infantile characteristics of a variety of different animals (e.g., large eyes, broad face, flattened nose and so forth—in other words, "cute"). We may be able to overcome our nurturing and/or protective inclinations in this case, but the inclinations nevertheless exist. They have presumably been selected during the course of our evolution because personal fitness is enormously enhanced by positive responsiveness to our own infants. That is, it seems reasonable that among our ancestors, those possessing a tendency to respond positively to stimuli of this sort produced relatively more successful offspring, so that *Homo sapiens* is now composed of individuals who generally respond in this way.

On a purely mechanistic level, there is no greater block between DNA and behavior than between DNA and bone structure, for example. Genes ultimately code for structural proteins, which influence the properties and interconnections of cells. DNA is just as capable of influencing nerve cells as bone cells, and if we grant that behavior arises from the activity of nerve cells in some environment, then behavior, also, is susceptible to genetic influence just as is skeletal structure.

There are no experimental data concerning genetically mediated behavior tendencies in human beings, because of the ethical constraints upon such manipulations with our species. However, abundant evidence exists for genetic influences on behavior in other animals, ranging from single-gene effects (Bastock, 1956; Rothenbuhler, 1967) to extensive hybridization studies (Clark et al., 1954; Sharpe and Johnsgard, 1965). For example, two species of African parrots differ in the way they carry nesting materials: members of one species use their beaks exclusively whereas members of the other tuck the materials into their rump feathers. A genetic component for this behavior is suggested by the actions of cross-species hybrids. These animals show intermediate behaviors, picking up strips of paper in their bills, placing them in the feathers, only to take them back into their bills, then dropping them on the ground and so on (Dilger, 1962). Unfortunately, these hybrids are infertile, thus precluding any precise analysis of number of genes, dominance–recessiveness and so forth. But, the fact that genes are involved in this complex behavior pattern and that their influence is substantial is abundantly clear.

Heritability. Some of the most potent evidence linking genotype to behavioral phenotype comes from studies of artificial selection, in which human experimenters substitute for "nature," deciding which individuals shall be reproductively favored. Selection of this sort has been standard procedure for centuries among animal and plant breeders. For our purposes, it is noteworthy that artificial selection has also been found effective in modifying the distribution of *behavioral* traits, in studies ranging from mating speed and directional preference in fruit flies (Hirsch and Erlenmeyer-Kimling, 1962; Manning, 1963) to aggressiveness in chickens (Cook et al., 1972). A classic study of selection for "maze-bright" and "maze-dull" rats succeeded in deriving statistically distinct strains within only two generations (Tolman, 1924). These differences remained after many generations with no further experimental manipulations (Searle, 1949).

For directional selection in general, let S (the selection differential) represent the difference between the mean of the initial generation with respect to a particular trait and the mean of those individuals chosen to be parents of the next generation, and let R (the response to selection) represent the difference between the mean of the initial generation and the mean of the first offspring generation. In this case, $R/S = h^2$ is a measure of the responsiveness of the trait to selection, i.e., its heritability (Figure 5).

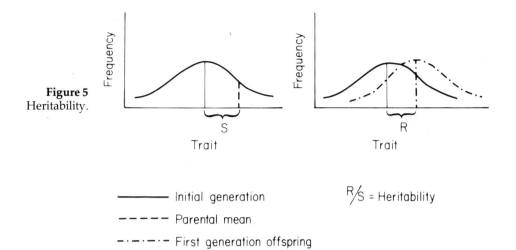

Figure 5
Heritability.

———— Initial generation

– – – – Parental mean

– · — · — · – First generation offspring

R/S = Heritability

Heritability in this sense is a special case of the more general "regression toward the mean." Heritability, h^2, is the same as the regression slope when offspring is regressed on midparent (a parental average). Heritability may be defined in several ways, but it is always a characteristic of population variances rather than individual characteristics. In any event, the important point here is that behaviors have been shown to have heritabilities of greater than zero. Heritability is also a function of the environment, but the fact that behavior is susceptible to evolution by natural selection makes it an appropriate concern of evolutionary biology. Behavioral genetics is a growing area of research, e.g., Ehrman and Parsons (1976), and is treated more systematically in the next chapter.

Biology of altruism. Altruism is a paradox for evolutionary theory because it seemingly requires a decrease in the reproductive success of the individual concerned. If a particular gene, or set thereof, increases the probability that its carrier will behave in such a manner as to *decrease* its representation in succeeding generations, then how can it evolve? One possibility is group selection, treated earlier in this paper—but group selection remains problematic.

One of the exciting breakthroughs in theoretical population genetics was the recognition that natural selection, operating on individuals, can explain the evolution of apparent altruism (Fisher, 1930; Haldane, 1932; Hamilton, 1964). Indeed, Hamilton's insights and their enormous implications for the evolutionary analysis of social behavior [see, especially, Hamilton (1975)] have provided much of the intellectual impetus for the field now designated "sociobiology." Basically, Hamilton recognized that parental care of offspring is but a special case of a more general phenomenon: concern for relatives. This evolutionary mechanism has been termed *kin selection* (Maynard Smith, 1964) and provides a reasonable explanation for the behavior of those group members who assist other group members in securing relatively scarce resources (e.g., food, protection) at some apparent personal cost. Since natural selection operates through the representation of genes in succeeding generations, any one individual can pass on its own genes either by raising offspring *or* by helping a relative (with whom some genes are shared by common descent) to reproduce. Thus, if two individuals are sufficiently related, then one individual may best further its own ultimate reproductive success by helping the other, even at some apparent immediate cost. More precisely, altruism via kin selection should evolve in this manner if $K > 1/r$, where K equals the ratio of the benefit to the altruist's relatives as a result of the behavior in question to the cost suffered by the altruist, and where r equals the coefficient of relationship between altruist and beneficiary. In this formulation, of course, benefit and cost are both measured in terms of units of fitness. The coefficient of relationship r is measured by the proportion of genes shared by virtue of common descent. For example, in a sexually reproducing, diploid species, each parent shares $\frac{1}{2}$ of its genes with each offspring. Similarly, on average, adults share $\frac{1}{4}$ of their genes with grandchildren, full siblings share $\frac{1}{2}$, and cousins share $\frac{1}{8}$.

This theory represents an important extension of evolutionary thought in that it substitutes "inclusive fitness" for simple Darwinian fitness as the ultimate arbiter of adaptive significance. Whereas Darwinian fitness is concerned only with the production of successful offspring, inclusive fitness recognizes the importance of *all* relatives, devalued in proportion as these relatives are genetically more distant. Kin selection was originally used to explain the epitome of altruism among animals—the evolution of sterile worker castes in bees, wasps and ants (Hamilton, 1964). Subsequently, cogent empirical data have been adduced in support of this interpretation (Trivers and Hare, 1976).

For the social scientist, kin selection is particularly important in that it provides a unified, coherent theory for the biology of nepotism—an apparently universal human trait. It also offers a whole new perspective on human mating systems, one whose possibilities have barely been explored and which offer an exciting future to social scientists with an evolutionary orientation. Furthermore, these evolutionary considerations suggest possible insight into the biology of female–male differences in behavior (Trivers, 1972), parent–offspring conflict (Trivers, 9174), sibling rivalry (Barash et al., 1978), parental solicitude for offspring (Barash, 1976) and xenophobia (Hamilton, 1975). In fact, an evolutionary approach to altruism does not require relatedness among the individuals concerned. Altruism can be selected between unrelated individuals, provided there is a sufficiently high probability of *reciprocity* (Trivers, 1971), namely, when costs are low and benefits high, and when individuals can recognize one another and can expect to interact again in the future. Although reciprocal altruism has been reported in baboons (Packer, 1977), its greatest impact most assuredly will be in its application to human behavior. These concepts are only a small sampling of the rich trove of ideas and possibilities available to the social scientist who wishes to explore the implications of evolutionary biology for human social behaviors. For instance, Morgan (1979) has found that in the four most active whaling boats in an Eskimo village, the captain-to-crew coefficients of relationship were as high as .50. Further, even the kinship terminology itself may reflect actual patterns of genetic relatedness (Greene, 1978). Hartung (1976) discusses the relevance of biology to inheritance patterns, concluding that since male offspring are high risk and high benefit from the parents' point of view, under conditions of polygyny, wealth is most effective when transmitted through the male line. Finally, Alexander (1974), Kurland (n.d.) and Greene (1978) discuss the implications of female promiscuity (which will affect the *average* certainty of paternity) with respect to social structure, especially with respect to instances of the avunculate.

Hybrid Vigor   The past few years have seen a dramatic increase in the number of sociological works which have incorporated various aspects of biology and evolutionary theory. Two recent collections (Fox, 1975; Bateson and Hinde, 1976) characterize the potential integration of these fields by the diverse backgrounds of both the contributors and their topics. Tiger (1975) reviews studies that have included somatic factors (particularly hormones) as correlates of behavior. Blurton Jones (1976) considers cultural inheritance from an evolutionary perspective [see also Dawkins' (1976) treatment of "memes" as the unit of cultural transmission]. The approaches used by Clutton-Brock and Harvey (1976, 1977, 1978) in their analyses of primate societies may prove especially fruitful in generating hypotheses about the evolutionary history of human social structure. They discuss correlations among a wide variety of variables such as population density, diet, sexual dimorphism, pair bonding, group size and breeding patterns. For example, polygyny is correlated with a high degree of sexual dimorphism.

In conclusion, we wish to emphasize that such terms as "altruism," when used by sociobiologists, carry no implication as to the cognitive or motivational state of the individual(s) concerned. The behavior is identified strictly in terms of its consequences for the distribution of genes in succeeding generations. Second, a concern with evolutionary biology does *not* ignore the undoubted role of such environmental factors as early experience, social learning and/or cultural tradition. In fact, tradition can be viewed as reflecting underlying biological adaptive strategies (Greene and

Barash, 1976). A final example is offered by Rozin (1976:66) where he concludes, "The avoidance of milk institutionalized in Chinese cuisine is no doubt in part a cultural adaptation to high lactose intolerance."

Cross-fertilization between evolutionary biology and the social sciences may well result in hybrid vigor. In any case, it certainly seems worth pursuing, with an open mind and a maximum amount of understanding.

References   Alexander, R.D. 1974. The evolution of social behavior. *Annual Review of Ecology and Systematics* 5:325–383.

Alper, S.J., Beckwith, S.L., Hunt Chorover, J., Inonye, H., Judd, T., Lange, R.V., and Sternberg, P. 1976. The implications of sociobiology. *Science* 192:424–427.

Barash, D.P. 1976. Some evolutionary aspects of parental behavior in animals and man. *American Journal of Psychology* 89:195–218.

Barash, D.P., Holmes, W.G., and Greene, P.J. 1977. Exact versus probabilistic coefficients of relationship: Some implications for sociobiology. *American Naturalist* 122:355–363.

Barlow, G.W. 1973. Competition between color morphs of the polychromatic Midas Cichlid *Cichlasoma citrinellum. Science* 179:806–807.

Bastock, M. 1956. A gene mutation which changes a behaviour. *Evolution* 10:421–439.

Bateson, P.P.G., and Hinde, R.A. (eds.) 1976. *Growing Points in Ethology.* Cambridge: Cambridge University Press.

Blurton Jones, N. 1975. Ethology, anthropology, and childhood. In R. Fox (ed.), *Biosocial Anthropology.* London: Malaby Press.

———. 1976. Growing points in human ethology: Another link between ethology and the social sciences? In P.P.G. Bateson and R.A. Hinde (eds.) *Growing Points in Ethology.* Cambridge: Cambridge University Press.

Boorman, S.A., and Levitt, P.R. 1973. Group selection on the boundary of a stable population. *Theoretical Population Biology* 4:85–128.

Campbell, D.T. 1975. On the conflicts between biological and social evolution and between psychology and moral tradition. *American Psychologist* 30:1103–1126.

Clark, E., Aronson, L.R., and Gordon, M. 1954. Mating behavior patterns in two sympatric species of xiphophorin fishes: Their inheritance and significance in sexual isolation. *Bulletin of the American Museum of Natural History* 103:135–226.

Clark, L.R., Geier, P.W., Hughes, R.D., and Morris, R.F. 1967. *The Ecology of Insect Populations in Theory and Practice.* London: Methuen.

Clutton-Brock, T.H., and Harvey, P.H. 1976. Evolutionary rules and primate societies. In P.P.G. Bateson and R.A. Hinde (eds.) *Growing Points in Ethology.* Cambridge: Cambridge University Press.

———. 1977. Primate ecology and social organization. *Journal of Zoology* 183:1–39.

———. 1978. *Readings in Sociobiology.* San Francisco: Freeman and Co.

Cook, W.T., Siegel, P., and Hinkelmann, K. 1972. Genetic analyses of male mating behaviour in chickens. 2: Crosses among selected and control lines. *Behaviour Genetics* 2:289–300.

Coser, L. 1971. *Masters of Sociological Thought.* New York: Harcourt Brace Jovanovich.

Crook, J.H. 1965. The adaptive significance of avian social organizations. *Symposia of the Zoological Society of London* 14:181–218.

Dawkins, R. 1976. *The Selfish Gene.* Oxford: Oxford University Press.

Dilger, W.C. 1962. The behavior of lovebirds. *Scientific American* 206:88–98.

Dobzhansky, T. 1970. *Genetics of the Evolutionary Process.* New York: Columbia University Press.

Ehrman, L. 1966. Mating success and genotype frequency in Drosophila. *Animal Behaviour* 14:332–339.

Ehrman, L., and Parsons, P.A. 1976. *The Genetics of Behavior.* Sunderland, MA: Sinauer Associates.

Eibl-Eibesfeldt, I. 1961. The fighting behavior of animals. *Scientific American* 205 (December): 112–122.

Fisher, R.A. 1930. *The Genetical Theory of Natural Selection.* Oxford: Clarendon Press.

Fox, Robin (ed.) 1975. *Biosocial Anthropology.* London: Malaby Press.

Gadgil, M. 1975. Evolution of social behaviour through interpopulation selection. *Proceedings of the National Academy of Science* 72:1199–1201.

Greene, P.J. 1978. Promiscuity, paternity, and culture. *American Ethnologist* 5:151–159.

Greene, P.J., and Barash, D.P. 1976. Genetic basis of behavior–especially of altruism. *American Psychologist* 31(May): 359–361.

Haldane, J.B.S. 1932. *The Causes of Evolution.* Ithaca: Cornell University Press.

Hamilton, W.D. 1964. The genetical evolution of social behaviour, Parts I and II. *Journal of Theoretical Biology* 7:1–52.

———. 1975. Innate social aptitudes of man: An approach from evolutionary genetics. In R. Fox (ed.) *Biosocial Anthropology.* London: Malaby Press.

Hartung, J. 1976. On natural selection and the inheritance of wealth. *Current Anthropology* 17:607–622.

Hinde, R.A. 1970. *Animal Behaviour: A Synthesis of Ethology and Comparative Psychology.* 2nd ed. New York: McGraw-Hill.

Hirsch, J., and Erlenmeyer-Kimling, L. 1962. Individual differences in behavior and their genetic basis. In E.L. Bliss (ed.) *Roots of Behavior.* pp. 3–23. New York: Harper and Row.

Huxley, J.S. 1942. *Evolution, the Modern Synthesis.* London: G. Allen and Unwin.

Kruuk, H. 1972. *The Spotted Hyena: A Study of Predation and Social Behavior.* Chicago: University of Chicago Press.

Kurland, J. n.d. "Matrilines: The primate sisterhood and the human avunculate." Unpublished manuscript.

Lehrman, D.S. 1970. Semantic and conceptual issues in the nature–nurture problem. In L.B. Aronson, E. Tobach, D.S. Lehrman, and J.S. Rosenblatt (eds.) *Development and the Evolution of Behavior,* pp. 17–52. San Francisco: W. H. Freeman.

Levins, R. 1970. Extinction. In M. Gerstenhaber (ed.) *Some Mathematical Questions in Biology,* Vol. 2 of Lecture on Mathematics in the Life Sciences, pp. 77–107. Providence, RI: American Mathematical Society.

Lewontin, R.C. 1970. The unit of selection. *In Annual Review of Ecology and Systematics,* pp. 1–18. Palo Alto: Annual Reviews.

Manning, A. 1963. Selection for mating speed in *Drosophila melanogaster* based on the behaviour of one sex. *Animal Behaviour* 11:116–120.

Maynard Smith, J. 1964. Group selection and kin selection. *Nature* (London) 201:1145–1147.

———. 1975. *The Theory of Evolution.* Baltimore: Penguin Books.

———. 1976a. Group selection. *Quarterly Review of Biology* 51 (June):277–283.

———. 1976b. Evolution and the theory of games. *American Scientist* 64(1):41–45.

Maynard Smith, J., and Price, G.R. 1973. The logic of animal conflict. *Nature* (London) 246:15–18.

Mazur, A. 1973. A cross-species comparison of status in small established groups. *American Sociological Review* 38:513–530.

Mech, L.D. 1970. *The Wolf: The Ecology and Behavior of an Endangered Species*. Garden City, NY: Natural History Press.

Moment, G. 1962. Reflexive selection: A possible answer to an old puzzle. *Science* 136:262–263.

Morgan, C.J. 1979. Eskimo hunting groups and the possibility of kin selection in humans. *Ethology and Sociobiology* 1:83–86.

Packer, C. 1977. Reciprocal altruism in *Papio anubis*. *Nature* 265:441–443.

Petit, C. 1958. Le determinisme genetique et psycho-physiologique de la competition sexuelle chez *Drosophila melanogaster*. *Bulletin Biologique de la France et de la Belgique* 92:248–329.

Petit, C., and Nouaud, D. 1975. Ecological competition and the advantage of the rare type in *Drosophila melanogaster*. *Evolution* 29:763–776.

Rothenbuhler, W.C. 1967. Genetic and evolutionary considerations of social behavior of honeybees and some related insects. In J. Hirsch (ed.) *Behavior–Genetic Analysis*, pp. 61–111. New York: McGraw-Hill.

Rozin, P. 1976. The selection of foods by rats, humans, and other animals. *Advances in the Study of Behavior* 6:21–76.

Schaller, G.B. 1972. *The Serengeti Lion: A Study of Predator–Prey Relations*. Chicago: University of Chicago Press.

Schaller, G.B., and Lowther, G.R. 1969. The relevance of carnivore behavior to the study of early hominids. *Southwestern Journal of Anthropology* 25:307–341.

Searle L.V. 1949. The organization of hereditary maze-brightness and maze-dullness. *Genetic Psychology Monographs* 39:279ff.

Sharpe, R.S., and Johnsgard, P.A. 1966. Inheritance of behavioral characters in F_2 mallard × pintail (*Anas platyrhyneohos* L. × *Anas acuta* L.) hybrids. *Behaviour* 27:259–272.

Sociobiology Study Group of Science for the People. 1976. "Sociobiology—another biological determinism." *BioScience* 26:183–186.

Stebbins, G.L. 1971. *Processes of Organic Evolution*. 2nd ed. Englewood Cliffs, NJ: Prentice-Hall.

Tiger, L. 1975. Somatic factors and social behaviour. In R. Fox (ed.) *Biosocial Anthropology*. London: Malaby Press.

Tolman, E.C. 1924. The inheritance of maze-learning ability in rats. *Journal of Comparative Psychology* 4:1–18.

Trivers, R.L. 1971. The evolution of reciprocal altruism. *Quarterly Review of Biology* 46:35–57.

———. 1972. Parental investment and sexual selection. In B. Campbell (ed.) *Sexual Selection and the Descent of Man*, 1871–1971, pp. 136–179. Chicago: Aldine.

———. 1974. Parent–offspring conflict. *American Zoologist* 14:249–264.

Trivers, R.L., and Hare, H. 1976. Haplodiploidy and the evolution of the social insects. *Science* 191:249–263.

van Lawick, H., and van Lawick-Goodall, J. 1971. *Innocent Killers*. Boston: Houghton-Mifflin Co.

van den Berghe, P.L. 1974. Bringing beasts back in: Towards a biosocial theory of aggression. *American Sociological Review* 39:777–788.

Wade, N. 1976. Sociobiology: Troubled birth for a new discipline. *Science* 191:1151–1155.

Wiens, John A. 1966. "On group selection and Wynne-Edward's hypothesis." *American Scientist* 54:273–287.

Wilson, E.O. 1975. *Sociobiology: The New Synthesis*. Cambridge: Harvard University Press.

Wright, S. 1931. Evolution in Mendelian populations. *Genetics* 16:97–158.

———. 1943. Isolation by distance. *Genetics* 28:114–138.

———. 1968. *Evolution and the Genetics of Populations,* Vol. 1: Genetic and Biometric Foundations. Chicago: University of Chicago Press.

———. 1969. *Evolution and the Genetics of Populations,* Vol. 2: The Theory of Gene Frequencies. Chicago: University of Chicago Press.

Wynne-Edwards, V.C. 1962. *Animal Dispersion in Relation to Social Behaviour.* Edinburgh: Oliver and Boyd.

Concepts of Behavior Genetics and Misapplications to Humans

Jerry Hirsch, Terry R. McGuire, Atam Vetta

11

Historically, the study of behavior and the study of heredity have shared contradictory relationships. Experimental behaviorists long denied the relevance of heredity, whereas for mental testers heredity was of overriding importance (Chase, 1980). With the advent of behaviorism, experimental psychology spent half the century trying to found a science on the denial of heredity, thus making it impossible to understand the diversity and individuality that characterize members of diploid cross-fertilizing species (Hirsch, 1963). Because all conspecifics were assumed to be born alike, they were expected to behave alike in similar circumstances (Hirsch, 1967). By assumption, behavior was independent of heredity. That was the context in which was launched the approach since called Behavior Genetics (Hirsch and Tryon, 1956). During the past 20 years many developments have converged to produce the work summarized by Ehrman and Parsons (1976). We are not concerned here with a review of the literature; instead, we shall consider basic concepts of behavior genetics and some misconceptions that have impeded progress.

Failure conceptually to appreciate and to integrate three fundamentals of biology—individuality, interaction and norm of reaction throughout ontogeny—underlies the long confusion. It is a fact that members of cross-fertilizing species are genotypically unique. Moreover, although it is a platitude to say that heredity and environment *interact* to produce the phenotype, it is just that interaction that has thwarted attempts to build for ideal organisms, models of behavior analogous to those built for ideal systems. Not only do genotypes differ in response to a common environment, but one genotype varies in response to different environments. Therefore, we need concepts to encompass behavior-genetic relations that are neither isomorphic nor independent: isomorphism might have justified the naive reductionism that led behavior genetics to racism, and independence might have justified behaviorism's naive environmentalism.

Individuality and Diversity

The understanding of individuality and diversity is essential to the understanding of behavior genetics and its appropriate application. Ordinarily, members of a cross-fertilizing, sexually reproducing species possess a diploid, or paired, set of *chromosomes.* Most species whose behavior we study are sexually dimorphic. The genetic basis of this dimorphism resides in the distribution of the heterosomes, a homologous pair of sex chromosomes *(XX)* being present in the mammalian female and an unequal pair *(XY),* in the mammalian male. Sexual dimorphism guarantees that any population will be variable to the extent of at least two classes.

Chromosomes other than sex chromosomes are called *autosomes.* Every autosome is normally represented by a homologous pair whose members have identical genetic loci. Alternative forms of a gene any of which may occupy a given locus are termed *alleles.* If an individual receives identical alleles from both parents at homologous loci, he is said to be homozygous for that gene. If he receives two alleles that differ, however, he is said to be heterozygous for that gene. The process by which a gene changes from one allelic form to another is called *mutation.*

When a gene is represented in the population gene pool by two allelic forms, the population will be genotypically polymorphic to the extent of at least three classes. That is, individuals may be homozygous for either of two alleles or heterozygous for their combination.

Study of populations has revealed that often extensive series of alleles exist for a locus. Well-known examples are the three (actually more) alleles at the ABO-blood locus in man and a dozen or more alleles at the white-eye locus in *Drosophila.* In general, for each locus having n alleles in the gene pool, a population will contain $n(n + 1)/2$ genotypic classes. Mutation ensures variety in the gene itself.

Sexual reproduction involves meiosis—a complex cellular process resulting in a meristic division of the nucleus and formation of gametes (reproductive cells) having single genomes (a haploid chromosome set). One homolog in every chromosome pair in our diploid complement is of paternal origin and the other is of maternal origin. In meiosis, the homologs of a pair segregate and a gamete receives one from each pair. The assortment to gametes of the segregating homologs occurs independently for each pair. This process ensures diversity because it maximizes the likelihood that gametes will receive unique genomes. For example, gametogenesis in *Drosophila willistoni* produces eight alternative gametic genomes, which, if we represent the three chromosome pairs of this species by *Aa, Bb* and *Cc,* we designate *ABC, ABc, AbC, aBC, Abc, aBc, abC, abc.* In general, n pairs of chromosomes produce 2^n genomes (if we ignore the recombination of gene linkages that actually occurs in crossover exchanges between chromosomes). Man, with 23 chromosome pairs, produces gametes with any of 2^{23} alternative genomes. This makes vanishingly small the chances that even siblings (other than monozygotes) will be genetically identical. Since the gamete contributed by *each* parent is chosen from 2^{23} alternatives, the probability that the second offspring born to parents will have exactly the same genotype as their firstborn is $(1/2^{23})^2$, or less than 1 chance in over 70 trillion! The probability that two unrelated individuals will have the same genotype, then, is effectively zero.

The argument for the genotypic uniqueness of members of populations is even more compelling, since other conditions such as physiological systems and ontogenic development contribute significantly to this already great *individual* diversity. However, natural selection works to eliminate diversity in prodigious quantities and to maintain a narrow fit to the available niche. For example, rodents (rats, mice, hamsters, etc.), of which there are over 300 genera and almost 3000 species, have litters varying in size from one or two up to 15 or 16 with an average below ten. Taking, for convenience, the number eight, which we obtain in some of our mouse and rat colonies, we can calculate how a population might grow:

Generation	Parents	Offspring	Population				
N_0		2					
N_1	2	8	8 + 2	=	10 =	5 × 2 pairs	
N_2	10	40	40 + 10	=	50 =	25 × 2 pairs	
N_3	50	200	200 + 50	=	250 =	125 × 2 pairs	
N_4	250	1000	1000 + 250	=	1250 =	625 × 2 pairs	
N_5			6250				
N_6			31,250				
N_7			156,250				
N_8			781,250				
N_9			3,906,250				
N_{10}			19,531,250				

In general,

$$N_t = N_0(1 + p)^t$$
$$N_{10} = 2(1 + 4)^{10} = 19,531,250 \approx 20 \text{ million}$$

Given good conditions they reach sexual maturity in a few weeks, closer to 30 than to 60 days, and gestation lasts only about 20 days. So it is possible to have over three generations a year and individuals can live two or more years. It is no exaggeration whatsoever to say that the reproductive capacity of a single couple might reach 20 million within the time of their own possible lifespan, because not only can their grandchildren be actively reproducing within the first year, but they themselves can have three or four litters in a year. Of course, it was precisely this insight transmitted by Malthus to both Darwin and Wallace which provided the key to evolution. Darwin even calculated that the slowest breeding mammal, the elephant, would have produced 15 million descendants from a single couple in five centuries. The message of the Malthusian calculation is simple: the reproductive capacity of any species is sufficient to flood the planet, and yet none of them does. Selection pressure is intense. Only a small proportion of the possible progeny survive in each generation.

However, man in civilization is doing ever more to limit reproduction and preserve the diversity, and through technology is spawning an ever increasing variety of cultural niches to accommodate his diversity. We are becoming maybe the most cosmopolitan species in the history of the animal kingdom. This is *not* a claim that human evolution has stopped—only that the pattern of selection pressures is no longer tailoring our species to a narrow niche of aggressive hunting and food gathering.

Concepts in Quantitative Genetics

Polygenic Traits Versus Major Gene Effects

In transmission genetics (the study of the inheritance of genes), a distinction is made between so-called major gene effects and polygenic effects. The study of the inheritance of major genes is the domain of classical Mendelian genetics, while the study of the inheritance of traits with continuous variation and polygenic correlates is the domain of quantitative genetics.

A major gene can be defined as an allele that alters in some distinctive way the "normal" or wild-type expression of a trait. The expression of a major gene is an either–or effect with either the wild-type or the "deviant" phenotype being manifested. The heterozygote may, however, show an intermediate phenotype. If appropriate matings are made, the major gene will show Mendelian segregation ratios. Examples of major genes in man are sickle-cell anemia, Huntington's chorea (a degenerative disease of the central nervous system) and phenylketonuria.

Polygenic traits are ones in which there is no obvious wild-type expression. Instead, these traits show continuous variation among all members of a population that is not due solely to environmental influences. Examples in man are height, pigmentation and intelligence. Polygenic correlates are often rated on a finer scale than are major gene effects. A trait like height, which is studied as a polygenic trait, may also be studied, in some cases, as a major gene effect. For example, "normal" height is the wild-type phenotype for a major gene like achrondoplasia (human dwarfism).

By definition, polygenic traits are specified by a number of loci. These loci are usually independently assorting and each has two or more alleles. The loci act as if they form a related system so that each allele adds or subtracts a certain quantitative increment to the trait being measured. Polygenicity does not imply that there are any underlying interlinked biochemical systems between alleles, perfect additivity of alleles, or the presence or absence of dominance. Polygenic systems may act in an additive manner, but this does not imply that any one allele adds one inch to height or five IQ points to intelligence, even though the mathematicogenetic models make it appear that such is the case.

The Case of One Locus with Two Alleles

To illustrate the thinking and mathematics behind quantitative genetics, we now consider the simplest case of one gene having two alleles at its locus. We also assume a random mating population with no migration, selection or mutation. That is, the population is in Hardy–Weinberg equilibrium, so that the genotypic frequencies are constant from one generation to the next. The two alleles are A_1 and A_2 with frequencies of p and q, respectively.

Since the population is in Hardy–Weinberg equilibrium,

$$p + q = 1 \tag{1}$$
$$p^2 + 2pq + q^2 = 1 \tag{2}$$

The frequencies of the three genotypes (A_1A_1, A_1A_2 and A_2A_2) are given by the square of the allelic array [Equation (1)]. This gives the genotypic array [Equation (2)].

The Average Effect of a Gene

Earlier we stated that polygenic systems are those genetic systems that act as if each allele adds or subtracts a certain increment to the phenotypic expression of a trait. The average effect of a gene is the estimated increment that a given allele from a parent contributes to the progeny phenotype. Parents do not transmit genotypes to their progeny. Genotypes are broken up by segregation and independent assortment. Therefore, new genotypes form in every generation. Predictions of progeny genotypic values can be made only if the parental genotypic values can be expressed in terms of genic values (i.e., the part of the genotypic value due to a single allele).

Each genotype has a corresponding observed phenotypic value designated here by Y_{11}, Y_{12} and Y_{22} (Table I). The genotypic value for each genotype is measured on a scale as deviations from a midpoint. The midpoint (MP) is defined as the scale value exactly intermediate between the phenotypic values of the two homozygotes A_1A_1 and A_2A_2. Thus, the genotypic values of the homozygotes are equal but opposite in sign. The genotypic value of the heterozygote is defined as d. (See Figure 1.)

Breeding Value

Since parents transmit only half their genes to their progeny, the mean genotypic value of their progeny is a function both of the

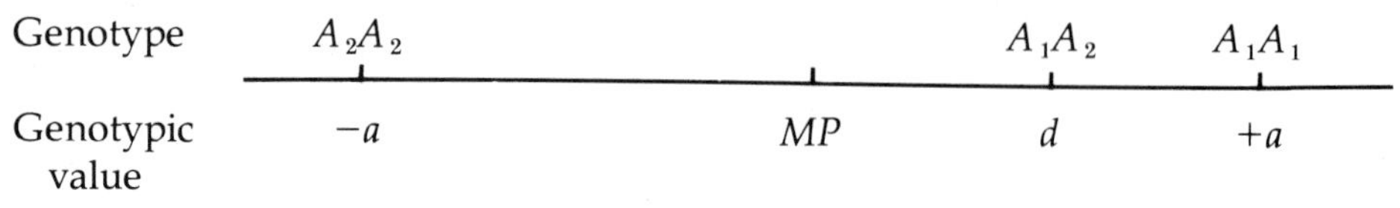

Genotype	A_2A_2		A_1A_2	A_1A_1
Genotypic value	$-a$	MP	d	$+a$

In terms of dominance relationships:

if $d = 0$, there is no dominance.

if $d > 0$ and $d < |a|$, there is partial dominance.

if $d = |a|$, there is complete dominance.

if $d > |a|$, there is overdominance.

Figure 1
Arbitrarily assigned genotypic values [after Falconer (1960)].

parents' alleles and of the average gene effects. The value assigned to an individual, as measured by the mean genotypic value of the progeny, is the breeding value or additive genetic value. The breeding value can be measured directly and, like the average effect of allele substitution, is a population parameter.

The additive genetic, or breeding, value can be expressed in terms of the average gene effects. It is simply the sum of the average effects of each allele at a locus. If more than one locus is involved, the breeding value is obtained by the summing of the average effects over alleles at all loci. This is the additive portion of the genotype and is the most important, since it determines the resemblance between relatives. The common elements relatives can share are independently acting genes, not unique combinations.

Dominance Deviation

For a trait in any population, it is possible to calculate the genotypic value of an individual as the deviation from the trait-scale midpoint and to calculate the breeding value from the mean of his (or her) offspring values. The observed difference between the genotypic value is the dominance deviation. For one locus with two alleles, the genotypic value is composed solely of the additive genetic value and the dominance deviation: $G = A + D$. (Since both the additive genetic value and the dominance deviation are expressed as deviations from the mean, the genotypic values must be expressed the same way, Table I.)

A most important distinction is that between dominance as it applies to alleles at a locus and dominance deviation as described here. The presence of dominance deviation does depend on the presence of dominance at a locus (i.e., if $d = 0$, there is no dominance deviation, e.g., Figure 1), but it also depends on the allelic frequencies in the population. The dominance deviations are given in terms of allele frequencies in Table I.

The dominance deviation is a population parameter and not a measure of the amount of dominance because it depends on both allelic frequencies and the magnitude of d. Unlike dominance, which is manifested only in the heterozygote, dominance deviation is found in all genotypes.

The dominance deviation and the additive genetic values are uncorrelated. Therefore, knowing the additive value of any genotype does not help to predict the amount of its dominance deviation.

Epistatic Interaction Deviation

When only one locus is involved, the genotypic value can be expressed in terms of the additive value and the dominance deviation value: $G = A + D$. With two or more loci, the genotypic value can be expressed as the additive and dominance values summed across all loci: $G = \Sigma A + \Sigma D$. If there is interaction between the loci, a third term, an interaction term, has to be introduced. Hence, $G = \Sigma A + \Sigma D + \Sigma I$ (or just $G = A + D + I$).

These interactions are of several types, and the number of types of interactions increases with the number of loci. For two loci there are three types of interaction: interaction between additive values *(AA)*, interaction between dominance deviation values *(DD)* and interaction between additive and dominance deviation values *(AD)*. For more than two loci, the number of interactions rapidly increases. Thus, for three loci, there are also interactions among all three additive values *(AAA)*, between two additive values and one dominance deviation value *(ADA)* and so forth. Since these separate interactions are difficult to measure, all interactions are usually clustered under the symbol I.

Variance

The study of genetics is properly the study of variation and of variance. Where a trait shows no phenotypic variance, there is no evidence that it has genetic correlates. One important aspect of

Table I
Genotypes with Dominance Deviation Values

Genotype	Frequency	Phenotypic value	Genotypic value	Genotypic value taken as deviation from the mean	Additive genetic value	Dominance deviation
A_1A_1	p^2	Y_{11}	a	$2q(a - pd)$	$2\alpha_1 = 2q\alpha$	$-2q^2d$
A_1A_2	$2pq$	Y_{12}	d	$a(q-p) + d(1-2pq)$	$\alpha_1 + \alpha_2 = (q-p)\alpha$	$2pqd$
A_2A_2	q^2	Y_{22}	$-a$	$-2p(a + qd)$	$2\alpha_2 = -2pq\alpha$	$-2p^2d$

quantitative genetics is the partitioning of the total phenotypic variance into smaller variance components.

The most common partitioning of variance is the division of total phenotypic variance into environmental and genotypic components. This partitioning is of little interest to geneticists but is used a great deal by psychologists.

The first partitioning of phenotypic variance is into genetic and environmental components: $(V_p = V_g + V_e)$. The estimation of these two components is not easy. One technique involves the use of isogenic populations—either homozygous inbred lines or the F_1 cross between two such inbred lines. These isogenic populations must be reared in a variety of environments. Since all individuals in a single population have the same genotype, any variation between them must be due to environmental differences. Heterogenic populations must be reared in the same variety of environments. The heterogenic population variance is due to both genetic and environmental causes. The difference between the variances of the heterogenic $(V_g + V_e)$ and isogenic (V_e) populations provides the estimate of the total genetic variance.

Heritability

No discussion of quantitative genetics would be complete without a consideration of heritability, especially since heritability is used in the human intelligence literature without regard for its conceptual basis. There are two types of heritability, broad (H^2) and narrow (h^2), each with a different conceptual basis and with a distinct and different usage. They are unfortunately confused and the symbol (h^2) is often misused to represent both of them.

Broad heritability (H^2) is the ratio of the total genetic variance (plus any genotype–environment correlation) to the total phenotypic variance: $(H^2 = V_g/V_p$ where $V_g = V_a + V_d + V_i)$. Since the genetic variance is a function of the allele frequencies of the gene correlates of a trait, any estimate of H^2 is valid only for a specified population (i.e., specified allele frequencies) and a particular environmental variance. Broad heritability is not a fixed quantity. On the contrary, it is a population descriptor that varies with allele frequencies and with changes in the environment.

Broad heritability is most often misused by psychologists in assuming it is a nature–nurture ratio or index to the causes of a trait. Heritability, however, describes the apportionment of variance: it does not describe how much of a trait is determined by heredity for any individual. Nor does it describe the average influence of heredity in determining the level of trait expression in a population. Broad heritability estimates only the contribution of genetic factors (additive, dominance deviation, interaction and genotype–environment covariance) to the total phenotypic variance for one trait in a specified population. Broad heritability is of little interest to geneticists and is only used (or misused) as described above.

Narrow heritability (h^2) is the ratio of additive genetic variance to the total phenotypic variance. Its value, like that of H^2 depends on the allelic frequencies in the population and applies only to a specified environmental variance. Narrow heritability is one of the most important parameters in quantitative genetics, since it can be used to predict the results of selective breeding for a given level of trait expression in a particular environment.

Only in one case, where $d = 0$ and there is no interaction variance, do broad and narrow heritability have the same value. It is clearly wrong to use the terms interchangeably unless the above two conditions are explicitly stated. In most cases, H^2 and h^2 estimate different values, and H^2 can be used at best only as an estimate of the upper limit of h^2.

Resemblances Among Relatives

Genetically, the relationship of resemblance among members of a family is based on a probablity of sharing identical alleles at each locus. Progeny receive one homologue of every chromosome pair from each parent. Therefore, an offspring shares with each parent 50% identical alleles with a probability approaching unity. *On average*, siblings also share half their alleles, but their relationship is more complex, because it is what we usually mean by probabilistic. Given in the gene pool four alleles at a locus and two parents, each heterozygous for a different combination of two of the four alleles, consider, for example, the mating $A_1A_2 \times A_3A_4$, which can produce progeny of genotypes A_1A_3, A_1A_4, A_2A_3, A_2A_4. A pair of siblings could have 16 possible genotypic combinations, such as,

1. (A_1A_3, A_1A_3) 3. (A_1A_3, A_2A_3)
2. (A_1A_3, A_1A_4) 4. (A_1A_3, A_2A_4)

Combination 1 has 100% identity; 2 and 3 have 50% identity; and 4 has 0% identity. Since the other 12 possible combinations have a similar distribution of percentages of identity, the average identity is 50%. Note, however, that unlike parent–offspring identity, which has no range and only one value, the sibling identity value is averaged over a range from 0 to 100%. The same relationship prevails at every independent autosomal locus. Relatives such as half-siblings, half-cousins and grandparent–grandchild are less closely related because they have a smaller range and lower average probabilities for sharing identical alleles. Attempts to estimate h^2 for a trait (in some population) are best made by means of studies of the resemblances of relatives, because it is the additive gene effects that relatives share. At least, that is the usual recommendation. Therefore, we next consider how this is done and how the results thus obtained can be interpreted.

Parent–offspring correlation. Parent–offspring correlations can be used to estimate the narrow heritability. It is easier to use the regression of the offspring on the parents than intraclass correlations since we are dealing with pairs of observations rather than with observations between groups:

$$b_{op} = \text{cov}(op)/V_p$$

where b_{op} is the regression of offspring on parent, $\text{cov}(op)$ is the covariance of parent and offspring, V_p is the parental variance.

The covariance between the parent and the offspring is the sum of the cross-products of the genotypic values. If we ignore epistatic interaction, the genotypic value of the parent is $G = A + D$. The genotypic value that an offspring shares in common with a parent is $\frac{1}{2}A$, since the child inherits half the parental alleles and none of the parental dominance deviation.

$$\text{cov}(op) = \Sigma\,(\tfrac{1}{2}A)(A + D)$$
$$\text{cov}(op) = \tfrac{1}{2}\Sigma(AA) + \tfrac{1}{2}\Sigma(AD)$$

since additive and dominance deviation values are uncorrelated:

$$\text{cov}(op) = \tfrac{1}{2}(AA)$$

The covariance of A with A is simply the additive variance. Thus, the regression of offspring on parent gives an estimate of one-half the narrow heritability:

$$\text{cov}(op) = \tfrac{1}{2}(AA) = \tfrac{1}{2}V_a$$
$$b_{op} = \text{cov}\,(op)/V_p$$
$$b_{op} = \tfrac{1}{2}V_a/V_p$$
$$b_{op} = \tfrac{1}{2}h^2$$

The measurement of the regression of the offspring on the parent gives an unbiased estimation of the narrow heritability. This is one of the easiest sets of measurements to make, but to be valid the measurements have to be made on both parent and offspring at the same age under the same environmental conditions and, of course, with replication of genotype observations. This may be practical for fast-maturing species but is certainly not so for man.

Midparent–offspring correlations. A second way to look at the resemblances between parent and offspring is to look at the resemblances between the offspring and the mean value of the parental trait expression. This mean value is usually designated the midparent. The covariance between the midparent and offspring also estimates $\tfrac{1}{2}V_a$. The regression of the offspring on the midparent estimates h^2, since the variance of the midparent is only one-half the variance of the single parent:

$$b_{op} = \frac{\tfrac{1}{2}V_a}{\tfrac{1}{2}V_p}$$
$$b_{op} = h^2$$

Midparent–offspring correlations have the same disadvantages for human studies as single-parent–offspring correlations. In addition, they require that additional measurements be made so that the scores of both parents are known.

Half-sib correlations. When one is dealing with the correlations among siblings, its often easiest to compare the variances between and within the families. Thus, one uses the intraclass correlation (t) rather than regression.

The between-group or between-family variance is that variance common to all members of a group or family. The within-family variance is that variance among family members and is a measure of the uniqueness of individuals.

The intraclass correlation can be used to estimate the heritability as illustrated in the path diagram in Figure 2. The correlation between the phenotypic values of the half-sibs Progeny 1 and Progeny 2 is a function of the alleles that they share in common and the relationship between those common additive genetic values and their phenotypes. Half-sibs have an average genetic relationship of $\frac{1}{4}$ ($r = \frac{1}{4}$). The regression of phenotype on the additive genetic value is the square root of the heritability ($\sqrt{h^2} = h$). The intraclass correlation between half-sibs estimates $\frac{1}{4}h^2$.

The correlation between half-sibs is another unbiased estimator of the narrow heritability. It is easier to measure half-siblings at the same age, but they are fairly rare. In addition, it is difficult to equalize the environments of half-sibs to make the measurements of the traits meaningful, and there remains the problem of replication.

Full-sib correlations. The problem of estimating h^2 becomes much more complicated in the case of resemblance between full-sibs.

Figure 2
Path analysis of half-sibs (parents not related). The correlation between the half-siblings 1 and 2 is the product of the paths connecting the two siblings: $t = \frac{1}{4}h^2$. Another way of saying this is that the correlation between the phenotypes of the sibs is the product of their average genetic relationship ($r = \frac{1}{4}$) and the relationship between the phenotype of each sib and his corresponding additive genetic value h.

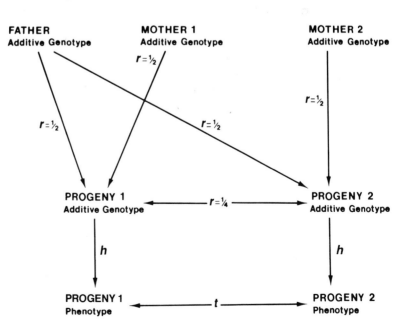

Full-sibs have an average additive genetic correlation of $r = \frac{1}{2}$, so it seems logical that they would estimate $\frac{1}{2}h^2$, since half-sibs estimate $\frac{1}{4}h^2$. As explained above, however, full-sibs inherit alleles from both parents, so that they have the possibility of having the identical genotype at any given locus. Full-sibs have not only one-half of their additive genetic variance in common but also share one-quarter of their dominance deviation variance. Since full-sibs are more highly related than one-half, the intraclass correlation gives a biased estimate of h^2.

Full-sib correlation is one of the easiest to measure. It is easy to locate full-sibs, the environments can be fairly well equalized, and often sibs can be measured at the same age, but there remains the problem of replication. Since the full-sib correlation is biased by dominance deviation variance, it can be used only as the upper limit to heritability.

Difficulty of measurement. In experimental studies, one attempts to set up a series of replicated controlled matings to get several different estimates of the heritability. A common mating scheme is to mate a number of sires to a greater number of dams. This will give a series of full-sib families for each dam, both full- and half-sib families for each sire, and unrelated families among sires. By a nested analysis of variance, estimates of heritability based on full- and half-sib correlations can be obtained. The half-sib estimate is unbiased but imprecise; the full-sib estimate is more precise but biased. In general, an average of the two estimates of h^2 is taken as a rough estimate of the heritability.

For human studies, such nested analysis is nearly impossible. Controlled human matings with replication are not feasible. Such a nested system might be possible in polygamous cultures or with second marriages where there are children by each marriage, but this offers little hope for human heritability estimates. The other available techniques also have severe limitations. Full-sibs are the easiest to measure but provide a biased estimate. Half-sib pairs are difficult to locate and have the problem of the controlling of environments. Parent–offspring correlations are useful but only if measurements are obtained at the same age.

Even with well-designed studies, the estimation of h^2 is not very accurate and the standard error is usually quite large. Klein, DeFries and Finkbeiner (1973) have presented tables of standard errors for different methods of estimating h^2. The numbers of subjects that would have to be measured are quite large. For example, to get an estimate of $h^2 = 0.6$ within 95% confidence intervals, for any method appropriate to human populations, would require measurements on a minimum of 800 individuals from 400 different families. To our knowledge, no studies of this magnitude have been attempted in human populations.

Heritability is an important parameter in quantitative genetics applied to agriculture. If the h^2 of a trait in a population is known then some prediction can be made about the response of that population to selective breeding for some expression of that trait in the environment in which the heritability was calculated. Heritability values (h^2 and H^2) are not nature–nurture ratios. There are no such ratios, since each genotype is unique and has developed a phenotype through continued idiosyncratic interaction with the environment.

Theoretical Misconceptions

Our misconceptions are due to the piling up of errors in theoretical and methodological foundation literature. In what follows we give a few examples and correct several misconceptions.

A literature has built up that, though incorrect, is widely believed to provide answers to an unanswerable question: What are the proportional contributions of heredity and environment to trait expression in human populations and to differences among races in the expression of those traits? The readers have been informed that the unfortunate situation, in which Jensen revived the discredited argument for "Negro" racial inferiority by claiming that both "intelligence" itself and average IQ differences between races were 80% genetic, is "the most important paper in [psychology] since Pavlov and Freud . . . a masterful summary of evidence that has been gathering for several decades" (McConnell, 1970). This occurred in an intellectual climate permeated by the myth of two cultures: "A distinction often made between science and the humanities is that in science, a cumulative discipline, one need study only the latest paper on any subject to obtain all the background necessary for further investigation" (Bonner, 1961). We have since learned to our chagrin, however, that believers of this fallacy also assumed that scientists act with an integrity and a humility, which Jensen (Hirsch, 1976) and others, (Stoker, 1976, see Burt discussion below) have *not* shown.

Formula Error in Determining Heritability from Twin Data

Jensen (1967) presented the formula $h^2 = (r_{MZ} - r_{DZ})/(1 - \rho_{oo})$ without any theoretical justification that it measures heritability, broad or narrow. In this formula, r_{MZ} and r_{DZ} are phenotypic correlations between monozygotic and dizygotic twins respectively and can be observed directly. However, ρ_{oo}, the genetic correlation between sibs, cannot be observed. It can be obtained from their phenotypic correlation if heritability is known, which of course it is not.

To overcome this difficulty Jensen (1967) suggested that the formula $\rho_{oo} = (1 + \rho_{pp})/(2 + \rho_{pp})$, where ρ_{pp} is the genetic correlation between mates, should be used to find ρ_{oo}. He gives Li (1955, Chapter 13) as reference for this formula. It, however, does not appear there and when consulted, Professor Li replied (private communication to AV) that he had never seen it before it was brought to his notice. This formula lacks theoretical justification. Moreover, it does not resolve the problem of finding genetic correlation. In order to use it, we require the genetic correlation between mates which can be obtained from their phenotypic correlation only if heritability is known. Thus, to use Jensen's formula for finding heritability of a trait, a previous estimate of that heritability is required.

How did Jensen (1967) resolve the dilemma? He assumed that the genetic correlation between mates is .25 without revealing how this figure was obtained from their phenotypic correlation of .6. The value of ρ_{DZ}, actually ρ_{oo}, which Adams et al. (1976) recently used, is based on this *assumed* genetic correlation. The value of .8 for the broad heritability of IQ, so often quoted by Jensen and others, is also based on this value. It is difficult to find a scientific justification for the method or to have any faith in estimates of heritability based on it.

Genotype–Environment Interaction

Jinks and Fulker (1970) described a method for estimating genotype–environment interaction from twin data. Using this method, they concluded that no such interaction exists for IQ. Jensen (1970) applied their method to studies of monozygotic twins reared apart (see below) and also concluded that no such interaction exists. Jensen's replication and the nonexistence of genotype–environment interaction for IQ are often cited. Two points concerning this method need to be stated clearly, and Professor Jinks has generously accepted both.

To begin, there was a slip in the algebra on p. 314 of Jinks and Fulker's paper. When their error is corrected and incorrect covariance values are replaced by correct ones, there is no unambiguous interpretation of the zero covariance of sums and differences from MZ twin scores (on which their estimate of zero heredity–environment interaction depended). Their method should always yield zero correlation between genotype and environment if the distribution of twin scores is bivariate normal, i.e., the result is an artifact. Thus investigators, who find no correlation between the sums of twin IQ scores and their absolute differences, only confirm something that is expected on statistical reasoning with no genetical meaning. It is therefore not surprising that all replications of the method show heredity–environment interaction for IQ to be approximately zero. Needless to say, this proves nothing except that the twin distribution for IQ might be approximately bivariate normal.

Secondly, Jensen's (1970) replication combined data from four well-known studies. Not only does his attempt fail because of the faulty method, but also because pooling those data was unjustified.

Norm of Reaction

Interaction and norm of reaction describe aspects of the complex genotype–phenotype relationship. The latter focuses on the fact that *a* genotype may develop different phenotypes in different environments. The former includes the latter and considers at one time many genotypes and many environments. For an array of genotypes and various sets of environmental conditions, it calls attention to how, out of the variety of possible distributions of phenotypic outcomes, the particular one obtained will depend on which genotype develops under which conditions. Haldane analyzed the interaction concept and formulated its quantitative interpretation. He showed that m genotypes in n environments generate $(mn)!/m!n!$ kinds of interaction. McGuire and Hirsch (1977) show that the proportion of these permitting generalization is small and diminishes as m and n grow. The latest failure to justify a generalized superiority–inferiority hierarchy (Plomin et al., 1976) does so by baldly asserting the following nonsense: "This truism for the individual (heredity–environment interaction) is simply false for individual differences in a population."

Within and Between Population Heritabilities

The independence of mean and variance of a normal distribution is a well-known statistical fact. On the relationship between the heritability of a population and the mean difference among populations, the position is succinctly stated by Bodmer (1975), who says, "Heritability measurements within a population bear no relationship to the question of genetic differences between populations." Yet DeFries (1972) claims that such a relationship exists. His solution is illusory, however, and the results of his proposed analysis would be uninterpretable, because the formulas used make the following assumptions: (1) that the conditions under which human populations breed are comparable to the controlled conditions of animal and plant breeding experiments; (2) that the variances of two populations compared are equal; (3) that populations are mating randomly; and (4) that populations share a common environment. *None* of the foregoing assumptions can be justified. Human breeding conditions are not controlled. In the case of IQ, where DeFries (1972) used Falconer's formulas, the assumption about variances is not valid. Even Jensen (1972) reported the phenotypic variance of IQ in the American black population to be about two-thirds of that in the white population. Furthermore, with respect to IQ, both populations mate assortatively, not randomly, which will result in correlation between genotypes. Also, the two populations have different environments and might have different coefficients of assortative mating. There is no gainsaying that, so long as heredity and environment interact or are correlated, both of which occur with human intelligence, heritability cannot be defined.

Misapplication of Heritability

Heritability, broad as well as narrow, is a technical term in quantitative genetics. Moran (1973) in a brief but excellent note pointed out that this precise concept cannot be used when genotype–environment covariance is present. Moreover, if the environmental component is correlated with families, Fisher's (1918) model cannot be used. Since Morton (1976) has now alleged that "comments by Moran on genotype–environment covariance . . . were subsequently corrected," by Holroyd, it is important for it to be known that Moran was correct and Holroyd was confused. Moran's (1973) simple analysis shows that, "for characteristics such as human intelligence in which genetic and environmental components are correlated, 'heritability' cannot be defined. . . ." Holroyd (1975) has objected, contending that "there is no logic for . . . [Moran's] statement since if heritability (h^2) is defined as the ratio of the total genetic variance to the total phenotypic variance. . . . This simply puts the covariance term in with the non-genetic variance which, in fact, is the usual procedure in Psychology" (Jensen, 1972). Holroyd's "correction" was based on what he *alleged* psychologists usually do—include the genotype–environment covariance with the nongenetic variance—and he cited Jensen as his authority. Jensen (1972), however, had stated exactly the opposite of what Holroyd attributed to him, for he had said, "Since most estimates of heritability of intelligence are intended to reflect the existing state of affairs, *they usually include the covariance in the proportion of variance due to heredity*" (italics added).

So we see that use of heritability in human behavior genetics has been indiscriminate and counterproductive. In quantitative genetics, heritability in the narrow sense (h^2) is defined as the ratio of additive genetic variance to phenotypic variance in the absence of either correlation or interaction between genotype and environment. However, when correlation exists, either (1) between genetic and environmental contributions to trait expression or (2) between environmental contributions to trait expression in both members of a parent–child or sib pair, heritability is *not defined*. Furthermore, when heritability can be defined, for example in well-controlled plant and animal breeding experiments, it has *no* relevance to measured differences in average values of trait expression between different populations: heritability estimates throw no light upon intergroup comparisons!

Obviously, heritability as genetically defined is not suited to the requirements of behavior genetics, for which other concepts will have to be developed. It also needs to be clearly understood that "High or low heritability tells us absolutely nothing about how a given individual might have developed under conditions different from those in which he actually did develop. Heritability provides no information about norm of reaction" (Hirsch, 1970).

The Misunderstanding of Regression

Since regression of offspring score from parental value toward the population mean has so often been misconstrued as providing evidence for genetic determination of trait expression [see Vetta (1975) for examples], we explain why that is a misinterpretation. Consider the simplest conceivable case of complete genotype–phenotype isomorphism, no dominance and panmixia, and let a group of fathers be selected to reproduce whose average value on a trait is x, measured as a deviation from the population mean. They will have offspring whose average value on the same trait scale is $\frac{1}{2}x$. The observed regression arises because both sexes contribute in reproduction, but we selected fathers only. Since mothers were unselected, their average deviation value on the trait is zero. The average progeny value is the average of the two parental values, or $(x + 0) / 2 = x/2$. However, if we select the sexes so that x is the average for both mothers and fathers, then the progeny average will be $(x + x) /2 = x$, and there will be *no* regression to the mean. That is, when the genetic contribution from both parents is taken into account, regression to the mean is not an index of genetic determination and genetic determination does not imply that there will be regression to the mean.

Jensen (1973), comparing the IQs of sibs of chosen groups of children from two ethnic groups, showed some confusion concerning sibling regression to the mean. Thoday (1973) clarified this confusion.

A Classic Revised Since 1918, Fisher's paper, "The correlation between relatives on the supposition of Mendelian inheritance," has been recognized as the source of the variance analysis technique—used for quantitative genetic and behavior–genetic analyses of phenotypic variance. Besides being received as a technical *tour de force*, it was considered to be a conceptual landmark, because it was supposed to have reconciled what was previously believed to be irreconcilable—the biometric and Mendelian points of view. Also, it has been widely believed that Fisher analyzed the components of the total variance in a Mendelian population by showing that Mendelian inheritance will lead to the observed correlations. This notion, however, is misleading because it has achieved, among geneticists and others, a status not unlike that of Vedas among Hindus. It is revered but not read. Few geneticists would claim to have read it and even fewer to understand it.

Fisher assumed a large number of independent factors having similar effects with partial dominance. He investigated correlations among relatives assuming that the population was mating at random and developed a model of assortative mating for a population in equilibrium. He showed that assortative mating will increase the genetic variance and obtained formulas for correlations between relatives. His model involves three parameters: μ the phenotypic correlation between mates, c_1 the ratio of total genetic variance to phenotypic variance and c_2 the ratio of additive genetic variance to total genetic variance. For a population mating assortatively μ is usually known; c_1 and c_2 can be obtained from the parent–child and sib correlations. Of course, what Fisher actually did was to use observed phenotypic parent–child and sib correlations to estimate values of c_1 and c_2 for the population. He did not show that the Mendelian inheritance will lead to the observed correlations.

Burt and Howard (1956) appear to have been the first to use Fisher's model to analyze IQ data. Actually it is not correct to say that they *used* his model. As already stated, the purpose of the model is to estimate the parameters c_1 and c_2. Burt and Howard, however, *assumed* the values of those parameters. Unfortunately many behavior geneticists have used their papers as a guide for the application of Fisher's model. [It is now revealed that in addition to unsubstantiated data, Margaret Howard as well as another phantom collaborator may have been invented by Cyril Burt. See Gillie (1979).]

The 1918 paper was Fisher's first major paper in genetics and apparently he did not appreciate fully the implications of his model. His formulas for parent–child and sib correlation are not correct for his model. Moreover, the correct formulas for these correlations for *his* model suggest another interpretation when the value of c_1 exceeds one, as was the case in the example Fisher drew from the Pearson and Lee data on human height and span. Fisher assumed additive deviations to be the only causes of resemblance between parent and child and thus failed to take account of the correlation between the additive and dominance deviations of parent and progeny. However, Wright (1952) has pointed out that, "Assortative mating introduces a correlation between dominance deviations of parents and offspring and between dominance deviations of either and additive deviations of the other."

It has now been shown that in Fisher's model of assortative mating there is a (small) correlation between additive and dominance deviations of parent and child. Thus, the assumptions on which Fisher obtained his formulas for parent–child correlation $[= \frac{1}{2}c_1 c_2(1 + \mu)]$ and sib correlation $[= \frac{1}{4}c_1(1 + c_2 + 2c_2 A)]$ are not correct for *his* model. Recently it has been possible to obtain formulas that are better for Fisher's model (Vetta, 1976). In Fisher's notation these are

$$\text{parent–child correlation} = \tfrac{1}{2}c_1 c_2 [1 + A(1 - A)^2]$$
$$+ \tfrac{1}{2}c_1(1 - c_2)A(1 - A)$$
$$\text{sib correlation} \quad\quad = \tfrac{1}{2}c_1 c_2 [1 + A(1 - A)^2]$$
$$+ \tfrac{1}{4}c_1(1 - c_2)$$

In both formulas the first term represents the contribution of additive deviations to correlation and the second term the contribution of dominance deviations. The contribution made by dominance deviations is smaller for parent–child than for sib correlation, because $A(1-A) \le \frac{1}{4}$. *This is another reason why the concept of heritability (defined as additive variance/phenotypic variance) cannot be applied to human populations mating assortatively.*

If the coefficient of assortative mating μ is known, values of c_1 and c_2 can be obtained from parent–child and sib correlation formulas. Effectively, the difference between the two correlations gives a fraction of the dominance variance. The formulas given here and those obtained by Fisher, however, are for genetic correlations that are not known and phenotypic correlations have been used instead. If the environments of sibs are more alike than those of parent and child, the difference between phenotypic correlations will also contain a fraction of the environmental variance. When the phenotypic correlational difference is too large to be explained by the amount of dominance variance in the population, the value of c_1 will exceed one. Thus, such a value, far from being evidence for no environmental effects, as Fisher believed, actually indicates their presence. However, a value less than one for c_1 does not, of itself, exclude environmental effects. It could mean that the contributions of dominance deviations, as well as of environmental effects, are small.

Phenotypic and Analytic Complexity

Johnson's (1974) dissertation provides a paradigm for serious human behavior–genetic analyses. The unexpected problems and analytic subtleties, to cope with which the literature and prior experience had left us totally unprepared, provided a most sophisticating but duly sobering experience. A consideration of some of the problems and results from this unique investigation can be of immense heuristic value. Only the most salient and general features are considered here. Thompson (1968) has distinguished three features of behavior: it is complex, continuously variable and developmentally fluid. It is the third property of ontogenetic flexibility, reflecting norm of reaction, that contributes so much confusion to the long agonized debate over the heredity–environment pseudoquestion. Accordingly, as a heuristic exercise from the behaviorist's perspective, a human trait, embodying the first two properties but not the third, was studied, thus circumventing the intractable problem of estimating the proportion of trait variation attributable to postnatal environment—a phenotype stable from birth to death whose expression is uninfluenced by where an individual grows up. The human fingerprint (dermatoglyph) is one such trait. It has a fascinating complexity and is interindividually variable but intraindividually postnatally stable in expression. It provides an intergenerational transmission–genetic perspective for studying segregation and assortment of similarities and differences in trait expression.

Table II
Distributions of Loop (L), Whorl (W) and Arch (A) Pattern Types
Cumulated over Ten Fingers in Johnson's Total Illinois Sample and in That
Sample Subdivided by Generations

Generation	Cumulated over ten fingers		
	L	W	A
Parent	.66	.28	.06
Offspring	.67	.27	.07
Total of both	.66	.27	.06

Observations were made on 10,580 individual fingerprints of
1,058 subjects in 212 nuclear families (both parents and two or
more offspring). For ease of exposition our discussion considers
only analysis of the dermatoglyphic pattern-type trait. It illustrates
well the problems besetting this complicated field.

Analysis of three widely recognized alternative forms of trait
expression—loop, whorl and arch—(shown in Table II) yields their
distributions both throughout the entire sample and across the two
generations separately. Also Table III shows a comparison with

Table III
Comparison of Population Distributions from Independent Studies by
Johnson (1974), by Ford–Walker and by Holt (Holt, 1968)

Pattern Type	Study	Fingers of Left Hand				
		1	2	3	4	5
L	Johnson	.63	.55	.72	.63	.87
	Ford–Walker	.64	.56	.74	.61	.85
	Holt	.68	.61	.76	.64	.86
W	Johnson	.32	.31	.16	.34	.11
	Ford–Walker	.31	.33	.17	.37	.12
	Holt	.27	.30	.16	.33	.12
A	Johnson	.05	.14	.12	.03	.02
	Ford–Walker	.06	.11	.09	.03	.03
	Holt	.04	.10	.09	.03	.02

Figure 3
Distributions for ten fingers of proportions of parental mating type
combinations (pie chart areas coded by shading for six pattern-type combinations). Distributions for ten fingers of proportions of offspring pattern
types (heights of bars) and proportions of parental mating combinations
from which offspring descended (shade-coded areas of bars).

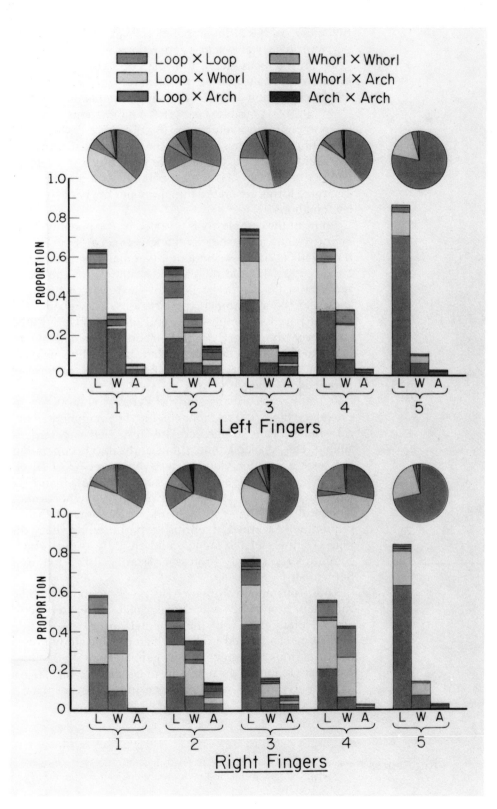

two other studies at the population level. The data clearly reveal a polymorphism stable across generations and populations.

When the focus shifts from the population to the family pedigree level of analysis, other problems arise. Three alternative forms of trait expression on each of ten fingers generate a sample space of $3^{10} = 59,049$ possible pattern combinations of fingerprint phenotypes for individuals and $(3^{10})^2 = 3^{20} = 3,486,784,401$ parental mating possibilities. Because the ten fingers do not show perfect correlation of trait expression, for each finger in every family the parents have been classified separately as a mating combination. The three forms generate a minimum per finger of six such parental combinations.

Some of the complexity is revealed by the phenotypic analysis in Figure 3, showing results for ten fingers separately. For each finger it presents (1) the distribution of parental mating combinations by pattern type, (2) the offspring distribution of the three pattern types, and (3) the proportions of each pattern type among offspring of the six parental combinations. The relative frequencies both of parental combinations and of their offspring phenotypes vary over the several fingers. Though the data do not show dermatoglyphics to be independent of heredity, neither do they suggest any obvious rule of transmission of pattern type from parent to offspring.

A *sine qua non* for any study of heredity is proof positive of the presumed biological relationship, i.e., ascertainment of the biological validity of the designated kinships, such as parent–offspring, sibling, etc. Available time, funds and subject cooperation permitted testing on four blood factors the members of 38 of the 212 families—about one-sixth of the sample. No less than 13%, that is, five out of the 38 families, have children who cannot be the biological offspring of at least one of the putative parents. Subsequently we learned of a British report (Philipp, 1973) disqualifying, as fathers of the family children, 30% of husbands (private communication from Professor Tizard of London to J.H., 30 September 1975).

Unfortunately, in addition to its preoccupation with heritability, the extant human behavior–genetics literature is vitiated by being almost totally devoid of fundamental control observations. *Every* difficulty encountered in the dermatoglyphic study must be faced in any serious human behavior–genetic analysis. Moreover, such work cannot ignore the ontogeny of behavior, which, in contrast to dermatoglyphics, is most sensitive indeed to postnatal environmental conditions.

References

Adams, B., Ghodsian, M., and Richardson, K. 1976. Evidence for a low upper limit of heritability of mental test performance in a national sample of twins. *Nature* 263: 314–316.

Bodmer, W.F. 1975. Resolution of genetics, race and intelligence. *Genetics Society of America* 15 (July): 6.

Bonner, J.T. (ed.) 1961. In D'Arcy Wentworth Thompson. *On Growth and Form*, Introduction, p. x. Abridged Edition. Cambridge: Harvard University Press.

Burt, C., and Howard, M. 1956. The multifactorial theory of inheritance and its application to intelligence. *Brit. J. Stat. Psychol.* 9: 95–131.

Chase, A. 1980. *The Legacy of Malthus: The Social Costs of the New Scientific Racism.* Urbana-Champaign: University of Illinois Press (originally published 1977).

DeFries, J.C. 1972. Quantitative aspects of genetics and environment in the determination of behavior. In L. Ehrman, G.S. Omenn, E. Caspari (eds.) *Genetics, Environment and Behavior*, pp. 6–16. New York: Academic Press.

Ehrman, L., and Parsons, P.A. 1976. *The Genetics of Behavior.* Sunderland, MA: Sinauer Associates.

Falconer, D.S. 1960. *Introduction to Quantitative Genetics.* New York: Ronald Press.

Fisher, R.A. 1918. The correlation between relatives on the supposition of Mendelian inheritance. *Trans. R. Soc. Edinb.* 52: 399–433.

Gillie, O. 1979. Burt's Missing Ladies. *Science* 204: 1035–1038.

Hirsch, J. 1963. Behavior genetics and individuality understood: Behaviorism's counterfactual dogma blinded the behavioral sciences to the significance of meiosis. *Science* 142: 1436–1442.

———. 1967. Behavior–genetic, or "experimental," analysis: The challenge of science versus the lure of technology. *Amer. Psychol.* 22:2, pp. 118, 119.

———. 1970. Behavior genetic analysis and its biosocial consequences. *Seminars in Psychiatry* 2: 89–105, p. 13.

———. 1976. Jensenism: The bankruptcy of "science" without scholarship. *U.S. Congr. Rec.* 122—73: E2671-2; 74: E2693-5; 75: E2703-5, E2716-8, E2721-2. (Originally published in *Educational Theory* 25: 3–27 (1975).)

———. 1978. Evidence for equality: Genetic diversity and social organization. In W. Feinberg (ed.) *Equality and Social Policy*, pp. 143–162. Urbana–Champaign: University of Illinois Press.

Hirsch, J., and Tryon, R.C. 1956. Mass screening and reliable individual measurement in the experimental behavior genetics of lower organisms. *Psychol. Bull.* 53: 402–410.

Hirsch, J., and Vetta, A. 1978. Gli errori concettuali nell' analise genetico-comportamentale. (The misconceptions of behavior genetics.) *Ricerche di psicologia.* Numero speciale dedicato a genetica e psicologia, anno II n. 5 gennaio 1978, Franco Angeli Editore, Milano.

Holroyd, R.G. 1975. On Moran's note on heritability. *Ann. Hum. Genet.* (London) 38: 379.

Holt, S. 1968. *The Genetics of Dermal Ridges*, pp. 185 and 186. Springfield, IL: Charles C. Thomas.

Jensen, A.R. 1967. Estimation of the limits of heritability of traits by comparison of monozygotic and dizygotic twins. *Proc. Natl. Acad. Sci.* (USA) 58: 149–156. p. 151.

———. 1970. IQs of identical twins reared apart. *Behav. Genet.* 1: 133–148.

———. 1972. *Genetics and Education*, p. 111. New York: Harper & Row.

———. 1973. *Educability and Group Differences.* New York: Harper & Row.

Jinks, J.S., and Fulker, D.W. 1970. Comparison of the biometrical, genetical, MAVA and classical approaches to the analysis of human behavior. *Psychol. Bull.* 73(5): 311–349. pp. 314.

Johnson, R.P. 1974. Phenotypic variation, fingerprints, and human behavior: An application of the family-pedigree paradigm. *Diss. Abstr. Inter.* 35(1): 546–B.

Klein, T.W., DeFries, J.C., and Finkbeiner, C.T. 1973. Heritability and genetic correlation: Standard errors of estimates and sample size. *Behav. Genet.* 3: 355–364.

Li, C.C. 1955. *Population Genetics.* Chicago: University of Chicago Press.

McConnell, R.A. 1970. The future revisited. *BioScience* 20(16): 903–904.

McGuire, T.R., and Hirsch, J. 1977. General intelligence (g) and heritability (H^2, h^2). In F. Weizman and I.C. Uzgiris (eds.) *The Structuring of Experience.* pp. 25–72. New York: Plenum Press.

Moran, P.A.P. 1973. A note on heritability and the correlation between relatives. *Ann. Hum. Genet.* (London) 37: 217.

Morton, N.E. 1976. Letter. *Science* 194(4260): 9–10.

Philipp, E.E. 1973. Discussion in *Law and Ethics of AID and Embryo Transfer,* p. 66. Ciba Foundation Symposium 17 (new series). Amsterdam: Elsevier, Excerpta Medica, North-Holland.

Plomin, R., DeFries, J.C. and Loehlin, J.C. 1976. Genotype–environment interaction and correlation in the analysis of human behavior. *Psychol. Bull.* 84: 309–322.

Stoker, S. 1976. Fact, fiction and fraud. (Review of J. Hixon, 1976, *The Patchwork Mouse. . . .) Nature* 264: 126–127.

Thoday, J.M. 1973. Review of A.R. Jensen, 1973. *Educability and Group Differences. Nature* 245: 418–420.

Thompson, W.R. 1968. Genetics and social behavior. In D.C. Glass (ed.) *Biology and Behavior: Genetics,* pp. 79–101. New York: Rockefeller University Press.

Vetta, A. 1975. A note on regression to the mean. *Social Biology* 22: 86–88.

———. 1976. Correction to Fisher's correlations between relatives and environmental effects. *Nature* 263: 316–317.

Wright, S. 1952. The genetics of quantitative variability. In E.C.R. Reeve and C.H. Waddington (eds.) *Quantitative Inheritance,* p. 18. London: H.M.S.O., Agricultural Research Council.

Nonvocal Social Signals and Clinical Processes

Robert M. Adams

12

Nonverbal behavior that communicates information to other persons is currently receiving much attention from a variety of research disciplines, including communication, social and clinical psychology, psychiatry and human ethology. The 1977–1978 *Subject Guide to Books in Print* lists 56 titles under nonverbal communication. Recent reviews have included general overviews (Weitz, 1974; Leathers, 1976; LaFrance and Mayo, 1978; Harper et al., 1978) and reviews of specific topics such as gaze (Argyle and Cook, 1976), interpersonal spacing (Altman, 1975), body movement and posture (Spiegel and Mochotka, 1974) and facial expression (Ekman and Friesen, 1975; Izard, 1971). The level of the reviews has ranged from critical analyses of the empirical literature to what Harrison (1975) has termed "psychopornography."

In recent years several authors [e.g., Ekman and Friesen (1968)] have seen the relevance of nonvocal (i.e., other than speech or speech-related) behavior to the causes, assessment and treatment of the problems that bring individuals to clinical practitioners. Here I intend to provide a general overview of some of the existing literature in this area as well as a more detailed look at a specific problem area—that which has been referred to as *assertiveness*. Assertiveness was selected as an area of research that appeared to have clear parallels in the dominance systems discussed extensively in the ethological literature on humans and nonhuman primates.

An assumption implicit in the discussion of deviant nonvocal social signals in relation to interpersonal problems is that there are a set of behavioral signals that are relatively uniform within the culture and perhaps to some extent across cultures. Eibl-Eibesfeldt (1975) has been one of the strongest advocates of the universality of nonvocal signals, citing the crosscultural similarity of a large number of behaviors. While other authors [e.g., Birdwhistell (1970)] argue against universality, the argument is typically in support of culturally determined forms of the behavior and at least predicts relative uniformity of signals within the culture to which individuals must adapt. While this latter is sufficient for our purposes here, it would be rather surprising if there were no universal signals for greeting, nonaggressive intentions, threat or the like, even if the superficial details of the signals varied greatly. And in fact the case for at least universality of facial expressions of emotion, albeit with different "display rules," appears rather strong (Ekman, 1973). The form of exchange of information at such basic levels is too important a matter to be left to chance cultural development and conditioning. There can be little ambiguity in such an important communication mechanism.

A second assumption important to the overview presented here is that nonvocal social behavior has greater than trivial importance in the process of interpersonal communication. This assumption has broad general support from any review of nonverbal behavior. More specific research has addressed the relative contributions of verbal and nonverbal behavior in conveying information. Studies such as those of Argyle et al. (1970), Mehrabian and Ferris (1967), Levitt (1964) and Waxer (1974, 1977) show that what is said can be of less importance than how it is said, even beyond such paraverbal cues as voice tone. While a numerical "importance ratio" that would be consistent across situations and messages would be difficult to derive, it appears from these studies not only that nonverbal signals are important, but that they may in fact lead to an interpretation of a message that is opposite to the verbal content.

What follows is limited to that behavior termed nonvocal and omits behavior termed paralinguistic or paraverbal. This omission does not constitute a comment on the importance of these behaviors. Voice tone, loudness, duration and latency of speech, patterns of silence, speech disturbances and the like often have high communicative value.

No discussion of definitional problems with such terms as communication, emotion and mental illness has been attempted. Such discussions deserve chapters, even volumes. It is hoped that the reader will be able to fit the discussion presented here into his or her own particular definition of terms that have been left open-ended.

And finally, any paucity of conclusions should be interpreted as a need for, and a plea for, further empirical research into the areas discussed. In general I attempt to show the interrelationship of the areas of nonvocal communication, human ethology and therapy, particularly behavior therapy, as well as the value of establishing such an interrelationship.

Nonvocal Signals as Causes of Behavior Problems

With regard to nonvocal social signals as causal factors, it appears that marked deviation from the norms for social interactions results in failure of the individual to establish and maintain rewarding social relationships. The result of such failures may be general anxiety, frustration, depression and feelings of failure and rejection, resulting perhaps in further reaching problems, such as the inability to obtain or hold employment. Argyle et al. (1974) describe this process as a "vicious circle of rejection and withdrawal" and distinguish between those social skill deficiencies that lead to problems and those that are thought to be secondary to some "deeper" problems.

To the extent that adequate interpersonal adjustment is a matter of sending and receiving appropriate social signals at appropriate times, the opportunities for violating the rules and risking rejection are limited only by the number of rules. Whether conforming to some rules is more important than others, whether violations are simply additive, whether there is a proportion of persons to be satisfied or whatever the formula that yields the threshold value of interpersonal inadequacy, there are clear examples of normative patterns of nonvocal social signals. These patterns have been derived or are being derived in behavioral areas such as looking and eye contact, facial expression, posture and body movement or kinesics, use of space or proximics, touch and physical characteristics. Combinations of these behaviors make up such molar categories as territoriality and dominance–submission relations.

A great many problems have been suggested as being the result of exhibiting inappropriate nonvocal social signals, either in their incidence or form or timing, as well as failing to recognize or properly interpret the signals of other individuals. Frequently these occur in the process of some social ritual that, instead of progressing through an orderly course to a satisfactory outcome, ends in problems. Zegans (1967) has observed, with regard to settling disputes, that "some few children never seemed able to accommodate this social ritual and became involved in more violent fighting" (p. 736). Bandura (1973) suggests a similar outcome in the case of individuals who submit to affronts until pushed beyond the limits of their tolerance. Observations of children (Blurton Jones, 1967) indicate that some do not appear able to distinguish the signals of rough-and-tumble play from those of hostility. Zegans (1967, p. 737) suggests with regard to paranoids that they "may not have been able to distinguish the gestures of playful agression from real hostility."

It would seem intuitively reasonable to expect a deficiency in either sending or receiving nonvocal signals to be accompanied by a deficiency in the other, or that the two are inextricably related. Conversation and turn-taking in conversation provide an example of complex behavior that is accompanied by a well-established exchange of nonvocal behaviors which includes patterns of gaze (Argyle and Ingham, 1972; Duncan, 1975, Kendon, 1967). While white subjects look more while listening than while speaking, the pattern is reversed in black subjects (LaFrance and Mayo, 1976). As the authors point out, the likely outcome of an interracial conversation is interrupting, awkward silences and perhaps worse as neither participant is likely to be aware of the cause of the discomfort.[1]

Male–female interactions present a great variety of potential problems resulting from nonvocal social signals, both in the area of courtship–dating interactions and as a result of widespread changes in the roles of women in our culture. Complex nonvocal signals are exchanged in male–female dating relations and failure to comply with established norms may lead to rejection and perhaps eventual disruption of heterosexual patterns of behavior. Literature on women's status in society, although not always methodologically rigorous, has emphasized nonvocal behavior as a major factor in their persistence in subordinate roles. Henley (1977) reviews studies citing such contributing behavior as tolerance of greater intrusions into personal space and more frequent touch, longer durations of gaze and more frequent smiling. Interestingly, although women do appear to smile more (Mackey, 1976), their smiles may be more likely to be directed at other women (Adams and Kirkevold, 1979). While these behaviors are said to have caused problems with regard to social roles, further problems may arise for individuals who incur resentment as they alter their traditional behavior patterns, as for example by "smile boycotts" (Firestone, 1970). Variance from gender-characteristic behaviors as a source of difficulty is also predicted by male problems ranging from "sissiness" to transsexuality [see, for example, Barlow (1974)]. It is interesting to note that the behaviors that define a girl as a "tomboy" do not ordinarily lead to analogous problems.

Complex combinations of nonvocal behaviors have also been suggested as causes of problems in interpersonal adjustment. Concepts such as territoriality and dominance hierarchy have often been taken relatively intact from ethology and applied to mental health processes by both ethologists and mental health workers. Singh and Gang (1974), for example, have argued that schizophrenia may be a result of defects in handling of "aggression and biosocial tendencies such as territoriality" (p. 161) and Kellett (1973) contends that specific types of psychosis may be associated with territorial societies. Esser and Deutsch (1977) report a regression to more primitive territorial and dominance behaviors, though not differentially associated with specific diagnostic categories. With regard to deviance in molar categories such as territoriality, it is difficult to ascertain the direction of cause and effect between the behavior and the disorder, or whether some other factor such as institutionalization is responsible for the observed deviations. Jonas and Jonas (1974) have noted interesting parallels between psychosomatic ailments in humans and a variety of responses of threat in nonhuman species. White (1970) has summarized much of the literature on these complex instances. Often the analogies

---

[1]No judgment of "deviance" or prescription for change is implied here. The same holds for mixed-sex interactions and gender-related behavior.

from animal behavior are less well detailed than one would wish, and the postulations of deficits in such systems as being causes of maladjustment need further empirical documentation.

Conclusive evidence for inadequacies in handling nonvocal signals as the cause of adjustment problems is difficult to establish. As in the case of most other causes of adjustment problems, the bulk of evidence available is the unsystematic recall of the client and his or her friends and family. Strong circumstantial evidence comes from treatment data: when a change in some behavior pattern reverses a failure to establish and maintain social relationships, one may infer the possibility that deviations in that behavior pattern were the cause of the problem. Of course, other interpretations are tenable. One of these is that both the failure of personal relationships and the specified deviant behavior are the result of a third problem. This has often historically been conceived as the overt behaviors being "symptoms" of some deeper underlying problem, a view that will not be discussed here.

Use of Nonvocal Signals In Assessment
The most frequent focus of the study of nonvocal behavior in relation to clinical issues has been on the assessment of clinical problems. Hill (1974) recalls an earlier time when psychiatrists confidently "recognized the slow movement, flexed posture, diminished motility and lack of spontaneous and associative movement, the immobile facial expression of the retarded depressive; the decreased or restricted general motility but increased peripheral movement of the agitated depressive; the rigid bodily postures and precise movements of the tense obsessional; the protracted handshake, the searching looks, the persistent eye-to-eye contact of the paranoid; and the lack of these and the failure to adopt congruent postures and to make congruent movements of the schizophrenic" (p. 227). While clinical practitioners have traditionally been concerned with the verbal behavior of clients as the primary means of assessment, there has been a growing emphasis on the overt nonvocal behavior of the client, not only for assessing problems, but for defining them. This behavior-as-problem approach has largely been identified with behavior therapy. But while behavior therapy assessment has recently received considerable attention [(e.g. Cimenaro et al. (1977), Hersen and Bellack (1976), Mash and Terdal (1976)], little attention has been focused closely on the nonvocal cues a client gives in the client–therapist or other social interaction. Such cues may indicate broader deviations in behavior or emotional state and may give direction to clinical intervention. Most material dealing with assessment continues to emphasize self-report, either through interviews or paper-and-pencil instruments. Only in the case of children's problems has there been a primary emphasis on observed behavior to define the need for and goals of intervention, but rarely has this behavior been in the class of nonvocal social signals.

An important and often unstated assumption with regard to

nonvocal behavior and assessment relates to the relative validity of nonvocal and verbal behavior as measures of the emotional state of an individual. Birdwhistell (1974), for example, acknowledges but rejects the extreme position that only the body, and not the language, tells the truth because the body is "natural." While nonvocal cues will not here be considered a direct and unadulterated communication pathway to the emotions, in many cases they appear to be less altered to fit the demands of the situation than verbal behavior [see, e.g., Ekman and Friesen (1968)]. Further validity is lent to nonvocal behavior by default. Traditional methods of assessment, such as projective technqiues and probing into historical factors, have not proven altogether fruitful, and standard diagnostic categories do not correlate strongly with symptoms or even with the type of treatment used.

A variety of nonvocal social behaviors has been associated with various mental disorders. These findings are almost invariably reported as quantitative rather than qualitative deviations from normal, although Grant (1970) has reported that one of his behavior categories, the shoulder shrug, did not appear in a group of hospitalized schizophrenics observed. Other work by Grant (1970) has focused on nonvocal behavior during interviews with students, recently hospitalized mental patients, and long-termed hospitalized schizophrenics. Of the groups of behavioral elements labeled Flight, Assertion, Relaxation, and Contact, the number of Flight elements increased with severity of illness. In addition, the patient groups showed fewer behavioral elements and behavior persisted longer within a category.

In other studies of hospitalized individuals, Horowitz (1968) has reported decreased personal space; Hinchliffe et al. (1971) and Waxer (1974) have found much less eye contact by depressives; and Rutter and Stephenson (1972) have found less looking during interviews by both depressives and schizophrenics, at least under some conditions (Rutter, 1977). Sainsburg (1955) and Waxer (1977) have found differences in hand movements and other nonvocal behaviors associated with high anxiety. A variety of other nonvocal social behaviors ranging from smiling for no apparent reason to physical assault are frequently found imbedded in assessment scales with other behaviors [e.g., Mariotto and Paul (1974)] and not analyzed independently.

A related group of recent and ongoing studies of institutional populations show great promise in revealing the details of the relationship of nonvocal behavior to various mental disorders and environmental variables. (Fairbanks et al., 1977; McGuire et al., 1977; McGuire and Polsky, 1980; Polsky and Chance, 1979; Polsky and McGuire, 1979). Although Polsky and McGuire present a detailed catalog of behaviors observed, the focus of these reports has been on combined categories of behavior. However, they emphasize an approach that "attempts to look at behavior within psychiatric wards in much the same manner as an ethologist would study a new [animal] species" (Fairbanks et al., 1977, p. 193).

Although most assessment studies have focused on emission of nonvocal behavior, Lorr and Hamkin (1970) have included recognition of facial expression as part of a general assessment battery. While the above are examples from studies designed specifically to examine nonvocal behaviors in the more severely disturbed, other examples are found in specific studies of these populations. An issue that awaits clarification is the degree to which selected nonvocal behaviors vary relative to all other behavior. In depressive patients, for example, there appears to be a reduction in virtually all social behavior.

Research in the association of nonvocal behavior with general emotional state in nonclinical populations has been more common than that with disturbed individuals (Gladstein, 1974). These studies have often been reviewed along with other measures of emotions, as for example by Izard (1971, or 1972), Dittman (1973) and Strongman (1973), or with other reviews of nonverbal behavior. Anxiety is a class of emotion with great clinical relevance and has been examined in some detail. Jurich and Jurich (1974), for example, report significant correlations for lack of eye contact and postural measures with finger sweat print and global ratings of anxiety. And, Clevenger and King (1961) relate behaviors such as swaying and irrelevant arm movements to public-speaking anxiety. It is likely that there will be considerable overlap between nonvocal behavior associated with anxiety and that associated with classes such as submission, nonassertiveness or Grant's "Flight" which includes scratching and head grooming.

It should be emphasized that much of what is mentioned here is information to which the therapist (and many other individuals for that matter) is already attuned in clients, but that is regarded simply as "clinical intuition." Only in rare instances, if at all, would one expect to find behaviors that are unique to some particular emotional state or class of disturbance. More often the behaviors vary simply in intensity, frequency, duration, sequencing and accompaniment by other behavior.

Training of Nonvocal Social Behavior

The training of nonvocal social behavior has been applied to deficits in such interpersonal relationships as dating and marital interactions, withdrawal in hospitalized groups, shyness, and especially assertiveness. Assessment and training in these areas are typically included under the broader heading of "social skills training" [e.g., Argyle et al. (1974), Hersen and Bellack (1976), Hersen and Eisler (1976) and Twentyman and McFall (1975)].

The most effective techniques used in training of social skills are largely those drawn from the armamentarium of behavior therapy (Craighead et al., 1976; Leitenberg, 1976). These include in various combinations, instructions and coaching, modeling, role-playing and feedback and reinforcement, often employing videotape. The needs of clients are ordinarily assumed to be the result of behavioral deficits or failure to learn appropriate social skills, and the training of new behaviors is the strong suit of behavior therapy. Major problems in social skills training appear to be assessment of deficits or maladaptive behaviors and generalization of training to nontherapy situations. In general, the identification of target behaviors is a major part of the battle, as training techniques have proven quite effective and social relationships appear to improve markedly after training.

As regards relevant nonvocal social behaviors, then, their identification is critical. Virtually every discussion of social skills training notes their importance and, frequently, that these behaviors change with training. Identification of specific behaviors, however, is still in the beginning stage, as indicated by examination of the literature on assertiveness.

Assertiveness   Lately assertive training has become the preferred treatment for a great variety of problems of interpersonal relationships. This trend has brought a proliferation of workshops, training centers and books for the professional and nonprofessional audience. Assessment of the need for and effectiveness of assertive training requires reliable and valid measures of assertiveness and, as indicated in recent reviews by Rich and Schroeder (1976) and Bodner (1975), these have not kept pace with the mushrooming use of assertive training. Particularly absent are adequately validated specific units of client behavior that serve as indicators of assertion or submission.

Several strictly nonvocal indicators of assertiveness have been cited in previous accounts with varying degrees of empirical support. Among these are body movement, head orientation and facial expression (Laws and Serber, 1975; Serber, 1972), although with minimal supporting data. A lower frequency of smiling in assertive subjects has both support (Eisler et al., 1975) and a lack of support (Eisler et al., 1973b). Decreased personal space has been shown to result from assertive training (Booraem and Flowers, 1972). Greater duration of looking at a coactor by more assertive subjects has both support (Eisler et al., 1974; Galassi et al., 1974, 1976; Hersen et al., 1973, 1974; Serber, 1972) and a lack of support (Eisler et al., 1973a, b, 1975). Only three of the above studies (Eisler et al., 1973b, 1975; Galassi et al., 1976) can be seen as directly assessing the validity of the behaviors in question against some criterion behavior or test. The others range from simple declarations that some behavior is assertive to changes in the behaviors as a function of assertive training. The former should be accepted with more caution than the latter, but changes as a result of training indicate that a behavior is modifiable by the training—not necessarily that it is a part of the assertiveness conglomerate. Add to these problems the methodological bias that occurs when the same observers rate both the target behaviors and the criterion behavior, and the identification of nonvocal indicators of assertiveness in behavior therapy would not appear solidly established.

The categories of eye contact and duration of looking, the most frequently mentioned nonvocal behaviors, pose particular difficulties with regard to assertiveness. Even apart from the difficulty of measurement [see Argyle and Cook (1976) for a review of results and methodological problems], studies of visual interaction indicate greater complexity of interpretation than is apparent in the clinical literature.

First, eye contact is in part a function of duration of speaking and listening, with less looking while talking (Argyle and Ingham, 1972; Kendon, 1967). Talking more, however, has been said to indicate assertiveness. Second, looking independent of eye contact has been implicated as an indicator of low status in both humans and nonhuman primates (Abramovitch, 1976; Anderson and Willis, 1976; Chance, 1967; Efran, 1968; Exline, 1971; Exline and Messick, 1967; Waterhouse and Waterhouse, 1973). If visual interaction is to be included among indicators of assertiveness, gaze aversion would appear to have greater validity, being seen as part of what Chance (1962) has termed a "cut-off" act.

A rich source of information on nonvocal behavior is the area of human ethology [see Blurton Jones (1972), Fox and Fleising (1976), McGrew (1972), McGuire and Fairbanks (1977)], characterized by unobtrusive naturalistic observation of observable features of behavior, cross-species comparisons and, currently, by the absence of concepts such as "innate behavior," which are anathema to learning-oriented behavior therapists. Behavioral categories established by human ethologists are of great potential value to the study of interpersonal relationships such as assertive–submissive ones, having been generated by direct, systematic observation. The behaviors are typically those for which function has been established by their effect on the behavior of a second subject and by the context in which they occur. The initial descriptive approach of ethology is further demanded by the fact that, as Brannigan and Humphries (1972) report, while most people can label behavior as belonging to some category of emotional expression, few people can accurately describe the components when given only the category label. This may be compared with generating lists of nonverbal assertive behaviors from the recall and impressions of clinicians, even though they may be assumed to be more astute and objective observers than most.

While assertiveness is a class of behaviors that is not often mentioned in the human ethology literature, there appear to be strongly analogous categories such as those observed in agonistic encounters, threat and dominance, and correlate categories such as submission and flight. While psychologists are careful to draw a distinction between assertion and aggression, the area has been, as McGrew has noted, a "terminological hodgepodge." Blurton Jones (1972) has labeled frown and nose wrinkle as aggressive behavior and McGrew (1972) has observed frown, wrinkle and head forward in agonistic encounters. Grant (1965, 1969, 1970) has labeled wrinkle and head forward as aggressive and/or assertive, and chin in and evade (a rapid head turn) as submissive and/or flight behaviors. As evidence of the interrelationships that are often overlooked, Adams et al. (in preparation) have shown a strong relationship in dyadic conversations between frown, head forward and nose wrinkle, and high overall ratings of assertiveness, and a strong relationship between chin in and evade and low ratings of assertiveness. The overall assertiveness ratings were by observers who had been instructed in standard psychological definitions of assertiveness (Alberti and Emmons, 1970; MacDonald, 1975; Rimm and Masters, 1979; Wolpe, 1969) and were not involved in ratings of other behavior categories.

The assertiveness literature has been built largely around verbal and paraverbal measures, which is perhaps one source of frequent failure of assertiveness training to generalize to nontraining situations and/or tasks [e.g., Hersen et al. (1974)]. Sending back a rare steak and most other verbal responses are likely to be highly situation-specific (Eisler et al., 1975). The nonvocal behaviors associated with assertiveness, however, should not be specific to any particular situation. The finding by Adams et al. of a high correlation between ratings of overall assertiveness made with and without sound demonstrates the importance of strictly nonvocal behavior in the responses of observers.

A major problem in identifying behaviors that indicate assertiveness is the absence of established criteria against which to validate them. Self-report measures present near-classic problems with regard to such variables as demand characteristics and reactivity. When high self-report scores are not associated with high behavioral scores, both ethology and behavior therapy tradition would favor the direct measures. Overall ratings of assertiveness are frequently used as validation criteria for other measures, but the criteria for the ratings are vague and the cues used by raters can be easily biased by instructions. Further difficulties may arise when the same persons rate both overall assertiveness and other indicators. Even if validity of overall ratings is assumed, no specific behavior is provided on which treatment programs may focus for evidence of improvement.

Further validity problems arise from the situations that are used to elicit behavior for study. There is a need to avoid the demand characteristics and other factors which threaten the external validity of role-playing situations. Ideally subjects might be observed across a broad sample of their day-to-day activities, focusing, for example, on interactions in which there is known to be or from which there emerges a dominant and a subordinate individual. Such studies have been carried out with children, again from an ethological perspective, using indicators of dominance such as who supplants whom and who has the toy at the end of the interaction [e.g., Ziven (1977)]. Considerations of cross-situationality raise the added issue of whether assertiveness or dominance can legitimately be considered a "trait" that should be expected to be consistent across settings.

Finally, there is a need to identify behaviors that are specific to nonassertiveness or submission, rather than assuming that this is simply the absence of those behaviors labeled assertive. Evade, for example, likely overlaps greatly with gaze aversion, which is associated with low dominance rank in primates (S.A. Altmann, 1967). Primate studies indicate that dominance status may be as obvious from the behavior of low ranking animals as from the behavior of high ranking animals, a controversial issue discussed by Deag (1977), Gartlan (1968), Rowell (1974) and Wade (1978). Extension of these lines of research in naturally occurring human interactions may well lead to a conclusion that making an assertive response is often of less consequence than not making a submissive one.

One may hope that the study of human social interactions in this area will some day be subject to the quantitative approach that Maxim (1976) has carried out with rhesus monkeys. By utilizing a psychophysical procedure in which each monkey's response served as a "rating" of the other monkey's previous response, an interval scale of dominance and submission behaviors was obtained. Interaction then could be examined in terms of the specific magnitude of, for example, the submission response evoked by a particular magnitude of dominance response. Among the many possible extensions of this approach is a consideration of the efficiency of teaching a client to make the minimal effective assertive response in any given situation.

Therapist Nonvocal Behavior

While attention has thus far focused exclusively on the nonvocal behavior of the client, the nonvocal behavior of the therapist is also of importance in the interaction. One major category of therapist influence is his or her reactions to the client's behavior. Showing approval or disapproval is particularly critical in those techniques in which the therapist acts almost exclusively as listener. Any signal in such a situation carries greater impact by virture of its rarity, and almost certainly alters the course of events through its reinforcing or punishing effect [see, e.g., Greenspoon (1955), Rosenfeld and Baer (1970), Verplanck (1955)]. Assessment of the presenting problem and its origins is then altered as a result.

A second major category of therapist influence through nonvocal signals is in the area of the therapist's interpersonal skills such as warmth (Smith-Hanen, 1977). A great variety of signals such as facial expression, posture and pattern of gaze convey warmth or liking or similar information to a client and this almost certainly affects the course of events in therapy. This effect may appear at a level as gross as how often the client continues to attend sessions, but is almost certain to affect the course of therapy (Truax and Mitchell, 1971).

Methodological Problems   A wide variety of methodological problems present themselves in research on nonvocal behavior, some of which have been discussed elsewhere in this chapter. Their consideration leaves little doubt as to the reasons for the overwhelming amount of research that is conducted in laboratories or with paper-and-pencil techniques.

Initial problems concern the selection of behavioral units and the level of complexity to be used. These can range, for example, in social encounters from an approach to a "social interaction" of measured duration, or from a smile to one of a great many types of smiles. Once units are established for further examination they must be defined in a manner that allows high interobserver agreement, a very complex issue in itself including, for example, adjustments for the rate of agreement by chance alone. Actual measurement of frequency and duration presents further problems as sampling methods must be selected to present valid representations, often different for different measures and for behaviors of different rates and durations [e.g., Adams and Markley (1978), J. Altmann (1974)].

These methodological problems become even more involved when the function of behavior is addressed. The function of behavior is established in part by its effects on a second individual and by the situation in which it occurs, including prior behavior of another individual. Often the same behavior functions differently in different situations, and when exhibited in combination with other behavior. All of this implies the need to examine not only the behavior of a target subject, but situational factors and complex sequences, including the behavior of other individuals.

External validity or generalizability of research findings also presents major problems. Comparisons of hospitalized individuals are often confounded by drugs or simply the effects of institutionalization. Interviews are far different with subjects from clinical populations than with normals, as the former are not "blind" with regard to the general aims of the research. Similar biasing effects also arise from interviewers and observers who are aware of the subjects' group membership. In general most settings for study, either clinical or analog, present "demand characteristics" (Orne, 1962) that may influence findings as strongly as the independent variables.

Other problems of significance in research on nonvocal behavior include terminology in describing and classifying nonvocal behavior and its function. This complicating factor arises in part from the fact that researchers come from a variety of disciplines, each with its own core terminology and frame of reference. A related issue is the communication problem involved in attempting to stay abreast of current research which appears in the journals of all the involved disciplines. From this it is not surprising to find so little cross-referencing. Even with regard to observational methodology there is surprisingly little recognition of work from an ethological perspective by that from applied behavior analysis and vice-versa (Peterson, 1975).

Elaboration of some of the potential problems in observational research is not presented here to discourage further research, but to aid in avoiding pitfalls. Whatever the questions that arise regarding repeatability and generality of findings from observational studies, they are not likely to be worse than those of other research areas. Bronfenbrenner (1977) comments that "much of contemporary developmental psychology is *the science of the strange behavior of children in strange situations with strange adults for the briefest possible periods of time*" (p. 513). Elms (1975) has discussed the "crisis of confidence in social psychology"; and the diagnostic research and outcome research in clinical psychology offer numerous conflicts and controversies. The observational methodology of ethology applied to nonvocal social signals appears to hold more promise for external validity than most other approaches to social behavior and clinical processes.

Nowhere is the scientific challenge to human ethologists greater or the need for application so essential as in the area of clinical processes. Psychology in all its diversity, including its therapeutics, may finally be established on a firm foundation of the biology of behavior if we are up to the work and dedication it will require. The quick answers of expedient studies on fashionable topics are *not* science. Short-term gains will have to be relinquished for long-term increments in understanding and closure by means of detailed observations of behavior (both normal and atypical) in realistic situations.

References   Abramovitch, R. 1976. The relation of attention and proximity to rank in preschool children. In M. R. A. Chance and R. R. Larsen (eds.) *The Social Structure of Attention*, pp. 153–176. New York: Wiley.

Adams, R.M., and Kirkevold, B. 1979. Looking, smiling, laughing and moving in restaurants: Sex and age differences. *Evnironmental Psychology and Nonverbal Behavior* 3: 117–121.

Adams, R.M., and Markley, R.P. 1978. Assessment of the accuracy of point and one-zero sampling techniques by computer simulation. Paper presented at the Animal Behavior Society Meeting, Seattle.

Adams, R.M., Allmaras, J.A., and Allmaras, M.G. Assertive behavior: Components derived from human ethology. In preparation.

Alberti, R.E., and Emmons, M.L. 1970 *Your Perfect Right*. San Luis Obispo, CA: Impact.

Alevizos, P., DeRisi, W., Liberman, R., Eckman, R., and Callahan, E. 1978. The behavior observation instrument: A method of direct observation for program evaluation. *Journal of Applied Behavior Analysis* 11: 243–257.

Altman, I. 1975. *The Environment and Social Behavior: Privacy, Personal Space, Territory, Crowding*. Monterey, CA: Brooks/Cole.

Altmann, J., 1974. Observational study of behavior: Sampling methods. *Behaviour* 48: 1–41.

Altmann, S.A. 1967. Structure of social communication. In S. A. Altmann (ed.) *Social Communication Among Primates*, pp. 325–362. Chicago: University of Chicago Press.

Anderson, F.J., and Willis, F.N. 1976. Glancing at others in preschool children in relation to dominance. *Psychological Record* 26: 467–472.

Argyle, M., and Cook, M. 1976. *Gaze and Mutual Gaze*. New York: Cambridge University Press.

Argyle, M., and Ingham, R. 1972. Gaze, mutual gaze and proximity. *Semiotica* 6: 32–49.

Argyle, M., Salter, V., Nicholson, H., Williams, M., and Burgess, P. 1970. The communication of inferior and superior attitudes by verbal and nonverbal signals. *British Journal of Social and Clinical Psychology* 9:222–231.

Argyle, M., Trower, P., and Bryant, B. 1974. Explorations in the treatment of personality disorders and neuroses by social skills training. *British Journal of Medical Psychology* 47: 63–72.

Bandura, A. 1973. *Aggression: A Social Learning Analysis*. Englewood Cliffs, NJ: Prentice-Hall.

Barlow, D.H. 1974. The treatment of sexual deviation: Towards a comprehensive behavioral approach. In K. S. Calhoun, H. E. Adams, and K. M. Mitchell (eds.) *Innovative Treatment Methods in Psychopathology*. New York: Wiley.

Birdwhistell, R.L. 1970. *Kinesics and Context*. Philadelphia: University of Pennsylvania Press.

———. 1974. The language of the body: The natural environment of words. In A. Silverstein (ed.) *Human Communication: Theoretical Explorations*. New York: Wiley.

Blurton Jones, N. G. 1967. An ethological study of some aspects of social behaviour of children in nursery school. In D. Morris (ed.) *Primate Ethology*, pp. 437–563. Chicago: Aldine.

Blurton Jones, N. G. (ed.) 1972. *Ethological Studies of Child Behaviour*. New York: Cambridge University Press.

Bodner, G. E. 1975. The role of assessment in assertion training. *Counseling Psychologist* 5: 90–96.

Booraem, C. D., and Flowers, J. V. 1972. Reduction of anxiety and personal space as a function of assertion training with severely disturbed neuropsychiatric inpatients. *Psychological Reports* 30: 923–929.

Brannigan, C. R., and Humprhies, D. A. 1972. Human nonverbal behaviour, a means of communication. In N.G. Blurton Jones (ed.) *Ethological Studies of Child Behaviour*, pp. 37–64. New York: Cambridge University Press.

Bronfenbrenner, U. 1977. Toward an experimental ecology of human development. *American Psychologist* 32: 513–531.

Chance, M.R.A. 1962. An interpretation of some agonistic postures: The role of "cut-off" acts and postures. *Symposium of the Zoological Society of London* 8: 71–89.

———. 1967. Attention structure as the basis of primate rank orders. *Man* 2: 503–518.

Cinemaro, A.R., Calhoun, K.S., and Adams, H.E. (eds.) 1977. *Handbook of Behavioral Assessment*. New York: Wiley.

Clevenger, T., and King, T. R. 1961. A factor analysis of the visible symptoms of stage fright. *Speech Monographs* 28: 296–298.

Craighead, W.E., Kazdin, A.E., and Mahoney, M.J. (eds.) 1976. *Behavior Modification: Principles, Issues, and Applications*. Boston: Houghton Mifflin.

Deag, J.M. 1977. Aggression and submission in monkey societies. *Animal Behaviour* 25:465–474.

Dittman, A.T. 1973. *Interpersonal Messages of Emotion*. New York: Springer.

Duncan, S.D., Jr. 1975. Language, paralanguage and body motion in the structure of conversations. In T. R. Williams (ed.) *Socialization Communication in Primary Groups*, pp. 282–311. The Hague: Mouton.

Efran, J.S. 1968. Looking for approval: Effect on visual behavior of approbation from persons differing in importance. *Journal of Personality and Social Psychology* 10: 21–251.

Eibl-Eibesfeldt, I. 1975. *Ethology: The Biology of Behavior.* 2nd ed. New York: Holt, Rinehart & Winston.

Eisler, R. M., Hersen, M., and Miller, P.M. 1973a. Effects of modeling on components of assertive behavior. *Journal of Behavior Therapy and Experimental Psychiatry* 4: 1–6.

Eisler, R.M., Miller, P.M., and Hersen, M. 1973b. Components of assertive behavior. *Journal of Clinical Psychology* 29: 295–299.

Eisler, R.M., Hersen, M., and Miller, P.M. 1974. Shaping components of assertive behavior with instructions and feedback. *American Journal of Psychiatry* 131: 1344–1347.

Eisler, R.M., Hersen, M., Miller, P.M., and Blanchard, E.B. 1975. Situational determinants of assertive behaviors. *Journal of Consulting and Clinical Psychology* 43: 330–340.

Ekman, P. 1973. Darwin and cross cultural studies of facial expression. In P. Ekman (ed.) *Darwin and Facial Expression: A Century of Research in Review.* New York: Academic.

Ekman, P., and Friesen, W.V. 1968. Nonverbal behavior in psychotherapy research. In J.M. Shlien (ed.) *Research in Psychotherapy,* Vol. III. pp. 179–216. American Psychological Association, Washington, DC.

Ekman, P., and Friesen, W. 1975. *Unmasking the Face.* Englewood Cliffs, NJ: Prentice-Hall.

Elms, A.C. 1975. The crisis of confidence in social psychology. *American Psychologist* 30: 967–976.

Esser, A.H., and Deutsch, R.D. 1977. Private and interaction territories on psychiatric wards: Studies on nonverbal communication of spatial needs. In M.T. McGuire and L.A. Fairbanks (eds.) *Ethological Psychiatry: Psychopathology in the Context of Evolutionary Biology,* pp. 127–152. New York: Grune & Stratton.

Exline, R.V. 1971. Visual interaction: The glances of power and preference. *Nebraska Symposim on Motivation,* pp. 163–206.

Exline, R.V., and Messick, D. 1967. The effects of dependency and social reinforcement upon visual behavior during an interview. *British Journal of Social and Clinical Psychology* 6: 256–266.

Fairbanks, L.A., McGuire, M.T., Cole, S.R., Sbordone, R., Silvers, F.M., Richards, M., and Akers, J. 1977. The ethological study of four psychiatric wards: Patient, staff and system behavior. *Journal of Psychiatric Research* 13: 193–209.

Firestone, S. 1970. *The Dialectic of Sex.* New York: Bantam.

Fox, R., and Fleising, U. 1976. Human ethology. *Annual Review of Anthropology* 5: 265–288.

Galassi, J.P., Galassi, M.D., and Litz, M.C. 1974. Assertive training in groups using video feedback. *Journal of Counseling Psychology* 21: 390–394.

Galassi, J.P., Hollandsworth, J.G., Jr., Radecki, J.C., Gay, M.L., Howe, M.R., and Evans, C.L. 1976. Behavioral performance in the validation of an assertiveness scale. *Behavior Therapy* 7: 447–452.

Gartlan, J.S. 1968. Structure and function in primate society. *Folia Primatologica* 8: 89–120.

Gladstein, G.A. 1974. Nonverbal communication and counseling/psychotherapy: A review. *Counseling Psychologist* 4:34–57.

Grant, E.C. 1965. An ethological description of some schizophrenic patterns of behaviour. In F.A. Fenner (ed.) *Proceedings of the Leeds Symposium on Behavioural Disorders.* Dagenham, England: May and Baker.

————. 1969. Human facial expression. *Man* 4:525–536.

————. 1970. An ethological description of nonverbal behavior during interviews. In S.J. Hutt and C. Hutt (eds.) *Behaviour Studies in Psychiatry*, pp. 61–72. New York: Pergamon.

Greenspoon, J. 1955. The reinforcing effect of two spoken sounds on the frequency of two responses. *American Journal of Psychology* 68: 409–416.

Harper, R.G., Wiens, A.N., and Matarazzo, J.D. 1978. *Nonverbal Communication: The State of the Art.* New York: Wiley.

Harrison, R. 1975. Body language revisited. *Journal of Communication* 25: 223–224.

Henley, N. 1977. *Body Politics: Sex, Power, and Nonverbal Communication.* Englewood Cliffs, N.J.: Prentice-Hall.

Hersen, M., and Bellack, A.S. (eds.) 1976. *Behavioral Assessment: A Practical Handbook.* Oxford: Pergamon.

Hersen, M., and Eisler, R.M. 1976. Social skills training. In W.E. Craighead, A.E., Kazdin, and M.J. Mahoney (eds.) *Behavior Modification: Principles, Issues, and Applications.* Boston: Houghton Mifflin.

Hersen, M., Eisler, R.M., Miller, P.M., Johnson, M.B., and Pinkston, S.G. 1973. Effects of practice, instructions and modeling on components of assertive behavior. *Behavior Research and Therapy* 11: 443–451.

Hersen, M., Eisler, R.M., and Miller, P.M. 1974. An experimental analysis of generalization in assertive training. *Behavior Research and Theraphy* 12: 295–310.

Hill, D. 1974. Nonverbal behaviour in mental illness. *British Journal of Psychiatry* 124: 221–230.

Hinchliffe, M.K., Lancashire, M., and Roberts, F.J. 1971. A study of eye contact changes in depressed and recovered psychiatric patients. *British Journal of Psychiatry* 119: 213–215.

Horowitz, M.J. 1968. Spatial behavior and psychopathology. *Journal of Nervous and Mental Disease* 146:24–35.

Izard, C.E. 1971. *The Face of Emotion.* New York: Appleton-Century-Crofts.

————. 1972. *Patterns of Emotion.* New York: Academic.

Jonas, A.D., and Jonas, D.F. 1974. The evolutionary mechanisms of neurotic behavior. *American Journal of Psychiatry* 131: 636–640.

Jurich, A.P., and Jurich, J.A. 1974. Correlations among nonverbal expressions of anxiety. *Psychological Reports* 34: 199–204.

Kellett, J.M. 1973. Evolutionary theory for the dichotomy of the functional psychoses. *Lancet* 1:860–863.

Kendon, A. 1967. Some functions of gaze-direction in social interaction. *Acta Psychologica* 26: 22–63.

LaFrance, M., and Mayo, C. 1976. Racial differences in gaze behavior during conversations: Two systematic observational studies. *Journal of Personality and Social Psychology* 33: 547–552.

LaFrance, M., and Mayo, C. 1978. *Moving Bodies: Nonverbal Communication in Social Relationships.* Monterrey, CA: Brooks/Cole.

Laws, D.R., and Serber, M. 1975. Measurement and evaluation of assertive training with sexual offenders. In R.E. Hosford and C.S. Mos (eds.) *The Crumbling Walls* pp. 165–172. Champaign, IL: University of Illinois.

Leathers, D.R. 1976. *Nonverbal Communication Systems.* Boston: Alyn and Bacon.

Leitenberg, H. (ed.) 1976. *Handbook of Behavior Modification and Behavior Therapy.* Englewood Cliffs, NJ: Prentice-Hall.

Levitt, E.A. 1964 The relation between abilities to express emotional meanings vocally and facially. In J. R. Davis (ed.) *The Communication of Emotional Meanings.* New York: McGraw-Hill.

Lorr, M., and Hamkin, R.M. 1970. Estimation of the major psychotic disorders by objective test scores. *Journal of Nervous and Mental Disease* 151: 219–224.

MacDonald, M.L. 1975. Teaching assertion: A paradigm for therapeutic intervention. *Psychotherapy: Theory, Research and Practice* 12: 60–67.

Mackey, W.C. 1976. Parameters of the smile as a social signal. *Journal of Genetic Psychology* 129: 125–130.

Mariotto, M.J., and Paul, G.L. 1974. A multimethod validation of the inpatient multidimensional psychiatric scale with chronically institutionalized patients. *Journal of Consulting and Clinical Psychology* 42: 497–508.

Mash, E.J., and Terdal, L.G. (eds.) 1976. *Behavior-Therapy Assessment: Diagnosis, Design, and Evaluation.* New York: Springer.

Maxim, P.E. 1976. An interval scale for studying and quantifying social relations in pairs of rhesus monkeys. *Journal of Experimental Psychology: General* 105: 123–147.

McGrew, W.C. 1972. *An Ethological Study of Human Behavior.* New York: Academic Press.

McGuire, M.T., and Fairbanks, L.A. 1977. Ethology: Psychiatry's bridge to behavior. In M.T. McGuire and L.A. Fairbanks (eds.) *Ethological Psychiatry: Psychopathology in the Context of Evolutionary Biology,* pp. 211–219. New York: Grune & Stratton.

McGuire, M.T., and Polsky, R.H. 1980. An ethological analysis of behavioral change in hospitalized psychiatric patients. In S.A. Corson, and E. Corson (eds.) *Ethology and Nonverbal Communication in Mental Health.* New York: Pergammon.

McGuire M.T., Fairbanks, L.A., Cole, S.R., Sbordone, R., Silvers, F.M., Richards, M., and Akers, J. 1977. The ethological study of four psychiatric wards: Behavior changes associated with new staff and new patients. *Journal of Psychiatric Research* 13: 211–244.

Mehrabian, A., and Ferris, S.R. 1967. Inference of attitudes from nonverbal communication in two channels. *Journal of Consulting Psychology* 31: 248–252.

Orne, M.T. 1962. On the social psychology of the psychological experiment: With particular reference to demand characteristics and their implication. *American Psychologist* 17: 776–783.

Peterson, L. 1975. A neglected literature and an aphorism. *Journal of Applied Behavior Analysis* 8: 231–232.

Polsky, R.H., and Chance, M.R.A. 1979. An ethological perspective on social behavior in long-stay hospitalized psychiatric patients. *Journal of Nervous and Mental Disease* pp. 167: 658–668.

Polsky, R.H., and McGuire, M.T. 1979. An ethological analysis of manic–depressive disorder. *Journal of Nervous and Mental Disease* 167:56–69.

Rich, A.R., and Schroeder, H.E. 1976. Research issues in assertiveness training. *Psychological Bulletin* 83: 1081–1096.

Rimm, D.C., and Masters, J.C. 1979. *Behavior Therapy: Techniques and Empirical Findings* 2nd ed. New York: Academic Press.

Rosenfeld, H.M., and Baer, D.M. 1970. Unbiased and unnoticed verbal conditioning: The double agent robot procedure. *Journal of the Experimental Analysis of Behavior* 14: 99–105.

Rowell, T.E. 1974. The concept of social dominance. *Behavioral Biology* 11: 131–154.

Rutter, D.R. 1977. Visual interaction and speech patterning in remitted and acute schizophrenic patients. *British Journal of Social and Clinical Psychology* 16: 357–361.

Rutter, D.R., and Stephenson, G.M. 1972. Visual interaction in a group of schizophrenic and depressive patients. *British Journal of Social and Clinical Psychology* 11: 57–65.

Sainsburg, P. 1955. Gestural movements during psychiatric interview. *Psychosomatic Medicine* 17: 458–469.

Serber, M. 1972. Teaching the nonvocal components of assertive training. *Journal of Behavior Therapy and Experimental Psychiatry* 3: 179–183.

Singh, M.M., and Gang, R.G. 1974. An ethological model of schizophrenia—A preliminary investigation. *Diseases of the Nervous System* 35: 157–165.

Smith-Hanen, S.S. 1977. Effects of nonverbal behaviors on judged levels of counselor warmth and empathy. *Journal of Counseling Psychology* 24: 87–91.

Strongman, K.T. 1973. *The Psychology of Emotions.* New York: Wiley.

Spiegal, J.P., and Mochotka, P. 1974. *Messages of the Body.* New York: The Free Press of Macmillan.

Truax, C.B., and Mitchell, K.M. 1971. Research on certain therapist interpersonal skills in relation to process and outcome. In A.E. Bergin and S.L. Garfield (eds.) *Handbook of Psychotherapy and Behavior Change.* New York: Wiley.

Twentyman, C.T., and McFall, R.M. 1975. Behavioral training of social skills in shy males. *Journal of Consulting and Clinical Psychology* 43: 384–395.

Verplanck, W.S. 1955. The control of the content of conversation: Reinforcement of statements of opinion. *Journal of Abnormal and Social Psychology* 51: 676–688.

Wade, T.D. 1978. Status and hierarchy in nonhuman primate societies. In P.P.G. Bateson and P.H. Klopfer (eds.) *Perspectives in Ethology* Vol. 3, Social Behavior. New York: Plenum Press.

Waterhouse, M.J., and Waterhouse, H.B. 1973. Primate ethology and human social behavior. In R.P. Michael and J.H. Crook (eds.) *Comparative Ecology and Behavior of Primates.* New York: Academic Press.

Waxer, P. 1974. Nonverbal cues for depression. *Journal of Abnormal Psychology* 83: 319–322.

Waxer, P. 1977. Nonverbal cues for anxiety: An examination of emotional leakage. *Journal of Abnormal Psychology* 86: 306–314.

Weitz, Shirley (ed.) 1974. *Nonverbal Communication.* New York: Oxford University Press.

White, N.F. 1970. *Ethology and Psychiatry.* Buffalo: University of Toronto Press.

Wolpe, J. 1969. *The Practice of Behavior Therapy.* New York: Pergamon Press.

Zegans, L.S. 1967. An appraisal of ethological contributions to psychiatric theory and research. *American Journal of Psychiatry* 124: 729–739.

Ziven, G. 1977. Facial gestures predict preschoolers' encounter outcomes. *Social Science Information* 16: 715–730.

Speculations on the Adaptive Significance of Self-Deception

Joan S. Lockard

13

When Wallace (1973) proposed his model of human deceit as an evolutionary mechanism, his basic assumption was that an accurate appraisal of one's environment is essential for high fitness. He reasoned, therefore, that one individual might increase his own relative fitness by causing a second (nonrelative) to misinterpret the environment.

Thus, if two individuals are searching for food that is scarcely sufficient to support one of them alone, either one might raise his own fitness by convincing the other to search in barren places.(p. 2)

Wallace illustrated this concept by having an individual perception of his world represented by a small circle (Figure 1), the radius of which was a measure of his own inaccuracy in seeing the world as it "really is," i.e., in terms of more objective criteria, physical and or psychological. The radius of a second larger circle, encompassing the first, depicts the extent to which another individual could increase such misperception or misinterpretation by the first person to the relative benefit of the second person. The degree of genetic advantage to the latter was a function of the relatedness of the two individuals involved, i.e., the deceiver accrued a greater increment in its inclusive fitness if the deceived were a nonkin.

Self-deception in the Deception of Others

Trivers (1976) carried this idea further by stating, in the foreword of Dawkins' book, *The Selfish Gene*, that since deceit is fundamental to animal communication (obviously including human communication) then there must be strong selection to detect deception. He goes on to suggest that the probability of detection, in turn, ought to select for a degree of self-deception, rendering some facts and motives unconscious so as not to betray, by subtle signs of self-awareness, the deception being perpetuated. The implications of this idea were evident in Trivers' paper on parental investment and sexual selection (1972), where he emphasized that male and female reproductive strategies would never be identical even when ostensibly cooperating in a joint task.

Figure 1

The centers of circles 1 and 2 represent persons 1 and 2; the radius of each circle (r_1 and r_2) equals each person's usual misperception of a given situation in the world of situations (the circumferences of circle 1 and circle 2, respectively). Person 2 deceives person 1 such that the latter's misperception of the world (circumference 3) is increased by radius R. Total misperception of person 1 equals $r_1 + R$ [adapted from Wallace (1973)].

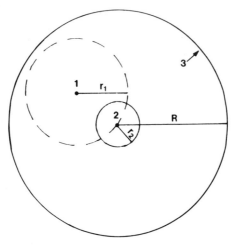

In any case, the cost of the copulation itself is always trivial to the male, and in theory the male need not invest anything else in order to copulate. If there is any chance the female can raise the young either alone or with the help of others, it would be to the male's advantage to copulate with her. By this reasoning one would expect males of monogamous species to retain some psychological traits consistent with promiscuous habits. A male would be selected to differentiate between a female he will only impregnate and a female with whom he will also raise young. (p. 145)

It is quite likely that the male would be more successful in this mixed strategy if he could convince both females of his intended fidelity. Moreover, if he himself is self-deceived as to his motives, then his behavior would undoubtedly be even more convincing. Self-deception would also be advantageous in the event of intended desertion by the male or subsequent cuckoldry by the female.

At any point in time the individual whose cumulative investment is exceeded by his partner's is theoretically tempted to desert, especially if the disparity is large. This temptation occurs because the deserter loses less than his partner if no offspring are raised and the partner would therefore be more strongly selected to stay with the young. Any success of the partner will, of course, benefit the deserter. (p. 146)

The adaptive benefit of self-deception is further implicated in the discourse of yet another paper by Trivers (1974) on the topic of parent–offspring conflict.

According to the theory presented here, socialization is a process by which parents attempt to mold each offspring in order to increase their own inclusive fitness, while each offspring is selected to resist some of the molding and attempt to mold the behavior of its parents (and siblings) in order to increase its inclusive fitness. (p. 260)

It again seems reasonable that if the individuals involved were unaware of their intent, the more convincing may be their argument and the greater the likelihood of achieving their ends.

Sincerity and Self-Deception Alexander (1974) indicated another facet of this intriguing subject by speculating that natural selection may have consistently favored tendencies for humans to be unaware of what they are really doing or why they are doing it. In his concluding argument for parental manipulation as a biological concept, he proposed that if parental pressures for altruism in offspring have, during human history, led progeny to reproductive success, then such behavior represents a valuable social asset, even when it derives from an inability to recognize the reproductively selfish intent of the behavior.

In a paper on the search for a general theory of behavior, Alexander (1975) again addresses the concept of human deceit.

> Consider two monogamous pairs cooperating or living in close proximity for some reason that represents reproductive advantage for both couples. If any resources are limited, any of the four individuals gains by securing for himself or his mate or both a disproportionate share. The profit in such behavior will depend on the likelihood and the significance of the risk to them of breaking up or reducing the effectiveness of the cooperation. When the relationship of individuals of the two sexes is considered, the same problem exists. Either male would gain reproductively by fathering as many of the total number of offspring as possible. Either female would gain, if she does not lose paternal behavior or her offspring in the process, by having her offspring fathered by the more fit of the two males. Any behavior of any of the four individuals short of full exhibition of whatever realization exists regarding such potential gains, and short of the behavior required to realize them, constitutes compromise and constitutes lying to the extent that the motivation is in fact part of the involved individual's consciousness. (p. 97)

He goes on to say that it is not difficult to be biologically selfish and still appear to be sincere if one is sufficiently ignorant of one's own motives. An individual who is convinced he is right with moral and ethical "mandates from heaven," in acting in any way he may feel is necessary to exist within the social group, is functioning in an adaptive manner since his survival depends on his sociality. Alexander emphasizes the importance of the concept of self-deception in understanding how man interprets his universe by stating:

> He will not see in himself what he does not wish to see, or what he does not wish his neighbors and fellows to see; and he is reluctant to see in other organisms what he will not see in himself. All of biology, all of science, all of human endeavors have been guided to some large extent by this circumstance. (p. 97)

In a similar vein, I mentioned in 1977 that proximal and distal explanations of the same behavior may often be superficially inconsonant with one another. I suggested that it is quite likely that much of recent human evolution has entailed deceiving oneself into increasing one's fitness by providing proximal reasons (e.g., physiological or cultural) to champion why it is one behaves in certain ways. For example, global concepts such as "being in love with your spouse" or "caring for your children" help span the difficult moments of a lover's quarrel or a defiant offspring.

In another commentary on the possibility of animal consciousness (Lockard, 1978), I propose that in those species where
individual identification of conspecifics has been essential for
survival, preadaptations for some degree of cognitive processes
may also be manifested. Moreover, if, in addition to cognition, a
species also exhibits social deceit, the capacity for consciousness or
perhaps more importantly its possible antithesis, subconscious-
ness, is probable. If, in deceiving conspecifics, an organism were
more successful (in terms of a greater increment in inclusive
fitness) if self-deceived as to the actual motive for the deception,
then possessing a subconscious would indeed be adaptive.

Therefore, of those animals possessing cognition, species likely to have
consciousness as well would be ones where the mating system was
polygamous and the infancy period quite extensive. In other words,
animals which compete for mates, where the male and female mating
strategies are dissimilar, and where the rearing of offspring may often
have to be borne by one parent either by default (i.e., the death of the
other parent) or by design (i.e., desertion by the other parent), are good
candidates for possessing consciousness and by inference, subconscious-
ness. (p. 584)

Self-Deception in Coping with Life

Krakauer (1975) wrote about other aspects of self-deceit, which are
quite old to the psychological literature, i.e., rationalizations. He
suggests that ego defenses (in the Freudian sense) include memory
repression, reaction formation (containment of unacceptable feelings by overemphasis of their opposites), repression of emotion,
denial of an unacceptable area of external reality, projection
(attributing one's own unacceptable attitudes to others), turning
against the self, dependent identification with another person and
regression to immaturity. He proposes self-deception as an unconscious function that enables the ego to consciously justify existence
and maintain self-control.

Krakauer (1978) goes on to say that self-deception is common to
all human beings and, thus, must have adaptive significance. In
this regard, he takes Freud's three centers of mental function (id,
ego and superego) and suggests that the evolving intellect (ego) of
early hominids became separated through natural selection from
the nonconscious functions in order for individuals to better cope
with life problems.

There are two distinct non-conscious centers of function that provide
behavioral channeling; the id, the inherited generator of emotions, goals
and instinctual drives and the superego, the learned unconscious which
replaces the missing "fixed" instincts of other species with values and
modes of behaviors acquired early from parents and culture. Ego functions
include perception, memory, thought, imagination, feelings (affect), and
control of the voluntary muscles.

Krakauer further reasoned that egos which are separated from
their unconscious have less emotional involvement and therefore

can think better. In his view, the function of the ego is to feed back ideas and information to the unconscious centers, mediate their responses and take action. Self-deception is the supposedly evolved mechanism by which control of the id and superego are maintained, and rationalization is the conscious means whereby ego resolves any conflict of motivation among the three centers of mental function. The psychoanalytic term "defenses of the ego" is purported to describe the adaptive aspect of self-deception. The conscious mind is supposedly defended by ego from directives of the id that are too strong, e.g., "get love" and "get more power" or from feelings of the superego that are too much to bear, e.g., "I am no good" and "Nobody can love me."

Self-Deception and Neurophysiological Correlates of Consciousness

This idea of self-deception as a "gating process" whereby some information is admitted to consciousness is an intriguing idea and one for which there may already be some supportive neurophysiological data. From studies on lateralization of higher cortical function, Puccetti (1977) suggests that research on commissurotomy patients argues for bilateral organization of consciousness. In particular, some of the confusion rests with the difficulty in separating the specific focusing of attention that is thought to be a property of more rostral (thalamic) portions of brain stem from the more generalized arousal and sleep wakefulness functions of the reticular formation of poutine midbrain.

Ojemann (1977) has provided evidence for lateralization of thalamic mechanisms along a verbal-visual-spatial dichotomy but with left thalamic (verbal) alerting mechanisms dominant. An assessment of areas of thalamus involved in language was undertaken in a series of 37 patients undergoing ventral lateral thalamotomy for Parkinsonism or dystonia (17 left and 20 right-hemisphere-dominant subjects) over the course of several years. The methodology included standard tests of specific behaviors presented to awake patients visually as slides or auditorially from prerecorded tapes during neurosurgical operations. Information on thalamic function was obtained during trials of stereotaxic electrical stimulation of the thalamus (only appropriately selected patients who had given written consent for the stimulation studies were used as subjects). Repetitive trials were employed in the standard tests so that some trials could be used as measures of control performance (nonstimulation trials) randomly interspersed with trials where stimulation occurred at selected thalamic sites. In that way the effects of stimulation were separable from those of the operating room environment. The tests also included controls for alteration in perception of input or disturbance of motor output. For example, the short-term verbal memory task involved an input, storage and output phase. Input to memory was object naming. A standard verbal distraction was then provided by counting backwards by threes from a pictured 2-digit number greater than 30. Following the six-second distraction, retrieval from short-term memory was cued by the word "recall" appearing on the screen. Each patient had been trained to give back the name of the previously pictured object of the trial. Stimulation occurred during either the input, storage or output phases of the test on selected trials, on both the input and output phases together in other trials, and these were randomly interspersed with trials without stimulation.

The data indicated that stimulation during input to short-term verbal memory decreased later retrieval errors. The same current applied to the same sites blocked retrieval of material already in short-term memory, whereas smaller currents at these same sites accelerated memory processes other than speech. Anomic naming errors were also evoked from lateral thalamus and interpreted as defects in retrieval from long-term memory (Ojemann, 1979). This interpretation was based on a high negative correlation between the severity of the language disturbance after a thalamic lesion and a measure of the stimulation-evoked short-term memory changes that made up the specific alerting responses in the same patient. This apparent gating response in ventral lateral thalamus determines access to memory at any point in time and modulates the likelihood of later retrieval. These effects are strongly lateralized, in that nonhemisphere-dominant thalamic stimulation shows none of these results for verbal material, though they are present for visual–spatial information. The converse is true for hemispheric-dominant thalamus (Ojemann, 1977).

Albert et al. (1976) showed that more generalized arousal mechanisms may also be lateralized, predominantly to the left brain. In that study, 47 patients with unilateral cerebral vascular lesions (with equivalent degrees of hemiplegia) showed a significant reduction in levels of consciousness following left-hemisphere lesions compared to right. Some 57% of the left-hemisphere-damaged, but only 25% of the right-hemisphere-damaged patients had a reduced level of consciousness following strokes, as assessed by response to painful stimuli, presence of spontaneous movement, specific reflexes, the ability to be aroused from sleeplessness and the ability to follow verbal commands. Earlier studies (Serafetinides et al., 1965) on changes in consciousness during intracarotid sodium amythal injections also implicated left-brain mechanisms, although these studies were not confirmed (Rosadini and Rossi, 1967). A more recent study by Dimond (1976), using the same commissurotomy patients referred to by Puccetti, indicated that the left hemisphere of these subjects was less capable of performing a vigilance task than was the right hemisphere.

Whitaker and Ojemann (1977) have summarized the information on the question of coconscious brains, or the bilateral organization of consciousness, by stating that no matter how one analyzes the dual and independent control over certain behaviors in commissurotomy patients, it is quite clear that in measures of attention, vigilance, language function and awareness of sensory stimuli, the right and left hemispheres are not equivalent.

Self-Deception and Facial Expressions of Emotions   Along these same lines, but with only speculative neurophysiological implications, Ekman (1971), in studies of pancultural facial expressions of emotion, suggested that universal facial expressions occur through the operation of a "facial affect program." This program is supposed to specify a relationship between distinctive movements of the facial muscles and particular emotions, such as happiness, sadness, anger, fear, disgust and surprise (Table I). He called this theory *neuro-cultural* because it emphasizes two very different sets of determinants of facial expressions, one which is

Table I
Facial Appearance of Six Emotions[a]

	Upper face	**Eyes**	**Lower face**
Happiness	No distinctive brow–forehead appearance	Eyes may be relaxed or neutral in appearance, or narrowed with crow feet apparent.	Outer corners of lips raised and possibly back; may have pronounced nasolabial fold, lips opened and teeth showing
Sadness	Brows drawn together or down in the middle and slightly raised at inner corners; forehead shows small horizontal and vertical wrinkles in center area	Eyes either glazed, with drooping upper lids or tense and pulled up at inner corner; eyes may be looking downward or showing tears	Mouth open and with partially stretched, trembling lips, or closed with outer corners pulled slightly down
Surprise	Raised curved eyebrows; long horizontal forehead wrinkles	Wide opened eyes with schlera showing above and often below; skin stretched above eyelids	Dropped-open mouth; no stretch to lip corners but lips parted
Fear	Raised, flattened and drawn together brows; short horizontal and/or vertical forehead wrinkles	Eyes opened, staring and raised more than in surprise; schlera may show above but not below iris	Mouth corners drawn straight back; lips stretched
Anger	Brows pulled down, inward, and appear to thrust forward; strong vertical forehead wrinkles above eyes	No schlera shows in eyes; lid tightening may be sufficient to appear squinting	Either the lips tightly pressed together or an open, squared mouth with lips raised and/or forward
Disgust	Brows drawn down but not together; short vertical creases in forehead; horizontal and/or vertical wrinkles on nose	Lower eyelids pushed up, raised but not tensed	Deep nasolabial fold and raising of cheeks; mouth either open or closed with upper lip raised; tongue may be visible forward in mouth

[a]Adapted from Ekman (1971).

responsible for universals and the other for cultural differences. In this respect, *neuro* referred to the facial affect program: the relationship between particular emotions and the firing of particular patterns of facial muscles. He regarded this program, at least partly, as innate and one that could sometimes be activated with relatively little prior cognitive processing or evaluation. The term *cultural* referred to the other set of determinants: the events that elicit, the rules that control and the consequences of emotion. These latter determinants were regarded as learned and may vary in different societies.

The facial affect program is hypothesized to link each of the emotions in Table I with a distinctive pattern of neural impulses sent to the facial musculature such that the result is a distinctive facial appearance. These emotions are considered primary or basic states. Ekman distinguished them from what he called secondary, blended or multiple emotions. He goes on to say that without postulating the existence of blended expressions that present various mixtures of the primary emotion, it would be impossible to account for the host of complex facial expressions of emotions and of emotion words, which far exceed the small list of primary emotions. For instance, some mixture of happiness and anger (primary emotions) may account for the blend emotion of "smugness."

Plutchik (1962) began the research on the language of emotion to show that a limited number of primary emotion labels could account for a large number of complex blends. Nummenmaa (1964) and Ekman and Friesen (1969) documented more extensively that blends of facial expressions do occur. They showed that still photographs of the face could convey information about two primary emotions to observers, and subsequently verified which parts of the face conveyed each of the primary emotions. Ekman (1971) proposed that blends could be manifested in three ways: (a) by a very rapid succession of two primary facial expressions of emotion, (b) by a division of labor across different muscle groups so that one emotion is shown in one area of the face while another is shown in another facial area, or (c) by a division across the right and left side of the face—the product of two sets of muscular movements that has an appearance dissimilar from each.

It was further suggested (Ekman, 1971) that there are display rules whereby blends of primary facial expressions are manifested. The idea that man can and typically does exercise some control over his facial expressions of emotion is not a new idea [e.g., Asch (1952) Hebb (1946), Honkavarra (1961), Klineberg (1940), Murphy et al. (1937), Tomkins (1962, 1963)], but Ekman and associates (Ekman and Friesen, 1969) have described ways by which facial behavior may be controlled. This control can be affected by means of intensifying, deintensifying, neutralizing or masking a felt emotion with a facial configuration associated with a different emotion. It is hypothesized that the manipulation of facial appearance is operative in most social situations, and that the display rules governing such masks are a matter of habit. It is observed that rarely will a person pause to consider what display rule to follow; in fact, the operation of display rules is supposedly more noticeable when they are violated than when properly applied.

Searching again for possible neurophysiological data which may be available, but on the control of facial movements, a recent study by Mateer and Kimura (1977) has suggested that all aphasic speech disturbances, even in fluent speech, are associated to some degree with impairment in acquisition and performance of complex, sequential nonverbal oral movements. Ojemann and Mateer (1980) studied the effects of cortical stimulation on nonverbal oral–facial movements in four neurosurgical patients. The patients were trained preoperatively to mimic simple oral–facial postures in response to slide pictures of the movement. The facial postures consisted of the terminal position for simple movements such as lip protrusion or tongue lateralization. A measure of both the ability to produce the same repetitive oral–facial movement and to produce a sequence of different oral–facial movements was obtained. Oral–facial movements were recorded by videotape, along with markers indicating the onset and termination of stimulation. The tapes were evaluated blindly, without the use of the stimulation marker channel. The findings indicated the presence of discrete areas in the language-dominant hemisphere for sequencing facial movements. It is centered principally in frontal and parietal cortex, immediately anterior and posterior to motor strip (Figure 2). Not only is this area concerned with oral–facial movements, but there is also evidence from other sources to involve it in the control of complex movement and gestures, including the manual communication system of the deaf (Kimura, 1976).

Figure 2
Left cerebral hemisphere: D = electrode locations at which sequential motor movements altered by electrical stimulation; F = final motor pathway; electrode locations of which all oral movements altered by electrical stimulation in four patients [adapted from Ojemann and Mateer (1980)].

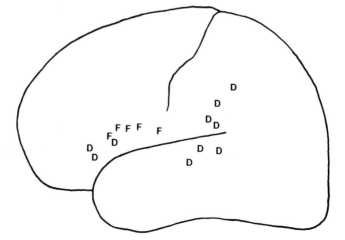

Self-Deception and Body Language

On a more global scale, in addition to facial expressions, gestures and even gait provide useful cues about the moment-to-moment motivation, including self-deception, of individuals. In this regard, Morris (1977) has indicated there are many occasions in our social lives when we wish to hide our true feelings but somehow fail to do so. He gives an example of a beareaved mother who is trying to conceal her sadness from her children by "putting on a brave face," as if she were wearing a mask of false expressions over a face of true ones. He continues by stating that the case of the bereaved mother is one where the deception failed because there was no great pressure for it to succeed and where, possibly, there was a positive advantage for it failing to deceive.

If the bereaved mother were too successful in concealing her grief, she would be criticized for her lack of feeling. Equally, if she failed to display some visible inhibition of her grief, she would be said to lack courage and self-control. Her "brave face" is therefore an example of pseudo-deception, where the deceiver is happy to be found out. Either consciously or unconsciously, she wants her forced smile to be read as forced. (p. 106)

Morris speculates as to what would happen if the pressure to deceive were greater, say, as in the case of a defendant in a murder trial who knows he is guilty but desperately protests his innocence. It was proposed that he would lie with his verbal statements and attempt to match his words with equally convincing body action. A problem arises, though, in that the defendant can control some parts of his body better than others.

The easy parts to discipline are those whose actions he is most aware of in ordinary day-to-day signalling. He knows most about his smiles and frowns—he sees them occasionally in a mirror—and his facial expressions will come at the top of his self-awareness list. So he can lie best with his face. (p. 106)

Compared to the face, the defendant's general body posture is more likely to betray his deceit in that he is not always fully conscious of the degree of stiffness of his stance or the degree of slump or alertness. Nevertheless, the value of these body postures as clues is greatly reduced by social rules that require certain rather stereotyped poses in specific contexts. Hand movements are less restricted and may, therefore, be more useful in deception since most social situations allow gesticulations.

It would seem, then, the best way to deceive is to restrict one's signals to words and facial expressions. Usually, whole-body lying is difficult for most individuals because of a lack of practice, in that they are rarely called upon to indulge in bouts of sustained, deliberate deceit. A deliberate lie is often clumsy in execution and only the observer's ineptitude saves one from discovery. Again, however, if one is self-deceived as to their own motivations, then unconscious role-playing may well be effectual.

Personality Correlates of Self-Deception

In a recent study by Monts and associates (1977), an attempt was made to study personality correlates of interpersonal self-deception. The authors hypothesized that among intimately associated groups, certain relationships between a person's attributes of insecurity, authoritarianism, repression and self-esteem should correlate with certain degrees of self-deception. They tested their hypothesis with 24 female and six male college students who were given evaluation scales purported to measure interpersonal self-deception, security–insecurity, ego-defensiveness, repression-sensitization and self-esteem. The investigators reasoned that an insecure person will hide from himself as long as possible the conscious recognition of rejection or loss of respect; that high authoritarians rigidly define which attitudes and emotions are appropriate to which situation and tend to suppress or deny those which are incompatible with the self-conception; that if the interpersonal contacts of the intimately associated individuals were threatening in some form, repressors would tend to avoid or deny the potential threat and sensitizers would be unduly alerted and overinterpret the potential threat, and that individuals with high self-esteem would either take on a defensive mode that allowed a strong self-protective facade or would recognize their limitations and adjust realistically to them, i.e., self-esteem would correlate positively with self-deception in the former case and negatively with self-deception in the latter.

The procedures of the study required that each individual rate himself (self-perception), rate another (other-perception) and rate how another would rate himself (reflected self-perception) in terms of a seven-trait word scale, where the items of the scale were indicated by the following words: kind, irresponsible, efficient, quiet, tense, individualistic and sophisticated. The results of the ratings were then plugged into a formula

$$\Sigma \; \frac{1}{K} \, (|OP - SI| - |RS - |SI|)/7$$

where OP equalled other perception, SI equalled self-perception, and RS equalled reflected self-perception. The only type of discrepancy that the authors regarded as theoretically meaningful was in terms of self-deception indicating an individual's overestimation of another's perception of him. For example, if an individual assessed himself as "seldom irresponsible," which was equivalent to a value of 1, and another individual also rated him as "seldom irresponsible" with a value of 1, but the individual perceived another as rating himself "irresponsible about half the time," assigning a value of 3; then, the resulting equation, $|1 - 1| - |3 - 1| = 0 - 2 = -2$, would indicate discrepancy, but no self-deception which, as proposed by the authors, requires a positive value greater than zero.

The findings of this study indicated that interpersonal self-deception as measured by the investigators was positively associated with repression-sensitization, negatively associated with insecurity and authoritarianism, with an ambiguous outcome in terms of self-esteem. Interpersonal self-deception was interpreted as enhancing security and self-esteem; repressors were regarded to engage in interpersonal self-deception more than sensitizers, and authoritarians were viewed as self-deceiving interpersonally less than nonauthoritarians. In summary, they suggested that the study focused upon the relationship between personality variables and one's defensive mechanisms, namely, the distortion of an individual's perception of others' perception of him. Though their results were not regarded as conclusive, their interpretation suggested that the personality of an individual both influences the operation of defense mechanisms and is influenced by them. It was proposed that certain personality characteristics predispose a person to self-deceive in interpersonal contexts, but interpersonal self-deception may itself be instrumental in fostering certain personality characteristics.

A very different study by Bear and Fedio (1977) on neurological patients suggests that personality variables and degrees of self-deception are intercorrelated. Patients with unilateral (involvement of one cortical hemisphere only) temporal lobe epilepsy were contrasted with normal subjects and patients with neuromuscular disorders in the evaluation of specific psycho-social aspects of behavior. Equivalent true–false questionnaires containing 18 traits were completed by both subjects and observers. Most of the traits are listed on the horizontal axis of Figure 3, and included such characteristics as humorlessness, dependence, obsessionalism, emotionality, guilt, anger, sadness and aggression. Each of the 18 traits was sampled by five items composed by the two authors and judged representative by three additional professionals. In addition to the 90 trait-derived items, ten questionnaires were modified from the lie scale of the MMPI. The latter items were included with the hypothesis that, in contrast to the trait items, they would not discriminate temporal lobe epileptics from comparison groups. Two 100-item questionnaires were employed: a personal inventory that the subject completed about himself and a personal behavior survey (consisting of a third-person version of the same items as the first scale) completed by a long-time observer. Four groups totalling 48 subjects were evaluated, 15 patients with right

Figure 3
Traits are ordered by decreasing ability to separate epileptic from nonepileptic subjects (analysis of variance). Mean scores over all traits are shown at right. LT indicates left temporal epileptics; RT, right temporal epileptics; N, contrast group with neurologic disease; and C, control group [graphs adapted from Bear and Fedio (1977)].

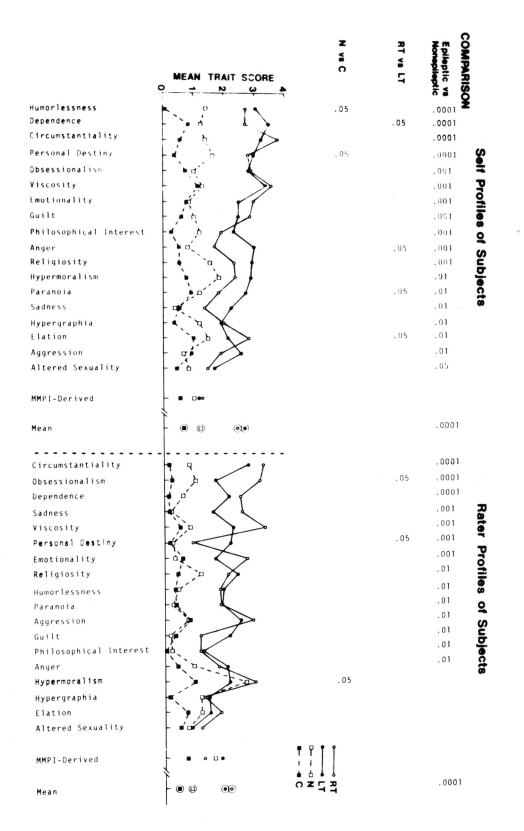

temporal lobe epilepsy, 12 patients with left temporal lobe epilepsy, 12 normal adults and 9 neuromuscular disordered patients to contrast with the epileptic patients.

The data were subjected to analysis of variance and indicated that epileptic patients self-reported a distinctive profile of humorless sobriety, dependence and obsessionalism. As indicated in Figure 3, the right temporal lobe epileptics displayed emotional tendencies in contrast to ideational traits of left temporal lobe patients. Right temporal lobe epileptics also exhibited denial traits while left temporal lobe patients demonstrated an overemphasis of dissocial behavior. The investigators suggested that the results identified psychological features, self-reported or observed, which reliably distinguished patients with temporal lobe epilepsy. The data were interpreted to support a hypothesis that sensory-affective associations are established within the temporal lobes, and that in man there exists an asymmetrical hemispheric representation in the expression of affect.

Genetically Programmed Self-Deception and Evolutionary Stable Strategies

So far in this discourse, the adaptive advantage of self-deception has been implicated in the process of accruing more relative fitness by being better able to deceive others, and by being better able to cope with life more generally. Also, some proximal neurophysiological mechanisms have been alluded to which could possibly be instrumental in these processes. However, it occurred to me that perhaps an even more profound human deception than either lying to others or a self-fulfilling self-deceit was operating, namely, genetically programmed self-deception. Ironically, it was while reading the last chapter of Dawkins' book (1976) that this idea crystallized. I was puzzled why after such a readable presentation of genetic evolution in his first ten chapters, Dawkins felt it necessary to propose "memes" (long-held ideas) as the basic unit of a parallel evolution, i.e., culture. In contemplating some likely explanations of his meme hypothesis—e.g., a note on which to end a profound book, a way of suggesting some hope for the future of mankind, or in rebellion to being a robot for genes (i.e., a gene machine)—a more awesome possibility presented itself. What if the most successful (in terms of inclusive fitness) gene machines are those who think (through self-deception) they know what genetic evolution is all about, but really do not? What better way for gene machines to look out for their genes than to have a little knowledge of how genetic evolution works but not enough to drastically change the biological programs. For if the robots were truly cognizant of such intricacies, could they not, in time, restructure the genetic processes and thus modify the genes themselves? Such interference would undoubtedly violate one of the three basic characteristics of gene survival, namely, *copying fidelity*.

In the application of this idea, it is *not* necessary to hypothesize a genetic conspiracy, since mere competition among organisms for available resources would result in the differential representation of genes in future populations. Yet in this competition, would not gene machines quite likely evolve who were optimally versatile (in terms of an "open genetic program" (i.e., requiring experiencial information for its execution) to reap the most from the environment but who could not undermine the successful genetic replicators? In asking a colleague to work with me in putting this question in terms of an evolutionary stable strategy, ESS [e.g., see Maynard Smith (1976)], Morgan (1977) was instrumental in the following expose:

First, let us define three reproductive strategies: (1) Ignorance is Bliss (IB). This IB strategy is characterized by complete unawareness that we are merely automato acting in our genes' interests. The IB strategist reproduces as much as possible. (2) The Rebel (R). The Rebel knows he/she is a gene machine, and just won't put up with it. The Rebel refuses to reproduce or if it decides to do so, changes some of its genes first. (3) The consenting Adult (CA). The CA strategist knows he/she is a gene machine, and strikes a compromise, reproducing a little, because it does feel good and there are all those biological predispositions to do so.

The first problem is whether the Rebel strategy can spread differentially. No. Obviously, if you don't reproduce, you don't leave genes behind, or if you reproduce with modified genes, then the characteristics of the most successful replicators are validated.

Now, how about the IB and CA strategies? CA cannot be an ESS *unless* we make some more assumptions. In particular, we might assume that CAs are ecologically better adapted than IBs, and that this adaption will be genetically transmitted to their offspring. Each CA offspring will then be more valuable than an IB offspring, in the sense that it will be more likely to survive into and through adulthood and leave yet another generation of genes behind. It will also be of more value to relatives, hence of greater weight in terms of inclusive fitness. In working these givens through with some numbers, let us assume that if two IBs mate, they produce three offspring, worth 15 genetic units each. If two CAs mate, they have two offspring, worth 20 genetic units each. Now suppose we have an IB/CA cross. Then the offspring are worth 17.5 each. But how many are there? Suppose the primitive "animal urges" of the IB mate are strong enough so that the CA strategist is tricked, manipulated or seduced into having three offspring? Then the following payoff matrix results.

	IB	CA
IB	3(15) = 45	3(17.5) = 52.5
CA	3(17.5) = 52.5	2(20) = 40

Inspection of this table clearly shows that an IB strategist is better off mating with a CA strategist than with another IB strategist, so IB is not a pure ESS. Similarly, a CA strategist is better off mating with an IB than another CA, so CA is not a pure ESS. The only stable ESS is some mixture of the two strategies.

The fractions of the population of IB and CA when an ESS is reached can be ascertained by taking the numeric values of each possible cross and solving for the fractions via three simultaneous equations:

Let i and c be the fraction of the population of IB and CA, respectively, and OC the genetic outcome (i.e., fitness) of their crosses when each cannot tell the difference between themselves from the outside. From the IB by CA table above

$$45i + 52.5c = OC$$
$$52.5i + 40c = OC$$

Therefore, $45i + 52.5c = 52.5i + 40c$
$$12.5c = 7.5i$$
$$c = \tfrac{3}{5}i$$

Since $i + c = 1$
$$i + \tfrac{3}{5}i = 1$$
$$i = \tfrac{5}{8}$$
$$c = \tfrac{3}{8}$$

An ESS is reached, then, when the IBs comprise $\tfrac{5}{8}$ of the population and the CAs, $\tfrac{3}{8}$. If this outcome were reality, it would seem that Dawkins himself was subject to self-deception in the closing sentences of his book:

We are built as gene machines and cultured as meme machines, but we have the power to turn against our creators. We, alone on earth, can rebel against the tyranny of the selfish replicators. (p. 215)

However, some among us may prefer to take comfort in a statement by West-Eberhard (1975):

The claim that a farmer who saves his brother's life benefits by the consequent increase of genetic alleles like his in the population, through kin selection, does not detract from the biological validity of the farmer's assertion that he did it to get help milking the cows.

In sending me this quotation, Adams (1978, personal communication) would contend that the converse is true as well. I suggest that perhaps the greatest self-deception of all is our believing we will ever really know!

Epilogue   A recent article (Crow, 1979) suggests the possibility that some genes do in fact violate Mendel's rules and circumvent natural selection to favor their own survival. In sexual reproduction the parental genes are continuously reshuffled and thereby exposed equally often (statistically) to selection pressures operating on individuals. A few genes (e.g., segregation distorter genes in *Drosophila*) cheat in meiosis and in so doing, undermine the system by reducing its fairness. Crow vividly illustrates the impact of such cheating by querying what would happen if such deception were to arise on one of the chromosomes determining sex. He speculates that if a similar complex were to be located on the Y chromosome, nearly 100% of the progeny would be expected to be males and that a population of flies, so affected, would become extinct within a few generations. However, even if a meiotic-drive system were not harmful in its own right—e.g., as the segregation distorter genes above or those that are known to cause a variety of tail abnormalities in some populations of house mice—it reduces the efficiency of the evolutionary process. Although there are many refinements of meiosis (e.g., "policing genes") which render such cheating unlikely, some genes still manage to beat the system.

It is also ironic that since Dawkins' statement of optimism in his book on the selfish gene (1976)—about our possibly being in control of our own destiny through cultural evolution—he has more recently (1978) emphasized that replicators (e.g., genes) survive by virtue of their effects not only on individuals (via their phenotypes) but also on the larger world outside the body wall through what he calls "extended phenotype." He further suggests that the study of animal communication and most of ecology could be viewed as branches of extended embryology. It occurs to me that a very bad pun may very well sum up our genetic plight: "Oh what a tangled web we weave when first we practice to deceive."

References   Adams, R.M. 1978. Personal communication.

Albert, M.L., Silverberg, R., Reches, A., and Berman, M. 1976. Cerebral dominance for consciousness. *Arch. Neurol.* 33:453–454.

Alexander, R.D. 1974. The evolution of social behavior. *Annual Review of Ecology and Systematics* 5:325–383.

———. 1975. The search for a general theory of behavior. *Behavioral Science* 20:77–100.

Asch, S.E. 1952. *Social Psychology*. Englewood Cliffs, NJ: Prentice-Hall.

Bear, D.M., and Fedio, P. 1977. Quantitative analysis of interictal behavior in temporal lobe epilepsy. *Arch. Neurol.* 34:454–467.

Crow, J.F. 1979. Genes that violate Mendel's rules. *Scientific American* 240:134–147.

Dawkins, R. 1976. *The Selfish Gene*. New York and Oxford: Oxford University Press.

———. 1978. Replicator selection and the extended phenotype. *Z. Tierpsychol.* 47:61–76.

Dimond, S.J. 1976. Depletion of attentional capacity after total commissurotomy in man. *Brain* 99:347–356.

Ekman, P. 1971. Universals and cultural differences in facial expressions of emotion. Paper presented at the Nebraska Symposium on Motivation, pp. 207–283.

Ekman, P. and Friesen, W.V. 1969. Nonverbal leakage and clues to deception. *Psychiatry* 32:88–106.

Hebb, D.O. 1946. Emotion in man and animal: An analysis of the intuitive processes of recognition. *Psychological Review* 53:88–106.

Hamilton, R.D. 1964. The genetical evolution of social behaviour I. *Journal of Theoretical Biology* 7:1–16.

Honkavarra, S. 1961. The psychology of expression. *British Journal of Psychology* 32:1–96.

Kimura, D. 1976. The neural basis of language qua gesture. In H. Whitaker and H.A. Whitaker (eds.) *Studies in Neurolinguistics*, Vol. 2, pp. 145–156. New York: Academic Press.

Klineberg, O. 1940. *Social Psychology*. New York: Henry Holt.

Krakauer, D. 1975. The species-specific framework of man and its evolution. In T.R. Williams (ed.) *Psychological Anthropolgy*. The Hague: Mouton.

———.1978. The adaptive significance of self-deception. Personal communication.

Lockard, J.S. 1977. Panhandling as an example of the sharing of resources. *Science* 198:858.

———. 1978. Commentary: Speculations on the adaptive significance of cognition and consciousness. *The Behavioral and Brain Sciences* 4:583–584.

Mateer, C., and Kimura, D. 1977. Impairment of non-verbal oral movements in aphasia. *Brain and Language* 4:262–276.

Maynard Smith, J. 1976. Evolution and the theory of games. *Amer. Sci.* 64:41–45.

Mayr, E. 1974. Behavior programs and evolutionary strategies. *Amer. Sci.* 62:650–659.

Monts, J.K., Zurcher, L.A., Jr., and Nydegger R.V. 1977. Interpersonal self-deception and personality correlates. *Journal of Soc. Psych.* 103:91–99.

Morgan, C.J. 1977. Personal communication.

Morris, D. 1977. *Manwatching: A Field Guide to Human Behavior*. New York: Harry N. Abrams, Inc.

Nummenmaa, T. 1964. *The Language of the Face* (Jyvaskyla Studies in Education, Psychology and Social Research 9). Jyvaskyla, Finland: Jyvaskylan Yliopistoyhdistys.

Murphy, G., Murphy, L.B., and Newcomb, T.M. 1937. *Experimental Social Psychology*. Rev. ed. New York: Harper Brothers.

Ojemann, G. 1977. Asymmetric function of the thalamus in man. *Annals of the N.Y. Academy of Science* 299:380–396.

———. 1979. A review of the neurologic basis of human cognition, with special emphasis on language. *Allied Health and Behavioral Sciences* 1:341–384.

Ojemann, G., and Mateer, C. 1980. Cortical and subcortical organization of human communication: Evidence from stimulation studies. In H. Steklis and M. Raleigh (eds.) *Neurobiology of Social Communication in Primates*, pp. 111–131. New York: Academic Press.

Plutchik, R. 1962. *The Emotions: Facts, Theories, and a New Model*. New York: Random House.

Puccetti, R. 1977. Bilateral organization of consciousness in man. *Annals of the N.Y. Academy of Science* 299:448–476.

Rosadini, G, and Rossi, G.F. 1967. On the suggested cerebral dominance for consciousness. *Brain* 90:101–112.

Serafetinides, E.A., Hoare, R.D. and Driver, M.V. 1965. Intracarotid sodium amylobarbitone and cerebral dominance for speech and consciousness. *Brain* 88:107–130.

Tomkins, S.S. 1962. *Affect, Imagery, Consciousness*, Vol. 1, The Positive Affects. New York: Springer.

———. 1963. *Affect, Imagery, Consciousness*, Vol. 2, The Negative Affects. New York: Springer.

Trivers, R.L. 1972. Parental investment and sexual selection. In B. Campbell (ed.) *Sexual Selection and the Descent of Man*. Chicago: Aldine.

———. 1974. Parent–offspring conflict. *American Zoologist* 14:249–264.

————. 1976. Foreword. In R. Dawkins, *The Selfish Gene*. New York and Oxford: Oxford University Press.

Wallace, B. 1973. Misinformation, fitness and selection. *American Naturalist* 107:1–7.

West-Eberhard, M.J. 1975. The evolution of social behavior by kin selection. *Quarterly Review of Biology* 50:1–33.

Whitaker, H.A., and Ojemann, G.A. 1977. Lateralization of higher cortical functions: A critique. *Annals of the N.Y. Academy of Science* 299:459–473.

Biological Evolution
of Culturally Patterned Behavior

Jerome H. Barkow

14

Culture was the great selective pressure which shaped our species. From at least *Australopithecus* on, the environment to which we were adapting was a cultural one (Barkow, 1973a; Durham, 1976; Geertz, 1965; Montagu, 1962). Our species and our culture developed simultaneously in what Dobzhansky (1963) termed a "feedback reciprocal relation"—the more we were capable of culture, the more culture we generated and the more we grew dependent on it for adaptation and survival; so the more we were selected for "cultural capacity" (Spuhler, 1959), which in turn led to greater development of culture . . . and so on. Human personality is therefore the result of selection for traits compatible with a cultural way of life.[1]

Is culture *still* a selection pressure today? The current wisdom proclaims it is not. The Neolithic Revolution is thought to have gradually severed the cybernetic tie between cultural and biological evolution. Technology and large-scale, complex social organization have generated an accelerating culture change whose speed is already thought to have left our Pleistocene brains in a permanent state of future shock. Popular writers such as Robert Ardrey have made much of how the apparent ending of the feedback between biological and cultural evolution means that our hunting-and-gathering brains must cope with a world of nation–states and nuclear weapons. Yet it has not been demonstrated that the feedback has, indeed, ended.

Physical anthropologists have frequently looked at local adaptation to climate and altitude, but not at the possibility of genetic adaptation in response to distinctive sociocultural environments. Because the ability of human groups to interbreed makes us

---

[1] For purposes of the present argument it is necessary only to accept that culture was in itself adaptive: it does not matter whether one feels that it was adaptive because it made us better hunters, in the manner of Tiger and Fox (1971), or because it enabled us better to compete with neighboring groups, as Durham (1976) argues.

unequivocally a single species, we assume that our populations do not differ in the genetic bases of their behavior. Presumably, the cessation of the positive feedback between biological and sociocultural evolution has left all groups with the same level and type of psychological potential. This presumption is basic to the social–behavioral sciences, where it is known as the "psychic unity of mankind," defined by Harris (1968, p. 15) as " . . . the belief that in the study of sociocultural differences, hereditary (genetic) differences cancel each other out, leaving 'experience' as the most significant variable."[2]

The psychic unity presumption means that human biopsychology is taken as a constant—everywhere the same. Thus, researchers have only very recently begun to wonder about the effects particular cultures may have on the biological fitness of their participants. Blurton Jones and Sibley (1978), for example, discuss whether "Bushman women maximise their reproductive success by spacing births widely and foraging seldom." The more general question they are really asking is whether some cultural norms (in this case, those dealing with fertility) lead to biologically adaptive behavior. This kind of problem is considered by the various contributors to the Chagnon and Irons (1979) collection and by Barkow (1977, 1978).

This chapter asks a slightly different question: Does the variability of our cultures mean that different populations are exposed to different selection pressures? For example, take a behavioral trait such as honesty. Suppose that in culture A being honest confers a fitness advantage, but in culture B there is no such benefit due to honesty. Does this mean that "genes for honesty" will increase in frequency in population A but will remain relatively rare in population B? If so, then the two populations will come to differ in the genetic substrate of their respective behavior patterns. When the cultural anthropologist comes along, with his presumption of the psychic unity of mankind, he will automatically ascribe the behavior differences between the two populations to an environmental or experiential variable—for example, differing child socialization practices. But in slighting the possibility of genetic differences, will he not be making an error? Can biological evolution "track" culture, in this manner? If it can, then the psychic unity of mankind is a mere unexamined assumption, rather than sound justification for seeking our explanations in the environment and not in endogenous factors.

[2] Harris' definition is now standard, even among cross-cultural psychologists [cf. Cole et al. (1971, pp. 214–216)]. Although the term meant for Boas what it does for Harris, for others (e.g., Morgan, Tylor) it simply meant that all races go through the same series of biocultural stages but that, since some races are more advanced than others, biologically determined behavioral–cultural differences among human groups do exist. See Harris (1968, pp. 137–141) or Stocking (1968, pp. 115–119) for further discussion of this point.

Our answers to these rhetorical questions must await the resolution of three complex issues, issues which themselves are questions: (1) Do some societies really confer a reproductive advantage on those with particular behavioral or personality traits? (2) Are there grounds for expecting such a reproductive advantage to result in microevolution (the selection of traits in an isolated population)? (3) If genetically based behavioral differences across populations do exist, what will be their effect on sociocultural evolution?

Cultural Values and Reproductive Advantages

Few studies bear on the question of whether, for some societies, individuals with particular behavioral characteristics do indeed enjoy a reproductive advantage over others. Does society A somehow permit the more intelligent to have more children than do others? Or does the reproductive advantage go to the most patient, or to the most aggressive, or to those who show some other trait? Most likely, various combinations of characteristics result in biological success, even within a single society, and no single trait is invariably associated with having many children and grandchildren. But because so few empirical data are available to help resolve this complex issue, I have reanalyzed material originally collected for quite different purposes. The results are available in more detailed form elsewhere (Barkow, 1977), and here I will merely summarize.

The original research had involved a comparison of two Hausa-speaking communities. Previous work had established that these two closely similar groups differed along the dimension of emotional inhibitedness. A combination of ethnographic differences and a quantitative analysis of the manifest content of a Thematic Apperception Test had shown that the Muslim community deeply valued the personal trait of emotional inhibitedness, and that its members were, indeed, relatively inhibited. However, the non-Muslim group neither valued nor reflected emotional inhibitedness to the same extent. The theoretical prediction was made that individuals who fit more readily into their own culture—the "conformers"—should enjoy a reproductive advantage over those who adjust less well. In the context of this study, this meant (a) there should be a positive correlation between number of living children and degree of emotional inhibitedness for the Muslim community (which values that trait), but (b) a correlation of zero between these two variables for the non-Muslims (who are neutral with respect to emotional inhibitedness). The two hypotheses were confirmed. While the results were statistically significant, the small absolute size of the association between number of children and inhibition score for the Muslim community means that the study is best described as "suggestive."

The anthropological literature actually yields a better reason than this empirical study for expecting that, in some societies, individuals with particular behavioral traits have a reproductive advantage over others. It has long been established that some ecological adaptations are associated with distinctive sets of value/ personality attributes. These attributes are apparently necessary for the ecological adaptation and, as a result of poorly understood processes of sociocultural evolution, tend to be associated with them. In 1959, Barry et al. published a cross-cultural survey in which they found that high food-accumulating societies (pastoralists and farmers) stressed obedience and responsibility in their child-training practices, while low food-accumulaters (hunter–gatherers and fisherfolk) emphasized independence and self-reliance. For example, it is easy to understand that a farmer who fails to plant in the traditional fashion runs a much greater risk of crop failure than one who uses the time-tested procedures. For farmers, obedience counts. Similarly, it is reasonable to suppose that a solitary hunter who is not independent and self-reliant is likely to fail—at least over the long term.

However, do individuals whose values are better suited to their subsistence economy actually have greater reproductive success than others? Although this seems plausible, there is little supporting evidence. Durham (1976) argues that cultural traits that tend to increase the fitness of their bearers are more likely to be propagated than other traits, simply because their bearers have more offspring than do other individuals. Thus, Durham presumably would conclude that the mere fact that certain value patterns are associated with particular subsistence economies implies that these values increased fitness.

Edgerton (1971) has also found that certain personality attributes are associated with particular ecological adaptations. He compared personality traits of four East African peoples, each of which included a pastoral segment and a horticultural segment. He accounted for his findings in terms of ecological adaptation: for example, the farmers tended to express anger less freely than did the pastoralists, a difference apparently related to the fact that an angry farmer must live with the long-term consequences of his anger while a pastoralist can argue and then move on. Similarly, pastoralists valued the ability to make quick decisions, a necessity for a herdsman who must frequently decide where and when to move his animals. The question is *Did these differences affect reproductive success?* Once again, no data are available to answer this question.

However, there is at least one human population in which a personality trait does appear to directly affect reproductive success. This group is the Yanomamö, studied primarily by Napoleon Chagnon (1968) and stereotyped as the prototypical warlike people. Female infanticide leads to a shortage of women, who must be won through warfare and then protected from the raids of others. Mortality among males through violence is exceptionally high. Gomila (1975), briefly reviewing the Yanomamö in the course of a discussion of fertility differentials, concludes that "with the

Yanomamö, access to reproduction is a direct function of the violence of individuals, which assures them easier access to wives and lets them best protect these wives" (p. 179). His implication is that there might well be microselection for whatever qualities make for a successful warrior. However, Durham (1976), also citing Chagnon (1968, 1974), has a slightly different conclusion. Discussing the village heads, he believes that they are able "to influence the behavior of their followers in ways that include raids on neighboring villages for women" (1976, p. 109). Since these village headmen sire a disproportionate share of the offspring of the villages, in effect the traits that make them successful headmen are apparently being selected for (assuming for the moment that these traits are heritable). But Durham feels that it is not so much the ability to be a successful warrior as the ability to manipulate others which increases reproductive success.

The lesson is that even where personality attributes do seem to affect reproductive success, we must not jump to the conclusion that we know what these personality attributes are. For example, high aggressivity among the Yanomamö may well be adaptive, but it is also possible that the most aggressive individuals are the most reckless and are quickly selected out of the population through a higher mortality rate. Bigelow (1973), in discussing the influence of intergroup warfare on human evolution, suggests that it resulted in selection not primarily for aggressivity but for high self-control and general symbolic ability. Factors leading to an increase in fitness must be established empirically, not conjecturally.

Reproductive Advantage and Microevolution

Let us assume for the moment that research will demonstrate that certain personality traits do, in specific societies, lead to reproductive advantage. This does not necessarily mean that microevolution of the personality attributes is taking place. Several questions must first be answered: (1) To what extent are the populations in question relative genetic isolates? (2) For how many generations has the process been taking place, and how many generations would be required for meaningful genetic change? (3) Are the personality attributes able to be inherited, and to what extent?

Genetic isolation. If a particular culture is generating a particular selection pressure, then that pressure will affect gene frequencies much more rapidly if it is coterminous with a breeding population. For example, in the Hausa case (summarized earlier), it was found that individuals who conformed to their culture's value of emotional inhibition had a slight reproductive advantage over the nonconformers. The study demonstrated this relationship in only a single community, however, and it may not hold elsewhere in Hausaland. At the same time, almost half of the villagers had been living in the community for five years or less, so population mobility was obviously very great. This local selection pressure, affecting some hundreds of individuals out of a total breeding population in the millions—there are perhaps 30 million Hausa speakers in West Africa—could hardly have been having any appreciable effect on gene frequencies.

Similarly, in Edgerton's East Africa study it is unlikely that microevolution for qualities related to success in farming or herding was taking place. Individuals frequently moved between the two means of livelihood, and some of the qualities required for the one kind of economy were quite opposed to those favored by the other. It may be that selection was actually occurring for both sets of behavioral attributes—to the extent that they were under independent genetic control and did not cancel each other. Since even then selection would have been intermittent, it would obviously have been much weaker than if each economy were associated with a single, genetically isolated population. In practice, genetic selection of culturally favored behavioral traits seems likely to lead to appreciable microevolution only if the populations involved are fairly isolated.

Number of generations involved. Culturally determined selective pressures obviously must endure more than a single generation if gene frequencies are to be meaningfully affected. In the Muslim Hausa example, for instance, the particular effect may have resulted from the psychological relationship between the Muslim and non-Muslim communities, with the former taking the latter as a "negative reference group" (Barkow, 1973b). Since the non-Muslim settlement was recent, the selection pressure could not have been older than perhaps two generations.

How long would it take for culturally provided selection actually to affect gene frequencies so that a particular behavioral trait underwent microevolution? Let us assume that the trait in question results from the operation of a single gene (unlikely) whose effects are little influenced by environmental factors. How long would it take, and how strong a selection pressure would be necessary, before the frequency of the gene/trait was seriously affected? Since I am not a physical anthropologist, it is fortunate that Loehlin et al. (1975, p. 45), in the course of a discussion of race and intelligence, supply this calculation. They assume, for illustrative purposes, that two populations have been separated for approximately 25,000 years or 1,000 generations:

Suppose that at the beginning of this period a given gene of intermediate dominance is at low frequency in both populations, say .01. In one population the gene remains at this frequency, but in the other there is a selection in its favor of .01, that is, possessors of the gene have a 1% reproductive advantage over nonpossessors. At the end of 1,000 generations, the frequencies of the gene in the two populations will be .01 and more than .99.

In short, it would take only a very slight reproductive advantage to drastically change gene frequencies over time. Of course, the above example required 25,000 years but stronger selection pressures would presumably require much less time and, in any case, one does not need to reach gene frequency differences of .01 and .99 before suggesting that two populations have meaningful genetic differences between them. The problem with this example is that for it to be applicable to culturally induced selection of behavioral traits, these traits would have to be single-gene effects. It is exceedingly unlikely that such characteristics as being readily socialized into obedience or independence or self-reliance are single-gene effects. Human behavioral traits are likely to be products of a large number of coordinated genes (polygenic) and their full variance (as I shall discuss shortly) is probably not under genetic control at all.

Wilson (1971, 1975a), arguing on the basis not of mathematical calculation but of research reports on species ranging from *Drosophila* to rodents, finds that genetically determined behavior within a population can be drastically altered by selection in *less* than ten generations. Certainly, professional dog breeders are able to change the temperaments of particular breeds in a relatively small number of generations, although Scott (1968) warns us that the behavior genetics of canines is not comparable to that of human beings. These examples, in any event, involve artificial and therefore very strong selection. One can only conclude that it is *possible*, on the basis of genetic theory and experience with other species, for selection to operate on the genetic bases of behavioral traits within relatively brief spans of time—that is, between ten and 1,000 generations.

One final factor that may affect the length of time required for selection to alter a behavioral trait has to do with the nature of its genetic substrate. Some traits may be determined by a pattern of dominant and recessive genes. Such traits will evolve quite slowly, since recessives in the heterozygous condition are not readily selected out. Many human behavioral traits, however, are probably produced by a number of genes, selection for which has an additive effect. In such cases, selection can gradually strengthen or weaken the traits in question. Of course, the behavior genetics of personality dispositions is almost wholly unknown, so that discussion of their rate of microevolution is necessarily speculative in nature.

Behavior and genetic control. For culturally induced natural selection of a behavioral attribute to take place, that attribute must be *heritable*. The concept of heritability is both slippery and controversial. Strictly speaking, it has to do with "what proportion of the variation of [a trait] is genetic, i.e., is attributable to the genetic differences among individuals in the population" (Loehlin et al., 1975, p. 74). Heritability does *not* refer to the extent to which a trait is under genetic control, i.e., able to be inherited. A trait may be 100% under genetic control but still have zero heritability. Heritability refers to the extent to which the *variability* of a trait is under genetic control, i.e., the extent to which the variability of its expression reflects the variability of its genetic substrate.

Let us take a trait under strong genetic control. Suppose that the culture of the population in which it appears has selected for it so powerfully, and for so many generations, that the entire population is now homozygous with respect to this trait. In other words, everyone in the population has the gene or genes that underly it. The trait has zero heritability because none of the variability in its expression is related to genetic variability, despite the fact that it has a genetic basis. The kind of microevolution with which this paper is concerned cannot take place because it already *has* taken place—no more genetic variability is left and there are no more alternative alleles for selection to work on.

Suppose the population in question is that of the entire human species. Suppose all human behavioral traits are under genetic control but that their heritability is zero for lack of genetic variability. In such a case, cultures may select for particular behavioral attributes without, however, influencing gene frequencies at all. Behavioral microevolution will not take place. If we wish to argue that it does occur, therefore, we must first demonstrate that the trait in question is heritable, i.e., that some of the variability in its expression reflects genetic variability. This requirement presents formidable empirical difficulties.

But let us assume, for the moment, that some human behavioral traits are heritable. Let us further assume that some cultures and ecologies are selecting for these traits. These two simple assumptions lead to a startling conclusion: if they are accurate, then biological evolution, under certain circumstances, will track cultural evolution.

Genetic Tracking of Culture

Genetic tracking of culture means that traits initially favored by purely cultural pressures are in the end selected by evolution (Wilson, 1971, 1975a, 1975b). In other words, if a culture happens strongly to favor passive behavior, then there is apt to be genetic selection for passivity. If the culture values aggressive behavior, then there may be microevolution in favor of greater aggressiveness. This concept is *not* the same as the Lamarckian notion of the inheritance of acquired characteristics: the genetic tracking of culture is a special case of what C.H. Waddington (1953, 1961, pp. 91–97) termed the "genetic assimilation of an acquired character" or "canalization." Rather than borrowing Waddington's original example of genetic assimilation among *Drosophila*, let us adapt a hypothetical high-altitude case from Gregory Bateson (1972).

Somatic genetic assimilation. We begin by moving a man from sea level to 10,000 feet. At first his heart will beat rapidly and his breath will be short, but eventually he will acclimatize to the high altitude.

However, as Bateson points out, our man will have paid a considerable price for his acclimatization. The physiological mechanisms associated with the adaptation have now been used up, making him less able to meet other emergencies: he has lost much of his somatic flexibility. Let us suppose, however, that he continues to live at the high altitude, along with others originally from sea level, and that they constitute a high-altitude community. The biological selection system will favor those individuals with maximum somatic flexibility and capacity to meet emergencies, so that there will be a gradual accumulation of genetic variants consistent with permanent adaptation to high altitude. The physiological changes that members of the first generation had had to make now become part of the genetic make-up of their descendants. No longer is a large portion of the body's somatic flexibility and ability to meet emergencies taken up with the mere business of breathing.[3]

Yet, if we examine the lung capacity of a member of the first generation and compare it with that of the 25th generation, we may find little difference. Both individuals will be adapted to high altitude and it may not be possible, depending on the ingenuity of the physiologists, to determine which is which. However, this is not a case of the inheritance of acquired characteristics; it merely looks like it, hence Bateson's "pseudo-Lamarckian" label. This is natural selection for a trait that is initially within the range of possible somatic adaptation, in response to the advantage of having the capacity for somatic adjustment freed from the *stress* of acclimatization to high altitude. Selection has taken place in terms of what Bateson (1972, p. 358) calls the "economics of flexibility."

Cultural genetic assimilation. The genetic assimilation of cultural values and norms might operate in a manner similar to the above example, since certain ecological adaptations strongly favor certain sets of values and personality attributes. In a hunting–gathering ecology, for example, most males will become hunters, an occupation requiring independence and self-reliance. However, those individuals slightly more capable than others *genetically* of acquiring these values would have had less of their capacity for ontogenetic personality adaptation "used up" and will have more psychological flexibility for their existence than do other individuals. This increased flexibility might then yield a reproductive and/or survival advantage, so that there would be selection for those genetically best suited for the hunter–gatherer values. Thus, we would have selection for a trait that is initially within the range of possible psychobiological adaptation of the species-selection gen-

---

[3] This example is hypothetical—there is no clear evidence that any human group has genetically assimilated the trait of high-altitude acclimitization. For a discussion of the relevant literature, see Bennett et al. (1975, p. 170) and Baker (1978).

erated by a cultural environment as a consequence of the adaptive advantage of freeing personality adjustments from some of the stress of socialization. This assumes, of course, that increasing psychological efficiency increases fitness, perhaps by leaving more energy for courtship, parental care or the learning of other skills.

In the high altitude adaptation example from Bateson, given two men of equally high vital capacity, a physiologist would find it impossible to tell which of these had experienced less somatic stress in achieving his acclimatization. Similarly, a psychologist, given two hunters equally independent and self-reliant, might find it difficult or impossible to determine which of them was the product of 1,000 generations of hunting–gathering and which the son of a horticulturalist simply adopted by his present group. Conceivably, the psychologist or psychiatrist might develop measures of psychological flexibility or ability to cope with emotional emergencies, but the task would not be easy.

Additional empirical difficulties. We are now faced with a new potential means of measuring heritability: genetically determined variability in the *ease* with which an individual acquires (ontogenetically) a particular behavioral trait. The measure would be similar to the psychologist's concept of *latent learning*, a term referring to the fact that it usually requires fewer trials for an organism to relearn a forgotten task than it took to learn that task originally. The empirical difficulties of attempting to measure the relative ease with which individuals are socialized into particular traits are apparent. But genetic tracking of cultural characteristics creates more empirical problems.

Genetic tracking occurs because both cultural socialization pressures and biological selection are operating in precisely the same direction. Moreover, they are likely mutually to reinforce one another. Applying Bateson's "economy of flexibility" model to sociocultural evolution, we would expect the culture to tend to accomodate itself to the general psychobiological traits of the group. Cultures, after all, may be thought of as patterned expressions of human psychobiological dispositions. While we have little understanding of the processes of sociocultural evolution, we do know that it seems to channel the psychobiological dispositions of its participants in ways that help to perpetuate the society (Barkow, 1975; Kardiner, 1945). A farming society, for example, might channel the competitive-aggressive tendencies of its young men into rivalries over prowess in hoeing or clearing land—or in the size of harvests. A hunting–gathering society might channel these same dispositions into competition in the hunt. Presumably, societies which fail to so channel such dispositions are likely to experience difficulty in inducing individuals to take up crucial roles and in controlling disruptive emotions.

The result of such selection is an empiricist's nightmare: culturally patterned behavior, rather than reflecting genetically based psychobiological group differences, is much more likely to mask them. Suppose we have a society with a genetically higher-than-average aggressive tendency. Cultural evolution might channel this aggressivity into system-maintaining pursuits, such as competition in hunting or farming or winning high position in the priesthood, or perhaps into displays of oratorical ability. The actual level of overt violence could be considerably lower than that of a society with a smaller proportion of "aggressive" genes. In short, *we cannot equate overt cultural behavior with any underlying genetic predispositions:* ethnography does not equal genetics.

Genetic tracking in other species. If genetic tracking of cultural traits can occur in *Homo sapiens,* then it follows that the process can also take place in any social species with a local tradition of behavior. Though social ethologist John H. Crook (1972) is primarily concerned with nonhuman species, it is intriguing to note how closely his argument follows the one I have been presenting for human groups. Crook notes that social organization in many species is fairly flexible, responding to ecological pressures, and that this organization is not irrelevant to natural selection:

Because a major requirement for biological success is for the individual to adapt to the social norms of the group in which it will survive and reproduce it follows that a major source of genetic selection will be social, individuals maladapted to the prevailing group structure being rapidly eliminated. Social selection is thus a major source of biological modification. In advanced mammals it is perhaps of as great an importance as natural selection by the physical environment. (p. 77)

If Crook's argument is valid for social mammals in general, then it is likely to be valid for our own species in particular (though we are not likely to be "rapidly eliminated"). While Crook does not explicitly discuss a genetic assimilation process, it is implicit in his assumption that most of the members of a social group are potentially able to adapt to a changed social organization on-togenetically, and that selection for the new behaviors follows. But, note that the flexibility of social organization which he discusses is *not* a function of genetic assimilation but is its converse. Genetic tracking of culture (or, in this case, protoculture) will minimize flexibility in the interests of efficiency of ontogenetic adaptation. We must look elsewhere for selection for flexibility in behavior and social organization, a search which will be resumed later, under the topic Phylogenetic Implications.

Behavioral Differences Among Infants and Empirical Research

So far, the discussion has repeatedly suggested that, while genetically influenced behavioral differences across human populations may exist, it is difficult to demonstrate their evolution empirically. There *is* evidence, however, that they do indeed exist; this evidence is indirect in that it deals not with adult behavior but with infant behavior.

D.G. Freedman, in his ethological and evolutionary study of human infancy (1974), reviews cross-cultural studies of the behavior of newborns, including his own comparative research across seven ethnic groups. His most striking findings involve a comparison of Caucasoid and Chinese–American infants between 32 and 75 hours old. Freedman and his wife Nina administered a series of standardized behavior scales and tests to the infants, measures consisting of such items as ability to follow a face and voice, speed with which an infant ceases to cry after being picked up and so forth. Multivariate analysis showed that the chief distinguishing factors between Chinese and American infants involved temperament and excitability. Though there was overlap on all scales between the two groups, the Chinese infants were on the average considerably calmer, quieter and more passive. For example:

In an item called *defensive movements*, the tester placed a cloth firmly over the supine baby's face for a few seconds. While the typical European–American infant immediately struggled to remove the cloth by swiping with his hands and turning his face, the typical Chinese–American infant lay impassively, exhibiting few overt motor responses. Similarly, when placed in the prone position, the Chinese infants frequently lay as placed, with face flat against the bedding, whereas the Caucasian infants either turned the face to one side or lifted the head. (pp. 150–152)

Freedman summarized by saying, "The Chinese–American newborns tended to be less changeable, less perturbable, tended to habituate more readily, and tended to calm themselves or to be consoled more readily when upset" (p. 154). However, the two groups were equal in motor and sensory development and central nervous system maturity.

Freedman's results were essentially the same when he compared Japanese and Caucasian infants in Hawaii—and Navaho and Caucasian infants in New Mexico and Arizona. (Since the Navaho are ultimately descended from a Siberian population, Freedman places them with the Chinese and Japanese in the category "Oriental.") He argues that the differences in infant behavior between the Orientals and the Caucasoids persist through so much dietary and social class variation that they must reflect differences in respective gene pools. He appears to favor an explanation of his hypothesized gene pool differences in terms of chance (genetic drift, the "founder principle" in particular), but he also raises the possibility that some "selective forces" (p. 172) may have operated. He cites a number of studies which suggest that the later childhood behavior of Oriental children remains consistent with the calm infant temperament finding, and he even briefly considers that some aspects of Oriental culture may reflect this genetically based temperament. In a later paper (1976), Freedman argues that the culture-and-personality school completely misunderstood the relation of the cradleboard to Navaho personality. Rather than the cradleboard causing the calm and rather passive Navaho personality structure, the innately calm temperament of the Navaho infant may have made cradle-boarding possible in the first place!

Freedman's study does not demonstrate the selection of psychobiological traits by culture. Freedman begins with traditionally defined ethnic groups and searches for differences among them. Finding differences, he must then try to account for them and it is not accident that he is largely driven for explanation to chance factors in evolution, rather than selection pressures. Freedman did not, after all, *begin* with genetic isolates that he had reason to suspect differed psychobiologically. Thus, his research is not directly applicable here, though it is informative: Freedman provides some optimism about the possibility of finding genetically based behavior differences among populations; he gives us a workable methodology, and by implication he gives us a hint that the psychobiological variables we should be looking for may well have more to do with temperament than, say, cognitive processes. It would be interesting to see Freedman apply his methods to Yanomamö infants after first having made some predictions based on Yanomamö culture and the possibility that a tendency toward successful physical violence may increase fitness in that society.

Empirical Procedures I have stressed pitfalls awaiting those who would challenge the psychic unity of mankind on empirical grounds or those who would hypothesize that evolution can track culture. Still, scientists should not shun problems merely because they are difficult. A research design for a study of the microevolution of psychobiological traits might proceed in this manner:

1. Establish the extent to which the population in question is a relative genetic isolate. We would not expect substantial genetic assimilation of culturally favored traits if only a small proportion of the total breeding population were subject to the culturally induced selective pressure at any one time. This step would begin with the collection of genealogies.
2. See whether individuals who conspicuously manifest the ideal values of the culture enjoy a reproductive advantage over others. Here, we need a sensitive ethnographic understanding of the society coupled with a study of fertility differentials.
3. Working the previous step backwards, determine empirically which individuals enjoy a reproductive advantage over others. Enlisting the techniques of psychological anthropology, ask in what ways are these people distinct from others.
4. Determine the length of the period during which the traits revealed by the previous two steps have been associated with greater reproductive success. Obviously, if the association is recent then there is no reason to expect these traits to have been genetically assimilated. Such a finding would not mean that the process of genetic assimilation was not *now* occurring, however, provided the traits were definitely heritable.
5. Establish that these traits found to be associated with reproductive success are heritable within each of the groups to be

studied. This is by far the most difficult yet most essential task of any test of the hypotheses concerning a genetic assimilation of culturally acquired characteristics.

6. Given the traits revealed by the previous steps, see if it is possible to make any predictions regarding the behavior of newborn infants. Some behavioral traits, such as temperament, seem to be of great constancy during the lifetime.

7. Reversing the previous step, see whether careful comparative observation of newborn infants suggests behavioral traits that might be associated with reproductive success in adulthood. Review the data on fertility differentials and on basic values to see if a connection can be made.

8. Ask whether individuals now in adulthood, who were adopted out of the home culture as infants, manifest traits common in the original culture but unusual in the adoptive society. (This is probably the step least likely to be successful, given the great lability of human behavior. Possibly it would be necessary to devise psychiatric assessment instruments measuring remaining capacity for personality adaptation in order to garner evidence that adapting to the host culture had been psychobiologically stressful.)

9. Repeat steps 1–7 but in terms of traits which are *dis-valued* by the society, in terms of traits that are associated with reproductive failure and in terms of traits that are conspicuously absent from newborn infants in the home culture. (Evolution, of course, works by selecting out at least as often as it does by selecting in.)

These procedures would hardly be simple to follow. Clearly, a multidisciplinary team would be required. But following these steps might make it possible to evaluate whether the genetic assimilation of culturally acquired characteristics was likely to be occurring.

In addition to the ambitiousness of this research task, there will be other difficulties. I have been writing of "fertility differentials" and "reproductive success" as if their determination were a simple, routine matter. But as Durham (1976, p. 99, citing Lewontin) points out: "It is not at all obvious what and when one should count [measure] to get a reliable indication of an individual's long-term genetic success." This problem results in part from the modern biologist's concepts of kin selection and inclusive fitness [explained lucidly in Wilson (1975a)]. Behavioral traits may tend to increase the frequency in the population of the genes an individual carries even when they lead to the individual's own death. This apparent paradox results from the fact that he shares his or her genes with others. If self-sacrifice results in the preservation of those gene-sharers (by saving close relatives, for example), so that the net result is an increase in the gene poll of the frequency of those genes which favored the self-sacrificial action, then this kind of "altruism" will be selected for. Evolution causes organisms to strive to maximize not their individual lifespans but their genetic representation in the gene pool—that is, their inclusive fitness.

In our own species, there may be subtle behavioral traits that increase inclusive fitness and which are encouraged by particular cultures. If a man marries late in life so that the kin-group's resources be devoted to the success of his older brother (with whom he shares a minimum of one half of his genes), might he not thereby be increasing his inclusive fitness? These are complex questions and it may be that traits that favor inclusive fitness, but not necessarily reproductive success, will go unrecognized by the researcher.

Phylogenetic Implications

If the genetic tracking of culture can occur at all, why has it not reached its limit, leaving our species with a rigid psychobiology? Why does our species have more than a single culture with matching behavioral predispositions, a single set of social behaviors and a single tool-kit? After all, highly specific behavioral predispositions would presumably have been more efficient than a generalized "capacity for culture."

Bateson (1972, p. 361) discusses a situation, described by him as "very rare in nature," in which "a population faces a stress which changes its intensity unpredictably and very often—perhaps every two or three generations." He explains that

under such variable circumstances, it might pay the organisms in survival terms to acquire the *converse* of the genetic assimilation of acquired characteristics. That is, they might profitably hand over to somatic homeostatic mechanisms the control of some characteristic which had previously been more rigidly controlled by the genotype.

Bateson is considering somatic rather than behavioral traits but his point still applies. If our early environment required frequent changes in behavior and social organization, our generalized capacity for culture might have resulted from this sort of "negative" genetic assimilation of culturally acquired behavioral characteristics. For example, Butzer (1977, p. 584) writes,

In the general context of the Pleistocene it appears that adaptations to new environments, or periodic and long-term environmental stress, involved concomitant cultural innovation and biological evolution. Environmental changes triggered cultural responses that favored biological evolution, which in turn affected the biological capacity for culture.

It is tempting to interpret Butzer in the light of Bateson and so conclude that our generalized cultural capacity resulted from periods of genetic assimilation of cultural acquired traits alternating with periods of "negative" genetic assimilation when flexibility was favored. Thus, we slowly accumulated the ability to adapt more-or-less efficiently to diverse environments requiring diverse sets of behaviors and social organizations. Of course the stresses leading to selection for behavioral flexibility need not have been entirely environmental. Bigelow (1973), for example, following Keith (1949), would argue that they resulted from frequent inter-group warfare.

It is even more tempting to suggest that some of our ancient cousins may have fallen into a genetic-assimilation trap. When environmental change finally overtook them, they had already genetically assimilated a single culture and social organization so thoroughly that they lacked the ontogenetic flexibility to adapt to the new situation. Instead, the stress destroyed them. Was this the fate of those australopithecine groups who were contemporaries of *Homo erectus* and, therefore, not in our line? Unfortunately, at present there seems to be no way in which to evaluate this speculation empirically.

Note, though, that the periodic negative genetic assimilation process—that presumably gave our ancestors their behavioral flexibility—was itself limited by other factors. Flexibility of be-havior was adaptive because it permitted the transmission of social tradition (culture) from generation to generation. Social tradition results in more rapid adjustment to diverse and changing envi-ronments than does biological evolution (speciation). However, cultures evolve and their evolution can cause them to drift away from the production of behavioral phenotypes that maximize the fitness of their participants. The more malleable the potential behavior of the individuals involved, the more this drift process may take place unrestrained. Eventually, drift might cancel out the fitness advantage conferred by cultural capacity in the first place. This cancellation has not happened because the tendency for cultures to drift away from the production of fitness-enhancing behavioral phenotypes constitutes a selection pressure itself—one opposed to total behavioral flexibility. Richerson and Boyd (1978) suggest that a number of our behavioral traits, including the largely invariant sequences of Piagetian cognitive development, result from selection against the fitness-reducing effects of cultural drift. Early language acquisition, independent as it is of any particular cultural tradition, would probably be another flexibility-limiting trait. Thus, we see that whereas negative genetic assimilation would have tended to increase behavioral flexibility, culture drift would have tended to limit it. Although our ancestors may not have genetically assimilated specific cultural traits, they quite likely were selected for very general, drift-reducing (fitness-enchancing) behavioral characteristics (Barkow, 1979). The "negative genetic assimilation" process did not make us into a *tabula rasa*.

Political Implications   Despite the difficulties involved, I have emphasized the empirical testing of the genetic assimilation of culturally acquired characteris-tics and of the related "psychic dis-unity" hypotheses. What would happen if a psychic dis-unity hypothesis were found to be true? For example, suppose a difference in temperament between two New Guinea peoples does exist, and this difference were found to be related to a difference in ethos between the two groups. For the sake of simplicity, let us assume that this difference is heritable within each society, is associated with an endocrine difference between the two groups, and that the trait in question has been, in one group of people but not the other, clearly linked to reproductive success for many generations. What then? Would the amount of racism in the world increase? Would this finding be used to support *apartheid* in South Africa or discrimination against francophones in British Columbia? Because so much emotion is raised by the suggestion of psychobiological differences across human populations, and because anthropology's Social-Darwinian past has made it sensitive to charges of racism, the following statement is appended. Readers uninterested in political controversy may consider this chapter concluded.

The social and behavioral sciences (including anthropology) are strongly environmentalistic in outlook. Explanations in terms of genetic differences are usally rejected out-of-hand. Not in *this* half of the century, at least, do anthropologists relate group differences in behavior to group differences in evolutionary biology. Why not?

It is frequently argued that not only do *no* such relationships exist, but that any attempt to assert the possibility of their existence is *morally wrong* in that it potentially gives aid and comfort to the racists (those who would claim that some human groups are biologically inferior to others). As I understand it, the argument is that any endogenous group differences are inevitably taken to imply a dimension of superiority–inferiority. From there it is supposedly a short step to ranking groups in order of their biological merit, moving on to notions of the "master race" and finally to a restocking of the slave pens, a rekindling of the pilot lights in the ovens of Dachau. To suggest that group differences could in any way be related to biology, it is felt, is to tamper with the bolt in our barrier against racism. Playing the sorceror's apprentice here can only strengthen those who secretly mourn Hitler's defeat. After all, there are plenty of environmental explanations for group differences in behavior without invoking the dangerous *djinn* of biology.

Those who feel I am overstating the emotionality of these arguments might wish to review the controversy surrounding the publication of E.O. Wilson's (1975a) *Sociobiology*.[4] Neither the

[4] The reader unfamiliar with the controversy will find a judicious summary in a news article by Nicholas Wade (1976) in the journal *Science*. One major attack against Wilson is to be found in a letter by E. Allen et al. (1975) to the *New York Review of Books*, with Wilson's (1975c) reply. Later and more careful attacks by Allen and others are to be found in Sociobiology Study Group of Boston (1977), while Ruse (1979) provides a calm defense. Another attack together with Wilson's reply (1976) appeared in *BioScience*, while he has also published a more general discussion

moral fervor nor the academic credentials of those attacking the relating of genetics to group differences in behavioral or psychobiological attributes is open to question. Nevertheless, I reject their arguments. Psychobiological groups differences, if they exist, are likely to be related to local cultures and *not* to universalistic criteria of inferiority–superiority; still less are they likely to be found among our traditional geographic "races" (as opposed to local genetic isolates). The possibility of microevolution of human psychobiological traits is an empirical question, which deserves to be answered empirically, without prejudice. I confidently assert that the result will be a stronger, not weaker bolt in our barrier against racism.

Racist simplifications are best demolished not by denying the relationship between human biology and human culture but by more fully understanding it. Any believer in the biological inferiority of various groups who finds this paper comforting is simply a fool. As for those who feel that the possibility of comforting such fools is so horrendous as to preclude all discussion of biology and behavioral differences at the group level—well, I must disagree with them.

References   Allen, Elizabeth, et al. 1975. Letter. *New York Review of Books* 13 November 22:43–44.

Baker, Paul T. (ed.) 1978. *The Biology of High-Altitude Peoples.* New York: Cambridge University Press.

Barkow, Jerome H. 1973a. Darwinian psychological anthropology: A biosocial approach. *Current Anthropology* 14:373–388.

——. 1973b. Operationalizing the concept ethos. In W.M. O'Barr, D.H. Spain and M.A. Tessler (eds.) *Survey Research in Africa: Its Applications and Limits.* pp. 184–198. Evanston: Northwestern University Press.

——. 1975. Prestige and culture: A biosocial interpretation. *Current Anthropology* 16:553–572.

——. 1977. Conformity to ethos and reproductive success in two Hausa communities: An empirical evaluation. *Ethos* 5:409–425.

——. 1978. Culture and sociobiology. *American Anthropologist* 80:5–20.

——. 1979. Maladaptive consequences of human intelligence and culture. Unpublished manuscript.

Barry, Herbert, III, Child, Irvin L., and Bacon, Margaret K. 1959. Relation of child training to subsistence economy. *American Anthropologist* 61:51–63.

Bateson, Gregory 1972. *Steps to an Ecology of Mind*, pp. 346–378. New York: Ballantine Books.

---

of "the attempt to supress human behavioral genetics." Wilson is not arguing for the possibility of group differences in human psychobiology, as I am, but simply for the relevance of evolutionary biology and genetics to understanding the social behavior of animals and insects, our own species being included in the former category. He is nevertheless accused of having covertly racist motives. For a review of the related (though earlier) controversy over "racial" differences in intelligence in Great Britain and the U.S.A., see Loehlin et al. (1975, pp. 7–10).

Bennett, Kenneth A., Osborne, Richard H., and Miller, Robert J. 1975. Biocultural ecology. *Annual Review of Anthropology*, Vol. 4., pp. 163–181. Palo Alto: Annual Review.

Bigelow, Robert 1973. The evolution of aggression, cooperation and self-control. In J.K. Cole and D.D. Jensen (eds.) *Nebraska Symposium on Motivation 1972*, pp.1–58. Lincoln: University of Nebraska.

Blurton Jones, N.G., and Sibly, R. 1978. Testing adaptiveness of culturally determined behavior: Do Bushman women maximise their reproductive success by spacing births widely and foraging seldom? In *Human Behavior and Adaptation Symposium*, No. 18 of the Society for the Study of Human Biology. London: Taylor & Francis.

Butzer, Karl W. 1977. Environment, culture, and human evolution. *American Scientist* 65:572–584.

Chagnon, Napoleon 1968. *Yanomamö: The Fierce People*. New York: Holt, Rinehart and Winston. 2nd ed., 1977.

————. 1974. *Studying the Yanomamö*. New York: Holt, Rinehart and Winston.

Chagnon, Napoleon, and Irons, William (eds.) 1979. *Evolutionary Biology and Human Social Behavior: An Anthropological Perspective*. North Scituate, MA: Duxbury Press.

Cole, Michael, Gay, John, Glick, Joseph A., and Sharp, Donald W. 1971. *The Cultural Context of Learning and Thinking: An Exploration in Experimental Anthropology*. New York: Basic Books.

Crook, John Hurrell 1972. Social organization and the environment: Aspects of contemporary social ethology. In D.D. Quiatt (ed.) *Primates on Primates*. Minneapolis: Burgess. (Reprinted from *Animal Behaviour*, 1970, 18:197–209.)

Dobzhansky, T. 1963. Cultural direction of human evolution. *Human Biology* 35:311–316.

Durham, William H. 1976. The adaptive significance of cultural behavior. *Human Ecology* 2:89–121.

Edgerton, Robert B. 1971. *The Individual in Cultural Adaptation: A Study of Four East African Peoples*. Berkeley: University of California Press.

Freedman, Daniel G. 1974. *Human Infancy: An Evolutionary Perspective*. New York: Lawrence Erlbaum Associates.

————. 1976. Infancy, culture, and biology. Paper presented at the 75th Annual Meeting of the American Anthropological Association, Washington, DC, November, 1976.

Geertz, Clifford 1965. The transition to humanity. In S. Tax (ed.) *Horizons of Anthropology*. London: Allen and Unwin.

Gomila, Jacques 1975. Fertility differentials and their significance for human evolution. In F.M. Salzano (ed.) *The Role of Natural Selection in Human Evolution*. Amsterdam: North-Holland Publishing Company.

Harris, Marvin H. 1968. *The Rise of Anthropological Theory*. New York: Thomas Y. Crowell.

Irons, William 1976. Emic and reproductive success. Paper presented at the 75th Annual meeting of the American Anthropological Association, Washington, DC, November. (Reprinted as Culture and biological success. In N.A. Chagnon and W. Irons (eds.) *Evolutionary Biology and Human Social Behavior: An Anthropological Perspective*. (North Scituate, MA: Duxbury Press, 1979.)

Kardiner, Abram 1945. *The Psychological Frontiers of Society*. New York: Columbia University Press.

Keith, A. 1949. *A New Theory of Human Evolution*. New York: Philosophical Library.

Loehlin, John C., Lindzey, Gardner, and Spuhler, J.N. 1975. *Race Differences in Intelligence*. San Francisco: Freeman.

Montagu, A. (ed.) 1962. *Culture and the Evolution of Man*. New York: Oxford University Press.

Richerson, Peter J., and Boyd, Robert 1978. A dual inheritance model of the human evolutionary process I: Basic concepts and a simple model. *Journal of Social Biological Structure* 1:127–154.

Ruse, Michael 1979. *Sociobiology: Sense or Nonsense?* Dordrecht, Holland/Boston: D. Reidel.

Scott, J.P. 1968. Evolution and domestication of the dog. *Evolutionary Biology* 2:243–275.

Sociobiology Study Group of Boston (eds.) 1977. *Biology as a Social Weapon*. Minneapolis: Burgess.

Spuhler, J.N. (ed.) 1959. *The Evolution of Man's Capacity for Culture*. Detroit: Wayne State University Press.

Stocking, George W., Jr. 1968. *Race, Culture, and Evolution: Essays in the History of Anthropology*. New York: The Free Press.

Tiger, Lionel, and Fox, Robin 1971. *The Imperial Animal*. New York: Holt, Rinehart and Winston.

Waddington, C.H. 1953. Genetic assimilation of an acquired character. *Evolution* 7:118.

———. 1961. *The Nature of Life*. London: George Allen & Unwin Ltd.

Wade, Nicholas 1976. Sociobiology: Troubled birth for new discipline. *Science* 191:1151–1155.

Wilson, Edward O. 1971. Competitive and aggressive behavior. In J.F. Eisenberg and W. Dillon (eds.) *Man and Beast: Comparative Social Behavior*. Washington, DC: Smithsonian.

———. 1975a. *Sociobiology: The New Synthesis*, pp. 117–120, 145–147. Cambridge: Belknap Press/Harvard University Press.

———. 1975b. Some central problems of sociobiology. *Social Science Information* 14:5–18.

———. 1975c. Letter. *New York Review of Books,* 11 December 22(20): 60–61.

———. 1976. Academic vigilantism and the political significance of sociobiology. *BioScience* 26:183, 187–190.

———. 1978. The attempt to suppress human behavioral genetics. *Journal of General Education* 29:277–287.

The Biological Synthesis of Behavior

Joan S. Lockard

15

The important facets of Darwin's *The Origin of Species* were largely a function of the taxonomic achievements of that time (Mayr, 1942). So it was that the importance of systematics in the study of evolution came to be realized in the last half of the 19th century. The impetus of genetics during the first third of the 20th century overshadowed the necessity for systematics, manifesting even some contempt for the discipline. However, in 1940, Huxley introduced the term "new systematics" and the modern synthesis of genetics, biology, ecology, biogeography, paleontology and taxonomy was underway. It was finally realized that the intricacies of evolutionary phenomena could only be attained through the joint cooperation of all of these disciplines. However, the omission of the science of behavior was not to be corrected for another 30 years. Although the advent of classical ethology [e.g., Lorenz (1938)] occurred much earlier, scientific consensus and the acceptance of behavior was not achieved until the mid-1970s with the Nobel laureates in ethology of Lorenz, Tinbergen and von Frisch (Lorenz, 1974; Tinbergen, 1974; von Frisch, 1974). An insurgence of interest in the behavior of social species soon followed with the appearance of a major text on the subject of sociobiology (Wilson, 1975). Subsequently, the study of the behavior of the most social species of all, Man, was undertaken, perhaps seriously, for the first time in terms of evolutionary concepts of natural selection.

Although it would appear that the biological synthesis has finally incorporated behavior, the sincerity with which hominid behavior is being addressed is still lacking. While the study of infants and children in terms of ultimate causation is becoming more acceptable, the behavior of adults is still regarded almost exclusively in terms of proximal explanations. Apparently, it is difficult to be objective about one's own species. Whereas scientific detachment is largely achieved with nonhuman animals, and to some extent with human young, it is mainly absent in the study of human adults. The problem rests with the overwhelming complexity with which researchers view adult human behavior. The major obstacles are an inability to focus on obvious behavioral consistencies or to formulate meaningful questions specific enough to be testable. Also, it seems as though it is nearly inconceivable that our behavior could be a function of ecological determinants of the distant past. For example, the idea that the places we choose to live or aspire to reside has anything to do with the theory of habitat selection (Chapter 3) would still be unthinkable to most social scientists today. Moreover, that phenomena such as parental care, sibling rivalry or divorce could be understood in terms of biological concepts of reproductive success, competition for resources and different male and female mating strategies, respectively, would be viewed with disdain by the majority of the academic community.

Greeting Behaviors   Yet, there are glimmerings of some progress in the occasional study that attempts to treat the adaptive significance of human behavior. In particular, the description of human greeting by Kendon and Ferber (1973) and the subsequent research by Deutsch (1977) on face-to-face behavior come to mind. The attempt of the former study was to develop a description of how people greet one another. Six films of different greeting situations (an adult birthday party, a wedding, a Thanksgiving gathering, high school adolescents at a band practice, a Fourth of July picnic celebration and unstaged activities at a nursery school) were carefully reviewed numerous times. The films were prepared for analysis by having each frame numbered. A list was assembled of behavioral units of greeting that repeatedly appeared in the films. Ninety-two interactions were analyzed, revealing five categories of the greeting ritual: (a) distant salutation, (b) recipient's response, (c) initial approach, (d) final approach and (e) close salutation. The first category involved sighting of one individual by another, orientation and initiation of approach, and contained such behavioral units as the eyebrow-flick, head-toss display including smiling or laughing, head lower behavior, head nod and wave. The second category encompassed the head dip as the recipient's acknowledgement of the distant salutation by the actor, followed by an exchange of glances by both individuals. The third category was the actor's approach, often manifesting such behaviors as face orientation, eye aversion, body-cross and self-groom. The fourth category contained the final movements by the actor before the stationary greeting and included such behaviors as the smile, head set (i.e., head tilted slightly) and palm presentation. The final category consisted of a close greeting ceremony, first without body contact and subsequently involving either a hand shake or a more intimate embrace. In addition to the definitions of the various behaviors involved in greeting, the main contribution of the study was the pervasive finding of the consistency of the greeting ritual (Figure 1) and its frequent occurrence in everyday social interactions.

As mentioned earlier, one of the most difficult problems in the

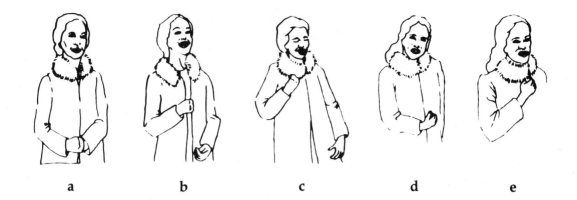

a	b	c	d	e

Figure 1
Human greeting ritual [adapted from Kendon and Ferber (1973)]: (a) sighting an acquaintance; (b) distance salutation involving eyebrow flick and head-toss display; (c) head-dip preceeding approach; (d) close salutation with head-set posture; (e) end of greeting ceremony with body cross and face-formation position.

study of human social behavior is narrowing the research subject sufficiently to permit systematic observations or experimental manipulations. Previous refuge in the rationalization that human behavior is complex more often than not addressed our inability to focus on the most relevant aspects of the research interest. The monograph by Deutsch (1977) on spatial structuring in face-to-face behavior illustrates well the scientific gain to be had in simplifying the object of concentrated study.[1] Building on Kendon and Ferber's greeting study (1973), a detailed spatial-temporal analysis of face-to-face interactions was investigated. The most important contribution of the investigation was the "geometry" of the research approach. A trapezoidal model was utilized in the study of the formation of conversational clusters of individuals (i.e., face-formations) that reduced complex temporal sequences of orientation, spacing and postural adjustments to understandable essentials.

Deutsch segregated a face-formation into three consecutive nonverbal behavioral components: (a) a *probe*, which is the expression of one's willingness to engage in a face-formation, (b) a *proposal* as to what spatial orientation arrangement among the participants will be maintained, and (c) an *acceptance* of the relative spacing and orientation of the other participants by not compensating for their maneuvers. A geometry of the face-formation was then developed where the space around the feet of each participant is depicted by a trapezoid, called a transactional segment. The *base* of the trapezoid (the shorter of its two parallel lines) is created on the ground by dropping an imaginary perpendicular line from the lateral extension of each shoulder of an individual and connecting the two points on the ground (Figure 2a). The *crown* of the trapezoid is a larger line parallel to the base. The base and the crown are connected by two lines (called *legs*) at a 45° angle to the

[1]The information cited on face-to-face behavior is taken from a review by the present author of Deutsch's monograph (1977) on this subject, which appeared in the *Human Ethology Newsletter*, 1978, No. 22.

base to complete the trapezoid. The transactional segment for each individual has a base of approximately two feet and is assigned a crown of six feet, spaced at a perpendicular distance of two feet from the base in accord with findings in the literature on personal space.

In the application of this model on the geometry of face-formation, Deutsch is able to reduce essentially 2,200 hours of detailed analysis of movie film of naturally occuring conversation clusters of individuals to the simple statement that for a face-formation to exist:

. . . each individual's transactional segment must overlap with at least one other person's transactional segment and the base of each individual's transactional segment must not be more than 90° out of phase with respect to the base of at least one other individual's transactional segment.

Figure 2
Face-formation [adapted from Deutsch (1977)]: (a) The personal space of an individual is depicted by a trapezoid on the ground where the base is formed by downward-projected perpendicular lines from the shoulder; the legs are the spaces to the side, and the crown is the area in front. (b) This is a closed face-to-face position of two individuals (as depicted on the ground) with no opening for another individual to join the dyad. (c) This is an open face-to-face position (L-shaped dyad) of two individuals with space available (bonding site) for another individual to join the group.

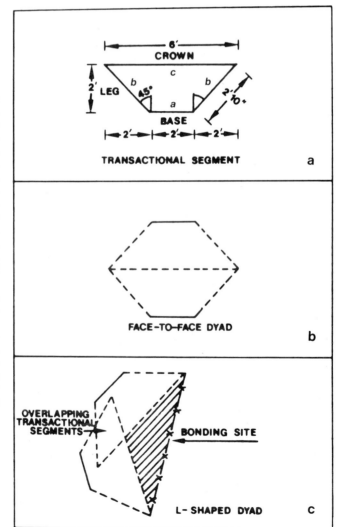

If after a face-formation is formed, a member inadvertently moves so as to change the spatial orientation, the other participants move so as to reestablish the formation.

Deutsch's model is also able to define the spatial arrangements under which a new member may join an already-formed face-formation, a potential participant may be excluded, a member may depart temporarily, or more permanent leave-taking may be initiated. If an individual is to be admitted, he probes the face-formation by stopping a short distance away while the crown of each member's transactional segment becomes nonoverlapping with respect to the segments of the other participants so as to open up a "bonding site" for the new member (see Figure 2c). The transactional segments become more overlapping if an individual is not to be admitted (Figure 2b). A member who departs briefly may return without going through a probe phase again if the other members have not compensated for his leave-taking by adjusting their orientation so as to close the vacated bonding site. If permanent leave-taking is to transpire, a rite of departure is commenced where oscillations of movements outward and then inward signal the member's intention before the "away phase" is evinced. Quantitative data on this last phase has been gathered in a recent study by the present author (Lockard et al., 1978) in which departure behavior in terms of nonverbal intention movements were systematically observed (reported in Chapter 1).

Mating Strategies   Another promising research area on a quite different topic—mating strategies—is illustrated by a series of experiments by Walster et al. (1973). The topic, "playing hard to get," was ingeniously investigated through the ploy of a computer-matching bureau. The authors reasoned from the folklore that the woman who is hard to get is a more desirable "catch" than the woman who is too eager for an alliance. They conducted five studies to demonstrate that males value hard-to-get dates more than easy-to-get ones. For example, in Study IV, the dating counselor told the male subjects that the computer had assigned them a date. Each subject was instructed to telephone his proposed match and ask her to go out with him. Actually all men were assigned confederates, half of which played easy-to-get and the other half hard-to-get. In the former case the confederate eagerly accepted a date, in the latter condition, the confederate replied:

"Mmm [slight pause]. No, I've got a date then. It seems like I signed up for that Date Match thing a long time ago and I've met more people since then—I'm really pretty busy all this week." She paused again. If the subject suggested another time, the confederate hesitated only slightly, then accepted. If he did not suggest another time, the confederate would take the initiative of suggesting: "How about some time next week—or just meeting for coffee in the Union some afternoon?" And again, she accepted the next invitation.

In the words of the authors, all five experiments failed. They subsequently proposed that two components, rather than the initial one, contributed to a woman's desirability: (a) how difficult the woman is for the subject to get, and (b) how difficult she is for other men to get. In a sixth study, they predicted that the selectively hard-to-get woman (i.e., a woman who is easy for the subject to get but hard for all other men to get) would be preferred to either a uniformly hard-to-get woman, a uniformly easy-to-get woman or a woman about whom the subject has no information. Their final hypothesis was supported by the data. It is interesting, in view of the fact that it took six studies to culminate in a positive outcome, the authors would suggest that the reason for the popularity of the selective woman was essentially self-evident: men ascribed to the selectively hard-to-get woman all of the assets of a uniformly easy-to-get woman and none of the latter's liabilities. Their discourse overlooked the essential biological conclusion from their findings, i.e., greater reproductive success for males who are assured of the fidelity of the women to whom they are mated than those who are not.

Whereas breeding systems in many different animal species have been studied in depth [e.g., Orians (1969), Wickler (1972), Williams (1975)], only recently has serious consideration been given to human mating strategies [e.g., Beach (1974), Dickeman (1980)]. The variety of current and historical marital systems across many different cultures [e.g., Coon (1971)] leaves in question whether Homo sapiens had at some time in the distant past evolved a "basic" breeding pattern. It could be argued that so vital an area of human function as breeding could not be left to chance factors. However, just as reasonably could be championed the idea that versatility in mating systems would be adaptive since adjustments to fluctuating ecological determinants of survival are essential.

The answer as to just what is the breeding system(s) of hominids may become less ambiguous if, as proposed by Trivers (1972), the mating strategies of males and females must be regarded as different even in the case of monogamy (although here they are undoubtedly more similar than in polygamous systems). If only reproductive span is considered, it becomes evident that females have fewer years than males in which to maximize their direct reproductive success, even though after menopause their inclusive fitness may still be increased. Therefore, a mating strategy that a male might adopt would be to breed as early as possible with a female of approximately the same age as the male until she reaches menopause, and then to abandon her to mate again with a much younger female still in her reproductive years. A female strategy might be to mate for life with a male possessing, or potentially capable of possessing in time, essential resources to help rear the young to reproductive age and subsequently (after menopause) to aid the offspring in their own reproduction, i.e., thereby increasing the grandmother's inclusive fitness. The male strategy, particularly if its resources were sufficient to support several mates and their offspring simultaneously, might be viewed as *facultative polygyny* and/or, if he were capable of only one mate and her offspring at a time, *obligatory serial polygyny*. In the same vein, the female strategy might be regarded as *facultative monogamy* for her and/or, if she were successful in keeping her spouse after menopause, *obligatory monogamy* for him.

In a recent study (Lockard and Adams, 1980a), we attempted to detect demographically such mating strategies by correlating by age the frequency of mixed-sex dyads relative to same-sex pairs in public shopping malls. Dyads rather than families were observed in order to minimize observational errors of parents and their offspring separating to shop and reuniting at a later time and location. It was assumed that the age of the dyadic members and the relative frequency of the three types of dyads (male–male, female–female and mixed-sex) would reflect mating strategies in the population at large. For example, an older male seen with a younger female (with an age difference of less than 18 years to statistically rule out the possibility of a parent–offspring sighting) would signify a different strategy than if the pair were of comparable age. It was predicted that at older ages males would be seen with younger females (e.g., some three to nine years younger) more often than expected by chance and certainly more frequently than older females would be seen with younger males.

Over 4,000 dyadic groupings in two large shopping malls in Seattle, Washington, were classified as to age and sex of individual members as they passed along a well-defined exit path. The observations were carried out where, and at a time when, a demographic cross section of a city was likely to be seen, and where there were no rigid constraints on the group composition that appeared. The data were subjected to computer analysis, and observed frequencies of specified age–sex dyads were compared by chi-square statistics to expected frequencies based on a binomial distribution. Mathematically significant mating strategies were then compared with the reproductive statistics (i.e., number of live births by parents' ages) of the locale to address the validity of the data.

As predicted (Figure 3b), the relative frequency of mixed-sex dyads in which the male is on the average six years older than the female begins to increase when the male's age is 21–23 years (Male Strategy 1), peaks at 27–29 years ($\chi^2 = 7.02$, df = 2 $p < .05$), declines ($p > .05$) again at 30–32 years and subsequently rises at age 39–41 years (Male Strategy 2; $\chi^2 = 16.00$, df = 2, $p < .01$), remaining high (e.g., $\chi^2 = 14.41$, df = 2, $p < .01$) until 51–53 years at which age it declines ($p > .05$) once more. In contrast, the frequency of mixed-sex dyads in which the female is six years older than the male is low at any age. Of the 200 mixed-sex dyads, collapsed across ages 18–60, in which one member was six years older than the other, in only 10% was the female the older

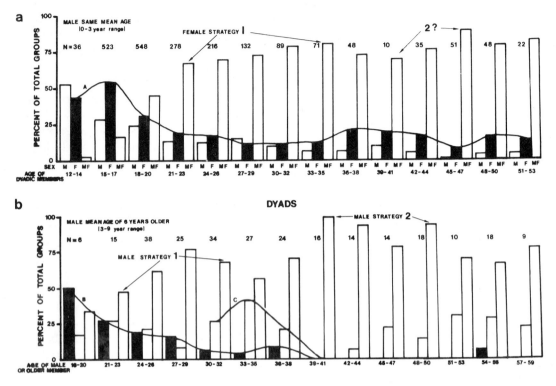

Figure 3

Mating Strategies [adapted from Lockard and Adams (1980a)]: (a) Dyadic members same mean age; A = a line connecting female–female dyadic histobars (F), with male–male histobars to the left (M) and mixed-sex histobars to the right (MF). A female mating strategy (1) is manifested between ages 21–35 and may continue at older ages, or a different strategy (2?) for some females may be operating from age 39 on. (b) One dyadic member is six years older than the other; B = a line connecting male–male dyadic histobars, with female–female and mixed-sex dyads, respectively, to the right. C = an increase of female–female dyads where one member is six years older than the other. A male mating strategy (1) is manifested for males between ages 21–33 years and another strategy (2) from age 39 to at least 51 years old, wherein the female member of the mixed-sex dyads is some six years younger on the average.

member. However, the frequency of mixed-sex dyads in which the female and male are of comparable ages (Figure 3a) increases ($\chi^2 = 35.43$, df = 2, $p < .001$) at age 21–23 years (Female Strategy 1) and remains high (e.g., $\chi^2 = 29.24$, df = 2, $p < .001$) from that age on, with the exception of a dip ($p > .05$) at approximately age 39–41 years (Female Strategy 2?).

When the reproductive statistics are analyzed for the same locale as that from which the dyadic data were gathered (Figure 4) it is found that males older than 32 years sired significantly often ($z = 2.88$, $p < .002$) children by females at least several years younger than they are. This outcome, in conjunction with the dyadic findings, supports the research hypothesis that males have different mating strategies than females. One interpretation of the data is that males in their lifespan may tend to mate seriously with more than one female, while females attempt to mate seriously with one male during their reproductive years and after menopause, either hold on to that male or obtain another male (with possibly greater resources than the first) to facilitate their inclusive fitness. For instance, the dip in frequency of comparably aged members of mixed-sex dyads at age 39–41 years (Figure 3a) may signify a parting of previously mated pairs (e.g., an increase in divorce rate) with a subsequent increase in newly composed dyads. The biological benefit to males of the more recently formed associations with *same-aged* females may be similar to that of the females, namely, to obtain assistance with rearing offspring of previous matings so as to facilitate the inclusive fitness of the males. This may be a "loser strategy" [e.g., Dawkins (1976)] by males 39 years or older in lieu of an ability to attract a "quality"

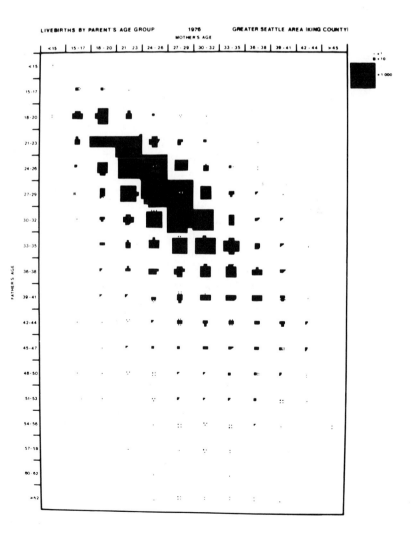

Figure 4

Frequency of live births by age of both parents for Seattle, Washington, 1976 [taken from Lockard and Adams (1980a)]. Mother's age at top, Father's age at left. Mean age of mother is 34 years for births where the father is 39 years or older.

younger female who could bear new offspring and possibly help rear the offspring the male already has or facilitate his existing offspring in the production of grandchildren.

A female, as well as a male, may have a "loser strategy" if, say, she is unable to attract a "male of means" either when she is younger or when she is older. In the former case, she may choose to mate with a male who is on a "quantity trip" (i.e., many females) in order to breed at all. In the latter case, she may choose a male who has limited resources in order to have at least some help in rearing her offspring if she has been deserted by (or has chosen to leave herself) the father(s) of her children. There is also the game of deception that could be played by either female or male given certain kinds of conditions as has been discussed in Chapter 13.

As an aside from the data of Figure 3b (line C) the finding that females in their reproductive years associate with older women may indicate that learning to rear offspring from more experienced mothers is taking place. This phenomenon may be similar to "aunting behavior" in nonhuman primates [e.g., Hunt et al. (1978)].

Parent–Offspring Groupings

Another fruitful research subject concerns parent–offspring associations, as studied demographically. Mackey (1976) investigated adult male grouping patterns in three countries (the United States, Mexico and Spain). His intent was to explore the parameters that could influence the behavior of men toward children. Observations of the associations of adults (by gender) with children classified by age and sex were gathered. An adult was judged to be in association with a child when there was a general orientation of one toward the other. A child was observed to associate with one of three kinds of adult groups: men only, women only or both men and women. A total of approximately 20,000 children were observed in three countries. All observations were conducted as inconspicuously as possible in areas of public access where either gender was equally likely to appear. In all three countries, a child was defined as a prepubescent while an adult was defined as a male or a female who is well into or who has finished puberty. The child category was divided into three age groups: 0–4 years, 5–7 years, and 8 years to puberty. The observations were subjected to chi-square analyses with statistical significance regarded as a probability less than .01.

It was found that regardless of country, the adult female associated with children more often that the adult male. There was, however, a very consistent percentage (14–18%) of the children who were with men-only groups during the time of day when adult males are not precluded from being with children. An age of child by adult group analysis revealed that for all three types of adult associations, generally the older children were underrepresented and the younger children were overrepresented. When the age distribution of children was compared among the three categories of adult groups, it was found that the older boys were overrepresented in the men-only groups. The incorporation of the maturing boys into male-only groups was not mirrored by a similar incorporation of the maturing girls into the women-only groups. Regardless of age, girls were always overrepresented in the women-only groups. In Spain, the girls were also overrepresented in the women and men groups, whereas in the United States boys were overrepresented in the women and men groups.

Mackey concluded that the level of parental "tending" by males, although not equivalent in frequency with females, was quite considerable in its own right. He went on to point out that adults of both genders will attend to children of both genders and that the adult male–boy dyad seems to illustrate a special relationship of association, which was not reflected in the adult female–girl dyad. He suggested that this lack of symmetry in the data for boys and girls is consistent with an evolutionary role that the male played as a hunter, and that adult male parenting behaviors have been influenced by past ecological parameters of food-sharing.

In a similar study restricted to the United States, Adams and Lockard (1980) were interested in a slightly different question of what is the most stable biological unit of human parent–offspring combination (i.e., mother–daughter, father–son and so forth). Over 10,000 groups in two types of public areas (shopping malls and zoological gardens) were observed and their composition recorded in terms of number, sex and estimated age of their members. Observation periods were restricted to evenings and weekends at the shopping malls, and weekends at the zoological gardens, to reduce the likelihood of a parent's presence being precluded by work. After the conduct of the study, some 2,000 parent–offspring groups were segregated by the criteria of at least 18 years differential between two members wherein one was 17 years of age or younger. In other words, family groups were defined as those with an individual up to age 17 accompanied by an adult at least 18 years older, but no more than 42 years older, to exclude most grandparents.

In the shopping mall data, whether analyzed by single-child only, youngest child or oldest child, the results were all the same. Only mother–offspring units, regardless of sex of child, increased in frequency with age of offspring from three to 17 years (Figure 5). Mother–daughter groups were most prevalent with mother–son, father–son, both parents present and father–daughter combinations evinced in order of descending frequency. The data also revealed that a child of two years of age was more than twice as likely to be accompanied by both parents as by a single parent, with mothers alone only slightly more likely than fathers alone. Older children especially over age 11, were generally more likely to be with a single parent, typically the mother, and boys and girls regardless of age were equally likely to be with both parents.

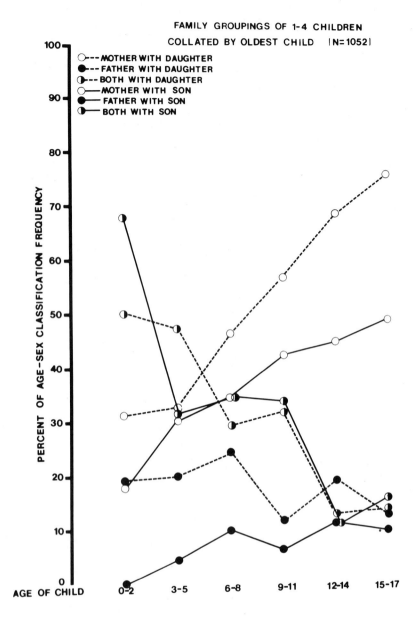

Figure 5
Single- and multiple-child family groupings at shopping malls [adapted from Adams and Lockard (1980)]: percent of total frequency for each age–sex–parent classification collated by oldest child.

The data from the zoological gardens (as illustrated by the collation of oldest child, Figure 6) indicated that groups with both parents present were the most prevalent. Mother–daughter units increased with age, while all other combinations were relatively infrequent.

As in many other mammalian species [e.g., Orians (1969), Mitchell and Brand (1972)] human mother–offspring units appear to be very stable. The strength of this outcome (from the shopping mall data) was surprising for older male offspring who were past the highly dependent age of childhood (i.e., greater than 12 years of age). This outcome was in spite of the relatively low frequency in which boys were observed in all other parent–child groupings.

In contrast to the shopping mall data, the predominance of both parents present in the leisure setting (zoological gardens on weekends) indicated a difference in parental roles in the two situations. The exceptions were mothers with very young children (0–2 years of age) and a similar burden that fathers bore with male offspring. The former speaks to the degree of maternal effort involved with very young children. The latter suggests some

Figure 6
Single- and multiple-child family groupings at zoological gardens [adapted from Adams and Lockard (1980)]: percent of total frequency for each age–sex–parent classification collated by oldest child (family groupings for child ages 12–17 years not shown, as N in these categories too small to be reliable).

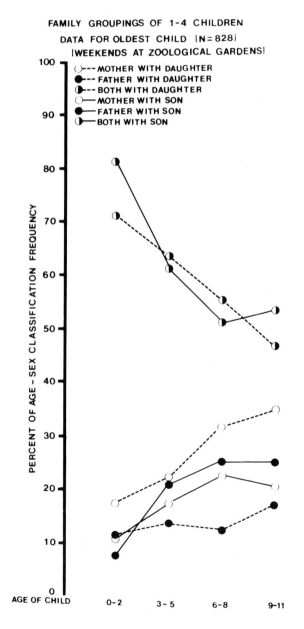

FAMILY GROUPINGS OF 1-4 CHILDREN

DATA FOR OLDEST CHILD (N=828)

(WEEKENDS AT ZOOLOGICAL GARDENS)

◐--- MOTHER WITH DAUGHTER
●--- FATHER WITH DAUGHTER
◑--- BOTH WITH DAUGHTER
◯— MOTHER WITH SON
●— FATHER WITH SON
◑— BOTH WITH SON

PERCENT OF AGE - SEX CLASSIFICATION FREQUENCY

AGE OF CHILD   0-2   3-5   6-8   9-11

tendency for gender identification to be operating, i.e., mothers with daughters and fathers with sons. The increasing frequency of mother–daughter units with age of child (in the leisure setting, Figure 6) is also indicative of this influence.

The prevalence of mother–daughter groupings when the daughter is of juvenile age may also address an easier assimilation of girls than boys into the adult society. This possibility is supported by a study on adoescent males (18–20 years old) by Lockard and Adams (1980d) in which a banding together of male subadults in same-sex groups of three or more members was found (Chapter 1). Also, the predominance at the leisure site of groupings including both parents suggest that at least for zoological gardens, such a setting may serve as an "extension of the home." The zoo, with its picnicing areas and quiet surroundings, may be an alternative to relaxing in the privacy of one's house.

The strong tendency (at either study site) for groupings, including both parents, to decrease with an increase in age of child is quite likely indicative of a decline in the need for care by both parents. This possibility is supported by another study by Lockard and Adams (1980b) in which it was found that the majority of children over the age of ten (particularly males) were not seen accompanied by a parent during the day in public places. Moreover, if male juveniles were seen with a male adult they were at greater than expected distances from the adult and greater than they would be if accompanied by a female adult. These relationships found between age of child and distance from parent are supportive of the findings in infant attachment research where proximity of child to parent declines with age [e.g., as reviewed in Lamb (1976)]. Although many studies have been done on attachment in a laboratory or home setting, most have included only the mother and infant. A few more recent studies have looked at father–infant attachment (Feldman and Ingham, 1975; Lamb, 1975; Ban and Lewis, 1974). Also, different behaviors have been used as measures of attachment such as exploration from a secure base, approach and nearness. The advantages of the studies by Mackey (1976), Adams and Lockard (1980) and Lockard and Adams (1980b) are that they not only confirm some of the trends that have been seen in infant attachment research but do so within a wider age range of children, a broader family context and a more natural setting. Moreover, the implicit assumption of the field studies is that in function, several of the behaviors of parent–offspring groupings (especially proximity) may have evolved biological benefits.

Carrying Behavior   Another topic of research, the data of which may come to have adaptive significance, is the sex-typical carrying behavior of adults (Haraszti, 1972; Hanaway, 1975). Most men carry books and similarly sized items at their side while women usually rest them on their hip or pelvic bones and cradle them with their

a

b

Figure 7
Gender-specific book-carrying positions [adapted from Scheman et al. (1977)]: (a) typical male carry with books at side; (b) typical female carry with books resting on hip and/or supported on upper torso by hand(s).

arm(s). Jenni and Jenni (1976) in their study on book-carrying behavior alluded to the possible role of anatomical differences in males and females which may contribute to gender-specific styles of carry. A study by Scheman et al. (1977) sought to quantify to what extent morphological differences between women and men affect the prevalence of the various styles. Not only were subjects' style of book-carrying noted, but their hip, waist and underarm measurements were also recorded. An attempt was made to develop a measure of "figure" that would most adequately account for the differences in style. An index of relative hip protrusion ("X area" = {hip − underarm} + {hip − waist}) was devised. The specific hypothesis tested was that women with hips that extended past the comfortable fall line of the arm along the side of the body would not show the side carry typically seen in males. In other words, the question was whether or not the physical protrusion of the hip is a limiting factor in the manner in which women carry their books.

The results of that study replicated (N = 1,181) the findings reported by Jenni and Jenni (1976) as well as those of Hanaway and Burghardt (1976) and Spottswood and Burghardt (1976). In kindergarten, there were no systematic differences in book-carrying style between boys and girls. Gender-trends in carrying behavior began to appear after age five (kindergarten) with males shifting predominantly to the side carry (Figure 7a) and females shifting away from it, first to the both-arm carry and later to a greater use of the one-arm front and one-arm, top-of-the-hip carry (Figure 7b). Style of carry differed significantly by sex and age and there was a significant interaction between the two factors.

The style of carry employed by children and teens who did not conform to the mean or "model" adult male or female "figure" seemed to mimic or model the gender-appropriate behavior. Such imitation was observed particularly in females who carried in the "female" style before their figure necessitated such a carry. It was noted that often these females would stand in such a manner as to throw their undeveloped hip out to the side to hold their books. The "figure" of males may develop more slowly and consistently than that of females. Significant differences in relative hip protrusion between males of different ages were only found when the boys were grouped by school types. Consistent with this outcome, the style of carry for males may also be more conservative, changing and varying less often. However, females seem to mature in spurts, changing dramatically in "figure" after puberty. Compatible with this idea, female styles appeared more variable and seemed to be influenced by physical change. It was found that the index of relative hip protrusion ("X area") partitioned styles of carrying most effectively in the high school population. There were, however, females who had a large "X area" (i.e., the hip measurement exceeded considerably the waist and/or underarm measurement) who carried on the side. This observation was particularly evident in the junior high school female population.

As with any behavior observed in public, the social context in which it occurred must be considered. School children are un-doutedly under some pressure to conform to the school norms. Hanaway and Burghardt (1976) suggest that the social presures and censures against sex-inappropriate behavior are possibly stronger for males than they are for females. Although the norm for any given school might appear to be asocial when compared to a population of schools, this suggestion seems viable for the data on junior high school students by Scheman et al. (1977). The book-carrying styles of junior high school males were sex-appropriate and corresponded with the physical-measurement index, whereas the female styles varied considerably and did not conform completely to the index values. It was observed that some of the other behaviors displayed by these females were also asocial. The current cultural pressures on females to become more inde-pendent (in the relatively liberal locale in which this study was conducted) could have resulted in their "going out of their way" to carry in the male style if this style were the asocial norm for this particular school or area.

It is safe to assume that style of book-carrying is a product of both physical and social factors and is not simply either a biological or cultural phenomenon. Although it may be valid to conclude that adult book-carrying behavior is, in part, a function of the mor-phological differences in the availability of space between the arm and hip of females and, subsequently, may have become overlaid with social-sexual connotations, there may well be other less obvious biological factors operating. In a recent study by the present author (Lockard et al., 1979) on adult female carrying behavior of infants (reported in Chapter 1) there was a strong tendency for mothers to carry their less-than-one-year olds on the left side. It was suggested that mother–infant bonding may be facilitated by such behavior. Whereas there may be little connec-tion between female book-carrying and female infant-carrying behavior, studies comparing the possibility of lateralized carrying of animate and inanimate objects (e.g., books, pets, dolls and stuffed animals) by young and older females may reveal biologi-cally meaningful similarities and differences.

Infant Releasing Displays

Another area of fruitful research that could be addressed in terms of evolved adaptations is the infant releasing displays of adult care-giving behavior. In a recent study of this phenomenon by Sternglanz et al. (1977), infant features were systematically varied via slides of facial line drawings. In contrast with previous studies, male adults were more attracted to features of babyness than were females. The investigators reasonably suggested that the discrepancy in data may be a function of their rating method of measuring infant attractiveness since preference for photographs of infants (Fuller and Reiling, 1976) and pupil dilation (Hess and Polt, 1960) were the methods utilized in earlier research. In more realistic settings, Berman and colleagues (1977) and Feldman et al. (1977) found that girls were more behaviorally and perceptually responsive to infants than were boys.

A study by Robinson et al. (1979) addressed responsivity to infants over a wide age–sex range of individuals in a field situation. Their research sought to determine interest in infants in a common public setting by using an unobtrusive measure, i.e., looking (versus not looking) at a stationary infant for at least two seconds by persons passing in a shopping center. The intent of the study was to ascertain if differential responsiveness to infants is a strong enough effect to be revealed in an everyday situation, with a heterogeneous population. The biological mother and father of a one-year-old female infant (dressed in yellow so as not to emphasize her sex) alternated in the care-taking role at the side of a pathway in an enclosed shopping mall (Seattle, Washington). Two trained observers (naive as to the research intent) recorded simultaneously, and alternated with every half-hour recording, either the age and sex of those who looked at the parent–child pair, or the age and sex of every person who passed by. Of the 4,559 individuals who walked along the pathway, 490 were observed to look at the parent–child pairs. As indicated in Figure 8, nine of the ten chi-square comparisons of looking, by age and sex of subject, reached statistical significance ($p < .01$). In general, regardless of the sex of the parent, female passersby were more likely to look at the baby than males. In decreasing order of probability, the age–sex groups most likely to look were females older than 59, females under 15, males over 59, females 15–29 and males under 15. The only group which appeared from the results to be clearly responding differentially to the sex of the parent was the under-15 male group, with some indication of this effect among the 30–59 females and 15–29 males.

There may be several reasons for differential interest in infants as a function of age and sex. Although explanations in terms of socialization and training in sex roles are probable, it is more than an accident of history that women have filled the child-care and perhaps other specific roles. The finding that both males and females over 59 years old look at infants is compatible with kin-selection theory. Adults of grandparent age would be interested in infants that probably reminded them of their own grandchildren and the genetic legacy to the next generation that they represent. The differential attention of the youngest male subjects to the father–infant pair, is also consistent with a biological interpretation. In male–male interactions, it has been shown that attention is directed toward the individual with the greatest status (Chance, 1967). The attention of the young males in the present research may have been directed toward the father as an adult male in addition to the gestalt of father–infant pair.

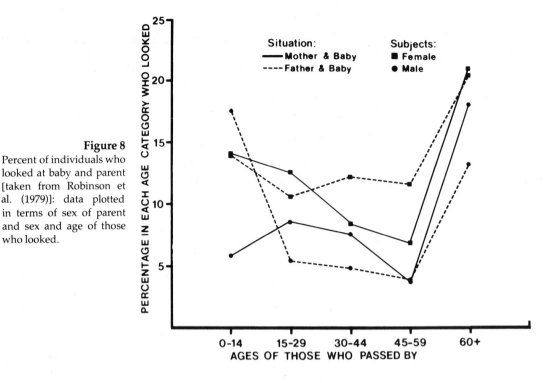

Figure 8
Percent of individuals who looked at baby and parent [taken from Robinson et al. (1979)]: data plotted in terms of sex of parent and sex and age of those who looked.

In a different context, the biological implications of looking behavior in terms of eye contact and gaze has also been an area of productive research. Argyle and Cook (1976) have suggested that there is a strong convention about not gazing at strangers in public places. Ellsworth and colleagues (1972) have indicated that the interpretation of a gaze depends upon contextual cues, and if these cues are unclear, as possibly in public, the stare may be ambiguous and hence disturbing. Scheman and Lockard (1979) attempted to ascertain whether the avoidance of staring (i.e., gaze-aversion in public) develops biologically or whether it bears a strong experiential component. Whereas the ability to gaze matures early in humans, the social implications of gaze may not develop until much later. Gaze-aversion was studied in 573 children in a large shopping center (Seattle, Washington). The observer stared continually at any child passing along a definable pathway. As shown in Figure 9, almost all infants (≤18 months of age) did not make eye contact with the observer. The majority of toddlers (greater than 18 months to five years old) established eye contact (for >1 second) but did not gaze-avert (i.e., a look of <1 second). The preponderance of school-age children (5–9 years of age) did gaze-avert (age x duration: $\chi^2 = 208.01$, df = 6, $p < .0001$).

The finding that toddlers stare for some length of time compared to the other two groups of children, suggests several possible explanations. If toddlers are indeed incapable of gaze-averting, or if they know how to, but social learning of its possible adult consequences (i.e., elicited aggression from others) does not transpire until age five or six years, then the features of small children as well as infants must have to be endearing to adults. Similar to the infant displays for eliciting care-giving, toddlers may manifest a nonviolent, defenseless posture that the adult, in turn, perceives as nonaggressive. To ascertain whether this is in fact the case, a study would have to be conducted in which toddlers, unaccompanied by protective adults, were given the opportunity to gaze-avert to a stranger. If the toddlers did gaze-avert, then such behavior might be biologically predisposed. If toddlers did not gaze-avert under those conditions, then a maturational and/or experiential process may be necessary for gaze aversion to be manifested. If it is a maturational process, then adults should show some positive affect toward an optimal gestalt of toddler features, which additional research could reveal.

The Challenge of Human Behavior

Although there are undoubtedly several other interesting topics that could be addressed, the major point of this overview would still be the same, namely, some progress is being made in studying human behavior in terms of evolved mechanisms. Several theoretical studies on human behavior are also indicative of this trend—for example, on the subjects of cultural selection for aggression (Durham, 1976) and the inheritance of wealth (Hartung, 1976), and as part of a 1978 symposium on natural selection and social behavior: kin selection and population fissioning (Chagnon, 1980),

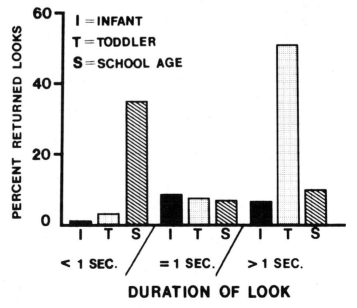

Figure 9
Percent of children who returned the observer's stare [adapted from Scheman and Lockard (1979)]: infant = <18 months of age; toddlers = >18 months to 5 years of age; school age children = 5–9 years of age; gaze-aversion = a look of <1 sec; gaze = a look >1 sec in duration.

lineage exogamy (Irons, 1980), paternal confidence and dowry competition (Dickeman, 1980), and an evolutionary perspective of neglect and abuse of children (Daly and Williams, 1980). In fact, all of the present volume (admittedly just a beginning) speaks to a change in attitude and method in the study of hominid behavior. Hopefully, the traditional idea that Man is a *tabula rasa* [e.g., Skinner, 1938] upon which proximal experiences write is indeed an idea in the past. The view that we are part of the greater biology of the animal kingdom, where phyletic origin and distant ecological pressures have influenced some of our present behavior seems scientifically a far more valid concept. It is intellectually foolish for us to continue to deny that we are a social primate by heritage (Chapter 2) with built-in predispositions to prefer certain habitats (Chapter 3), to choose certain mates (Chapters 7 and 8), to bear children and rear them in particular ways (Chapters 4 and 5), to develop certain behavioral signals (Chapters 1, 6 and 12), to be aggressive (Chapter 9), to be deceitful (Chapter 13) and to use our culture for our own biologically selfish ends (Chapter 14). On the other hand, an overemphasis of this position would be just as foolish. We are both a product of our evolutionary biology (Chapter 10) and our cultural experiences. In our zealousness for biological significance, we must be especially careful to guard against the misapplication of concepts of behavioral genetics (Chapter 11) and to consider both distal and proximal explanations of our behavior. Most assuredly, a synthesis of the sciences of behavior and biology is finally occurring, and those who are engaged in the study of Man must be up to the challenge it provides.

References   Adams, R.M., and Lockard, J.S. 1980. Parent–offspring groupings by age/sex classification in public. In preparation.

Argyle, M., and Cook, M. 1976. *Gaze and Mutual Gaze*. Cambridge: Cambridge University Press.

Ban, P.L. and Lewis, M. 1974. Mothers and fathers, girls and boys: Attachment behavior in the one-year-old. *Merrill-Palmer Quarterly* 20:195–204.

Beach, F.H. 1974. Human sexuality and evolution. In W. Montagua and W. Sadler (eds.) *Advances in Behavioral Biology*, Vol. II, Reproductive Behavior. New York: Plenum Press.

Berman, P.W., Monda, L.C., and Myerscough, R.P. 1977. Sex differences in young children's responses to an infant: An observation within a day-care setting. *Child Development* 48:711–715.

Chagnon, N. 1980. Predictions of population fissioning among the Yanomamö based on kin classification and kin relatedness. In R.D. Alexander and D.W. Tinkle (eds.) *Natural Selection and Social Behavior: Recent Research and Theory*. New York: Chiron Press.

Chance, M.R.A. 1967. Attention structure as the basis of primate rank orders. *Man* 2:503–518.

Coon, C.S. 1971. *The Hunting Peoples*. Boston: Little, Brown and Co.

Daly, M., and Williams, M. 1980. Neglect and abuse of children in an evolutionary perspective. In R.D. Alexander and D.W. Tinkle (eds.) *Natural Selection and Social Behavior: Recent Research and Theory*. New York: Chiron Press.

Dawkins, R. 1976. *The Selfish Gene*. Oxford: Oxford University Press.

Deutsch, R.D. 1977. *Spatial Structurings in Everyday Face-to-Face Behavior: A Neurocybernetic Model*. Orangeburg, New York: The Association for the Study of Man–Environment Relations.

Dickeman, M. 1980. Paternal confidence and dowry competition: A biocultural analysis of Purdah. In R.D. Alexander and D.W. Tinkle (eds.) *Natural Selection and Social Behavior: Recent Research and Theory*. New York: Chiron Press.

Durham, W.H. 1976. Resource competition and human aggression, Part I: A review of primitive war. *The Quarterly Review of Biology* 51:385–415.

Ellsworth, B.C., Carlsmith, J.M., and Henson, A. 1972. The stare as a stimulus to flight in human subjects: A series of field experiments. *Journal of Perspectives in Social Psychology* 21:302–311.

Feldman, S., and Ingham, M.E. 1975. Attachment behavior: A validation study on two age groups. *Child Development* 46:319–330.

Feldman, S., Nash, S.C., and Cutrona, C. 1977. The influence of age and sex on responsiveness to babies. *Developmental Psychology* 13:675–676.

Fuller. W., and Reiling, A.M. 1976. An investigation of Lorenz' "babyness." *Child Development* 47:1191–1193.

Hanaway, T.P. 1975. The development of gendered book-carrying behavior. Unpublished doctoral dissertation, University of Tennessee.

Hanaway, T.P., and Burghardt, G.M. 1976. The development of sexually dimorphic book-carring behavior. *Bulletin of the Psychonomic Society* 7:267–270.

Haraszti, L. 1972. Dimorphism in carrying books. Unpublished paper. University of Chicago.

Hartung, J. 1976. On natural selection and the inheritance of wealth. *Current Anthropology* 17:607–622.

Hess, E.H., and Polt, J.M. 1960. Pupil size as related to interest value of visual stimuli. *Science* 132:349–350.

Hunt, S.M., Gamache, K.M., and Lockard, J.S. 1978. Babysitting behavior by age/sex classification in squirrel monkeys (*Saimiri sciureus*). *Primates* 19:179–186.

Irons, W.G. 1980. Why lineage exogamy? In R.D. Alexander and D.W. Tinkle (eds.) *Natural Selection and Social Behavior: Recent Research and Theory*. New York: Chiron Press.

Jenni, D.A., and Jenni, M.A. 1976. Carrying behavior in humans: Analysis of sex differences. *Science* 194:859–860.

Kendon, A., and Ferber, A. 1973. A description of some human greetings. In M. Crook (ed.) *Comparative Ecology and Behaviour of Primates*. London: Academic Press.

Lamb, M.E. 1975. The sociability of two-year-olds with their mothers and fathers. *Child Psychiatry and Human Development* 5:182–188.

———. 1976. Proximity seeking attachment behaviors: A critical review of the literature. *Genetic Psychology Monographs* 93:63–89.

Lockard, J.S., and Adams, R.M. 1980a. Courtship behaviors in public: Different age/sex roles. *Ethology and Sociobiology*. In press.

Lockard, J.S., and Adams, R.M. 1980b. Parent–offspring proximity in public. In preparation.

Lockard, J.S., and Adams, R.M. 1980c. Serial polygyny evinced in public dyadic groupings classified by age and sex. In preparation.

Lockard, J.S., and Adams, R.M. 1980d. Peripheral males: A primate model for a human subgroup. In preparation.

Lockard, J.S, Schiele, B.J., Allen, D.L., and Wiemer, M.J. 1978. Human postural signals: Stance, weight shifts and social distance as intention movements to depart. *Animal Behaviour* 26:219–224.

Lockard, J.S., Daley, P.C., and Gunderson, V.M. 1979. Maternal and paternal differences in infant carry: U.S. and African data. *The American Naturalist* 113:235–246.

Lorenz, K. 1938. A contribution to the comparative sociology of colonial-nesting birds. *Proc. Int. Ornithol. Congr.* 8:207–218.

———. 1974. Analogy as a source of knowledge. *Science* 185:229–234.

Mackey, W.C. 1976. The adult male-child bond: An example of convergent evolution. *J. of Anthropological Research* 32:58–71.

Mayr, E. 1942. *Systematics and the Origin of Species.* New York: Columbia University Press.

Mitchell, G.D., and Brand, E.M. 1972. Paternal behavior in primates. In F. Poirier (ed.) *Primate Socialization.* New York: Random House.

Orians, G.H. 1969. On the evolution of mating systems in birds and mammals. *The American Naturalist* 103:589–603.

Robinson, C.L., Lockard, J.S., and Adams, R.M. 1979. Who looks at a baby in public? *Ethology and Sociobiology* 1:87–91.

Scheman, J., and Lockard, J.S. 1979. Development of gaze aversion in children. *Child Development* 50:594–596.

Scheman, J., Lockard, J.S., and Mehler, B.L. 1977. Anatomical influence on book-carrying behavior. *Bulletin of the Psychonomic Society* 95:367–370.

Skinner, B.F. 1938. *The Behavior of Organisms: An Experimental Analysis.* New York: Appleton-Century.

Spottswood, P.J., and Burghardt, G.M. 1976. The effects of sex, book weight, and grip strength on book-carrying styles. *Bulletin of the Psychonomic Society* 8:150–152.

Sternglanz, S., Gary, J.L., and Murakama, M. 1977. Adult preferences for infantile facial features: An ethological approach. *Animal Behaviour* 25:108–115.

Tinbergen, N. 1974. Ethology and stress disease. *Science* 185:20–27.

Trivers, R.L. 1972. Parental investment and sexual selection. In B. Campbell (ed.) *Sexual Selection and the Descent of Man, 1871–1971.* Chicago: Aldine.

von Frisch, K. 1974. Decoding the language of the bee. *Science* 185:663–668.

Walster, E., Walster, G.W., Piliavin, J., and Schmidt, L. 1973. "Playing Hard to Get": Understanding an elusive phenomenon. *J. of Personality and Social Psychology* 26:113–121.

Wickler, W. 1972. *The Sexual Code: The Social Behavior of Animals and Men.* Garden City: Doubleday and Co.

Williams, G.C. 1975. *Sex and Evolution.* Princeton: Princeton University Press.

Wilson, E.O. 1975. *Sociobiology: The New Synthesis.* Cambridge: Belknap Press of Harvard University.

Glossary
Definition of Scientific Terms

Terms Not Specifically Defined in the Text

Agonistic. Referring to any activity related to fighting, conciliation or retreat.

Allogrooming. Grooming or cleaning of another individual, in contrast to self-grooming of one's own body.

Altricial. Pertaining to young animals who are helpless for a considerable period following birth, in contrast to precocial offspring who are (for the same age) considerably more mature.

Commissurotomy. Surgical division of the fiber bundles connecting the two sides of the brain.

Conspecific. A member of the same species.

Convergent evolution. Similarity in a set of traits (not necessarily of homologous origin) as a function of similar ecological selective pressures.

Cursorial. Physically adapted for running.

Commensality. The state of symbiosis in which members of one species are benefited by coinhabiting with other species to neither their benefit or harm.

Dimorphism. The existence within the same species of two different forms or morphs.

Endogamy. Mating within one's own social group (inbreeding).

Evolutionary stable strategy. A strategy adopted by most members of a population which cannot be bettered by an alternative strategy.

Exogamy. Mating outside one's own social group (outbreeding).

Ethology. The study of animals in, and their adaptations to, their natural or usual environments.

Filiation. The state of being an offspring and its relation to its parent(s).

Homologous. Pertaining to like structures or traits via common ancestry, in contrast to analogous similarities in function.

Hypergamy. The tendency of members of one sex (usually female) to mate preferentially with those of the other sex (usually males with greater resources).

Isomorphism. Similarity in appearance or structure of organisms of different species.

Jural. Relating to right or duties.

Lek.   An area used repeatedly for communal courtship displays.

Meiosis.   Division of germ cells in which the number of chromosomes is halved to form gametes.

Morphology.   The study of anatomical or physical structures of organisms.

Oligotrophic.   Deficient nourishment or nutrition.

Ontogenetic.   Pertaining to the biological development of a single organism, in contrast to the phylogenetic or evolutionary history of a group of organisms.

Panmixia.   A random mating system wherein there are no barriers or restrictions as to the fertilization of ova by sperm.

Phylogenesis.   The evolutionary history of a species via natural selection.

Polyandry.   The tendency of the females of a species to mate with more than one male, in contrast to the opposite, polygyny; in either case, the male(s) may participate in rearing the young.

Polymorphism.   The coexistence of two or more functionally different castes or morphs within the same sex of a species (usually social insects).

Postorbital constriction.   Reduction of the bony bar on the side of, and behind the eye sockets of a skull.

Prognathous.   Extensive projection of either or both jaws.

Sagittal cresting.   Protrusion of the suture between the two parietal bones of the skull which serves to increase the area of origin of the temporal muscles.

Supraorbital torus.   Convex bony ridge over the eye sockets of a skull.

Swidden agriculture.   Impermanent or temporary cultivation of a piece of land.

Xenophobia.   Fear or distrust of strangers or nonfamiliar conspecifics.

Terms Commonly Referred to in the Text

Adaptation.   Any morphological structure, physiological process, or behavioral pattern that makes an organism more fit to survive and to reproduce in comparison with other members of the same species.

Aggression.   A physical act or threat of action by one individual that decreases the genetic fitness of another.

Character.   A particular trait possessed by one individual or species and not another.

Coefficient of relationship.   The degree of relatedness, symbolized by r, between two individuals which indicates the fraction of identical genes they have in common.

Communication (biological).   Action on the part of one organism that alters the probability pattern of behavior in another organism in an adaptive fashion to either one or both organisms.

Demography.   Growth rate and age/sex characteristics of populations and the processes that determine these characteristics.

Display.   A consistent behavior pattern that has evolved via natural selection to convey information unambiguously.

Ecology.   The systematic study of the interaction of organisms with their environment.

Evolution (organic). A change in gene frequencies within populations from generation to generation.

Gene. The basic unit of biological heredity.

Genetic fitness. The differential contribution to the next generation of one genotype in a population relative to other genotypes.

Genotype. The genetic constitution of an individual organism in contrast to its expression in a given environment (i.e., phenotype).

Graded signal. A signal that varies in intensity, frequency or both, thereby transmitting degrees of information.

Habitat. The natural or usual environment of particular organisms.

Inclusive fitness. The sum of an individual's own fitness in terms of direct descendants (i.e., reproductive success) plus all its influence on fitness in other relatives (i.e., via kin selection).

Kin selection. The differential selection of genes held in common with relatives other than offspring.

Monogyny. The tendency of a male of a given species to mate with only a single female for at least one breeding period.

Natural selection. The differential contribution of genes to the next generation by individuals of different genotypes belonging to the same population.

Niche. The range of environmental variables (e.g., temperature, humidity, and food items) within which a species can survive and reproduce.

Phenotype. The observable characteristics of an organism as expressed by its genotype interacting with environmental factors.

Polygamy. The tendency to acquire more than one mate. Polygyny: more than one female to a male. Polyandry: more than one male to a female.

Population. A group of organisms belonging to the same species and occupying a delimited area at the same time.

Preadaptation. Any previously existing anatomical structure, physiological process or behavior pattern upon which selective factors may operate to form new evolutionary adaptations.

Proximate causation. Immediate environmental conditions or internal physiology of the moment that affect the behavior of an organism (in contrast to ultimate causation).

Reciprocal altruism. The trading of altruistic acts by individuals at different times to their mutual benefit.

Reproductive success. The number of offspring of an individual that survive to reproductive age.

Selection pressure. Any ecological feature (e.g., food resources and predators) that results in natural selection.

Sexual dimorphism. Any consistent difference in size, shape and behavior between males and females beyond the basic functional portions of the sex organs.

Sexual selection. Epigamic selection, based on mate acquisition and competition therein between members of the same sex.

Society. A group of cooperatively organized individuals belonging to the same species.

Sociobiology. The systematic study of the biological basis of the behavior of social species.

Species.   A population of similar individuals that are capable of interbreeding freely with one another but not with members of other populations under natural conditions; the basic unit of biological taxonomy.

Ultimate (distal) causation.   The ecological determinants which have, via organic evolution, rendered certain traits adaptive and others nonadaptive (in contrast to proximal causation).

Index